HERMENEUTICS

Hermeneutics

An Introduction to
Interpretive Theory

Stanley E. Porter & Jason C. Robinson

WILLIAM B. EERDMANS PUBLISHING COMPANY
GRAND RAPIDS, MICHIGAN / CAMBRIDGE, U.K.

Published 2011 by
Wm. B. Eerdmans Publishing Co.
2140 Oak Industrial Drive N.E., Grand Rapids, Michigan 49505 /
P.O. Box 163, Cambridge CB3 9PU U.K.

Printed in the United States of America

17 16 15 14 13 12 11   7 6 5 4 3 2 1

Library of Congress Cataloging-in-Publication Data

Porter, Stanley E., 1956-
    Hermeneutics: an introduction to interpretive theory /
    Stanley E. Porter & Jason C. Robinson.
        p.   cm.
    ISBN 978-0-8028-6657-8 (pbk.: alk. paper)
    1. Hermeneutics.   2. Criticism.   3. Interpretation (Philosophy)
    I. Robinson, Jason, 1976-   II. Title.

    BD241.P67   2011
    121'.686 — dc23

                                                    2011017716

www.eerdmans.com

Dedicated to those seeking in earnest to understand

"What man needs is not just the persistent posing of ultimate questions, but the sense of what is feasible, what is possible, what is correct, here and now."

HANS-GEORG GADAMER, *Truth and Method*
(trans. Joel Weinsheimer and Donald G. Marshall
[2nd rev. ed.; New York: Continuum, 2002], xxxviii)

Contents

Acknowledgments

We wish to acknowledge first of all those who have had the most significant influence upon our interest in hermeneutics and interpretation.

Stanley Porter wishes to acknowledge the influence of a number of important teachers from whom he has learned much and benefited greatly. These include: Dr. Noel Fitch, Dr. Glenn Sadler, and Dr. William Spengemann in literary criticism; Dr. Herb Prince and Dr. Paul Whittemore in philosophy; Mr. Nigel J. C. Gotteri in linguistics; and Dr. Grant Osborne and Professor Anthony Thiselton in general hermeneutics. He also wishes to thank a number of colleagues who through conversation and other means have had significant influence upon his thought in these areas through the years. These include Dr. Dennis L. Stamps, Dr. Stephen Fowl, Dr. Mark Brett, Professor Markus Bockmuehl, Professor Arthur Gibson, Dr. David Rhoads, Professor Francis Watson, and Dr. Mark Boda. Dr. James Peterson and Dr. Andrew Gabriel each helpfully read one of the chapters, and Dr. Matthew Malcolm provided several useful insights. Porter also wishes to acknowledge the constructive input of a number of students and former students in his classes, hermeneutical or otherwise, who have helped him to think through such interpretive and hermeneutical issues. These include Dr. Jeffrey T. Reed, Dr. Scott Berthiaume, John Wesley Reed, Scot Snyder, Dr. Brook W. R. Pearson, Dr. Kent Clarke, Dr. Matthew Brook O'Donnell, Christopher Land, Jan Nylund, Beth Stovell, Brad Williams, who helped with research, and Andrew W. Pitts, who read through the entire manuscript and offered many valuable suggestions, and provided important research help. Porter would finally like to thank the students who have studied with him in various hermeneutics and related interpretation courses at various educational institutions where he has had the privilege to teach.

Jason Robinson wishes to thank Dr. Richard N. Longenecker and Dr. Stanley E. Porter for challenging his early interpretive views. He remembers having once delivered a seminar paper on the role of experience in art and theology, after which Stan asked simply, "Why have you accepted that particular hermeneutical approach over the others?" This was a disturbing question that troubled him — though he would never admit as much to Stan — for it became clear that he had not spent enough time looking at his own interpretive theory in a broader context. He also wishes to thank those who, through institutional and personal connections, introduced him directly to the Gadamerian and larger hermeneutical tradition. These include those he studied with at master's and doctoral level, including Dr. Jeff Mitscherling, Dr. Jay Lampert, and Dr. John Robertson. He wishes to thank all of them for the lessons they shared with him.

On a more personal level, we would like to thank those closest to us for their unstinting support. Stan would like to thank his wife, Wendy, for being a constant source of encouragement and help in enabling him to carve out time for completion of such a project, as well as reading it through in its entirety and making many helpful suggestions of content and style. Thanks! Jason wishes to thank his wife, Cynthia, for her unending editorial support on all his hermeneutics projects, including countless hours of reading and rereading the many drafts of this manuscript, and for being his life partner — that we are on this journey together makes me infinitely grateful.

Our hope and desire is that this book will be a fitting tribute to those who have helped us in our own hermeneutical thought, and an aid to others as they develop in theirs.

Preface

This project came about as the result of our common interests in hermeneutics and interpretive theory. Collaborative work on a dictionary of criticism and interpretation led to further discussion about possible research
topics in the area of hermeneutics. After discussion of a range of potential
topics, we decided to collaborate on this book to bring together recent
hermeneutical and interpretive thought in a single critical introductory
volume. One of the major ambitions of this volume was to create a constructive bridge between European hermeneutical foundations, especially
though not exclusively in the work of a number of German thinkers, and
recent North American hermeneutics, including biblical hermeneutics
and literary theory. The mix of figures and topics might strike some as un-
usual in that it gives roughly equal significance to many of the giants of
Western intellectual thought and contemporary authors whose work is still
in progress. These are areas that are usually kept apart and not brought
into interpretive dialogue in a single volume such as this one. Even some
very recent treatments have emphasized contemporary continental
thought, but at the expense of not giving equal weight to the North American and English-language tradition. This volume is not an inclusive survey
that runs the risk of moving too quickly over the surface of admittedly
complex issues and ideas, or a specialized volume on a single topic that
lacks the kind of breadth required by the topic, but a volume that provides
critical analysis of (admittedly restricted) major movements and figures in
hermeneutics and interpretive theory in the modern era, especially as
these interpreters and movements have had an impact on biblical and

theological study. This resulting effort has been collaborative in every sense of the word.

In planning the content of this volume, we readily noted that there were a number of major figures who had to be included in such a work, especially those thinkers who had had wide and sweeping influence on philosophy and hermeneutics. The more difficult task was to determine those other figures and movements that had had significant, and in some ways even equivalent influence. Some of these have become even more important in recent areas of applied hermeneutics. We recognize that there are other movements we could have included, but we believe the ones we have selected and exposited are those that continue to be productively utilized or responded to in continuing hermeneutical thought. Even after having determined all of the movements, within some of these it was difficult to focus on the one or two most significant figures for presentation. One of the criteria we used was the enduring significance of the contributor's thought, in terms of other thought being based upon, responding to, or being derivative from such a figure. We realize that some may object to several of our choices, but we believe each one is justifiable because of their individual and abiding contribution. Even though it may appear strange to treat a number of living scholars along with some of the giants of hermeneutical thought, we have weighed those figures discussed in this volume and believe their work merits their treatment here, as they represent schools of thought not represented as well by others. We also know that we have had to leave out many important thinkers. Our only excuse is that we believe we have included others equally as significant. We believe that we have reached a unique balance and synthesis of hermeneutical work represented in this volume. Our goal has been to present each of the movements included here by representing it in terms of the thought of the most significant figure or figures who represent that thought. We have chosen to do so not by simply quoting the individual authors at great length, as is done in some roughly equivalent hermeneutical works, but by analyzing and then synthesizing relatively large quantities of material so that the major ideas of their proponents are presented. We have provided useful and in some instances relatively comprehensive bibliographies to guide readers to our sources of information and further sources that can provide more detailed primary and secondary discussion. Virtually all of this secondary literature — due to the projected audience of the book — is in English, although these volumes often include reference to important material in other languages. Most of the positions and proponents included have application to a wide range of hermeneutical thought, but we have especially included those who have had a direct and immediate impact on the field of theology and biblical interpretation. The history of modern hermeneutics began with theological reflection, and in this volume we continue to discuss it in terms of its use in the broader field of theology.

Our envisioned audience for this work is anyone interested in hermeneutics and interpretive theory. More particularly, we believe this volume will be of use for those wanting a concentrated introduction to the movements and proponents included. This includes non-specialist scholars in the particular movements and persons, and especially graduate and advanced undergraduate students who are considering such hermeneutical positions and their representatives in detail. Our ideal audience is not the complete novice to the subject or the uninformed non-expert, nor necessarily the expert well versed in all areas of philosophy, hermeneutics, and other forms of critical theory. We believe that this volume will be most useful probably to advanced undergraduates — perhaps after an introduction to philosophy or principles of interpretation (often called hermeneutics) — and certainly to graduate students who desire a more detailed conspectus of major figures and movements in hermeneutics and interpretation. We believe that scholars may also benefit from this volume by its bringing together in one place a range of topics and its exposure to some figures and movements not readily encountered in other treatments of the subject. We also believe that we present some new ideas and configurations of thought that may challenge experts as well. We would also like to believe that others will find this volume useful as well. To facilitate such reading and use, we have written each chapter without footnotes, but with a bibliography at the end that provides access to the written sources we have used. We also acknowledge use of various websites, especially for factual and related information about the topics and hermeneuts discussed. We have chosen against using footnotes so that the presentation does not become distracted into secondary discussions. This is a genuine concern, as the topics introduced here are given to many different types of subsidiary topics. We have presented the major concepts of each hermeneutical position by means of the actual thoughts and beliefs of a major proponent of such a position — while admittedly quoting selectively in our presentation so as not to overburden our text. As a result, we have discussed in some detail the life and context in which the person lived, but we have concentrated on presenting their ideas as exemplified and found in their major writings. These should all be accessible through the bibliographies at the end of each chapter.

Both authors of this book have been interested in hermeneutics for a considerable length of time, and this joint effort reflects their desire to benefit from their cumulative experience and areas of expertise.

Stanley Porter's interests in hermeneutics (and philosophy) developed side by side with his study of English literature through both B.A. and M.A. programs. In the course of these studies, he became interested in the theoretical and philosophical issues related to hermeneutics and interpretive theory. As some will perhaps know, the study of English literature in the 1970s, at least in certain venues, was undergoing a theoretical reassessment that was interesting to watch and even more interesting to be part of. During further M.A. and Ph.D. studies, he had the opportunity to take courses in hermeneutics with such scholars as Grant Osborne and Anthony Thiselton. These courses cemented Porter's hermeneutical interests, to the point that, even though his doctoral research was in the area of Greek grammar and linguistics, he framed it as an exercise in hermeneutics, and continued to pursue these interests. Those reading this book, especially the chapters on structuralism and poststructuralist thought, will realize the intertwined connection between linguistics and hermeneutics. This time of study was also a period of important discussion with a number of fellow graduate students whose lively debate of interpretive issues — in formal seminars or in conversations over lunch — fostered continued interest in major questions regarding interpretation, normativity, foundationalism, and context. In the course of his teaching career, Porter has on several occasions taught courses and supervised students in the study of hermeneutics, as well as actively teaching in the area of interpretive theory and practice. As a result, he not only published his first monograph, in which Greek linguistics is framed as a hermeneutical endeavor, but has written a number of essays on literary interpretation, exegesis, and hermeneutics. He has also edited a number of works on various elements of interpretation, including a major dictionary on criticism and interpretation.

Jason Robinson was first introduced to the idea of hermeneutics in his first year of undergraduate study, when it at first did not seem all that important or interesting. It was merely one more course to complete in order to get a bachelor's degree. Even after he finished a B.R.E. in theology and a B.A. in philosophy, hermeneutics remained a vague and abstract concept, due in large part to the then current textbooks that made almost no sense to him. During his graduate study for an M.T.S. in theology and philosophy, and an M.A. and Ph.D. in philosophy, it became clear to him that he had not spent enough time looking at his own interpretive theory in a broader context — only reinforcing what he already believed to be self-evident. As a result, his interest in hermeneutics grew as he came to see its relevance, not only to how he read the Bible or engage his academic career but to his own developing worldview. During his graduate studies, from John Robertson, Robinson learned how the need for hermeneutics is universally relevant, even in the natural sciences. He learned about the hermeneutical priority of the question (over the answer), and about the openness to the new and different that a sincere thinker must encourage within himself, even when it is uncomfortable. From Jeff Mitscherling he learned to see the broader tradition in which hermeneutics, and all of the other disciplines, find themselves, and the value of a historical awareness. He learned to pay much closer attention to ancient philosophy and its ever-present influence in hermeneutics and in contemporary language and thought. He further learned how philosophical hermeneutics continues to struggle with the questions of Plato and Aristotle, and how the goal of becoming a better, moral, and wise person — to find the good — is not merely a philosophical ideal, but a hermeneutical imperative.

Hermeneutics and interpretive theory is a topic of increasingly recognized importance in the humanities, especially in theological circles, and even in the social sciences. We trust that this volume will represent major movements and ideas, and significant figures who hold to such ideas, in a way that makes them intelligible, understandable, and most importantly usable by those interested in hermeneutics.

ONE What Is Hermeneutics?

Introduction

Hermeneutics has a long and complex history with many surprising twists and turns. As a discipline in its own right it is relatively modern, yet the idea of hermeneutics may be traced as far back as the ancient Greeks. In its most basic sense hermeneutics refers to the many ways in which we may theorize about the nature of human interpretation, whether that means understanding books, works of art, architecture, verbal communication, or even nonverbal bodily gestures. Indeed, as we shall see in the following chapters, the nature of human understanding, and therefore our ideas about hermeneutics and interpretive theory, face a number of interesting challenges that make a complete description of "what it means to understand" difficult.

What do we mean when we say that we understand something? While most of us may pick up an apple and immediately know that it is red and that, if we take a bite, it tastes delicious, we are unable to answer how it is that we know what we know. Few of us stop to consider what is going on when we experience things. An apple is self-evident to each of us who holds one. We do not need to be convinced that it exists and that it has properties we see, taste, and touch. Yet what makes our interaction with the apple possible remains a mystery. From a hermeneutical perspective, this is not just a question about how our senses work in relation to our cognitive processes. Perhaps the eating of a candied apple at a fair or circus represents an experience that holds special meaning. If it does, then the question of perceiving the object, the candy apple, clearly involves a unique context — a history, an event, a specific micro-world — that only the individual involved knows. It is a context that influences how one experiences that object. And now, as we think about it, it is a context that conditions our recollection. In a similar way, our experiences of people, books, social events, and so on, are all conditioned by surrounding circumstances. We do not merely hold a book in our hands, see the letters on the page, and understand the sentences and paragraphs as they exist in front of us. We experience the meaning in relation to our own histories, desires, memories, imaginations, etc. Thus the question of what it means to understand becomes a very large one. Hermeneutics attempts to answer the question by examining closely the hidden realm of activity behind the scenes of our own lives. The aim is to make the structure, or perhaps the lack of structure, of human understanding as explicit as possible.

There are many different explanations as to what might be transpiring in the act of human understanding, e.g., sociological, psychological, biological, chemical, neurological. Some of these have met with more success than others. There are also many different hermeneutical descriptions, many of which do not agree with one another or with the more scientific explanations. One of the unique claims of hermeneutics is that it goes beyond the biological, psychological, etc., because it looks at what makes all of them possible. Most importantly, hermeneutics tries to avoid reducing "understanding" to its lowest common denominator, e.g., describing it only in terms of specific neural networks working in specific electro-chemical ways within the brain. Hermeneutics is successful only to the degree that it is able to include as much of what makes us human as possible, e.g., our social, historical, linguistic, theological, and biological influences. Broadly speaking then, to think hermeneutically means to ask what we mean by human understanding universally, i.e., what we all do naturally, regardless of our specific cultures, languages, or traditions. However, most hermeneutical descriptions also pay close attention to how our cultures, languages, and traditions influence the ways in which we understand. In short, hermeneutics asks three important questions. What is understanding? How might we describe it best? And how might we understand better?

"Hermeneutics" comes from the Greek verb *hermeneuein*, which means "to interpret" or "to translate." Today it refers to the science, theory, and practice of human interpretation. The term has an interesting historical association with the Greek god Hermes. Hermes, a character in the ancient

Greek poems the *Iliad* and *Odyssey,* played a number of interesting roles — one of them was to deliver messages from the gods to mortals. He was a medial figure that worked in the "in-between" as an interpreter of the gods, communicating a message from Olympus so humans might understand the meaning. In this way, Hermes, son of Zeus, was responsible for fostering genuine understanding — comprehension — which required more effort than if he merely transliterated (interpreting letter for letter, word for word without any modification or adaptation). Hermes had to interpret the meaning of the messages on behalf of his listeners and in doing so had to go far beyond merely repeating the intended truth. He had to re-create or reproduce the meaning that would connect to his audience's history, culture, and concepts in order to make sense of things. In like manner, hermeneutics tries to describe the daily mediation of understanding we all experience in which meaning does not emerge as a mere exchange of symbols, a direct and straightforward transmission of binary code, or a simple yes or no. Rather, meaning happens by virtue of a "go-between" that bridges the alien with the familiar, connecting cultures, languages, traditions, and perspectives that may be similar or millennia apart. The go-between is the activity of human understanding that, like Hermes, tries to make sense of the world and the heavens. It is an intricate and complex activity that sometimes gets things wrong. Our goal in this book is to consider some of the most popular ways in which this hermeneutical activity has been conceived and some of the things we may do to improve our chances of getting interpretation right.

In its earliest modern forms, hermeneutics developed primarily as a discipline for the analysis of biblical texts. It represented a body of accepted principles and practices for interpreting an author's intended (and inspired) meaning, as well as providing the proper means of investigating a text's socio-historical context. This form of hermeneutics was focused on the many dynamics that exist between author, text, and reader. It was assumed that in order to achieve a clear and accurate reading of a text one had to employ definitive rules of interpretation to clarify and safeguard the proper untangling of a rather obvious and commonsense relationship; that is, someone (at a specific place, at a specific time, with a specific language) had written something with the intention of having a later reader understand what he or she had in mind. In fact, the relationship between author, interpreter, and the interpreted material may seem so straightforward that some may doubt whether hermeneutics and interpretive theories are even necessary. After all, most of us engage in conversations daily without any

3

specific hermeneutical aids or external methods, and we read novels, newspapers, magazines, and the like with few serious difficulties or misunderstandings. However, as we shall soon see in the chapters that follow, making sense of this seemingly elementary relationship between author, text, and reader has proven to be extremely difficult, especially when the text in question may be thousands of years old and written in ancient languages. Engaging a text or person in close proximity to one's own historical and cultural situation is easier than if there are temporal, spatial, and linguistic gaps. Yet even when we intently look below the surface of our casual and everyday encounters we find a sense of otherness or distance between ourselves and the text or other person. How many times have we been sure that we understood what was just read or heard, only to discover later on that we had been entirely mistaken? Hermeneutics thrives upon the inherent ambiguity and otherness that we face daily, and is used to foster a common accord when there is misunderstanding or lack of agreement. Whether reading an ancient text such as the Bible — where hermeneutical questions continue to be important — or trying to make sense of a current best-selling novel, our interpretive experience will be one in which hermeneutical reflection is always relevant.

One of the ongoing debates in hermeneutics has been over which elements to emphasize in the tripartite relationship of author, text, and reader, for the purpose of bridging gaps in understanding — whether between (1) the author and his or her intention placed within the text, (2) the text and its cultural-historical context, or (3) the reader's present situation and socio-historically conditioned way of understanding the text. Focusing on one element over the others runs the risk of creating an imbalance or, at the very least, rendering an incomplete picture. For instance, emphasizing a search for an author's originally intended message will often mean that the circumstances that influence the reader's own perspectives on the text — that is, what the reader is likely to have "read into" the text, "between the lines" so to say — are potentially overlooked. Conversely, many contemporary hermeneuts (hermeneutical thinkers) accept the "death of the author" in favor of emphasizing the dynamics between reader and text for, it is argued, we simply do not have access to an author's original intention. This does not mean that we should entirely ignore the author, only that we should not regard authorial intention as something to be sought like a secret plot or mystery behind the words themselves. We may never fully put ourselves into the shoes of another, so there will always be some uncertainty. Moreover, some hermeneuts have gone much further and argued that the basic tripartite depiction of author, interpreter, and interpreted is flawed from the start. They have abandoned it for something they believe is more fundamental. One of the more popular versions of this approach argues that finding the "ideal" source of human understanding, attained through principles and rules of interpretation that offer methodologically sound and objectively reliable knowledge, is an impossible quest. Instead, what we should examine is our "way of being" in the world, for which method and objectivity have only minor roles to play at most.

Whether for legal, philological (the historical study of languages), or theological applications, early hermeneutical thinking was dominated by attempts to find the right method or technique for ensuring correct understanding. Since then the different hermeneutical applications have given way to more generalized hermeneutical approaches that go beyond the scope of disciplinary boundaries. Hermeneutics now applies to every subject area within the social, human, and natural sciences. It has ceased to be a special philosophy, method, or way of interpreting sacred literature, and has become a universal means of thinking by which we attempt to clarify the conditions of all human understanding. Strictly speaking, contemporary hermeneutics is not a discipline in the typical sense. True to its mediating heritage, hermeneutics does not attempt to establish itself as a philosophical scheme or discipline on its own. Rather, it endeavors to describe the already present structure of human understanding and to highlight the conditions for clearer insight and comprehension. Hermeneutics does not directly seek to set up a new way of seeing the world; that is, it does not prescribe how we "ought" to reflect upon and think about things (although there is a very real sense in which such changes may result from thinking hermeneutically), but to describe how we already do reflect and think.

Some contemporary hermeneutical investigations still function chiefly as the application of techniques and methods for the sake of facilitating understanding; that is, they continue to rely on prescribed rules and principles for bolstering a specific kind of reliable comprehension. As we shall observe, such attitudes and posturing toward interpretation, while perhaps serving valuable roles in their own right, have held more modest positions among contemporary hermeneutics, which perceives itself as describing what it is to understand in the first place, prior to any secondary and "externally applied" means toward truth. In sum, hermeneutics — once something characterized by specific tools of thought within a handful of disciplines — has become a general theory of understanding for all spheres of human awareness.

This fundamental shift represents a very important repositioning of interests in regard to the nature of human understanding. An obvious example is that most hermeneuts no longer try to answer what a particular passage "really means" in a complete and total way or what an author "really intended." Few today would be so bold as to claim to know "the Truth" beyond a shadow of doubt. This is due in large part to the perceived failure of the many previous interpretive theories and methods. Indeed, in surveying the history of hermeneutics and interpretive theory one cannot help but be struck by a growing sense of modesty and humility. The activity of interpretation and how we might best do it remains an open question. It is not surprising then that some, e.g., radical deconstructionists, have simply given up, or at the very least have become radically skeptical about ever having a comprehensive theory of interpretation or a hermeneutic.

Recent generations of hermeneuts are similar to the old in that they endeavor to bring about meaningful agreement — a sharing of a common meaning among people — but, unlike their predecessors, they seek to bridge the gap between interpreter and interpreted by illuminating the conditions under which agreement may be reached through dialogue in all areas of human pursuit, whether biblical, theological, philosophical, scientific, and so on. Hermeneutics does not and cannot guarantee the fixed meaning of a text, a laboratory experiment, or a work of art. Thus the very goals of hermeneutics, and not only the methods and practices, have been thrown open to debate and discussion. Part of the challenge in thinking about hermeneutics is deciding which debates and discussions are worthy of engagement, and which are unlikely to be fruitful. Our hope is that readers will find something of value in each chapter, and that the questions they take away will help inform their own field, discipline, or vocation.

So what might this general theory of human understanding offer us today? We shall answer this in due course. For now let us take note of the fact that hermeneutics is an umbrella movement with many different themes that have evolved into a surprising array of theories, most dramatically so since the late nineteenth century. Fortunately for students of hermeneutics, there is a strong tradition of shared interest in concepts and motifs such as language, creativity, experience, authority, history, tradition, freedom, application, knowledge, understanding, and science. So while there may be little in the way of universally accepted properties and even less that may be recognized as linear and gradual development in hermeneutics, i.e., clear steps of progress that have led uniformly to the present, there are still many common themes, historical stages, and enduring questions that we may critically examine.

For our purposes there are six distinct hermeneutical trends that, while overlapping in many areas, are worth examining in detail: romantic, phenomenological and existential, philosophical, critical, structural, and poststructural (deconstruction). In addition to studying these major hermeneutical movements, we will also examine what we consider to be some of the most influential and important adaptations of these interpretive theories, in order to gain greater insight into the intricate problems and questions in modern hermeneutics, as well as to become aware of the more practical difficulties experienced when one tries to apply hermeneutical theories theologically and biblically. To that end, we will examine hermeneutic phenomenology, dialectical theology and exegesis, theological hermeneutics, and literary hermeneutics. The dependency of these adaptations upon the major hermeneutical trends should become clear in their individual discussions. However, the order and style of presentation will not be as simple as these lists indicate. We focus upon key figures within each movement and integrate the approaches into an order that we think makes their relationships clear.

At this point, we wish to introduce the major trends and adaptations that we treat in this volume.

Romantic Hermeneutics

Romantic hermeneutics, associated primarily with the work of Friedrich Schleiermacher (1768-1834) and Wilhelm Dilthey (1833-1911), represents the first significant movement in what would influence many hermeneutical revolutions during the late nineteenth and twentieth centuries. Schleiermacher and Dilthey are exemplars of the author-oriented hermeneutical tradition that focused interpretive efforts on understanding the author and his or her socio-historical context over and above understanding the text on its own. Two of the most important developments fostered by romantic hermeneutics include a shift from regional or disciplinary-bound hermeneutics to a general hermeneutics and the development of methodological and epistemological ways of understanding that incorporate reconstructive approaches, most notably that of the author's original creative acts.

Prior to Schleiermacher, hermeneutics was divided into specialized forms, with biblical hermeneutics (virtually synonymous with exegesis as the objective study of texts) being preeminent among them. Due to Schlei- ermacher, followed closely by Dilthey, the notion of hermeneutics as a matter of practical exegetical operation between text and reader is general- ized to include much broader concerns related to the nature of human un- derstanding. Schleiermacher was the first to move hermeneutics away from being a corpus of rules that are applied to texts, to its being represen- tative of universal principles or laws of understanding that transcend indi- vidual occasions or applications. Wherever there is discourse, he proposes, hermeneutics as the "art of understanding" is necessary. By the end of the nineteenth century the idea of hermeneutics could no longer be consid- ered primarily a matter of biblical interpretation, for it had become a transdisciplinary activity. Still, Schleiermacher's romantic hermeneutics is applicable to biblical texts even though he denies that the interpretation of sacred literature has a special place among other literature or that it de- serves a unique interpretive method.

Dilthey is well known for his epistemological analysis (concerning the nature and scope of knowledge) of the human sciences, and as one of the first to stress a distinction between the human and the natural sci- ences. Dilthey, inspired by Schleiermacher, accepts the universal character of hermeneutics as something belonging to the essential nature of all the human sciences. Life itself, he claims, is hermeneutical. One of the key fac- tors in Dilthey's approach concerns concrete expressions of historical life and their interpretation through a methodology that provides objective understanding — a form of understanding said to be capable of acting as the foundational discipline for the human sciences. Hermeneutics is not only a general process according to Dilthey but a scientific and founda- tional method, and therefore something far in excess of mere rules and principles for the reading of texts.

Phenomenological and Existential Hermeneutics

Edmund Husserl (1859-1938) and Martin Heidegger (1889-1976) were the first major contributors to phenomenological hermeneutics. Of the two it is Heidegger who has had the most impact. While Husserl avoided work- ing directly with hermeneutics, his work has proven to be of inestimable value to all later hermeneutical thinkers, with the most obvious among them being Heidegger, along with Paul Ricoeur. Two of the most impor- tant developments in phenomenological hermeneutics include Husserl's descriptive method and critical examination of consciousness, and Heidegger's proposal that understanding and interpretation always arise from the perspective provided by one's own life-world or situation, including one's prejudices and presuppositions.

Like Dilthey, Husserl claims to offer a foundational theory of knowledge and method on which to ground other disciplines. His foundational science begins with what is originally and immediately present to consciousness, without relying on empirical evidence or data to confirm what we experience. Through his phenomenological method, he argues that it is possible to describe our consciousness of phenomena as they are in themselves, prior to interpretations, presuppositions, or explanations. We are thinking creatures and all that may be thought about exists to us as our "consciousness of something." Hence, for Husserl, because consciousness is always intentional, as directed toward something, then the only proper sphere for analysis will be the study of objects and the world as they appear to consciousness. How are things given in experience? How are the meanings of things constituted?

In contrast to Husserl, Heidegger argues that we should avoid a methodological stance toward fostering human understanding and clarity of interpretation. Instead, he argues that we should seek to disclose something more fundamental to our way of living. With Schleiermacher and Dilthey, the first major move of hermeneutics was toward providing a general hermeneutics, preoccupied with method and an epistemic desire to find correct, even objective interpretations. Heidegger rejects this path pioneered by earlier hermeneuts for a much more radical approach that begins with the forgotten existential question — What is the "meaning" of being? This is not a question of what we know and how we may guarantee interpretive accuracy. Rather, it is a question about our mode of knowing, a question about our living as knowers, not about the status or content of our knowledge *per se.*

Heidegger's hermeneutics is made possible because of our nature as existentially situated creatures. He argues that we are always already in the world and that we already understand it interpretively through our circumstances and our practical involvements. To understand, for Heidegger, is to understand in relation to one's own finite situation. It is not an act of our conscious awareness or intentionality, as it is for Husserl, or of our epistemological knowing or methodological investigation, as it is for romantic hermeneuts. Rather, Heidegger believes that hermeneutics is possible because we are beings-in-the-world. We are mortal and contingent creatures that are inaccessible through methods, rules, and techniques of interpretation. Heidegger's more existential approach is different from Husserl's methodologically rigorous phenomenology. The most obvious difference is that, contrary to Husserl's efforts to avoid presuppositions (and Schleiermacher's and Dilthey's desires to overcome the negative impact of one's own prejudices), Heidegger embraces a view of human understanding in which it, and all acts of interpretation, are inseparable from our situatedness. If correct, what this means for all prior hermeneutics and interpretive theories is that no matter how thorough and objective the interpretation may seem, it will always be at least partially determined by presuppositions and prejudgments — sometimes for better, sometimes for worse.

Philosophical Hermeneutics

Philosophical hermeneutics was initially developed by Hans-Georg Gadamer (1900-2002), a German philosopher widely accepted as one of the most important twentieth-century hermeneuts. According to Gadamer, previous hermeneutical thinking, excluding Heidegger's, mistakenly accepts the scientific ethos in an attempt to foster objectivity and method as all-important ways to achieving the most reliable insight possible. Gadamer argues against the claim that the best form of understanding is achieved either through technique or method for avoiding misunderstanding, as it is for Schleiermacher, or as a way of securing objective foundational knowledge, as it is for Dilthey. And against the models provided by the natural sciences, and mimicked by many disciplines in the social and human sciences, Gadamer proposes that understanding is not something we grasp through experimental isolation and interrogation but that which grasps us as an experience or event of meaning outside of our control. Method is a valuable tool but it is severely limited. Genuine understanding, for Gadamer, emerges when we begin to see what is questionable in new ways and open ourselves to a dialogue with the other, e.g., text, person, work of art. One of the chief virtues of Gadamer's philosophical hermeneutics is that it seeks to find willing dialogue partners, never merely passive audiences. Thus, unlike many current (especially scientific) interpretive methodologies, it does not treat given subject matters, texts, or people with dispassionate and neutralizing distance, but as mutually influential partners in an ongoing interpretive dance or play of give-and-take.

In Gadamer, the broader hermeneutical shifts from regional to general hermeneutics, and from epistemological to existential hermeneutics, are clearly evident. His most significant contributions to hermeneutics come from his unique emphasis on how understanding is mediated through language and tradition. Gadamer is perhaps best known for his distinctively dialogical (the logic of dialogue) approach to human understanding and his further expansion of the reach of hermeneutics. Like Heidegger, Gadamer began with the notion that all understanding is hermeneutical, where the hermeneutical function is our basic mode of being-in-the-world. Philosophical hermeneutics is not concerned with the fixed meaning of a text. Rather, it seeks to establish a dialectic or open-ended questioning and answering between the past and present, the text and the interpreter, without aiming at a final or complete interpretation. Understanding, for Gadamer, is more than a matter of taking a good look to see what is there. It is a product of asking questions, even if all we are given are propositional statements. We must risk our beliefs, assumptions, and desires, allowing ourselves to be caught up in the event of interpretation if we want to truly understand.

Hermeneutic Phenomenology

Paul Ricoeur (1913-2005), a French philosopher, was a phenomenologist with wide-ranging interests, especially in hermeneutics and language, the human subject, psychoanalysis, and religion. His writings are also wide-ranging, and his work in both North America and France has given him a unique perspective and platform for his hermeneutical philosophy. In particular, his philosophy took a decidedly hermeneutical turn, with the result that his work on language and hermeneutics merits serious consideration because of its linguistic grounding and literary application.

Ricoeur's hermeneutic phenomenology brings together and extends a number of major themes. These include an exploration of the nature of discourse in terms of narrativity; a recognition of and appropriation of the place of creativity; an appreciation of language as discourse; extension of his work on the human will by incorporating and modifying the work of speech-act theory as part of his human action model; and exploration of the issue of time.

Ricoeur's major hermeneutical contribution begins with what he identifies as the apparent conflict or dialectic between the concepts of explanation and understanding, and argues through to the conclusion that this dichotomy is more apparent than real. He does this through two major hermeneutical moves. The first is to consider language as discourse, especially written language, and the second is to consider the notion of what he calls plurivocity, by which he means plural meaning at every level of language, from the word to the discourse. The problem of language as discourse is as old as the ancients. According to Ricoeur, this problem stems from a fundamental distinction between language as code and language as it is used. Linguistics has concentrated on language as system or structure, rather than language as it is used, which has relegated discourse to a marginalized position. The neglect of discourse is the result of Ferdinand de Saussure's (1857-1913) fundamental dichotomy between *langue* and *parole*. For Ricoeur, *parole* is to be equated with discourse, whereas Saussure emphasized *langue* as the synchronic analysis of language systems.

A discourse is not a series of sentences, but a whole, according to Ricoeur. These multiple sentences lead to a plurivocity of the discourse typical of complex discourses. These discourses consist of a complex hierarchy of elements — seen in terms of the relation of the parts to the whole — that are recognized through a circular interpretive process. Further, understanding a text means that one must understand it as an individual text, not as a type. Any literary text also has a number of different potential meaning horizons. These are often posited through the metaphorical and symbolic extensions of meaning of the text. Ricoeur believes that it is logical probabilities that provide the validation of these potential horizons, rather than some kind of empirical proof, just as there are also ways of falsifying interpretations and determining that some are more probable than others. Ricoeur sees all of this as part of the hermeneutical circle, in which there is a circular relationship between a guess and its validation. Thus, Ricoeur notes that even though there may be several potential ways of understanding a text (the potential limited by the text itself), not all of the interpretations have equal validity.

Critical Hermeneutics

Jürgen Habermas (1929-) is responsible for what is commonly referred to as critical hermeneutics. His work on critical hermeneutics has less obvious relevance to the reading of texts, though it still applies, for it is meant to serve as a means of displacing distortions within communication and understanding and fostering the rationality inherent in interpersonal linguistic communication. Habermas's concern for distorted communication and interaction, most evident in his critical theorizing about both the conditions that create legitimacy crises and the necessary conditions for restoring legitimacy, is evidence of his persistent emancipatory interest to free society from domination, violence, coercion, and ignorance. Through his critical hermeneutics, Habermas believes we may be objective about given issues while working toward the public good, because we are able to move beyond the reign of regional biases and prejudices that lie hidden in our ideologies and unreflected assumptions about the world.

Habermas's unique perspective on critical thought within hermeneutics follows from his understanding of communicative rationality and is meant to supplement what he sees as reflective deficiencies in contemporary hermeneutics, specifically philosophical hermeneutics and its inability to adequately act as a critique of society. Habermas, like Heidegger and Gadamer, rejects any monological foundation upon which to base interpretation and understanding, i.e., universally binding and absolute methods. However, he is not as radical as they are, for he insists on a semifoundational approach that he believes makes it possible to subject tradition and our own prejudices to a critical and quasi-objective examination. Habermas argues that the only way to liberate ourselves from distortions and ideologies, and to recover legitimacy in the public sphere, is a kind of critical reflection that other hermeneuts have yet to offer.

Habermas agrees with Heidegger and Gadamer that communicative meaning is understood within tradition, but he desires to go further and to judge the tradition within which meaning arises. He accepts our situatedness as the starting point for all understanding while at the same time proposing a way to step out of our circumstances and conditioned ways of thinking. What is prior to our situation, he argues, is the claim to universally valid groundings. Whereas Gadamer describes the interpretive act as a fusion of horizons, Habermas argues that the horizon of reason is always already implicit. To ignore implicit validity claims is a serious mistake, for they are a necessary part of every fusion of horizons. By pulling truth and method closer together, Habermas offers methodical criteria for the successful analysis of communication, whereby he believes he overcomes the limited Gadamerian proposal that misses much-needed critical judgment and reflection.

Structuralism

Structuralism is a diverse field of study, which has had significant influence over a wide range of fields of academic and intellectual inquiry, including both the natural sciences and the arts and humanities. Structuralism made its major migration to North America in the 1920s, where it was popular for several decades as a hermeneutical model in fields including linguistics, literary criticism, biblical studies, and anthropology, among others. Structuralism continues to be a major force in such fields as anthropology and linguistics, but it has lost its influence or become transformed into various poststructural forms of inquiry in fields such as literary and biblical studies.

Structuralism has its origin in the linguistic theories of Ferdinand de Saussure. Several of the key notions in Saussure's thought include: (1) the arbitrary nature of the sign: Saussure distinguishes between the *signifié* (thing signified) and the *significant* (signifier), and he sees no necessary correlation between the concept and the sounds used to speak of it. They — sound and concept — are joined together into a unit that he called the sign. (2) *Langue* versus *parole*: Saussure sees *langue* as the sign system held in common by the users of a language, while *parole* is each user's personal and idiosyncratic use of that *langue*. *Langue* is the primary object of linguistic investigation. (3) Synchrony versus diachrony: Saussure defines synchrony as concerned with the grammatical form and the sound of a given language at a point in time, and diachrony as the changes that affect any language over time. Structuralism developed in a number of different ways in linguistic and anthropological circles. The best known of these have been the Prague school of linguistics, American structuralism, and French structuralism.

Daniel Patte (1939-) is probably the best-known and most rigorous biblical structuralist. Patte recognizes that there are a number of different structural approaches, but they all have common features that are important for interpreting a text. These include: the meaningfulness of structures, differentiation of syntagmatic and paradigmatic relations, and a linguistic model that realizes the arbitrary relation between the signifier (expression) and the signified (content) in terms of both form and substance (a distinctly Saussurian concept). This orientation leads Patte to adopt the semio-structural model of A.-J. Greimas (1917-1992) as his method, which he develops at some length along the lines of Greimas's generative trajectory.

14

Throughout his works, Patte's burden is to define and situate within the wider field of biblical exegesis a usable structuralist hermeneutics that can be employed to examine the texts of the New Testament, with the particular purpose of elucidating their religious or faith dimension. He sees structuralism as providing the means by which one can bring both exegesis and hermeneutic, a distinction that Patte makes at one point, into meaningful relation, whereby exegesis (the analysis of text) leads to hermeneutic (what the text means for the modern reader).

Poststructuralism

The most famous poststructuralist is Jacques Derrida (1930-2004). Derrida's work has become synonymous with deconstruction, which represents a collage of challenges and ideas that may only loosely be described as hermeneutics. In fact, Derrida is very pessimistic about the possibility of hermeneutics, whether phenomenological, existential, philosophical, critical, or otherwise. For him, Heidegger, Gadamer, Habermas, and the like had all failed to recognize their logocentric preoccupations (the misguided belief in an origin, ground, or ultimate generating source of truth and meaning). In the case of philosophical hermeneutics, Derrida believes that it — in a similar fashion to romantic hermeneutics — tries to uncover and make known the hidden meaning and truth of texts, and that it therefore reflects what he argues is Gadamer's belief in the possibility of complete and more or less stable understanding. While the legitimacy of Derrida's views against hermeneutics remains highly debated, his arguments serve to highlight many of the common assumptions made by deconstructionists, and hermeneuts more generally. That is, in his pessimism he articulates the nuances of his own position in relation to hermeneutics, while eliciting the same from Gadamer and his defenders.

The enduring debate between these two intellectual camps has proven to be very helpful to those trying to appreciate deconstruction in spite of its many popular mischaracterizations. Strictly speaking, deconstruction is not a philosophy, theory, or set of beliefs, and is therefore very difficult to understand. For the sake of convenience many refer to it as a literary method for reading texts, but deconstruction is not reducible to instrumentality, sets of rules and techniques, or even language. Deconstruction is something (really "no thing") that disrupts and destabilizes prevailing assumptions and attitudes, rather than something that tries to establish specific ways to truth. Where many thinkers identify coherent and unified truth, meaning, and the like, Derrida finds radical otherness and difference. For instance, when Husserl turns toward things in themselves as they appear in our consciousness, Derrida argues that the things themselves always escape us. When Habermas seeks out legitimacy through the rationality inherent in communication, Derrida dismisses his position as a remnant of misguided Enlightenment logocentrism. And when Gadamer turns to dialogue and the fusion of horizons, Derrida argues that there is always already interruption and rupture.

As a quasi-poststructural and quasi-postmodern approach ("quasi" because it is not at all clear just where or how deconstruction fits), Derrida's deconstruction criticizes notions such as the referentiality of language (that language accurately points to things in the world) and the objectivity of structures as mistakes typical of the entire Western metaphysical tradition. Derrida's deconstructive approach seeks out elusive, excluded, marginalized, and subverted meanings in order to make known what has been ignored, showing that what something seems to mean really means something else, often something other than what an author intended. However, deconstruction is not about proving that anything may pass for truth or nothing at all, only that there is no transcendentally signified, e.g., transcultural, transhistorical truth, or grounding like the sort assumed by traditional metaphysics. Derrida accepts that there is meaning we may know and agree upon, yet he insists that there may never be final and decidable meaning because meaning is always contextual, deferred, incomplete, and full of internal tensions and contradictions.

Dialectical Theology and Exegesis

Dialectical theology emerged in the early twentieth century as a hermeneutical response to disenchantment with theological liberalism, as an attempt to retain discussion of God within a modern critical environment. Karl Barth (1886-1968) is considered by many to be the most significant (Protestant) theologian since at least Schleiermacher, and the most prolific since Martin Luther (1483-1546). The dialectical theology that he championed throughout his intellectual career — a theology full of existential tensions and paradoxes — became the most significant response to the fall of theological liberalism in its attempt to address these issues. Barth makes some strong claims for hermeneutics, especially the relationship of biblical hermeneutics to general hermeneutics. He asserts that the common task of hermeneutics is to understand the words of the writers or speakers, using the tools of literary-historical exegesis. Biblical hermeneutics in fact has an advantage over general hermeneutics in that it must restrict its knowledge of the text to what is found in the text, rather than importing ideas from outside the text.

Central to the foundation of Barth's dialectical hermeneutic is the biblical testimony that "God has spoken." The revealed, written, and proclaimed Word is the threefold form of the Word. Important is Barth's belief that the Trinity *per se* is not part of revelation, but is what the church affirms about God. God as wholly other is the revealer who chooses to reveal himself in divine self-disclosure as Creator, Reconciler, and Redeemer. And finally, Barth's dialectical hermeneutics maintains that the Bible is not to be equated with the Word of God, but is a witness to revelation of what it means that the word was made flesh. The Bible, though the fallible product of human beings, has authority as a witness to God in Christ.

Rudolf Bultmann (1884-1976) is considered by many to be the most important New Testament interpreter and theologian of the twentieth century, as well as a significant hermeneut. Whereas Barth approaches these matters as a dialectical theologian, Bultmann approaches them as a dialectical thinker more heavily influenced by contemporary philosophy and historical-critically based exegesis of the Bible. Bultmann continues to exercise significant influence over New Testament studies, but less directly in hermeneutical circles. His adoption of dialectical theology and his powerful biblical scholarship provided a strong impetus for the movement.

Bultmann proposes that understanding is based upon a number of factors. Some of the most important of these include: (1) pre-understanding, or how understanding of a text is always determined by a prior understanding of it; (2) existential encounter, in which the interpreter is open to an existential encounter with the text; (3) questioning the text, whereby the interpreter formulates a particular question with a specific objective in mind for understanding the text; and (4) the hermeneutical circle, in which there is a reciprocal spiral of growing understanding as the interpreter brings his or her pre-understanding to interpretation, and that pre-understanding is confirmed, denied, or modified in dialogue with the text.

Bultmann is perhaps more popularly known for his "demythologization." As we shall see, in Bultmann's demythologization there are a number of correlations among Heidegger's philosophical thought (the desire to address the situation of contemporary humanity), liberal theology of the nineteenth century (an anti-supernatural presupposition based upon scientific naturalism), and the history-of-religions school of thought (the attempt to find common religious origins and explanations).

Theological Hermeneutics

The emergence of theological hermeneutics in the latter part of the twentieth century is an attempt to reconcile the centrality of theology in Christian interpretation with recognition of the complexity of hermeneutical thought.

Anthony Thiselton (1937-) is a significant figure in theological hermeneutics for a number of reasons. For many students of the Bible he has provided their first and sometimes only significant introduction to philosophical hermeneutics. His work in hermeneutics is characterized by thorough examination of the writings of the major philosophers, especially from Schleiermacher to the present, and detailed analysis of their arguments as he appropriates them for his theological hermeneutical stance. Besides his major works in hermeneutics, he is an accomplished New Testament scholar and has also profitably investigated the field of modern linguistics.

One sees in Thiselton's attempt to define the scope of theological hermeneutics several important characteristics of his work. One is wide exposure to the thought of other philosophers who might contribute to his theoretical understanding. In many if not all fundamental ways, the climax of Thiselton's work is seeing how his theological hermeneutics unites a number of horizons — between the Bible and theology, and between hermeneutical method and doctrinal practice. As Thiselton indicates, hermeneutics is an applied activity, in which understanding is seen in formative practice that is communal and public in nature and presuppositional in orientation.

Thiselton believes that hermeneutics is fundamental to the establishment of doctrine that is not simply abstract, theoretical, and overly general. Returning to and relying upon Gadamer, Thiselton approaches doctrine instead from the standpoint of asking hermeneutical questions from life. This is appropriate, because Christian confessions, such as the early creeds, reflect a life-context in which they are used. That life-context (as speech-act theory indicates) can result in truth claims, because confessional statements presuppose certain states of affairs.

Kevin Vanhoozer (1957-) has become a popular figure in the field of theological hermeneutics in North America on the basis of substantial treatments of major issues such as the question of meaning and the dramatic character of doctrine and his easily digestible and entertaining essays on several important and recurring themes in the field. Vanhoozer has raised the popular profile of theological hermeneutics especially as it relates to interpretation within the church. His theological hermeneutics is identifiable as postconservative and postfoundationalist, though affirming the canon as the basis of belief.

Both Thiselton and Vanhoozer are advocates of theological hermeneutics, and they have much in common in their appeal to philosophy and the doctrine of the church. However, there are also a number of interesting and obvious points of contrast in their approaches. Thiselton is biblically oriented and exegetically grounded, whereas Vanhoozer approaches the topic as a systematic theologian. The result is that their work approaches the topic of hermeneutics differently, with biblical exegesis providing the point of entry and evaluation for Thiselton, while Vanhoozer's major point of contact is contemporary theology. Thiselton is more overt in his knowledge and use of philosophy than is Vanhoozer. Thiselton's knowledge and documentation of philosophical writers is encyclopedic and exhaustive, while Vanhoozer tends to focus upon major thinkers, such as Gadamer, Ricoeur, and the major speech-act theorists (Austin, Searle, and Wolterstorff), who provide the framework for his thinking.

Literary Hermeneutics

Literary hermeneutics combines literary interpretation with recognition of major hermeneutical issues revolving around the author, the text, and the reader. Alan Culpepper (1945-) positions his literary hermeneutic in terms of two major emphases. The first is in relation to the metaphor of the text as window or mirror. Drawing upon the New Criticism, Culpepper wishes to reposition the study of John's Gospel, and by implication the New Testament as a whole, from being a window to being a mirror. The metaphor of the window is that the text serves as a point of access to the history of the community behind the Gospel, and behind that the life and teaching of Jesus. Instead, if the text is seen as a mirror, the metaphor shifts the point of focus from going beyond the text to seeing meaning reside between the observer and the mirror, or between the reader and the text. Therefore, rather than origins, historical background, and matters behind the text having preeminence, the focus is upon the text and its readers, both implied and real.

Culpepper's literary hermeneutic also emphasizes the implications of such a mirror-like repositioning. Culpepper develops for biblical studies a communications model that moves from the real author through the implied author to the narrator and the story, and then from the story to the narratee and the implied and real reader. Involved in the communication between implied author and implied reader is both explicit and implicit commentary. The narrator-narratee relation contains the world of narrative time, within which lies the story time. The story involves events, settings, characters, and plot, and stands at the center of the communications model. The major components of this communications model form the basic elements of Culpepper's literary and especially narrative-focused hermeneutics.

Culpepper defines a literary hermeneutics that is developed out of the materials of a number of forms of literary criticism current at the time. The influence of the New Criticism was significant, especially for defining narrative itself. However, the Chicago school was also important in helping to articulate formal and structural elements of the text, such as plot. There is also an influence from structuralism and narratology, as his literary hermeneutic attempts to define what it is that makes a narrative function. There is also the influence of reader-response criticism, especially in defining the role of the reader. To briefly summarize Culpepper's literary hermeneutics, Culpepper is concerned with the text as text, in terms of its major constituents, such as plot, character, and the like, and with the reader of the text, both within and outside the text.

The literary hermeneutics that Stephen Moore (1954-) develops is not the same kind of working model that Culpepper initiated and that has become enshrined in what is now known as narrative criticism. To the contrary, what Moore does is illustrate the consequences of literary criticism, especially as one moves down the interpretive path from the New Criticism to reader-response criticism to deconstruction and poststructuralism.

There are three important interpretive signposts that characterize Moore's literary hermeneutics. (1) The first significant signpost is Moore's observation that redaction criticism and literary criticism have much more in common than most scholars think. Narrative criticism is then better able to describe the thought of the text than is redaction criticism, which does not recognize the narrative nature of the text and hence does not describe the content of the text as well. (2) The second significant signpost concerns reader-response criticism. Whereas some forms of reader-oriented criticism lead to the disappearance of the reader, some more radical forms lead to the disappearance of the text itself. All reading, even of grammar, involves interpretation, to the point that there is no firm foundation for interpretation that does not involve assumptions. (3) The third signpost relates to Derridaean poststructural deconstruction. Derrida calls into question all of the major points of departure for interpretation. This "hard" form of deconstruction attempts to break completely with the foundations of criticism itself, with the interpreter becoming alienated from meaning, and an exile and an outsider to the interpretive task. With his theory of literary hermeneutical dependence, Moore thus accounts for how one gets from narrative criticism to deconstruction and poststructuralism.

Conclusion

This introduction has merely sketched the major figures and movements that will be treated in more detail in the following chapters of this volume, with a more detailed discussion of these major hermeneuts and their approaches to the major interpretive issues of their day. The range of their thought encompasses the broad scope of philosophical and hermeneutical issues of the last several hundred years, and addresses such fundamental issues as epistemology, metaphysics, and general questions of being, besides specific questions of interpretation and understanding within the realms of philosophy, linguistics, theology, and biblical studies, among others. We have not tried to be exhaustive in our approach by dealing with all of the contributors to this continuing hermeneutical debate. We have chosen to deal with those figures who are representative of the major areas of hermeneutical thought, especially as they have continued to have currency in ongoing hermeneutical discussion and development. This plan has guided our presentation of the subject matter of the book in a roughly chronological ordering. As a result, we begin with hermeneutics as it emerged from theological discussion during the Enlightenment, and continued to develop into a mode of philosophical thought in its own right. At this point, hermeneutics was firmly embedded within other areas of intellectual endeavor, including the field of theology and biblical studies, before emerging into its own light, where it has continued to function for the last century or more. However, as we have already seen in the brief summary within this chapter, hermeneutics has always continued to be in dialogue with many of the major philosophical and even theological or biblical interpretive trends of the day. This comes to the fore in a variety of recent hermeneutical thought that is influenced again by theological and related questions. In the course of our discussion of these major figures and movements, it will also become clear that hermeneutics has been in continuous and fruitful dialogue with many other influential intellectual movements of the last one hundred years, such as structuralism and literary interpretation. Their interplay also continues to provoke important hermeneutical developments. We do not claim to have provided an exhaustive study of hermeneutics and interpretive theory, but we believe that we have introduced the major figures and their thought within the fields of hermeneutics and interpretive theory as they have had a direct influence upon a variety of philosophical, theological, and biblical perspectives.

TWO Hermeneutics and New Foundations:
Friedrich Schleiermacher and Wilhelm Dilthey

Introduction

Friedrich Schleiermacher and Wilhelm Dilthey sparked the first major hermeneutical revolution, which changed forever the nature and scope of hermeneutics. Through them, hermeneutics was reborn in ways that none could have predicted. Redefining hermeneutics from being primarily a discipline-bound utility for safeguarding (legal, philological, biblical) interpretations into a more generalized view of human understanding, Schleiermacher and Dilthey were the first to emphasize what has become known as the author-oriented hermeneutical tradition. It is not enough, they argue, that we try to interpret a given text on its own, e.g., its structure, language, and/or cultural context. We cannot hope to understand the meaning of it except that we also try to understand the author, his or her socio-historical context, and the reader's participation in the present "hermeneutical circle" — a concept that has its genesis in this revolution. Interpretation involves historically conditioned and living beings, in terms of both the original creative act of a text and the current reader who tries to makes sense of that intentional act. However, we need not merely stop with an awareness of the author's subjective state or our own subjective influences, for if we are methodologically and epistemologically rigorous we may find a fuller — for Dilthey, an objective — understanding that is just as good as, or in some cases even better than, that of the original author. Hermeneutics, it was promised, could serve as the foundation for the human sciences, for wherever there was communicative misunderstanding, verbal or written, there hermeneutics offers clarity and enlightenment.

Friedrich Schleiermacher

Friedrich Schleiermacher (1768-1834) is often referred to by the distinguished title of "father of modern theology." Philosopher, philologist, pastor, and theologian, Schleiermacher's thought ushered in a new era of modern Protestant theology. His distinct approach to religion and his philosophical theology continue to offer much to those doing theology today. Regardless of whether one finds him persuasive or not, all subsequent theology has had to contend with him, and future theology will at least in part define itself in light of him. As the first to develop a general hermeneutics into a formal discipline of study that is methodologically self-conscious — in contrast to the specialized philological, legal, and theological hermeneutics that are typified by exegetical procedures — Schleiermacher's reputation as a significant figure in hermeneutics is well deserved. With his systematic approach based upon general principles of human language and thought, Schleiermacher offers us a universalized hermeneutics in which understanding is in many important respects "the *art* of understanding." Whether in his contributions to theology, philosophy of religion, or hermeneutics, Schleiermacher was one of those rare historical figures that we may rightly refer to as a pioneer.

Life and Influences

Schleiermacher was born in Prussian Breslau (Lower Silesia in southwestern Poland), into a family of Reformed (Calvinist) ministers. Both his parents, Gottlieb and Katharina-Maria, were also reared in clerical families. The mature Schleiermacher is sometimes referred to as belonging to the Reformed tradition in a broad sense, but one may rightly question the appropriateness of such a label. While his love for the church cannot be denied, his rejection of central expressions of orthodox Reformed theology is equally beyond dispute. Understanding Schleiermacher's significance for modern theology and biblical hermeneutics is therefore made difficult because of his awkward fit within a specific tradition and the controversies that surround his unique ideas.

24

Schleiermacher was first educated among the Moravians, first at the Moravian Brethren's school in Niesky (1783-1785) and then at their seminary in Barby (1785-1787). While he was at the Moravian seminary he began to question their pietist theology as being too narrow and intellectually inadequate. It was among the Moravian Brethren that he also started to question orthodox tenets of Protestantism such as Christ's nature and atoning sacrifice. These doubts would soon turn into outright rejection. Nevertheless, by that time Moravian pietism had already left its indelible mark on him, though it was not immediately evident when he left the seminary in frustration and disappointment to study philosophy at the University of Halle (1787-1789).

Since its seventeenth-century beginnings in German Protestantism, pietism has had significant influence throughout the Christian world. Pietists generally attempted to restore what they believed to be the authenticity and genuineness of sincere religious commitment as the call to a devout and holy life — to be "people of the heart" and of the Bible. Pietism stressed experience and holy living in order to correct the perceived frigidity created by overemphasizing the purity of doctrine that tends to intellectualize faith. Most often suspicious, even hostile, to claims of self-directed or autonomous rationality, closed systems of traditional theology, and strict adherence to doctrine, the pietistic emphasis on inward experience, including a preoccupation with individual conversion, could easily lead to the problem of religion being perceived as an entirely private and emotional matter. However, it also emphasized external aspects such as spreading the gospel, helping the needy, and exemplifying the practical side of Christianity generally.

While at Halle, Schleiermacher was able to explore in-depth the works of prominent philosophers such as Plato (428/427 BC-348/347 BC) — he would later make important translations of Plato's dialogues — and other ancient Greek philosophers, as well as Baruch Spinoza (1632-1677) and Immanuel Kant (1724-1804), all of whom served to greatly influence the development of his philosophical theology and the reconstruction of his Christian faith. During this time he was also increasingly influenced by the Enlightenment tradition and the growing Romantic movement. The influences of F. W. J. Schelling (1775-1854) and, in particular, his later relationship with Friedrich Schlegel (1772-1829) likewise proved to be important for Schleiermacher's theological development.

Having finished his studies at Halle, Schleiermacher served briefly as a private tutor to the family of Count Dohna in East Prussia (1790-1793).

Then, after his first and second successful theological examinations prescribed by his church, both of which resulted in undistinguished performances in dogmatics, Schleiermacher became assistant pastor in the Prussian town of Landsberg (1794-1796). After this brief pastorate he was then appointed Reformed chaplain at the Charité Hospital in Berlin (1796-1802) where he wrote his first book that earned him significant recognition, *On Religion: Speeches to Its Cultured Despisers* (1799). This first publication is well known for its revolutionary importance in the philosophy of religion, even more so than its theological import. Although it was addressed primarily to the "cultured despisers" of religion for the sake of rescuing religion, it still has theological relevance, especially insomuch as Schleiermacher offers his vision of the nature of religion in general.

After another short pastorate, Schleiermacher received his first academic post at the University of Halle (1804-1806) where he taught on such subjects as philosophical ethics, theology, New Testament exegesis, and hermeneutics. Then, beginning in 1810, as professor of theology at the University of Berlin, Schleiermacher taught such subjects as dogmatic theology, hermeneutics, practical theology, history of philosophy, ethics, dialectics, and New Testament theology and criticism. The competency and breadth of his intellectual pursuits are as impressive as they are uncommon, even among intellectuals.

Schleiermacher became known to the English-speaking world for this striking apologetic work, *On Religion: Speeches to Its Cultured Despisers,* and his most important dogmatic text, *The Christian Faith* (1821-1822). Both are widely considered classics along with the likes of John Calvin's (1509-1564) *Institutes* and Karl Barth's (1886-1968) *Church Dogmatics.* Next to Schleiermacher's significant theological influence are his contributions to the philosophy of religion and hermeneutics, though in the history of philosophy he is generally held to be a second-rate philosopher. At present, Schleiermacher's thought receives only modest scholarly attention for his interpretive method despite being widely recognized as the first to systematically formulate the basic principles of modern hermeneutics.

Romanticism and the Enlightenment

Schleiermacher's hermeneutical approach reflects his strong connection to the early German Romantic movement, and both his conflict with and his embrace of the Enlightenment tradition. Schleiermacher wrote during a time when Enlightenment ideas held wide audience and considerable influence. The eighteenth century had witnessed an outpouring of knowledge in virtually every field of human pursuit. This fostered new optimism and confidence in the powers of human reason and natural scientific inquiry, for Enlightenment knowledge was alone believed to be capable of conquering misplaced fears in dogmatic authorities, naïve superstitions, prejudices, and the like. It was an "age of reason" that had a new faith in science, technology, commerce, and the human ability for progress. Not surprisingly, this new confidence posed a number of critical problems for the church, including the undermining of essential ideas such as biblical inspiration, inerrancy, authority, and claims to ultimate truth. In fact, the church increasingly came under attack wherever it was perceived to block human reason, especially when it made knowledge claims based on revelation of God. The new enlightened faith attempted to displace the old as a full frontal assault on traditional authority and its claims to truth.

As a reaction to and break from Enlightenment rationalism, Romanticism, both theistic and atheistic, fostered the primacy of humane interests, imagination, creativity, the emotional and passionate nature, and human freedom. Often celebrating irrationality, though not itself necessarily always anti-rational, the romanticists sought a way of life and view of nature in contrast to the narrow rationality of the Enlightenment. They believed that neither human reason nor mechanistic science could adequately articulate or capture the full breadth of life, art, religion, and nature. Thus the German romanticists sought a new way of looking at the world that moved away from the mechanistic orientation of those such as Isaac Newton (1663-1727) and René Descartes (1596-1650) in which we may have certain and rational knowledge — for, it seemed to Newton and Descartes, the universe is fully determined and predictable. The romanticists saw the encroaching worldview of the age of reason as a dangerous force that threatened to reduce the dynamic nature of humanity and the world — life — into something quantifiable, uniform, bland, and ultimately controllable, objective, and mechanical.

Schleiermacher's works bear witness to his passionate effort to overcome many of the limitations imposed by scientific rationalism through his own pietist and romantic dispositions. For example, he argues that propositional theology, e.g., exegetical theology, is by itself a fruitless endeavor, and that any theology beginning with a metaphysics of a transcendent God who makes himself known through a rational, external, and objective revelation is groundless in method and content. He believes that true religion has been missed by dogmatizing theologians who seek timeless and fixed dogmas as sources of religion. Instead, true religion is a feeling, awareness, or consciousness of God, i.e., a "feeling of absolute dependence." This feeling of dependence constitutes the authentic human being. In this sense, according to Schleiermacher, religion is not a special method of knowing or way of acting but is innate to all experience. Part of the difficulty in appreciating just what this "feeling" means is that Schleiermacher does not offer a definition of it. By his own admission he cannot, for if one did, then such a description would risk becoming something that is objectifiable, something that "is" quantifiable. In Schleiermacher's account, Scripture is not the mediation of God's self-revelation to human beings, i.e., as if God could somehow be evident in the comprehension of sentences and their meanings, but is his direct communication to the self-consciousness of human beings through impressions. We cannot, for Schleiermacher, make this revelation to our self-consciousness objective or even strictly rational. It escapes our powers of reason and scientific investigation.

In response to his understanding of our consciousness or awareness of God as an essential element of human nature, Schleiermacher went on to revalue and redefine many central Christian ideas. While he personally held Christianity to be distinct among world religions, his ideas helped open the study of religion to non-theological and non-Christian ways. After all, if, as he claims, religious truth is not something found in doctrines or fixed dogmas but in human experience and piety, then even the Bible cannot hold an ultimate claim to religious truth. Instead, for Schleiermacher, we discover truth within a community and its experience of redemption. The real value of biblical stories is their ability to encourage and nourish the consciousness of God for those who hear them. One of the consequences of this is that if a literal interpretation of the biblical text is shown to be in error, e.g., the biblical witness does not agree with incontrovertible archeological evidence, then such an error does not mean we should be discouraged about the authenticity of the Bible. The nature of religious faith and truth does not depend on archeological evidence to verify it. Truth and meaning are behind the text and are what foster the feeling of absolute dependence. In this way, Schleiermacher's dogmatic theology is a systematic and consistent articulation of the teachings — written and oral expressions of religious affection — that prevail at a particular time and in a particular communal context. This protects religion from misplaced emphasis on the objectivity of orthodoxy, as well as the brutal skepticism of the Enlightenment. This also means that the subject matter of dogmatics is safe in the experiences of particular religious communities, rather than being entirely subjective and private religious experiences. However, because Schleiermacher's notion of religious knowledge is immediate self-consciousness, the emphasis is no longer on God or any externally existent being but on the experiences of humanity. This result is in many respects similar to the repositioning evident in the Enlightenment tradition.

Hermeneutical Method and the Art of Understanding

Schleiermacher was never primarily a biblical scholar, yet his theological program maintains a more significant place for biblical interpretation than many biblical scholars have acknowledged. Even so, as much as his hermeneutics has proven helpful for interpreting the Bible, his interpretive method is more properly applied to all experiences of interpretation. Hermeneutics, for Schleiermacher, is the application of general rules of understanding developed through close attention to the nature of human thought and language. As such, Schleiermacher's hermeneutics represents a radical shift in method, motive, and ideology, most especially in that he breaks free of the regulating ideals of authoritative interpretation, i.e., church tradition. Even so, while his hermeneutics is clearly not a biblical hermeneutics *per se,* Schleiermacher still appreciates that Christian communities will most often base themselves and their doctrines on the Bible, so an exegetically based theology, and therefore hermeneutics in some sense, must still have an essential role in the church along with dogmatics. This raises one of the more peculiar oddities in Schleiermacher's thought, namely his rejection of the Old Testament. He accepts that Christian communities will always be at least partially determined by their continual reference to the New Testament, but he rejects the Old Testament because he does not think it provides the same degree of guiding normative status as the New Testament. This view has been a difficult one to understand for both admirers and detractors of Schleiermacher.

Not surprisingly, Schleiermacher's persistent appeals to the subjectivities of human nature, i.e., our feeling of dependence as the ground of genuine religion, frequently caused many to feel uncomfortable with both his theology and hermeneutics. Sometimes described as "a theology of experience" that foolishly ignores more objective grounds of religion, Schleiermacher's hermeneutical method is indeed far more subjective, individualistic, and psychologizing (having to do with the human mind and mental processes) than traditional methodologies that attempt to provide objective-historical accounts of the Bible on its own terms. However, in fairness to Schleiermacher, this simple and often pejorative characterization fails to appreciate his deep historical and intersubjective commitments.

Schleiermacher's approach moves away from philologically centered interpretations based upon methods and procedures to more philosophical interpretations in which there is a heightened awareness of the act of interpretation itself and its historical groundings. The genesis for his rules of interpretation is independent of texts, e.g., their structure and context, because they are rules based first and foremost upon a general theory of how we understand. Hence, with Schleiermacher the hermeneutical task becomes less concerned with establishing textual meaning on its own and more concerned with comprehending the act of understanding itself. Hermeneutics in this manner is essentially an art of coming to understand another person. Even more fundamental than this, however, it is the art of avoiding misunderstandings.

Understanding is not something we stumble upon or something interjected into the gap of our lack of awareness of things. It requires a critical methodological effort to achieve. Schleiermacher's assumption is not that we understand as a matter of course, but that there is usually an existing misunderstanding or foreignness that we must strive to overcome. For instance, when interpreting the Bible we do not encounter it simply as it is and understand it as such. Rather we encounter it already predisposed to misunderstanding its meaning. We are alienated from it in some fundamental way. The temporal and cultural gap between us and the text's author are the negative grounds for this misunderstanding. More than merely with texts, we are also alienated from the world and others as well. This universalized notion of misunderstanding creates a critical need to have a rigorous hermeneutics. For if we are not only predisposed to misunderstand texts but all things we try to understand, then we must have a hermeneutical method for all life. Hermeneutics, then, is the art of understanding all communication.

Schleiermacher sees the task of interpretation as primarily a matter of both reconstructing and reproducing the past act of the author. To accomplish an interpretive reconstruction he proposes two interdependent approaches or means of interpretation that form the foundation of both the theoretical and universal character of his hermeneutics. The first concerns a grammatical or linguistic interest, and the second a psychological interest. Each may vary in importance depending upon the specific matter at hand, yet their relation to one another always remains one of continued dialogue in which neither is subjugated to the other. Alone, neither grammatical nor psychological procedures are sufficient for understanding.

Grammatical or linguistic interpretation — which is different from translation — includes philological, exegetical, and literary operations for the purpose of interpreting a text against the context of its original linguistic rules and structures. When interpreting what someone is saying, this kind of interpretation focuses on commonly shared features and rules of language, i.e., how things are said in particular situations and how those "sayings" relate to common rules or norms. For Schleiermacher, the meanings of words are related to how they are used and the governing rules for the use of the words. To understand the potential range of meaning in a word we must discover the rules governing the presuppositions behind it. Indeed the role of language for Schleiermacher cannot be easily underestimated, for it is crucial to his entire hermeneutical method. Only through the medium of language may we understand one another. However, linguistic interpretation alone is not enough. For instance, Schleiermacher recognizes that there are often ambiguities of linguistic meaning due to highly individualistic and therefore distinct contexts that cannot be easily understood; that is, there seems to be no way of tracing the words back to shared norms. However, even if we do know the linguistic norms, Schleiermacher believes that in order to truly know someone's intended (linguistic) meaning we must appreciate their psychological state as well.

Psychological interpretation considers the subjectivities and creativity of the individual author (or speaker). By identifying the meaning of a text with the subjectivity of the author, Schleiermacher accepts that there is always something behind the text to which we must look, i.e., the worldview and creative genius of the author. Hence, the act of interpreting cannot be a matter of merely applying philological rules and literary procedures through objective and rational reflection. Rather, interpretation is the art of understanding the individuality of the author, which is possible because of a "divinatory" method of sharing in a psychological commonality between the interpreter and interpreted, i.e., because the interpreter is somehow able to project him- or herself into the mind of the author. While an interpreter may gain a great deal of knowledge about the linguistic and grammatical elements, there must also be an intuitive reading between the lines, an empathetic projection of his or her own consciousness for the sake of reconstructing and reliving the originally intended meaning.

To understand a text, the interpreter must be in conversation with the grammatical, including the historical and cultural context, and the psychological aspects at hand. This dialogical movement between the grammatical and the psychological with regard for the text has no specific or detailed rules to follow, so interpreters must struggle to gain increasing awareness with each further rereading. In this way, the interpretive process moves from the reader through the text, in light of the temporal and cultural context of the work, toward the original intention of the author. Throughout the interpretive process, we are working against what Schleiermacher sees as a persistent inadequacy in texts, which we must overcome before we may truly grasp the inner form and meaning of the text as determined by the author and his or her life-context.

Despite the most rigorous and thorough applications of Schleiermacher's interpretive methods, readers will never be privy to all of the relevant knowledge or intentions of the author. Yet this does not deter or frustrate Schleiermacher's notion of interpretation. To the contrary, he argues that an interpreter may understand the text and its author as well or even better than the author understands himself. Like other romantic thinkers, he accepts that no matter how unique a person's writing (or spoken expression) might be, it will always reflect a wider cultural spirit (Geist) that may be discerned by the interpreter. When a reader approaches a text by making explicit the unconscious rules and conventions of the text's language, time, and culture, he or she may be in a better position than the author to understand it. Ironically, Schleiermacher finds that an author may not even be the best interpreter of his or her own work.

Schleiermacher is well known for his emphasis on the psychological aspect of interpretation, in which readers should attempt to mimic or align themselves with the minds of authors and reconstruct their intentions. Meaning, in this sense, is conceived as being a matter of an inwardly subjective state of mind that is somehow present in the outward manifestation of the text. Yet even when one takes up the stance of the author, and attempts to work out the meaning fixed by the author's intention, there will be an endless number of latent meanings. Both the inherent circularity of all understanding and the immensity of potentially relevant knowledge to help supplement any interpretation preclude a final interpretation.

The problem of inherent circularity is often described in terms of the "hermeneutical circle." In Schleiermacher's account, the hermeneutical circle is a continual and somewhat paradoxical reciprocity between parts and wholes, i.e., a text and the body of literature to which it belongs. We are able to understand a language or text only through a sense of individual elements or parts, but to do this we must have a sense of the whole, and vice versa. This implies a vicious circle that leads to tautologies (using different words to say the same thing) without any broadening horizon of meaning. How might one break into or out of the hermeneutical circle?

Schleiermacher's contention is that our initial understanding of a text is not a complete comprehension of either parts or wholes, but a form of intuition or awareness that offers a partial awareness of the whole context, i.e., author's life and intentions, balanced with the parts. This is possible because understanding does not happen all at once but comes in different degrees of success. At first an interpreter may not have any logical grounds for understanding, only an intuitive basis or sense of a whole. Upon this initial basis the reader builds interpreting refinements with each further examination. To employ either a grammatical or psychological approach to interpretation may very well lead to circularity problems, but, for Schleiermacher, through the dialogical relation of grammatical and psychological analysis the tautological dangers and insufficiencies of the circle are overcome. Consequently, the hermeneutical circle is not vicious and pointless, despite its persistent circularity. Rather, the art of understanding is a perpetually spiraling movement toward the approximation of meaning in which we strive to overcome misunderstandings stumbled upon at every turn.

Wilhelm Dilthey

Philosopher, historian, and humanist, Wilhelm Dilthey (1833-1911) succeeded Schleiermacher at Berlin but, while greatly indebted to him, he is not overshadowed by him. Whereas Schleiermacher is responsible for the birth of contemporary hermeneutics, Dilthey is responsible for developing a general hermeneutics encompassing the essential nature of the entire human or social sciences. For Dilthey, human life itself is hermeneutically accessible. Through a "hermeneutics of life" we may gain a greater appreciation of the comprehensiveness of lived experience, i.e., understand the meaning of our actions and even ourselves. For Dilthey, understanding is the interpretation of all expressions of inner life. Through his efforts, the discipline of hermeneutics evolved into the methodological foundation for all of the social and human sciences. To help secure this foundation, Dilthey developed his hermeneutics in order to show that the social and human sciences could be just as rigorous and objectively valid as the natural sciences, though in quite different ways.

Life and Influences

Relatively little has been written specifically on Dilthey's life. He was born in Biebrich, Germany, as the son of a Calvinist theologian. He enrolled to study theology at the University of Heidelberg in 1852, but after one year he left to study history and philosophy at Berlin. Dilthey defended his doctoral dissertation on Schleiermacher's moral principles in 1864. He briefly taught at Berlin, took up his first professorial chair at the University of Basel in 1866, and was called to the University of Kiel in 1868 and then to Breslau in 1871. In 1882, he returned to Berlin as successor of Hermann Lotze (1817-1881) to take up the chair that G. W. F. Hegel (1770-1831) once occupied. Dilthey's long career as a university professor ended when he retired fully from teaching in 1905. Today he is often hailed as the best and most significant example of the nineteenth-century hermeneutical tradition. Surprisingly, in spite of his substantial contributions and influence, Dilthey received only modest attention during his own lifetime. This is no doubt due in part to his lack of academic publications. At the time of his death, he had published only three books and various essays.

Dilthey's long academic career was devoted to an enormous range of subjects and his dozens of posthumously published volumes help prove his versatility in many intellectual fields. He produced important studies in literary criticism and made important contributions to aesthetics, moral philosophy, epistemology, and more. Dilthey also produced intellectual biographies of celebrated thinkers such as J. W. Goethe (1749-1832), J. C. F. Hölderlin (1770-1843), and his most popular, Schleiermacher and Hegel. Dilthey's major influences include Kant, Leopold von Ranke (1795-1886), J. G. Droysen (1808-1884), Schelling, and, in particular, Hegel and Schleiermacher. Scientific method as idealized in models of the natural sciences and the empiricism of John Stuart Mill's (1806-1873) *Logic* were also important in the development of Dilthey's thought.

As an important historical thinker, Dilthey is perhaps best known for his epistemological analysis of the social or human sciences, and as one of the first to stress the distinction between the human sciences *(Geisteswissenschaften),* including philology, religion, psychology, politics, economics, etc., and the natural sciences *(Naturwissenschaften),* including physics, chemistry, astronomy, etc. This distinction is now a standard division. One of his main claims is that the human sciences have a distinct subject matter just as empirical, objective, and scientifically valid as the natural sciences. Even so, unlike the natural sciences, the human sciences take

on their methodological starting point from the historical world constituted and formed by the human mind. To scientifically study an individual's historical world one must attempt to understand the whole person
and not just select elements — reflecting a fragmentary approach common
in the natural sciences. For Dilthey, the methodologies of the natural sciences cannot effectively work on the essentially unpredictable and irreducible nature of human beings.

In 1883, Dilthey published the first part of his major philosophical
work, *Introduction to the Human Sciences*. In it he approaches the problem
of interpreting human phenomena with a methodology that seeks a deeper
historical consciousness and appreciation of life itself. He explicitly rejects
the reductionist, mechanistic, and ahistorical approaches of the natural
sciences because he believes that imposing external categories of interpretation based on the particular methods of the natural sciences will fail to
do justice to the fullness of experience. Instead, Dilthey's foundational science for human studies was developed as a systematic method for gaining
concrete and historical knowledge of "expressions of inner life" that make
given conclusions objectively valid, without being entirely materialistic. To
understand life, Dilthey claims, one must understand it from categories intrinsic to the complexities of life experiences themselves.

Unlike the natural sciences, Dilthey approaches the nature of human
beings as far more than just biological facts to be quantified or data to be
organized. However, this does not mean there is something behind life.
There are no universal subjects located in any sort of transcendentalism or
metaphysical absolute. Unlike Schleiermacher, Dilthey does not appeal to
any mystically intuited "feeling of absolute dependence" or consciousness
of God. For Dilthey, there are only historical individuals within specific
communities for whom life unfolds contingently and changeably. Thus,
while understanding may still be as objectively valid as it is in the natural
sciences, it will be a different kind of objectivity, one that is more like interpreting a poem than doing physics.

Life and Lived Experience

Dilthey's conception of "life" is central to his philosophy and his study of
the lived experience of individuals within the context of their life-worlds.
From his notions of life and lived experience, Dilthey develops an epistemology for how we can achieve objectivity about an experience or set of

experiences. He argues that in their daily lives every person has life experiences that cannot be divorced from serious scientific study of humans. But this scientific study does not examine life-experiences as if they are modeled on the sort of experiences scientists use while they examine their research objects from a distance. Dilthey's philosophy of life is meant to offer a way of both examining and describing experiences such that they remain bound to the totality or comprehensiveness of our lives, including our values, morals, beliefs, social customs, laws, etc. To examine life-experiences presupposes someone in a given historical and cultural context that cannot merely be stepped out of in order to systematically examine them. In Dilthey's account, the distancing of the subject and object of study, as idealized in the natural sciences, is simply not possible when examining the complexities of life-experiences. It might seem like an obvious point, but in order to examine our experiences we must turn to an understanding of ourselves rather than to external things. Indeed, the implications for this sort of understanding are highly complex and significant.

Dilthey's primary methodology, his hermeneutics, is directed toward the human world — a theme reminiscent of the romantic movement — for the purpose of arriving at objectively valid interpretations of the concrete and historical expressions of inner life. Hermeneutics is about understanding or interpreting life, for to understand is to understand historical expressions. Unlike the supposedly neutral and indifferent (unprejudiced, dispassionate) stance of the natural scientific researcher who must typically isolate a subject matter in order to understand it through meticulous experimentation — removing it from its natural place in the world and placing it under a microscope — Dilthey formulates his notion of understanding life in terms of the complex nature of our cognitive, conative, and affective abilities. The objectivity of Dilthey's hermeneutical investigations does not consist of abstracted sense perceptions and observations cut off from historical and social influences. Rather, understanding is based on interpreting expressions of life, not external causation or physical laws. Dilthey sees that we all have individual experiences as well as sharing in communal experiences. These interdependent features of our lives support each other in a unity of meaning that is accessible to hermeneutics. That is, it is both our individual and communal experiences, together, that provide sensibility and make possible an objective examination. If all one had was one's own isolated experiences of life there could be no objectively valid interpretation of them.

Human Sciences, Understanding, and Expressions

The human sciences or studies, for Dilthey, are grounded in the relations of lived experience, expression, and understanding. He works with the problem of human understanding by continuing the romantic and idealist heritage grounded in the concept of spirit *(Geist)*, and proposes a hermeneutical program through a distinct historical method that includes all human phenomena or objectifications. For Dilthey, in order to appreciate our life-experiences we must develop our historical consciousness in ways that are lacking in the natural sciences. When people think of natural science, the most commonsense view is that it offers explanatory knowledge. By contrast, Dilthey argues that something other than "explanation" is possible in the human sciences, for they are disciplines of the "human spirit," *Geisteswissenschaften,* which term may be translated in many ways. It is generally translated as "human" or "social sciences," i.e., knowledge of humanity. More narrowly it is the "spirit sciences" or "sciences of the spirit," though this in no way implies something spiritual in a religious sense. *Geisteswissenschaften* or human sciences have come to include fields of study such as history, philosophy, sociology, religion, psychology, art, literature, politics, law, and economics. Dilthey's hermeneutics is meant to offer us critical access to the structure of the human spirit as it is expressed in all of these fields.

Dilthey's related concepts of "understanding" and "expression" are important to his philosophy generally and to his theory of interpretation in particular. Understanding *(Verstehen)* is used by Dilthey in a specific way unlike the explanatory knowledge of the natural sciences *(Verstand)*. Understanding, in Dilthey's sense, is essential to the human sciences as a comprehensive awareness of mental content, i.e., ideas, intentions, feelings, that manifest in given expressions, i.e., texts, words, gestures, art. We perceive meaning in the world, in communities, in ways that are not strictly empirical (involving sense-data), so uncovering the structures of meaning and making explicit the process that creates meaningful experiences will be distinct from "explanation." *Verstehen* involves both an empathetic and non-empathetic understanding of expressions of life as we come to understand the other, e.g., person, text, work of art, as another. This understanding of the other is quite unlike that in which we perceive the other as merely a means toward a desired end or goal, which tends to distract us from being truly attuned to expressions of life.

This understanding is not achieved through introspection but the interpretation of expressions of life that are the externalizations of experience. An expression is not just a feeling, which is what most people may infer from the notion of expression, but any manifestation of inner life, e.g., social customs, laws, writings. That we experience life as meaningful, and that we are capable of expressing and understanding that meaning, form the basis of Dilthey's epistemology for the human sciences. The very nature of experience itself, as evident in expressions for objective examination, is Dilthey's subject matter and basis for systematic investigation within the human sciences.

Again, it is not so much understanding manifested as explanatory knowledge that is important to Dilthey, but expressions or manifestations of experience, i.e., of mind, for we cannot penetrate beyond expressions to some kind of pre-experience or experience in itself. All we have are expressions upon which to reflect. Reflections or interpretations of expressions are possible because we all share in a social-historical world. If expressions were entirely subjective or based solely in individual experience we could not expect to make sense of them in any significant way. Hence, we may make sense of them because expressions are part of the socially and historically structured world in which all human beings are a part. And because we are able to make sense of expressions, regardless of whatever evaluative judgment may be reached, we have at least a minimal basis for reaching objective conclusions about those expressions.

Unlike the natural sciences in which there is an assumption of one day possibly exhausting knowledge about certain phenomena, i.e., knowing everything about electromagnetism, there is no such optimism when it comes to the objectivity of expressions in the human sciences. The very nature of experience is such that it is indeterminate. There will always be something left unsaid. For Dilthey, expressions offer objective access to subjective experience, but life expresses itself in many forms and its meaning is never absolute or final, for history itself is never final. As with Schleiermacher, Dilthey's notion of understanding is not something that occurs all at once, but something that comes with degrees of success. As breadth is added to our experiences and they are integrated into our unity of meaning, understanding will be progressively realized. Sometimes even past events may gain new meaning we did not previously recognize, as our currently expanding awareness increases with every new experience in the present.

Historicism

Various notions of history or historicism are evident throughout the academic disciplines. Dilthey's historicism is different from the positivistic belief in objective historical understanding, i.e., historical knowledge derived from uninterpreted observations and events. Indeed, a great deal of Dilthey's work is devoted to understanding the nature of history, for, as we have discussed, he believes we are historical beings and that everything that may be understood will be done so historically. Through a historical understanding he attempts to provide a new philosophical foundation for the human sciences that is quite different from many popular *a priori* epistemologies of history that attempt to organize the neutral data of human history (facts). As we have discussed, Dilthey's historicism begins with creating a foundation that develops our historical consciousness, which proceeds from the totality of our being and life-experiences. This means that the description of the world coming from the human sciences will be one about our participation in specific historical-social realities. Although he sympathizes with the empiricist school, which relies on observable phenomena in the world as the sole basis for making knowledge claims, this approach simply cannot offer the rich historical-social reality of his much fuller notion of historicism. Again, to be clear, Dilthey's philosophical foundation, with its basis in his dynamic historical paradigm, goes beyond empirical facts to an understanding of human experience that transcends the narrow truth realm of the natural sciences and all previous forms of historicism.

Dilthey argues that historical science is possible because we are ourselves historical beings who can understand our own inner historicity of experiences. Understanding the historicity of our experiences begins by focusing on particular historical individuals bound to particular contexts. To understand, for Dilthey, is a matter of understanding our historicity which is itself an expression of life. We experience life as temporal beings who have direct experiences of life as a whole or unity (shared common meaning) and as particulars (specific events and experiences), and all of this within the context of our past, present, and future. The common meaning or unity of meaning that we experience holds together the past and our anticipations of the future in the unified present. This is not a reflective temporal ordering we do to make sense of our experiences, but the implicit temporality of every experience. We understand life as inescapably tied to the past and future. It is the synthesis or joining of these times (past and future) in the present that gives us our historicity. We are not inextricably captive to our past (though we are dependent on it) or entirely preoccupied with our present, for we also have anticipations of the future. We are creators who live historically, both conditioned by it and conditioners of it. Dilthey's insistence on the distinct temporal character of historical experience and understanding is one of his major contributions to the history of philosophy.

Methodological Interpretation and the Hermeneutical Circle

Through his interpretive methodology, Dilthey proposes that we may reflect upon expressions of human existence and, in turn, answer how it is possible to understand in an objectively valid way, i.e., how we may understand life in terms of life. As we have seen, his hermeneutics is an attempt to form a foundation for the *Geisteswissenschaften* as a methodological understanding capable of offering an equivalent scientific credibility evident in the natural sciences.

In order to hermeneutically achieve a comprehensive and objective historical understanding of a text or expression, the dual operations of what Dilthey calls "elementary understanding" and "higher understanding" are needed. Elementary forms of understanding are essentially pragmatic forms of hermeneutical analysis, i.e., concerned with our interests and needs. This analysis is possible because of his belief that expressions in human activities manifest mental content. We may have elementary forms of understanding because expressions are tied to pragmatic affairs of everyday life in which all human activities are manifestations. The interpretation of street signals, facial movements, basic social norms, etc., all require elementary forms of understanding. This sort of understanding is not so much a reflective effort on our part but a form of understanding that does not require conscious effort because the expressions are understood immediately. However, when an expression is not immediately understood or there is need to make more complex interpretations, we require higher forms of understanding. These higher forms are the methical foundations of hermeneutics that presuppose lower forms of understanding for determining the significance of an expression. The higher forms of understanding include grammatical, psychological, and comparative reconstructions, which establish the basis for epistemological claims.

For Dilthey, meaning is always contextual, so we must understand in the light of a given context, i.e., a specific place and time. Dilthey's notion of the hermeneutical circle is, like Schleiermacher's, informed by the reciprocity of whole and parts. Meaning is grasped from the parts, or individual experiences, in light of the whole, and the sense of the whole is conditioned by the meaning of parts. The relation of whole and parts is grounded in lived experience as a matter of context and relation. It is something that can be objectively grasped in reference to one's own experiences.

Hermeneutics for Schleiermacher and Dilthey is essentially reconstructive, i.e., looking away from oneself while concentrating on the other person or expression. For Dilthey, the reconstruction of a person's inner world of experience is an essential re-experiencing of another's world. Without re-experiencing there can be no objective understanding. Through an empathetic re-creation that relies upon the unified meaning of our own experiences, we are able to effectively relive and understand, particularly as this relates to written expressions that may be examined repeatedly. Understanding a text, like understanding an expression, involves a circular working from a text to the author's biography, the particular historical context, and then back again. This is not meant to be a vicious circle leading to tautologies but a spiraling toward wider understandings. The text is an expression of its author, as the text and author are expressions of their socio-historical context.

Interpretation, as the application of understanding to a text, reconstructs the environment in which it was composed and places the text within it. Interpretation becomes more effective as we acquire more knowledge about the author. Thus temporal and cultural distance from an author makes reliable interpretations more difficult, but not impossible. For both Schleiermacher and Dilthey the interpreter's present life-world has a negative or inhibiting value, while simultaneously being the only available basis from which we may transplant ourselves into another's world. To do this we must overcome ourselves and the inhibiting prejudices and biases. Understanding is possible to the extent that we may methodologically untangle ourselves as much as possible from the present, and attempt an attunement or right relationship to the present of the other.

As with Schleiermacher, Dilthey focuses much of his attention on meanings associated primarily with an individual and his or her life-world, rather than with the medium of expression such as a text. Dilthey's later work emphasizes less of the psychologizing evident in Schleiermacher and concentrates more on the expressions of an author as both products of the socio-historical context and products of the individual author. Unlike

Schleiermacher, where grammatical interpretation largely characterizes the objective nature of the hermeneutical circle with which psychological analysis is combined, Dilthey perceives the hermeneutical circle in such a way that the objectivity of the grammatical analysis also applies to the psychological. Dilthey is more methodically conservative and avoids the more mystical, empathetic, and intuitive leaps Schleiermacher requires for understanding.

A Critical Appraisal of Romantic Hermeneutics

It would be an exaggeration to claim that hermeneutics began with Schleiermacher. But with him a specific hermeneutical problem arises, namely, that of broader human understanding. His conception of hermeneutics as the art of understanding provides a new horizon or worldview for hermeneutics in which it is no longer adequate merely to ask grammatical or linguistic questions with the expectation that understanding will arise from their answers. Prior to Schleiermacher, hermeneutics was divided into three main forms as philological, theological, and legal. He introduces a more general hermeneutics that can address questions of human (mis)understanding across these individual and often isolated applications. Schleiermacher's response to the universalized hermeneutical problem is meant to overcome not only misunderstandings that accompany ancient texts such as the Bible, as if historical and cultural distance alone were the sources of estrangement, but misunderstandings that accompany all human communication. Hence, with Schleiermacher, hermeneutics is no longer primarily a matter of rules to be applied to texts but principles or laws of understanding that transcend individual occasions or applications. Wherever there is discourse, the art of understanding is necessary.

Schleiermacher's romantic and philosophical inclinations meet in his appeal to the living relation of creative genius and general rules of understanding. Interpreting a text involves not only gaining knowledge of a text's social-historical context but entering into the perpetual dialogical relation of psychological and linguistic procedures. Both the text and its author are open to interpretation as readers attempt to go behind the text and reproduce the original intention of the author. Objectively, Schleiermacher's method seeks to know the language of the author as the author did. Subjectively, it seeks to know the internal and external aspects of the author's life. Schleiermacher believes that interpretation takes on a circular structure as a hermeneutical spiral in which we may arrive at an understanding of a given text and author that is even more complete than that held by the originator. This ambition may seem naïvely optimistic, but it is consistent with his belief that there is a larger cultural spirit to which the author belongs and about which we may come to know.

One of the more common criticisms concerning Schleiermacher's hermeneutics comes from his emphasis on psychological interpretation that attempts the reproduction of authorial intent. Since Schleiermacher, many hermeneuts have rejected authorial intent as the basis or norm of meaning because it leads to an undependable subjectivity that cannot offer objective truth, but only states of consciousness that are not very helpful or certain. His foremost theological critic, Karl Barth, argues that Schleiermacher reduces theology to anthropology (Barth, *Theology of Schleiermacher*). Schleiermacher's method of interpretation is susceptible to the same critique by locating fixed meaning in the intention of the author. This reduction is indicative of Schleiermacher's more general undervaluing of objective grounds of religion such as his rejection of the doctrine of biblical inspiration. He claims that Scripture does not deserve any sort of unique interpretive method but belongs in the same hermeneutical categories of grammatical and psychological analysis as all other texts.

Hans-Georg Gadamer (1900-2002) criticizes Schleiermacher for defining hermeneutics as the art or technique of interpretation and for his reconstructive approach to the intentions of an author (Gadamer, *Truth and Method*, 173-97). It will become clearer in Chapter Four that, for Gadamer, hermeneutics cannot be a technique or method of interpretation. Such a method or technique reflects a misplaced confidence in procedure. Further, Gadamer claims that hermeneutics cannot be a reconstruction of an author's intention because texts have their own independent and living meanings that are not fixed and limited by an author's intention.

Despite many of Schleiermacher's misplaced ambitions he deserves considerable credit for establishing a decisive turn within hermeneutics, one that helped many others such as Dilthey to rethink the nature of human understanding. With Dilthey the primary hermeneutical question became more than just how we should avoid misunderstanding, but how we should understand historically. His systematic investigation and interpretation of the richness of human experience, along with his struggle with the problem of historical understanding, expanded the universality of general hermeneutics in new and important ways.

Dilthey's notion of understanding in the human sciences depends on the unique ability of individuals to place themselves empathetically into the psychic life of others. This is a distinct form of understanding unlike that experienced by an individual coming to understand a natural object or phenomenon. Dilthey's philosophy of life examines life as it is irreducibly expressed, e.g., through signs and works, rather than as something that follows universal physical laws. We understand ourselves and others as we understand expressions of life, and we can understand expressions because there is always a certain kind of homogeneity.

Dilthey's method of interpretation depends on his key insight that the most fundamental expression is that of history. As a consequence, all other understanding must take place historically, even that of ancient texts. Dilthey claims that through the development of historical sense, as a unity or coherence of meaning, one transcends the prejudices of one's present. One's own historical consciousness makes objectivity in the human sciences possible through a transcending of the individual's relative experiences and awareness. Consequently, Dilthey's historical understanding concentrates much less on authorial intent than Schleiermacher's psychological analysis. Without carefully supplementing authorial intent with universal history, Dilthey believes hermeneutics risks becoming ahistorical and arbitrary. However, one may very well wonder just how certain or objectively valid the unity or coherence of meaning (universal history) is that is supposedly separate from the person understanding it.

For both Schleiermacher and Dilthey our present life-world or context is negative in that it creates unwarranted, biased, or prejudiced views. However, both Dilthey and Schleiermacher recognize that understanding depends on reference to something we already know. Yet this way of understanding implies we are already inclined to impose or merely bring along our biases and prejudices when trying to understand. If re-experiencing is the primary means of acquiring objectively valid understanding within the human sciences or of an ancient text such as the Bible, and understanding depends on reference to what one already knows, we cannot really be sure when complete objectivity has been gained. This problem is partially answered insofar as Dilthey's method is neither an entirely subjective nor an objective understanding, but something that occurs outside the strict bifurcation of subject and object. Dilthey's hermeneutics is a subjective process that offers access to an objective reality in degrees of determinacy rather than all at once. And while the empathetic association essential to both Dilthey and Schleiermacher entails the likely interjection of one's own conditioned and prejudiced understanding in reconstructing meaning, the historicity of Dilthey's method and the desire for authorial intent in Schleiermacher's are grounds for establishing objectivity that assists in overcoming subjectivity and arbitrariness — even if not entirely successfully on either account.

Dilthey failed ultimately to overcome the scientific style of reductionism exemplified in the natural sciences. At the time it seemed to Dilthey that the only way to offer credibility to historical knowledge would be to offer a dimension like that of the natural sciences. And while Dilthey freed historians and social scientists from the need to justify themselves on the basis of strict empirical science, his epistemological methodology does not go far enough. The specific force of this failure will become more evident under the later examinations of Gadamer and Martin Heidegger (1889-1976), both of whom approach hermeneutics from our ontology (the structure of our "being"). For example, Gadamer claims that neither the human nor natural sciences may achieve total objectivity. Gadamer credits Dilthey with expanding hermeneutics into a historical method and epistemology of the human sciences, but he believes that Dilthey failed to appreciate the radical difficulty in attaining objectivity and that he ultimately remains too method oriented. Gadamer is not alone in his pessimism toward gaining objective understanding. Since Dilthey, many have become suspicious of attaining absolutely objective knowledge in any area of human pursuit.

Conclusion

Schleiermacher and Dilthey are often considered exemplars of the author-oriented hermeneutical tradition because of their emphasis on the author and his or her social-historical context instead of the text itself. Schleiermacher is the more extreme case as evident by his proposal that we ought to try to locate authorial intent as the genuine source of a text's meaning. In response to these traditional author-oriented hermeneutics comes the charge, among others, that methodological hermeneutics is guilty of reductionism, i.e., of taking immensely complex events or materials and considering them under rubrics of either mind, context, or tradition without a more comprehensive approach. Nevertheless, while such criticisms seem justified and the methods of Schleiermacher and Dilthey seem limited and misguided in significant ways, they are still the radical forerunners that laid the foundation for hermeneutical thought throughout the twentieth century.

The common conception of biblical hermeneutics as primarily a matter of practical exegetical operation between text and reader was fundamentally and radically changed in Schleiermacher and Dilthey, so much so that, by the end of the nineteenth century, hermeneutics could no longer be primarily associated with biblical interpretation. Instead, a whole new universalization of the fundamental nature of hermeneutics manifested itself as a transdisciplinary quest for general understanding. Hermeneutics is still applicable to biblical texts, but for many people the interpretation of sacred literature no longer holds a special place among other literature or deserves a unique interpretive method. The relevance to biblical interpretation is not merely that hermeneutics provides a shift in emphasis but that it offers an entirely different way of approaching the Bible. Understanding Scripture is no longer something done with rules and procedures of exegesis alone, or with a unique sense of understanding that is applicable only to sacred literature. While we may view Schleiermacher and Dilthey's methods as lacking on many fronts, they are nevertheless responsible for establishing new foundations for hermeneutics through the perennial question: How do we understand?

REFERENCE WORKS

Barth, Karl. *The Theology of Schleiermacher,* ed. Dietrich Ritschl, trans. Geoffrey W. Bromiley. Grand Rapids: Eerdmans, 1982.

Bulhof, Ilse N. *Wilhelm Dilthey: A Hermeneutic Approach to the Study of History and Culture.* The Hague: Martinus Nijhoff, 1980.

Dilthey, Wilhelm. *Dilthey: Selected Writings,* ed. and trans. H. P. Rickman. Cambridge: Cambridge University Press, 1976.

———. *The Essence of Philosophy,* trans. Stephen A. Emery and William T. Emery. Chapel Hill: University of North Carolina Press, 1954.

———. *Hermeneutics and the Study of History,* ed. Rudolf A. Makkreel and Frithjof Rodi. Princeton: Princeton University Press, 1996.

———. *Introduction to the Human Sciences,* ed. Rudolf A. Makkreel and Frithjof Rodi. Princeton: Princeton University Press, 1989.

———. *Pattern and Meaning in History: Thoughts on History and Society,* ed. H. P. Rickman. New York: Harper & Row, 1962.

———. *Poetry and Experience,* ed. Rudolf A. Makkreel and Frithjof Rodi. Princeton: Princeton University Press, 1985.

———. "The Rise of Hermeneutics," trans. T. Hall. In *Critical Sociology: Se-*

lected Readings, ed. P. Connerton. Harmondsworth, UK: Penguin Press, 1976.

Ermarth, Michael. *Wilhelm Dilthey: The Critique of Historical Reason.* Chicago: University of Chicago Press, 1978.

Gadamer, Hans-Georg. *Truth and Method,* trans. Joel Weinsheimer and Donald G. Marshall. 2nd rev. ed. New York: Continuum, 2002 (1960).

Gerrish, B. A. *The Old Protestantism and the New: Essays on the Reformation Heritage.* Chicago: University of Chicago Press, 1982.

————. *The Prince of the Church: Schleiermacher and the Beginnings of Modern Theology.* Philadelphia: Fortress Press, 1984.

Hodges, Herbert A. *The Philosophy of Wilhelm Dilthey.* London: Routledge & Kegan Paul, 1952.

Makkreel, Rudolf A. *Dilthey: Philosopher of the Human Studies.* Princeton: Princeton University Press, 1975.

Niebuhr, Richard R. *Schleiermacher on Christ and Religion: A New Introduction.* New York: Charles Scribner's Sons, 1964.

Palmer, Richard E. *Hermeneutics: Interpretation Theory in Schleiermacher, Dilthey, Heidegger, and Gadamer.* Evanston, IL: Northwestern University Press, 1969.

Plantinga, Theodore. *Historical Understanding in the Thought of Wilhelm Dilthey.* Toronto: University of Toronto Press, 1980.

Redeker, Martin. *Schleiermacher: Life and Thought.* Philadelphia: Fortress Press, 1973.

Rickman, H. P. *Wilhelm Dilthey: Pioneer of the Human Studies.* Los Angeles: University of California Press, 1979.

————. *Dilthey Today: A Critical Appraisal of the Contemporary Relevance of His Work.* New York: Greenwood Press, 1988.

Schleiermacher, Friedrich. *The Christian Faith,* trans. H. R. Mackintosh and James Stuart Stewart. Edinburgh: T. & T. Clark, 1928 (1820-21).

————. *Hermeneutics and Criticism, and Other Writings,* trans. and ed. Andrew Bowie. Cambridge: Cambridge University Press, 1998.

————. *On Religion: Speeches to Its Cultured Despisers,* trans. Richard Crouter. New York: Cambridge University Press, 1988 (1799).

Stoeffler, F. Ernst. *The Rise of Evangelical Pietism.* Leiden: E. J. Brill, 1965.

THREE Phenomenology and Existential Hermeneutics: Edmund Husserl and Martin Heidegger

Introduction

Edmund Husserl and Martin Heidegger were the first major contributors to phenomenological and existential hermeneutics. As we shall see, Husserl proposes a foundational theory of knowledge and method upon which to ground other disciplines. His unique means of doing this is through a methodological consideration of what is originally and immediately present to consciousness. Husserl's phenomenological method is meant to describe our consciousness of phenomena as they are in themselves, prior to interpretations, presuppositions, or explanations.

Reacting in many ways directly to Husserl, Heidegger seeks to disclose something he believes to be more fundamental to our way of living by asking the question — What is the "meaning" of being? Such, for Heidegger, is a question about our mode of knowing, a question about our living as knowers, not about the status or content of our knowledge *per se.* We do not exist as conscious selves, as Husserl has it, with an intentional awareness "of phenomena." Rather, we exist among phenomena, engaged and interacting with the world such that we cannot rely on epistemological, methodological, or any other artificially imposed means of conditioning and clarifying human understanding. Hermeneutics, for Heidegger, describes how we interpretively understand prior to our use of methods and techniques. Moreover, and perhaps most controversially, Heidegger claims that hermeneutical understanding necessarily involves prejudices and biases — contra

Husserl — for we rely on them to make sense of things and our experiences of them.

Edmund Husserl

Edmund Husserl (1859-1938) is the central figure of the twentieth-century discipline known widely as phenomenology, literally "the science of phenomena." Phenomenology, from *phenomenon,* refers to what is "seen or observed." In its most basic sense this is a discipline concerned with what is given or what appears in our conscious awareness of things. That is, phenomenology is concerned with what is seen or directly experienced by human beings. What happens when we experience a tree, a person, a house? What is going on when we "know" or "understand" the world and others? Husserl's philosophical research is not hermeneutics. It is not even hermeneutically inclined in its methodology. Nonetheless, his phenomenology is of invaluable significance for hermeneutics indirectly and for the development of what might be called "phenomenological hermeneutics" directly. Husserl's influence is particularly pronounced in the hermeneutical developments of those such as Martin Heidegger, Hans-Georg Gadamer (1900-2002), and Paul Ricoeur (1913-2005), all of whom have taken up and expanded their own form of phenomenology. Husserl's thought is not hermeneutical, for he avoids taking an "interpretive" stance in many respects, focusing instead on things (phenomena) and our consciousness or experience of them. Naturally, it might seem odd to claim that Husserl's non-hermeneutical thought is important, even central, to the development of twentieth-century hermeneutics. Yet for those who responded to his challenge and adopted elements of his philosophical program into their own, often much different, perspectives, his "method" proved to be revolutionary, offering a radical new direction for hermeneutical thinking.

Like his contemporary, Wilhelm Dilthey (1833-1911), Husserl develops a universally valid foundation and theory of knowledge in contrast to the domination of the natural sciences and the persistent presumption of metaphysics that there is something behind reality. Unlike Dilthey, however, Husserl begins with the validity of logical formations, which, he argues, are ahistorical, while Dilthey begins with manifestations of life through which life is understood historically. Nevertheless, while their individual conceptions of philosophy diverge from the start, their shared desire to save philosophy from the domination of the natural sciences and to

49

offer universally valid foundations for understanding overlap. Both Dilthey and Husserl offer twentieth-century interpretive theories very important starting points from which to develop and define themselves. Not surprisingly then, their views still find wide audience among scholars and students today, both within and outside continental Europe.

Life and Influences

Husserl was born at Prossnitz, Moravia, in 1859. He began his university studies in 1876 at the University of Leipzig, where he studied astronomy, physics, mathematics, and philosophy. In 1878, he began mathematical studies at the University of Berlin under the mathematicians Karl Weierstrass and Leopold Kronecker. He did not complete his studies at Berlin but moved to Vienna where he did his doctoral dissertation in theoretical mathematics on the calculus of variation, receiving his doctorate in 1883. After a short return to Berlin, Husserl went back to Vienna in 1884, where he spent two years studying philosophy with the Austrian philosopher and psychologist Franz Brentano (1838-1917). Impressed by Brentano and his philosophy, Husserl decided to continue his studies in philosophy but to do so at the University of Halle, where he submitted his dissertation (or *Habilitation,* the second dissertation required for German university teaching) *On the Concept of Number* in 1887. It was at this same university that Husserl began his teaching career (1887-1901). He later taught at the University of Göttingen (1901-1916) and of Freiburg (1916-1928), after which he retired, but not before gaining a significant following. In 1937, because of his Jewish background, Husserl was ordered by the German authorities to leave Freiburg. This is only one example of the difficulties he experienced under the National Socialists. His death followed one year later, after he had become isolated, quite lonely, and sick with pleurisy.

Husserl published relatively little in his lifetime, but his extensive unpublished literary works are still being transcribed, edited, and published. After his death, 40,000 pages of manuscripts were taken from Freiburg to Louvain to prevent them from being destroyed. Since 1950, the Husserl Archives have continued to edit his collected works, *Husserliana.* A number of volumes have already been produced.

For the most part, scholars have been rather indifferent to Husserl's religious inclinations, preferring instead to focus on his philosophical method, which does not directly take up issues of religion. It is unclear how much interest Husserl had in religion, though it is fair to say he was at least modestly interested, if only because he had some religious associations. While Husserl was born into a Jewish family and later married a woman from the Prossnitz Jewish community, he did not embrace his Jewish heritage, but became an Evangelical Lutheran in 1887, was baptized as a Christian, and reportedly died as one. Still, any direct connections or relevance between his philosophical and possible theological concerns are tenuous at best, despite the discernible influence his phenomenology has had in the study of religion, theology, and philosophy of religion.

Husserl's Development

With his phenomenological method, Husserl argues that philosophy may become a rigorous science, which, as he sees it, is something philosophy has always mistakenly believed itself to be. In Husserl's account, only phenomenology may serve as the proper foundation for the sciences, including all other disciplines of inquiry, for it alone is able to offer the groundwork from which to begin all our investigations without falling into the shortsighted and uncritical dilemma of prior thinking. To that end, the preeminent concern for Husserl's foundational science is what is originally and immediately present to consciousness and, therefore, that which cannot be purely a matter of what is outside the mind, e.g., in the form of objective facts.

Husserl's philosophy is highly complex and has been misunderstood by many of his readers. Added to its complexity, despite the tremendous interest it has generated among scholars, is that there is no straightforward account or closed canon of Husserlian thought. Throughout his life, phenomenology continued to take shape, first as primarily descriptive, then as more of a static transcendental, and finally, a genetic transcendental phenomenology. Some scholars argue that there are large breaks in his thought and that the later Husserl should be seen as distinct from the earlier, but this view seems partially misleading and tends to overlook many of the important continuances in his thinking that are necessary to make sense of his mature thought. As first a trained mathematician and psychologist, Husserl's philosophy follows, in part, the paths taken in his prior mathematical work and study, but it does so as a redirected effort to find something he believes may only be properly philosophical. Husserl developed his phenomenological approach after he had become convinced of the inadequacy of psychologism (an account of logical laws or mathematical knowledge in terms of empirical descriptions of psychological or mental states). In both his early mathematical and his later philosophical studies, Husserl continues to seek a solid and absolute foundation for all the sciences.

Among his various publications, it is in his first major work, *Logical Investigations* (1913), that Husserl provides the foundation for phenomenology and breaks with his previous investigations, which were caught in psychologism. *Logical Investigations* is the first publication in which the notion of "phenomenological description" appears as Husserl's method of describing acts of experience and judgment that correlate with experienced objects, and our understanding of their meaning. Phenomenology is often referred to as a descriptive method because of its evidential and reflective approach. It was largely while he was at Göttingen that Husserl developed the formulations for his transcendental (or pure) phenomenology that are presented in his second major work, and perhaps his most influential, the first book of *Ideas Pertaining to a Pure Phenomenology and to a Phenomenological Philosophy* (1913; the second and third books were published posthumously). In his final major work, *The Crisis of European Sciences and Transcendental Phenomenology* (1936), he presents an existential notion of "life-world" (*Lebenswelt*) as part of his developing genetic phenomenology that considers the way the sense of things comes to be constituted in the mind.

Phenomenology

Husserl proposes that, in order to make philosophy a rigorous science, a critical analysis and description of the world of concrete "lived experience" must always take priority over the world as it actually exists. The basic reason for adhering to phenomenology is that one desires to live a rational and critical life. The goal is to overcome unexamined beliefs and assumptions about the reality of existent things that get in the way of a proper or correct knowledge of how we really experience the world. What is needed to capture the essences of everyday experiences and to gain the most fundamental knowledge is a science of the world of immediate or lived experience. Husserl argues that the natural sciences have already failed before they begin, for they start from presuppositions and perspectives of knowledge that they do not question. Phenomenology is supposed to overcome these false beginnings by asking how things are given in experience and how the meanings of things are constituted.

Husserl's phenomenology represents a definitive turn away from objectivity, the abstractions of scientific theorizing, and the metaphysical or transcendent (distinct from "transcendental"). For Husserl, theories and formulas simply cannot reveal the sort of truth or knowledge provided through his phenomenological method. Only in describing and analyzing the acts of human consciousness where the essences of things are disclosed may we find what is properly and essentially knowledge. Phenomenology in this sense is the science of consciousness. This, however, is not to say that phenomenology is stuck within the individual's closed sphere of consciousness without something more reliable or logical to make sense of its content. To know something is not to be a lone subjective island. Nor is it to be entirely distinct and separate from objective things we experience in the world.

More than merely a rigorous science, phenomenology is meant to be a totally rational science. "Rational" in this sense does not refer to formal logic in which symbols, mathematical precision, and rational arguments determine what is reasonable because they are believed to represent or correlate to reality in itself. It may seem obvious to most, but we do not experience the world in terms of logical symbols or rational arguments. While principles of correct reason may aid us in avoiding many mistakes of thinking, including many common fallacies we encounter in our daily lives, how we know the world "rationally" occurs long before these artificial forms of rationality are imposed. For Husserl, an analysis of consciousness reveals that phenomenological knowledge is prior to all other forms of knowledge, no matter how accurate we believe the other forms to be. His basic premise is that the world, as we know it, is always known in experience even though we have access to various scientific methods and procedures for qualifying and quantifying life. Further, he argues that we do not perceive our experiences themselves, as if they are out in front of us to examine, but we see through them to objects and events in the world. For instance, when I look at a tree I am not standing outside myself examining, categorizing, and scrutinizing my experience of a tree. I myself am simply perceiving the tree. These other "reflective" activities are added later and are therefore distinct from my conscious awareness of the tree. Phenomenology is meant to be a critical way of examining experience as it is, without distorting it by turning genuine experience into an abstraction.

Husserl's main description of consciousness is that it is fundamentally intentional. Consciousness is an act of always being directed toward objects in the world and not toward itself as self-consciousness. The central structure of consciousness is this "intentionality." The world is what we are conscious of, so it is always the object of mind. It does not matter if there is a world prior to or independent of human consciousness because we are only aware of the world as we experience it, as we are conscious of it. Phenomenology, at bottom, is an attempt to analyze the structures of "pure human consciousness" and how consciousness is always "of" something. In many important and precedent-setting ways, Husserl's analysis overcomes the bipolar stress of either subjective or objective knowledge. Phenomenological knowledge cannot be entirely subjective or objective because the subject (ourselves) and the world are always known together rather than separately. One might even claim, as Husserl does, that phenomenological research transcends the opposition between subject and object; that is, subjectivity is not the opposite of objectivity. Even so, this has not kept Husserl's life-work from being criticized on both sides of the philosophical divide. Some claim his method is too subjective while others are concerned that it is preoccupied with an impossible form of objectivity.

Epochē *and Eidetic Reduction*

As we have seen, Husserl's phenomenology is meant to be a radically descriptive and rigorous science devoted to describing "the things themselves." To focus on things themselves means to search for pure and absolute knowledge that may only be realized when we are able to describe the content or data of consciousness without prejudice, bias, or unexamined presuppositions. Husserl's investigation is often called "transcendental phenomenology" to denote the search for ultimate and foundational structures of experience, thought, and reality. It attempts to go beyond the surface of our ordinary experiences and find what is beneath what we take for granted as our everyday encounters. To accomplish this, Husserl proposes two main moves or methods, each one having several different operations. The first method is an attempt to describe phenomena as immediately apparent in experience through the "*epochē* reduction." The *epochē* is the "bracketing," "suspending," "canceling," or "placing in parenthesis" of the world, so that one might attend to what is present to consciousness and, therefore, allow for genuine knowledge of the world, the pure phenomena. The second method is called the "*eidetic* reduction," and is an attempt to offer direct intuition into the essential structures and meanings the mind utilizes when it contemplates an object.

54

To begin a phenomenological examination one must first employ the *epochē* method. *Epochē* is from a Greek word for "cessation" or "abstaining," e.g., of belief. Through this method one suspends judgment and belief in the natural world with the intent of being able to discern how certain beliefs, perceptions, expectations, and the like are structured. For Husserl, only phenomenological knowledge when it is absent of all assumptions of the existent world is certain to the individual. Hence, Husserl's discipline, which may only be done by the individual, begins with one pushing aside the outside world and focusing on things as they show themselves in experience, in essence, going back "to the things themselves" *(zu den Sachen selbst)*.

Bracketing is essential so that one may concentrate on meanings present in the mind, regardless of whether an object of contemplation actually exists, in order to lay open the structures of consciousness. With this method, Husserl proposes that one has the means by which all beliefs, assumptions, presuppositions, and commitments may also be set aside. And while questions concerning the actual empirical existence of objects or things in the world tend to get in the way of attaining knowledge, this does not mean phenomenology denies existence, only that it suspends concern for it.

The bracketing procedure is often referred to as the "transcendental reduction," and it is what makes the "*eidetic* reduction" possible. However, the *epochē* reduction is not, as the word implies, meant to reduce something to its basic or most fundamental principles but to allow access to the phenomenon in the least prejudiced or corrupted way. If I perceive the color red, I am experiencing the pure phenomenon, as an individual, and it is the scientific data that I must bracket or put aside. Red is never reduced to its basic color combinations, light spectrum analysis, etc., in experience. Experience is more than what emerges through scientific reductions.

Although phenomenology is not a description of the "real world" *per se* but our experiences of the perceived world, this does not mean that consciousness creates the world. Consciousness "is" the experience of the world. Further, meanings and values are not in things of the world independently of the human mind, because consciousness is essentially referential as consciousness *of* something. Husserl argues that consciousness contains ideal, unchanging structures and meanings that determine what object the mind is directed toward at a given time.

The *eidetic* reduction, also known as "*eidetic* intuition," is the extraction or disclosure of essences that are the intelligible structures of the phenomena found in consciousness. It is not enough that we only bracket the world and reflect upon the contingent content of our consciousness. In this sense, phenomenological analysis, as *eidetic* intuition, discloses the universal and necessary components or essences of consciousness, contents, and structures. Thus, by way of this intuition of essences (knowledge), phenomenology gains access to the features of consciousness and the relationship between lived experiences of consciousness and ideal objects.

Transcendental Phenomenology

Husserl's transcendental phenomenology undermines both scientific attitudes and philosophical theories because these are, he argues, imbued with prejudiced and uncritical constructions that cannot be the proper foundations for knowledge. For Husserl, ideal knowledge is intuition, namely, what is given in an experience of perception. He challenges all inquiries of science and philosophy to return to the things themselves through an analysis and description of acts of consciousness that are more foundational than, even prior to, scientific knowledge and theories.

However, while Husserl and his contributions to the phenomenological tradition are largely responsible for bringing about much of twentieth-century continental European thought, his specific phenomenological task or discipline has always lacked practitioners. Instead, Husserl's original method has often been overshadowed by existential phenomenology, largely because of Heidegger, and more recently by hermeneutical phenomenology, largely because of Gadamer and Ricoeur. In fact, Husserl had hoped for the continuance of his philosophy through his successor and former assistant (not his student as often believed), Heidegger. Unfortunately, it came as a great disappointment to Husserl when he read Heidegger's first major work, *Being and Time* (1927; dedicated in friendship to Husserl), that his destined successor had gone in a much different direction than his own phenomenology. Heidegger's distinct approach begins with the fact that we are, each of us, "being-in-the-world." According to Heidegger, we cannot possibly bracket the world in order to understand it or ourselves. Since Heidegger, many, such as Jean-Paul Sartre (1905-1980) and Maurice Merleau-Ponty (1908-1961), have argued that phenomenology cannot be merely the investigation of pure consciousness but must take into account the totality of the human situation. Existential phenomenology begins with an appreciation of our presence-in-the-world in ways not dealt with by Husserl's reductionist approach, while hermeneutical phenomenology begins with how we understand and interact with the world through the interpretive structures of experience. Neither the existential nor hermeneutical approaches are exclusive but tend to be mutually supportive, as evidenced first in Heidegger's thought.

In Dilthey, hermeneutics remains subsumed under an epistemological concern as the search for a certain kind of theory of knowledge and method. In Husserl, we find the same effort to establish a foundational theory of knowledge and method on which to ground all other disciplines. Hermeneutics to this point could not escape its methodological and epistemological preoccupations. With Schleiermacher and then Dilthey, the first major move of hermeneutics was to become a general hermeneutics, but in Heidegger we find the second major move of hermeneutics in which it begins to evolve in an entirely new direction. Both epistemological and methodological hermeneutics are challenged by Heidegger in his quest to answer the forgotten question — What is the meaning of being?

Martin Heidegger

Martin Heidegger (1889-1976) is quite simply one of the most important, original, and provocative philosophers of the twentieth century. Some see in Heidegger's work a new beginning for human thought that overcomes the mistaken avenues of belief, metaphysics, and inquiry that go as far back as the early Greeks. Others see in Heidegger's work something that, at bottom, is nothing but meaningless nonsense. In fact, many are initially put off by his often obscure and impenetrable style of writing that became even more cryptic toward the end of his life, while others find his almost mystical style refreshing and rewarding. Regardless of how one weighs the relative success or failure of his work, Heidegger's thought and influence cannot easily be ignored, especially in the study of hermeneutics. The effects of his thought are so broadly evident, from hermeneutics and deconstruction, to political theory, psychology, and theology, that a comprehensive list of those whose ideas have been directly influenced by him would be impossible. Heidegger's own work is characteristically that of Continental Philosophy or Contemporary European Philosophy, within which he is often regarded as the central figure of contemporary existentialist thought, even though he rejected his own association with it. Ironically, most existential thinkers have avoided the title because it stands for so much, or, in Heidegger's case, because it fails to say enough.

Life and Influences

Heidegger was born in Messkirch, Germany, in 1889. Raised in a Catholic family, he initially studied for the priesthood but after two years he left to pursue philosophy at the University of Freiburg. It was at Freiburg that Heidegger became familiar with Husserl's work, especially his *Logical Investigations,* and began to gain a thorough understanding of the phenomenological discipline that would profoundly influence his intellectual development.

In 1913, Heidegger completed his dissertation titled "The Doctrine of Judgment in Psychologism," and in 1915 he completed his *Habilitation* dissertation titled "Duns Scotus's Doctrine of Categories and Meaning," which earned him the right to teach in Germany. In 1919, Heidegger broke with Catholicism and by the 1920s he appears to have rejected religion entirely. Nevertheless, he continued, even under the banner of being a philosophical atheist, to seek a non-metaphysical god unbound to either the objectifying or subjectivizing tendencies that Heidegger continually criticized. Heidegger's theological interests are far-reaching, though he never arrived at any sort of confessional foundation. Gadamer claims that Heidegger's most famous and influential text, *Being and Time,* developed largely from his encounters with Protestant theology while he was at the University of Marburg in 1923 (Gadamer, *Philosophical Hermeneutics,* 214). Heidegger's theology, which may only loosely be labeled a theology (more aptly a negative theology), is directed toward a God that cannot be literally spoken of, and therefore one he never describes or portrays in any detailed way. Heidegger's critique of traditional theologies and their preoccupation with a God that is a "being" provoked numerous theologians such as Paul Tillich (1886-1965), in his *Systematic Theology* (3 vols. [1951, 1957, 1963]), to try to reconcile Heidegger's challenges to the traditional view of God and Christian theology.

Heidegger was appointed as Husserl's assistant in 1919. In 1923, he moved to Marburg to take up an associate professorship, which lasted until 1927 when he became a full professor. The following year he moved back to Freiburg where he succeeded Husserl as chair. He remained there until 1946 when he was removed due to his association with the National Socialists. In his career, Heidegger taught on various topics such as phenomenology, logic, time, and metaphysics, and on thinkers such as Plato (428/427-348/347 BC), Aristotle (384-322 BC), Thomas Aquinas (1225-1274), F. W. Nietzsche (1844-1900), Immanuel Kant (1724-1804), and G. W. Leibniz

(1646-1716). At Marburg, Heidegger interacted with distinguished theologians such as Rudolf Otto (1869-1937), Rudolf Bultmann (1884-1976), and Tillich. All of these were significantly influenced by Heidegger's thought. Between 1933 and 1934, after replacing Husserl as professor of philosophy at Freiburg, Heidegger became the university's first National Socialist rector. His specific political beliefs have been debated by scholars, but his involvement with Nazism is undisputed. After the war Heidegger was prevented from teaching in Germany for five years because of his involvement. Yet despite his political involvements, Heidegger continues to find vast audiences around the world. He died in 1976, having secured a place among the world's most influential philosophers.

Heidegger's Phenomenology

In 1927, Heidegger's *Being and Time* appeared, marking his decisive break with Husserl's transcendental phenomenology and the beginning of his own investigation of "fundamental ontology" (ontology, the study of our being, what it means "to be"). In Husserl's last major work, *The Crisis of the European Sciences,* he presents his existential notion of the life-world of everyday experience. Heidegger picks up on this and various other elements of Husserl's phenomenology, and begins his own ontological project of the lived world. Even so, quite unlike Husserl's phenomenology, which is meant to put philosophy on absolutely certain grounds similar to that of mathematics, Heidegger's phenomenology asks a question concerning being or the being question *(die Seinsfrage).* What is the meaning of being? What is it "to be"? To answer this, Heidegger proposes an analysis or "existential analytic" to reveal the structures of human experience and how we are related to the world and things in it.

The complex nature of Heidegger's project makes any simple explanation impossible. Because of this, many people have come away from reading *Being and Time* feeling more frustrated than enlightened. His obscure and strained syntax, along with his creation of new words, including the redefinition of common German words, makes reading *Being and Time* demanding — in any language. Heidegger was aware that his work would be difficult for others because, in his account, modern societies are not fitted to asking the question of being or to allowing being to reveal itself. Hence, on Heidegger's own terms, to appreciate his philosophy requires that we not only overcome his cryptic style and our own conditioned ways of thinking, but that we open ourselves to something he argues has been passed over and forgotten since the early Greeks. Added to these frustrations is that Heidegger never fully completed the book.

In contrast to Husserl, Heidegger is not interested in the structures of consciousness, essences, or even knowledge *per se*, but in an investigation into the meaning of being. Prior to any theory of knowledge, for Heidegger, is the question of being. But what kind of being do human beings have? For Heidegger, an analysis or description of pure consciousness misses the fundamental truth that we are always already being-in-the-world. The world cannot be bracketed or judgment about actually existent things suspended, for the meaning that things have is known in the context of our relationships to them within the world. Understanding and meaning occur prior to our reflection upon these relationships. Things are perceived and understood as they are encountered and practically used during the course of an ordinary day, and, therefore, known in ways that the act of bracketing would preclude.

With Heidegger, phenomenology becomes a radically interpretive enterprise in which understanding is never without presuppositions or preformed prejudices, for there is no neutral or unbiased starting place from which one may begin to understand. There is only the place and situation in which we always already find ourselves. Like Husserl, Heidegger also returns to the things themselves, but for him this is possible only through the forgotten question of being that we may learn to ask by analyzing the being we ourselves are. According to Heidegger, human existence has a hermeneutical structure that underlies all our interpretations including those of the ontic or natural sciences; that is, both scientific and cultural knowledge must be derived from the structure of being. Yet this does not mean being is a tangible thing as the word "structure" implies. Being is no-thing. Hence, understanding itself cannot be objectively grasped or employed as a faculty of the mind like a method or procedure for securing truth, for understanding is our fundamental mode of being-in-the-world. Human understanding in this sense is what always happens where we find ourselves as "thrown project" — as already in the world at a certain time and place with foreknowledge from previous experiences building upon themselves. That is, understanding happens as we work through the hermeneutical circle from our existential situatedness to a self-developed and aware interpretive stance. It is a stance, however, that is historical, finite, and always incomplete.

One of the ways we may ask the question of being is by way of historical reflection, but Heidegger rejects the notion of objective historical knowledge. Our history is not something that may be viewed or examined by a detached or unbiased attitude. What matters is not so much our history in terms of the facts and details of our past, but our historicity, our being historical. We are thrown into a world in which language, culture, and institutions of life are already given, so no matter where or when we find ourselves we will always be conditioned by our own historical situatedness. Dilthey's examination of the conditions for the study of history was particularly important for Heidegger's development and account of historicity. Like Dilthey, Heidegger argues that we understand life from out of life itself. In contrast to Dilthey's notion of understanding, which depends on the unique ability of humans to place themselves empathetically into the psychical life of others, Heidegger refuses to connect the problem of understanding with other minds. Rather, he argues that a more fruitful investigation will begin when we first recognize ourselves as being-in-the-world and that as such we are never detached observers.

To be being-in-the-world is to be more like actors than neutral and objective knowers. We are participants in and not observers of the world through an abstract and distanced perception of things. Heidegger repeatedly criticizes the ideal of a neutral or disinterested observer as the distortion created by epistemological and philosophical descriptions of human existence. Obviously, one cannot deny we live in a world of objects and people, yet, according to Heidegger, traditional notions of how we are to understand these relations have missed the fundamental starting point — our ontology. Understanding begins with our situatedness as being-in-the-world, rather than our knowledge of others or being-with-others. Being-in-the-world, as our primary way of existence, displaces the too-often privileged priority of one's own inner subjectivity. However, while we are individuals in the world we are also social beings. In fact, for Heidegger, we cannot understand ourselves except as being-with-others and as sharing a world. Ultimately, Heidegger's quest for the meaning of being is supposed to offer a single unified whole, but to examine the totality and disclose what it means to be, he works through fragmented parts, e.g., being-in, being-with, and being-there.

Dasein *and the Existential Analytic*

In Heidegger's view, humanity has fallen into a state of crisis due to its narrow approach to the world, a crisis that manifests itself through technologically and scientifically conditioned ways of thinking. The question of being has not been authentically asked, and because of our ignorance and forgetfulness of what being is — what we ourselves are — a more authentic style of existence has been missed and the world has been darkened. Heidegger did not initiate existential thought, but he did introduce a distinct forcefulness and existential seriousness that had not been evident previously. And although he was never a self-proclaimed existentialist, his thought combines traditional ontology and existential humanism in a dramatic new way. With him, hermeneutics is no longer concerned with methodology, epistemology, or even consciousness. Instead, hermeneutics becomes involved with fostering an authentic existence through Heidegger's ontological investigation into the meaning we have forgotten.

Heidegger claims that industrialized societies tend to foster a manipulative attitude toward life, which is caught up in inauthentic routine. This inauthenticity or "average-everyday" understanding cannot account for or really understand itself because it does not reflect on its own superficiality and dangerous activities. What is needed, Heidegger proposes, is an existential analysis that inquires into the meaning of "to be" that is present to us yet remains to be drawn out. This meaning will only be disclosed when we stop attempting to grasp at essences, facts, abstractions, and the like, and begin to live life without trying to dominate or manipulate it. As beings-in-the-world we are not spectators who find meaning by examining our lives as if they are laid out to be dissected. Rather, our care about the world and our actions within it are always prior to our thinking or examining. Knowledge in the scientific sense may only be supplemental to our distinct way of existence.

Following the Danish existential philosopher Søren Kierkegaard (1813-1855), Heidegger uses the term *Existenz* to describe the mode of existence distinct to humans. We are such that our being is an issue for us, according to Heidegger. But what kind of being do human beings have? Heidegger begins his analysis with his now famous term for humans that serves as the focus of his analysis — *Dasein* ("there-being" or "to be there"). The terms "humanity" or "human" imply too much and too little for Heidegger. For example, "human" does not accentuate the verbal form of "to be" that he claims is characteristic of *Dasein*. To be is not to be an entity or to be a being alongside other beings. To be is a distinctly separate aspect of *Dasein*. To be is to be immersed in everydayness and to "be there." To be there is to be disclosing, and, for Heidegger, if we may somehow get at this disclosedness we will have "to be" understood. To be human —

Dasein — is more than to be an independent self. To be is to be there — to exist in the present, fully interacting with one's possibilities and environment. Truth emerges when we are fully present. It is the perpetual movement of a revealing and a disclosing of what is concealed. We cannot "be" fully all the time, so truth will be revealed to us in part and then concealed shortly thereafter. We live our lives like a pendulum that swings into and out of an authentic understanding and awareness. Clearly, Heidegger's position is different from the widely accepted view among many philosophers in which truth is the final and correct correspondence of facts or logically valid arguments to the world. Indeed, Heidegger's philosophy is especially difficult to decipher, especially when he makes claims such as that thinking itself is not so much an act or process we may learn as it is a way of living, dwelling, being.

Heidegger explicitly rejects the subject-object schema prevalent in most prior philosophical thinking. To be a thing is to be objectively present, but to be *Dasein* is characteristically different. Being cannot be a matter of what it "is" because being has no properties or substance. Ordinary things or beings are evident to us, yet the being of beings, or what it is to be, is always partially manifest as well as hidden. To get at the nature of being requires discipline and patience, for it is not something we may pick up and manipulate with our hands. Heidegger sees the distinctive mode of human life as in contrast to everyday objects because we are not just objects. However, to investigate being one must investigate the human being insofar as it is or has being. In short, the path or window to the meaning of being is through *Dasein,* which provides the place and occasion for the being of beings. Whatever the meaning of being is, it is not a theory, concept, or fact. And however we conceive of being, it will always be prior to the subject-object schema.

Heidegger's existential analysis rests upon a distinction between the ontological and the ontic. The ontic or ontical is the factual world understood by the sciences. Ontic refers to beings or entities and any inquiry into them, such as the ontic sciences of chemistry, biology, and physics. *Dasein* is an animal and has ontic qualities, but it (he or she, more properly we) is unique, for it alone is concerned with the question of being and what it means "to be" — at least in our more authentic moments. None of the other animals inhabiting the earth are concerned with the meaning of being. *Dasein* is unique as ontologically concerned. Moreover, it (we) somehow has relation to its own being in such a way that it may consider its own being in contrast to other entities. For Heidegger, the question of being represents our decision to let the question be a question for us. It is a turn or a decision, an event, of recognizing a wedge between beings and being — an ontic-ontological difference. We are the beings who ask the question of what we are. We are not satisfied with just existing or of knowing entities as such. We alone are able to interrogate the nature of what it means to be.

This questioning is not at all easy, however, for, as we have seen, *Dasein* has no determinate essence or fixed set of properties to be examined. It is comprised of its possibilities. For Heidegger, we find ourselves "there" (out in the world as active selves) and by virtue of our own decisions we emerge as selves — realizing and actualizing our possibilities. We are not determined from birth — as if an essence preceded our existence — even though we are limited and dependent upon our own historical and cultural situations. *Dasein* is able to transcend its particular place and time. "To be" means there is always something outstanding, for *Dasein* aims toward what is not yet — it is always reaching outside of itself toward what is possible and therefore not yet determined. *Dasein* is not trapped within a mind or body, as if always trying to reach out of itself and into the world to grasp at and comprehend objects. It is always already out there dwelling, acting, and participating with objects in their multiplicity. For Heidegger, authentic life means constantly understanding and interpreting what it means to be as we think more fundamentally than is possible in the objective and methodological sciences — letting being reveal itself as being-in-the-world.

Part of what distinguishes our "to be" from mere objective presence, such as that of a rock or tree, is the particular temporality of our existence. Heidegger argues that temporality is the horizon upon which the meaning of being is projected. Our temporality makes the inquiry into being possible. As projection, *Dasein* is transcendent as it is always more (or other) than its actual circumstances. *Dasein* is always fundamentally oriented toward possibility rather than actuality, with the present as the basis for projecting possibilities. The transcendence of *Dasein* is temporality, for our mode of being is open to the past, present, and future. This temporality is not a linear or chronological time (sequential step of one moment after another) but a "being oneself" as one lives toward one's future possibilities while simultaneously knowing one's past and present. Heidegger's strong claim is that the being of *Dasein* is not merely temporal or within time. As strange as it may seem, for Heidegger our being *is* temporality.

Questions of Situation and Hermeneutics of Facticity

Heidegger's ontological phenomenology is a hermeneutics of life or what he calls "hermeneutics of facticity." Hermeneutics in this sense is an interpretation of the conditions and circumstances that determine or limit one's possibilities as being-in-the-world. In our everyday activity, we experience life as already partially interpreted and understood within the context of given relationships to people and things. Thus any attempt to interpret our facticity or the limiting conditions on our possibilities becomes an attempt to interpret interpretation. Our facticity is our being-already-in, so Heidegger's hermeneutics of facticity becomes a seemingly paradoxical self-reflective thoughtfulness. Through hermeneutics we are making understanding explicit and disclosing the nature of being to ourselves. The existential analysis of *Dasein* is itself engaged in an interpretation, a self-understanding of being. Through interpretation we do not make understanding or bring understanding to fruition, for understanding does not arise from the act of reflective interpretation. For Heidegger, interpretation makes explicit what is already understood as the working out of possibilities projected in understanding. Heidegger's hermeneutics has no single and isolated subject or object to be studied, only life itself from which we cannot extract ourselves to study at a distance. We are always intertwined with life in meaningful ways. To be *Dasein* is to be in the world we know as a whole or totality before we know it as parts.

Our initial relation to entities within the web of meaningful relationships is to their handiness or what Heidegger calls "ready-to-hand." Handiness is the primary mode of things that we later forget are handy because of our familiarity with them. If I assume that the pencil I am holding is first an object with various properties and qualities that I later recognize as having pragmatic value, thus becoming handy in writing, according to Heidegger I have reversed what is actually the case. Being-in-the-world is not just being with things spatially and knowing them as products with specific factual properties, but as useful and helpful. We live and dwell with things that matter practically; that is, they are ready-to-hand. I know the pencil first as something to be drawn with, and then, perhaps when it breaks, I become aware of its various properties. We care about things and how things work because they facilitate our potentiality — the awareness of our potential to be. That is, we are linked to things because we care. Yet this caring, as much as it is about our individual selves, is a social activity. We are radically individual and, simultaneously, inextricable from others.

We are individual selves and always involved socially. In fact, Heidegger argues that being-in-the-world is initially and for the most part fallen into a world of averageness or public everydayness.

Dasein has two ways of taking up existence or caring. Either we do so authentically or inauthentically. For the most part, we tend to fall prey to "the they" who do not make their possibilities their own. Yet Heidegger believes that it is out of choices made from our everyday inauthentic understanding that we are capable of more authenticity (though we may never achieve permanent authenticity). We often go day after day stuck in routines. We are lost to ourselves and our own possibilities. Heidegger's notion of authenticity involves our acting creatively and openly with each new day. However, whatever authenticity means today will be different tomorrow. This is because we know we have a potential future of our own that is not merely pre-existing. We are continually remaking our future possibilities by embracing different options and making new choices. It always remains an option for *Dasein* to take the encroaching future as one's own or to flee from it. To be authentic is to embrace possibilities rather than to follow predesigned or designated lifestyles. In Heidegger's account, our openness to the world is not a cognitive ability or an intentional grasp of concepts. It is a mood of readiness to experience the new and unexpected.

As being-in-the-world, *Dasein* initially and for the most part falls prey to inauthenticity. We see our inauthenticity manifest most clearly in our fleeing from the hostile notion of our annihilation, i.e., death. What is needed, Heidegger contends, is an understanding of what it means to live with death, not as an event, but as a possibility. *Dasein* knows itself as with a life to lead and with choices to make. It is always projecting upon possibilities and as such is oriented toward the not yet. If *Dasein* is oriented toward the next moment, then *Dasein* itself cannot be complete. It is always somehow never arrived at and in constant fragmentariness. It exists such that its "not yet" belongs to it. How may *Dasein* grasp its existence as a unitary whole if it is always not yet? Part of an understanding of the unity of being must involve an authentic relation to death. Our orientation to the not yet is an obstacle to grasping *Dasein*'s whole. However, through our understanding of death we may come to understand ourselves in a more unified or whole manner. An authentic attitude recognizes death as the possibility of a complete end in which there are no more possibilities. Death is never present. We never experience our own death as an event (because we are already dead). Yet our awareness of this abrupt end of all our possibilities informs us of our finiteness and helps make our existence our own.

Angst (dread or anxiety) is a unique mood that Heidegger claims confronts us with our own flight from the contingent finitude of the world. Anxiety brings one face to face with the thrown nature of being-in-the-world, i.e., that one is in the world regardless of choice or decision. Even so, we alone have the freedom to make our possibilities our own. In order to face our own lives in their entirety we must live with the possibility of the end of possibilities, having been called back to ourselves by anxiety. Accepting the possibility of my own death intensifies the "mineness" of existence. We often fear specific things such as sickness and accident. However, unlike fear that typically has an object or thing associated with it, e.g., something that will inflict pain or suffering, Heidegger argues that anxiety has none. Anxiety is unlike fear in that it cannot be set aside or overcome by removing obstacles in our lives. *Dasein* is distinguished not only because its being is a problem for it, but also because its understanding of mortality enforces an awareness of potentiality. Anticipation and anxiety free us and bring us face to face with the possibility to be ourselves. Authentic being is always being-toward-death.

Understanding and Interpretation

Heidegger's notions of understanding and interpretation are thoroughly intertwined with the meaning of being. *Dasein* always has a pre-ontological understanding of itself that is usually subsumed or covered over by "average everydayness." Yet *Dasein*'s understanding may develop and interpret itself (i.e., because anxiety brings us back to ourselves) such that it may disclose the structures that ground its everyday ontic existence. Hermeneutics, as a hermeneutics of our fundamental ontology (i.e., facticity, historicity), is a disclosure of being and, consequently, an entirely new form of understanding unlike that of Schleiermacher, Dilthey, and Husserl.

To understand is always to understand in relation to a situation. For Heidegger, we cannot describe understanding like a tool to be used or a specific act or technique to be played out, for it is in and through understanding that we exist. Moreover, to describe understanding we cannot begin with a method, theory of knowledge, analysis of consciousness, or even something we might first associate with language. Rather, we must begin with a disclosure of being. Heidegger argues that understanding may never be self-evident as if it were corresponding to facts in the world, for *Dasein* has no single object or fact to first comprehend. Instead, understanding is inherently circular or hermeneutical. It is an ongoing relation of *Dasein's* ontic, factual everydayness, and its ontological state.

The concept of a hermeneutical circle in Heidegger's account should not be confused with any object-subject relation or even with something formal in structure. His hermeneutical circle is best characterized in terms of pre-understanding and temporality. Structures of understanding involve a fore-structure that constantly projects upon that which is already understood and evident. It is an anticipatory structure or preliminary awareness ("fore-having," "fore-sight," "fore-concept") of meaning. As historical beings, we have anticipations and expectations of the future and its possibilities, as well as conditioned understanding from previous understanding. Hence, all existence is interpretive and all meaning takes place within a context of interpretation mediated by culture and language. What remains in interpretation is to work out "the things themselves" instead of allowing our pre-understanding to be guided by mistaken assumptions or illusions. Even so, this working out is not a technique or method meant to achieve understanding so much as a description of how understanding emerges as we constantly respond to our fore-projection and prejudgments. Understanding happens prior to our reflection because we are already participating, and therefore understanding, from a specific orientation and awareness about our situation and context. *Dasein* is an event, an occurrence, wherein understanding is "to be" in the world, which is always understood interpretively.

While understanding is ontological, i.e., as our facticity and historicity, it is also linguistic. In his famous "Letter on Humanism" (*Basic Writings* [1992]), Heidegger asserts that language is the "house of being." We always already find ourselves in this house, in language. Like understanding, language is not a tool to be used; it is the house in which we exist. The relation of language to thinking and being is a mysterious one, yet it is one that Heidegger argues is very important, for it is the vehicle through which the question of being may be examined. However, the problem of speaking of the relation between "being" and "humans" is that our traditional language invites us to conceive of the two as separate entities. It is no surprise then that Heidegger continually strains to create new terms and concepts to help clear the way for more original thinking.

After 1930, Heidegger took a different direction in his thinking that focused more on the interpretation of Western conceptions of being. During his early career he was mostly interested in the world, tools, and moods. Later, he became more preoccupied with questions of language, technology, thinking, and the need for creative experiences. Heidegger's ultimate quest was to find a new beginning in art and poetry that thinks more originally than metaphysics by questioning our common interpretations, simple adoption of doctrines, and uncritical assumptions. In poetic expression he claims there is a truer experience of being. Through his "step back" from traditional metaphysical thinking, Heidegger argues for the possibility of a new revelation of being through attunement. He considers artists and poets to have a privileged access or relation to the attunement of being. He looks to their radical thinking to find new words and expressions that break through (de-structure) previous philosophical views (e.g., the metaphysical tradition of the West) to ask questions that create a sense of the unfamiliar and find meanings of given phenomena — to let things show themselves.

While Heidegger's notion of interpretation makes it difficult to recognize the immediate implications for textual interpretation, the impact is significant. Foremost is the realization that when we interpret texts our presuppositions and biases will manifest themselves just as much as they do in our exegesis of life and the world. Our facticity and historicity cannot be overcome no matter how ardently we may try to approach a text without prejudices and preconditions. We cannot attend to a text as if it has pure meaning or significance in itself. To understand a text is never to unravel the intended meaning of the author or the fixed meaning of the text on its own. Rather, we will always understand the text out of the possibilities or horizons of our own being.

A Critical Appraisal of Phenomenological and Existential Hermeneutics

Schleiermacher's art of understanding is the first to develop as a general hermeneutics beyond the boundaries of traditional philological interpretations, where the act of interpretation and how we understand understanding are central. Dilthey's hermeneutics, as the foundation for the social sciences, is the first to develop the methodological and objective means he claims are capable of making the social sciences as rigorous and objectively valid as the natural sciences. To their credit, both are responsible for establishing new foundations for hermeneutics as a transdisciplinary quest through the question of how we understand. However, Heidegger's hermeneutics reveals how both Dilthey's and Schleiermacher's hermeneutics remain caught up in a futile attempt to establish grounds or foundations that they cannot deliver through maintaining hermeneutics as a way of knowledge. For Heidegger, this same misguided foundationalism is evident in Husserl's efforts to find a theory of knowledge and method on which to ground all other disciplines. Hermeneutics as existential phenomenology moves beyond understanding as knowledge, which typified much previous hermeneutics including that of Husserl, and continues to be found in subsequent foundationalist hermeneutics. Heidegger's work is not merely an extension of the question of how we know, which dominated prior hermeneutics. Instead, he questions the manner of being of *Dasein* that exists as a particular kind of situated understanding.

Heidegger's existential and phenomenological analysis redefines what it means to understand. By placing ontology at the very heart of hermeneutics, he alters what it means to interpret life and texts. For Heidegger, we may no longer naïvely accept the totality of the world as subject-object relations for our interpretive eye to gaze upon. Instead, there is something prior to all this, a more fundamental starting point for all our inquiries — the meaning and disclosure of being. The ontological turn offers a comprehensive universality as *Dasein*'s understanding that is not a consciousness of the world but being-in-the-world that comes face to face with its own mortality and contingency of existence. Heidegger's ontological quest is driven by basic issues beyond the historical horizons of the text and its author and, among other things, it "de-psychologizes" prior hermeneutics. Hermeneutics is the interpretation of the being of *Dasein* and an event of understanding that cannot be reduced to method, theories of interpretation, or an empathetic projection into another's life.

One of the more common criticisms of Heidegger's philosophy is that it is simply incoherent. What is being? What is *Dasein*? As his detractors point out, these things do not exist. We know what beings are (what people are), for they are observable, measurable, even quantifiable. The "to be" of *Dasein* is a nonsensical and misguided notion that fails to provide an adequately critical and rational basis for formulating a rigorous philosophical system. Indeed, Heidegger's attempt to describe a way of understanding that rejects the popular philosophical assumption of a Cartesian self (the conscious "I") tends to fall on deaf ears, especially among Anglo-American philosophers and theologians. Yet, while these same philosophers and theologians may agree with many of Heidegger's criticisms of previous hermeneutics — e.g., the failure to appreciate the nature and role of language — such agreement in no way serves as approval for Heidegger's own project.

Conclusion

Husserl's influence on hermeneutics has been enormous, although even those sympathetic to his phenomenological method have continued to criticize his foundationalism and his failure to better appreciate the nature of language and history. As we shall see, without Husserl, not only Heidegger but also Gadamer, Derrida, Habermas, Bultmann, and Ricoeur — to name only a handful — could not have been as successful in their attempts to develop a hermeneutical description of understanding. His phenomenological method helped usher in a new era for hermeneutical investigations in which the very notion of human consciousness and understanding took on new shape.

Heidegger's impact on theology and theological hermeneutics is significant, although the response to his work has been mixed. There have been many, especially in German circles, who have embraced especially Heidegger's later thought. However, many theologians have avoided Heidegger and his work because of his atheistic approach and his involvement with the National Socialists. Combined with the difficulty in understanding his work, these elements have kept many from fully appreciating his contributions. Gadamer, also an atheist, has often found wider acceptance among theologians, especially where there is an interest in hermeneutics. Heidegger's philosophy receives its fullest hermeneutical development in Gadamer, who resumes the ontological project by creating what is often celebrated as the most important and substantial work in twentieth-century hermeneutics.

REFERENCE WORKS

Bernet, Rudolf, Iso Kern, and Eduard Marbach. *Introduction to Husserlian Phenomenology.* Evanston, IL: Northwestern University Press, 1993.

Biemel, Walter. *Martin Heidegger: An Illustrated Study,* trans. J. L. Mehta. New York: Harcourt Brace Jovanovich, 1976.

Critchley, Simon, and William R. Schroeder, eds. *A Companion to Continental Philosophy.* Cambridge, MA: Blackwell, 1998.

Edie, James M. *Edmund Husserl's Phenomenology: A Critical Commentary.* Bloomington: Indiana University Press, 1987.

Gadamer, Hans-Georg. *Philosophical Hermeneutics,* ed. and trans. David E. Linge. Los Angeles: University of California Press, 1977.

Guignon, Charles, ed. *The Cambridge Companion to Heidegger.* Cambridge: Cambridge University Press, 1993.

Heidegger, Martin. *The Basic Problems of Phenomenology,* trans. Albert Hofstadter. Bloomington: Indiana University Press, 1982.

―――. *Basic Writings,* ed. David Krell. 2nd ed. New York: Harper & Row, 1992.

―――. *Being and Time: A Translation of Sein und Zeit,* trans. Joan Stambaugh. New York: State University of New York Press, 1996 (1927).

―――. *Discourse on Thinking,* trans. John M. Anderson and E. Hans Freund. New York: Harper & Row, 1966 (1959).

―――. *Introduction to Metaphysics,* trans. Gregory Fried and Richard Polt. New Haven: Yale University Press, 2002 (1935).

―――. *Poetry, Language, Thought,* trans. and ed. Albert Hofstadter. New York: Harper & Row, 1971.

―――. *The Principle of Reason,* trans. Reginald Lilly. New York: Harper & Row, 1991 (1955).

―――. *What Is a Thing?,* trans. W. B. Barton, Jr., and Vera Deutsch. Chicago: Henry Regnery, 1967 (1935-36).

―――. *What Is Called Thinking?,* trans. J. Glenn Gray. New York: Harper & Row, 1968.

Husserl, Edmund. *Cartesian Meditations,* trans. Dorion Cairns. Dordrecht: Kluwer, 1991 (1931).

―――. *The Crisis of European Sciences and Transcendental Phenomenology: An Introduction to Phenomenological Philosophy,* trans. David Carr. Evanston, IL: Northwestern University Press, 1970 (1936).

―――. *The Essential Husserl,* ed. D. Welton. Bloomington: Indiana University Press, 1999.

―――. *Husserl: Shorter Works,* ed. Peter McCormick and Frederick Elliston. Notre Dame, IN, and Brighton, UK: University of Notre Dame Press and Harvester Press, 1981.

―――. *The Idea of Phenomenology,* trans. W. P. Alston and G. Nakhnikian. The Hague: Nijhoff, 1964.

―――. *Ideas Pertaining to a Pure Phenomenology and to a Phenomenological Philosophy. First Book: General Introduction to a Pure Phenomenology,* trans. F. Kersten. The Hague: Nijhoff, 1982 (1913).

————. *Ideas Pertaining to a Pure Phenomenology and to a Phenomenological Philosophy. Second Book: Studies in the Phenomenology of Constitution,* trans. R. Rojcewicz and A. Schuwer. Dordrecht: Kluwer, 1989.

————. *Ideas Pertaining to a Pure Phenomenology and to a Phenomenological Philosophy. Third Book: Phenomenology and the Foundations of the Sciences,* trans. T. E. Klein and W. E. Pohl. Dordrecht: Kluwer, 1980.

————. *Logical Investigations,* trans. J. N. Findlay. New York: Humanities Press, 1973 (1913).

————. *On the Phenomenology of the Consciousness of Internal Time,* trans. John B. Brough. Dordrecht: Kluwer, 1991 (1928).

Macquarrie, John. *Martin Heidegger.* Richmond, VA: John Knox Press, 1968.

Robinson, James M., and John B. Cobb, Jr., eds. *The Later Heidegger and Theology.* New York: Harper & Row, 1963.

Stapleton, Timothy J. *Husserl and Heidegger: The Question of a Phenomenological Beginning.* Albany: State University of New York Press, 1983.

Steiner, George. *Martin Heidegger.* New York: Viking, 1978.

Tillich, Paul. *Systematic Theology,* 3 vols. Chicago: University of Chicago Press, 1951-1963.

FOUR Hans-Georg Gadamer's
Philosophical Hermeneutics

Introduction

In Hans-Georg Gadamer (1900-2002), the historical breadth of Wilhelm
Dilthey (1833-1911), the phenomenological description of Edmund Husserl
(1859-1938), and the ontological analysis of Martin Heidegger (1889-1976)
culminate in an original hermeneutical description of human understanding. Whereas Friedrich Schleiermacher (1768-1834) is often credited with
the birth of modern hermeneutics, it is Gadamer who championed its
twentieth-century development. His name has become synonymous with
philosophical hermeneutics, which, while not religious in focus, has been
very influential in many theological circles and particularly so in biblical
studies. Perhaps best known for the popular phrase "the fusion of horizons" and his contributions to the understanding of texts, Gadamer's work
revolutionized views about the nature of interpretation throughout the human and social sciences.

Concerned with the reigning scientific ethos in which objectivity
and method dominate the intellectual landscape of the West, and the embrace of that ethos by many in the humanities and social sciences, Gadamer offers a hermeneutical description of understanding that deflates the
superiority and almost absolute authority of the natural sciences. Convinced that the methods and techniques of the natural sciences are limited
means, Gadamer describes human understanding in terms quite unlike
those accepted by both the natural and human sciences. Understanding,
for Gadamer, grasps us in unexpected and unpredictable ways. It is an un-

derstanding made possible by our own historically conditioned ways of thinking, and one in which language plays a crucial role. Only when we begin to question the world and ourselves in ways that the natural sciences do not — perhaps cannot — may we begin to know broader, more encompassing experiences of truth. The objective truth of the laboratory fails to account for or make sense of the concrete and practical experiences we know every day. Gadamer believes that hermeneutics offers us the means for describing best the structure of human experiences of meaning and understanding, a structure too often ignored and misunderstood by science.

Gadamer and Philosophical Hermeneutics

The field of philosophical hermeneutics owes its very origins to the work of Gadamer, who titled his foundational work *Wahrheit und Methode: Grundzüge einer philosophischen Hermeneutik* (Truth and Method: Elements of a Philosophical Hermeneutics) (1960), a label not retained in the English translation. In this monumental work that influenced the entire course of interpretive thought in the last third of the twentieth century, Gadamer brought together both philosophical and hermeneutical interests to address questions of meaning and understanding.

Life and Influences

Born in Marburg, Germany, Gadamer's life-story spans over one hundred years and includes some of the most interesting though disturbing periods in human history. Gadamer lived through times of remarkable change, including having witnessed firsthand the greatest technological discoveries of the last century — providing him with important insights into both the good and bad of modern developments — yet his personal history is filled with many periods of sadness and difficulty. At a very early age, he had to cope with the death of his mother, the severe illness and institutionalization of his brother, and the First World War. Beyond his lonely and depressed childhood, Gadamer endured much more, including his struggle to survive polio at 22, the circumstances of his failed marriage, the sickness and death of his father, and, most visibly, the devastation and deprivation of World War II. But while these events overshadow Gadamer's biography, he also lived a privileged life of longevity and contribution to the world.

Gadamer began his university studies at the University of Breslau in 1918. Under Nicolai Hartmann (1882-1950) and Paul Natorp (1854-1924), he completed his doctoral dissertation on Plato at the University of Marburg in 1922. At the University of Freiburg in 1923, he first met Husserl and began his studies with Heidegger, and although Gadamer's early philosophical influences were Hartmann and Natorp, Husserl and Heidegger were more significant to his overall philosophical development. In 1924 he returned to Marburg to continue studying philosophy with Heidegger and classical philology with Paul Friedländer (1882-1968). He passed the state examination in classical philology in 1927. In 1928, under Heidegger's and Friedländer's guidance, he completed his *Habilitation* or second dissertation, titled "Plato's Dialectical Ethics." After his first appointment to a junior position at Marburg in 1928, and his simultaneous though temporary professorship at the University of Kiel (1934-1935), Gadamer was appointed professor at the University of Leipzig (1938-1947) and of Frankfurt (1947-1949), and then succeeded Karl Jaspers (1883-1969) at Heidelberg (1949). He retired from his chair in philosophy in 1968, after which he continued to lecture and travel, often venturing to North America as a visiting scholar. He had a long association with Boston College, among others.

Gadamer's involvement in academic politics during the 1930s and 1940s, and his relationship with the National Socialist party, which he survived by neither supporting Hitler nor openly opposing him, are occasionally matters of debate. For example, his signing of a declaration in acknowledgment of Hitler and the National Socialist state in 1933 has sometimes been an issue of contention. However, to be fair, there seems to have been little significant opposition to the declaration at that time — a notable exception including the Swiss theologian Karl Barth (1886-1968). All teachers in German universities and institutions of higher learning were expected to sign the declaration or be removed from their positions. Still, some scholars question whether his actions were indications of mere political accommodation or moral failure. For the most part — unlike Heidegger — Gadamer has escaped criticism for his political involvements or lack thereof.

Gadamer's religious disposition presents something of a mixed impression. Throughout his work, he makes clear reference to religious and theological issues, evidence of his knowledge of both Catholicism and Protestantism, even though he was never a Christian himself. While Gadamer's writings are intentionally agnostic in terms of a personal faith commitment, they reflect his thorough familiarity with many theological problems such as Augustine's notion of inspiration, so much so that one might argue that they provide the basis for key elements of his hermeneutics. At the very least, it is clear that biblical hermeneutics served as an important background to Gadamer's development of philosophical hermeneutics. Regardless of his own non-religious standing, Gadamer's philosophical hermeneutics has deeply and directly influenced contemporary biblical interpretation and aided in disentangling the unique difficulties posed to theologians trying to make sense of the biblical message for modern audiences. Indeed, far from indifferent or even intolerant, Gadamer's personal motif of always remaining open in conversation is testified to by his enduring sympathy toward religious and theological problems.

As we proceed through the rest of this chapter, some repetition of ideas and themes is unavoidable. The nuances of Gadamer's thinking are made clearer by approaching some ideas from various directions in order to better appreciate them. Some of Gadamer's concepts, such as the fusion of horizons, dialogue, play, and openness, build upon each other, yet represent the same basic notion, namely, how we interpret the world and everything in it. Thus, Gadamer's notion of dialogue helps to make sense of his views on play, while play helps to make sense of his notion of dialogue, and so on.

Not only did Gadamer play a key role in the development of hermeneutics, but he has also been a central figure in many important debates among the most well-known contemporaries on the subject. It is important to understand the basic ideas Gadamer is trying to express in order to better appreciate some of the unresolved tensions in hermeneutics, especially those involving Jürgen Habermas (1929-) and Jacques Derrida (1930-2004), two of Gadamer's most outspoken detractors.

Philosophical Hermeneutics

Like Heidegger, Gadamer is very concerned with the dangers posed to modern societies through the naïve acceptance of exclusively technological and scientific ways of thinking (of which there are many different forms). By accepting the prevailing ideals of modernity with its claims to truth through technique and method, Gadamer believes that many industrialized societies have unintentionally invited disastrous forms of moral and intellectual impoverishment. Whether it is in philosophy, theology, literary theory, or any other field, the ideals of modern objectivism, most prevalent in the natural sciences, have permeated cultural life and created forms of alienation and estrangement, closing off our access to important experiences of truth. Prior hermeneutical thinking, like so many ways of thinking, according to Gadamer, has tended to accept the scientific ethos in its attempts to foster objectivity and method as all-important and indispensable ways to truth. Moreover, Gadamer disputes the popular hermeneutical claims that the most reliable forms of understanding are achieved best through techniques for avoiding misunderstanding (as we have partially seen with Schleiermacher), or through securing objective foundational knowledge (as we have seen with Dilthey). Instead, Gadamer suggests that understanding occurs as something far more radical, when we begin to examine in new ways the object of our questioning and to work through our experiences of estrangement and alienation — the sense of "other" we encounter in new things, people, texts, works of art, etc., and the distance created by artificial boundaries of modern science. Understanding, for Gadamer, is not something we may employ or dominate, as if it were a thing to be achieved through the correct deployment of techniques and methods. Genuine understanding grasps us and dominates us in ways such that we are not in control of it. It is neither purely subjective nor purely objective. Through his philosophical hermeneutics, Gadamer wants to describe the concrete and universal nature of the hermeneutical problem that may only emerge when we are freed from the methodological and procedural assumptions that require us to control how we arrive at understanding, e.g., through experimentation, measurement, and theoretical principles. Such assumptions pervade convictions about ourselves, our experiences, our world, and our cultures. However, Gadamer's argument is not that we should fear these means of discovery, but, rather, that we need to find a more balanced and nuanced way of using them to supplement what exists as a more authentic and original experience of understanding.

Following Husserl and Heidegger, Gadamer argues that we are always more than just observers in the world. We are participants with something at stake whenever we risk asking a question or seeking truth. How we encounter things in the world will always be entangled with and inseparable from our interests, ambitions, concerns, and beliefs. Hence, if we are always somehow involved with what we are trying to understand, then the ideal of distanced and neutral objectivity in which we as subjects are merely blank slates awaiting impressions from the outside world of objects must be fundamentally misguided. What hermeneutics is trying to get at cannot be mapped out in explicit detail like a formula or mathematical equation. Human understanding must be experienced as a living activity in the moment. We cannot fully appreciate it unless we allow it to possess us intimately, opening ourselves to the other — new arrangements and relationships with texts, people, cultures, etc. In short, we cannot understand the world objectively except in a limited and awkward manner. It is an impossible ideal that fails to account for what actually happens to us when we experience the world. Thus, we must free ourselves of the prevailing goals of objectivism and also subjectivism. To that end, Gadamer proposes a new hermeneutics of experience in which the supreme maxim or code of conduct is holding oneself open in conversation. This kind of openness is meant to overcome the belief that we must control and isolate parts of the world in order to accurately and objectively know them. He believes that through the interactions we experience in conversation and dialogue we experience a more fundamental and universal way of understanding than that offered by objectivism.

Philosophical hermeneutics is much more than the practice of certain principles or the application of given techniques for discovering or uncovering the truth of written messages. An experience of truth, written or otherwise, is always more than we might take hold of or grasp fully. No matter how stringent our methods of investigation or how objective we think our mode of retrieving data may be, the living truth of the message in question or the experience at hand will always be more than these forms of seeing may disclose. For Gadamer, what is present in a text, conversation, or work of art is always detached from its origin and author. What this means is that our interpretation will always be a living and dynamic experience in which we do more than follow rules in the scrutiny and interrogation of a passive text. Interpreters must allow the text to draw them into its own world, even though interpreters will remain rooted in the present. And just like our living relationship to the truth of a text, our whole experience of life reflects the same universal hermeneutical dynamics. That is, any hermeneutical understanding, like that of reading a text, represents the same basic structure as our other experiences in life. Thus, Gadamer's description of hermeneutics in terms of what it means to understand is not only a matter of how we know classical texts, philosophical texts, works of art, and the like, but a way of disclosing what it means to have an experience of understanding universally. Clearly this is a bold claim.

The name "philosophical hermeneutics" is a bit misleading, for while Gadamer's approach is philosophical it is not a philosophy proper, especially in the sense of being a closed system of normative rules (what ought to be done). Gadamer does not develop his hermeneutics in order to prescribe how we ought to live our lives or as a program of principles for how we must think if we wish to do so accurately. Rather, hermeneutics is meant to describe how we already live and think, and to be a description of what happens over and above our doing or wanting. His investigation is an analysis and description of the inherent structure of understanding itself. It describes the basic mode of experiencing and understanding by virtue of our ontological structures, rather than offering a complete philosophical system that prescribes rules and norms for life, interpreting texts, proving something to be true, etc. Gadamer's work tries to overcome the many barriers to understanding while simultaneously trying to appreciate phenomenologically the concrete nature of our experiences — as they occur before we reflect on them.

Gadamer is well known for his distinctively dialogical (the logic of dialogue) approach to understanding and his further solidification of the expanded scope of hermeneutics. Like Heidegger, Gadamer begins with the notion that all understanding is hermeneutic and that the hermeneutic function is actually our basic mode of being-in-the-world. As it is with Heidegger, understanding cannot be either a methodological concept or something grounded upon the belief in neutral and unbiased knowledge, for we do not understand ideas, concepts, reasons, and so on, as if we were blank slates. Further, as already noted, hermeneutics cannot be the concern for unlocking the past and fixed meaning of a text, i.e., as located in authorial intent. Instead, Gadamer's hermeneutics is concerned with establishing a dialectic or open-ended questioning and answering between the past and present, and between the world and the interpreter. Knowledge is about more than simply taking a good look to see what is there. It is a product of asking sincere questions that we do not already know the answers to, answers that may surprise and even disappoint our expectations.

For Gadamer, we are beings-in-the-world, living lives already understood interpretively, prior to the application of techniques, rules, and principles of reason. To get at what it means to understand, Gadamer attempts to expose more original experiences of understanding that occur before our thinking and doing. These experiences of understanding may be finite, incomplete, and provisional, yet he argues that they cannot be pejoratively repressed or ejected from our awareness of things and the world, for that is how we know the world. The strong claim here is that we are intimately bound up with this prior and relative understanding. He believes that to try to do away with experiences of life that do not offer clear and present subject-matters to be weighed or measured for the sake of purely quantitative investigations is an impossible and misguided goal. Life does not fit in a test tube, and our experiences cannot be calculated by even the most advanced computer. What is meaningful, important, and life changing is most often, though not always, understood apart from these forms of mechanical seeing.

Philosophical hermeneutics continues the shift evident in Heidegger from thinking of understanding as a methodology of the humanities or as a chiefly reflective attitude upon life, toward a philosophical universality of understanding and interpretation. This hermeneutical universality is the comprehensive embrace of all experience in an ontological investigation, e.g., the experience of art, experience of philosophy, and historical experience. Hence, hermeneutics is meant to be a general or all-inclusive philosophical description that aids in our encounters with historical texts as well as in our encounters with the world. Whether in our interpretations of texts or life, hermeneutics is never about static and absolute interpretations, but is the current dialogue that binds together our language, experiences, and history. While Gadamer's hermeneutics has as its starting point Heidegger's hermeneutics of life or facticity, it is uniquely set apart as a hermeneutics of dialogue.

Truth and Method

Gadamer's earliest interests were in Greek philosophy, as evident by his first book, *Plato's Dialectical Ethics: Phenomenological Interpretations Relating to the Philebus* (the revised form of his 1928 dissertation). Through his studies of Plato (428/427-348/347 BC), Aristotle (384-322 BC), and other Greek thinkers, Gadamer discovered important elements that would help to shape his most influential and famous work, *Truth and Method* (1960), and to motivate his sustained hermeneutical purpose of demonstrating why the role of "practical reasonableness" (prudence or moral wisdom) remains an essential, though often overlooked, feature of human understanding. From Aristotle (it is perhaps Heidegger who deserves credit for introducing this Aristotelian notion to Gadamer), he learned to value the importance of both the practical and theoretical, a lesson Gadamer argues that the natural sciences and other "theoretically" driven interpretive theories have not yet recognized in full. *Truth and Method* represents part of

Gadamer's ambitious effort to draw attention to the critically important need for all of us to make wise and morally good decisions in our lives by finding a right relationship to modern technological developments and the natural sciences.

Until the publication of *Truth and Method* in 1960, Gadamer had published relatively little. After its release, he quickly found international notoriety and influence that would last throughout the rest of his life. In *Truth and Method*, Gadamer confronts what he sees as unnecessarily narrow approaches to understanding the world, especially those that claim (whether implicitly or explicitly) to be the sole avenues capable of leading to the highest forms of truth, i.e., the theoretical pursuits of understanding that characterize modern epistemology and are lionized in popular philosophical accounts of scientific methodology. Thus, *Truth and Method*, contrary to the implied meaning of the title, is not a book about how method may yield truth. It might have been more aptly titled *Truth Over and Beyond Method*.

Truth and Method is a large and complex work that weaves together a lifetime of scholarship and Gadamer's rare depth of insight into the history of philosophy. Its content is notoriously difficult for most readers to understand, not only because it is deeply entrenched in German thought but because of the daring originality of Gadamer's approach to hermeneutical understanding. The first of its three sections is primarily a critique of Kantian-based aesthetics and an analysis of how truth emerges in an experience of art. The second section is a critique of the methodological historicism of Dilthey (including those that came before him), followed by a third section that explores how meaning and truth are mediated through language — something thoroughly historical in nature. Gadamer's *magnum opus* is perhaps best known for the second and third sections in which the nature of language and tradition are given critical roles within his hermeneutical account, yet these sections rely on the first in which he describes the aesthetic experiences of truth and offers a critique of modern "subjectivized" aesthetic consciousness.

Both extremes of objectivity and subjectivity are mistaken descriptions of understanding according to Gadamer. Merely assuming the existence of such a dichotomy overlooks the dynamic nature and potential of human understanding. To overcome the mistaken starting point of an objective/subjective bifurcation — a division that characterizes the different forms of truth expressed by the human and natural sciences, i.e., where objectivity in the "hard" sciences prevails and subjectivity in the "soft" arts dominates — *Truth and Method* begins by describing some of the ways in which our experiences of art (a poem, painting, sculpture, etc.) reveal how we hermeneutically avoid the pitfalls of both objectivity and subjectivity, while remaining confident that what we know is true and reliable rather than radically relative and solipsistic, as if it is only one's own mind that truly exists. It often comes as a surprise to new readers of Gadamer that his main strategy to discredit the superiority of objectivism (and subjectivism in art) is grounded in our experiences of truth with art, a kind of truth or knowledge that is widely considered too subjective and relative to have any real value. How strange it first appears to read Gadamer's defense — rather exaltation — of the very destabilized forms of human understanding that method and objectivism are meant to overcome.

To defend the truth that comes through works of art as an example of human understanding that transcends the limited scope of objectivism, Gadamer attempts to dislodge the popular view that the work of art has only radically subjective value, e.g., it makes us feel good in the moment. He believes that there is much more at work in our (hermeneutical) experiences of art than mere entertainment. To our harm, Gadamer believes that the work of art has been segregated from society and hedged off from our everyday lives by invisible boundary lines defended by popular scientific and epistemological assumptions. In modern societies, most of us do not think of the work of art as speaking directly and meaningfully to cultural situations or as presenting us with important questions about ourselves and our social and political situations. Rather, works of art are often seen as little more than entertainment pieces to be enjoyed in museums, admired as historical markers, or even hung in homes as mere decoration. The value of art, so it seems, is only surface deep. Indeed, many may not regard a poem as a relevant commentary on contemporary life (preferring case study research and the newest statistical analysis), or a theatrical play as something to challenge one's personal decisions in life, e.g., what is the good life? (preferring the expert evaluations of psychologists and perhaps sociologists). Many would not think of a painting as something that dialogues with us, speaking to us meaningfully, even challenging us. In Gadamer's view, the work of art has lost its value in society because it has been falsely stigmatized as a subjective experience without any sustainable claims to importance.

Additionally, *Truth and Method* reveals Gadamer's concern that along with art many other forms of human experience have been dismissed as inferior to the dominant ideals of truth and rationality. Through a consideration of culture, common sense, judgment, and taste, Gadamer argues that the Enlightenment's ideal of scientific knowledge has divorced science and the claim of reliable and trustworthy knowledge from our everyday lives and compromised our abilities to be practically wise, i.e., to make good decisions in the concrete situations in which we find ourselves. As a consequence, when one has primarily a scientific or abstract outlook on the world (and self), he or she will be less able to know the right (the prudent, practically wise, morally excellent) way to act in a given situation; one will be less able to navigate the many demands encountered daily. For instance, too often we acquiesce to the authority of experts and informed judges when what is needed most is the exercise of our own practical reasonableness — common sense. To be fair, the natural sciences also involve many concrete and practical aspects, especially in laboratory experimentation, yet the ideals of knowledge as timeless, universal, necessary, and certain — which are closely associated with theoretical knowledge — remain far more important as qualities of genuine understanding than those of the practical, i.e., the temporal, particular, contingent, and probable sides of reality — which are most often rejected because of the close association with subjectivity. Gadamer believes advancing human understanding relies on a combination (or application) of both the theoretical and practical if we are to do it well.

Gadamer argues that the problem we are witness to today began when the human sciences (history, sociology, psychology, theology, religion, etc.) began modeling themselves after the natural sciences, doing away with subjective notions like common sense, e.g., practical knowledge or practical reasonableness, for what is seen to be more foundational and reliable. Gadamer's hermeneutics offers a defense of the human sciences against this remodeling. As such, it is far more focused on showing how other experiences of truth inform our lives than it is with showing how the methodological and epistemological biases of the present age fail in what they claim to offer. In many spectacular ways they have been successful, and there is much that has been gained from them. Even so, claims Gadamer, in regard to an appreciation of the nature of interpretation and human understanding, they remain desperately limited.

To be clear, Gadamer's criticisms are aimed at those structures that monopolize claims to truth. Philosophical hermeneutics is at odds with comprehensive claims to truth made through any inflexible attitude that sees itself as unbiased and prejudice-less. Such attitudes, Gadamer believes, reflect a blindness to one's situated and conditioned way of being-in-the-world. He is not opposed to modernity or science in a general sense, only to those parts that have forgotten the value of other experiences and claims of truth. Gadamer, the trained classical philologist (one who studies the historical development of languages and literature), was well schooled in the use of methods and the benefits they provide. As such he is uniquely qualified to see their inherent values and limitations.

One of Gadamer's central arguments in *Truth and Method* is that any inquiry or investigation believed to be without prejudice or bias is in denial of its own conditioned ways of understanding. To claim a presuppositionless starting-point, which all good scientists are expected to do, reflects an attitude that cannot succeed except in a limited manner. Gadamer — again controversially — defends the legitimacy and importance of our prior hermeneutical situatedness that includes our individual prejudices, biases, and traditions, for understanding always occurs in a larger historical context. To begin an investigation with the belief that one has an unbiased perspective begs further difficulties and misunderstandings, for our cultural and historical backgrounds make possible our experiences of the world — even in the isolation of the laboratory. Like Heidegger, Gadamer recognizes that one's present horizon — one's knowledge and experience — is the productive ground of understanding that may be partially transcended through exposure to other points of views. Truth, for Gadamer, is very much as it is for Heidegger. It is an event in which there is a revealing and a concealing, rather than a strict correspondence of facts or a transcription of empirical observations. What we know and believe to be true in the present will often change in light of shifting cultural values and beliefs. To understand means to constantly work through the hermeneutical circle waiting to arrive at a disclosure of truth, within which there are always new presuppositions and prejudgments in need of being challenged. Only when we embrace this basic nature does Gadamer believe that we will be able to partially transcend the potentially vicious circle. Objectivists, while seeking in earnest to transcend their historical and cultural conditioning, go too far according to Gadamer. They forget that these elements of our being cannot be entirely removed or erased, only worked through toward glimpses of truth. Understanding combines the theoretical and practical in such a way that we blend subjective and objective elements (for lack of better labels), as we spiral toward clarity of understanding.

Fusion of Horizons

Gadamer describes the structure of our experiences of understanding as an event in which we participate. It is not merely a thing we do but something that occurs when we encounter another person or thing. More specifically, within the hermeneutical event there occurs a "linguistic" fusing of the objective and subjective that creates new horizons of possibility, i.e., new meanings and understandings. These possibilities and new understandings are rooted in the present and effectively conditioned by the past. The fusion of horizons is the event of opening ourselves, our horizons, to others (other lives, questions, ideas). Understanding happens through a gradual and perpetual interplay between the subject matter and the interpreter's initial position — a fusion of one's own horizon and the horizon of the text or other. Within this fusion, Gadamer denies the possibility of any single and objectively true interpretation that could transcend all viewpoints, while he simultaneously rejects the notion that we are restricted to our own subjective point of view. Understanding (described in terms of the fusion of horizons) is never a static and absolute experience but an interplay of possibilities involving real risk taking — the universality of which binds together language, tradition, and experience. Gadamer sees the hermeneutic event or fusion of horizons as something that happens without our making or doing. We enter into the experience voluntarily and participate in it according to its own structure and rules, rather than merely our own wishful desires.

Gadamer argues that planned and methodological ways of interpretation provide only limited degrees of certainty. Moreover, such interpretations never capture the fully intended and original meaning of a text. To suppose they might is to miss the reality that there is always something outstanding, unsaid, and undisclosed. To understand, however, is not merely an act from one's subjectivity wherein the interpreter is only injecting his or her own biased views on a static text. Instead, understanding is a historical act wherein one is responding to his or her own tradition (relying on past experiences to make sense of the present) while rethinking what was believed to be true because of what is encountered currently in the text. This, for Gadamer, is a dialectical movement — a give and take, a questioning and answering — and is the model for all of our experiences in life. To understand is often a matter of negotiating a tentative truth or belief about what is presumed to be the most accurate meaning, given all of the available evidence. It is rarely ever final. This kind of understanding is most obvious when we encounter a reversal of expectations and find our prejudgments (based in our prior experiences) challenged and corrected by something new. In fact, for Gadamer, all understanding reflects this sort of ongoing and unending search for clarity and insight.

To truly experience this sort of clarity through dialogical understanding requires a giving over of self to the event (the experience of colliding horizons), and by doing so, allowing "the subject matter" *(die Sache)* to speak for itself. To truly allow a text or person to speak, we must be prepared to be confronted by the new and the unexpected, including that which contradicts our beliefs. Genuine understanding is possible when we allow ourselves to be interrogated by the subject matter through whatever new questions may be asked of us. Such an experience is negative inasmuch as it is unpredictable and even contradictory to our expectations. There is always a reciprocity in Gadamer's "fusion of horizons" and "dialogical understanding," for while simultaneously giving oneself over to be grasped by the hermeneutical event one is also incorporating or assimilating the subject matter into one's own horizon. We are neither entirely lost in the experience itself nor are we entirely in charge of what occurs.

The challenge of this hermeneutical experience is proportional to the degree that one is willing to become moved in the playful dialogue of understanding, i.e., the willingness of the interpreter to allow the interjection of his or her own historically situated understanding (his or her present horizon) by the experience of something alien. That which is foreign or alien, such as an ancient text, exists in such a way that it is beyond our ability to simply take information from it, i.e., absorbing the truth in a one-directional manner, grasping the meaning by merely reading the words on the page and stringing the meaning together. Interpretation and understanding are far more turbulent — more violent and demanding — than this acquisition model presents. For Gadamer, we begin to see meaning when we allow the fusing of personal and extrapersonal horizons to take place. If we consider this metaphor of a "fusion" for a moment we might imagine the great heat and glowing embers generated in the collision of two worlds that may be millennia apart. In the heated fires of interpretation what is presumed to be true will often be burned up in the combustion, unable to withstand the heat, while whatever emerges will frequently be a new and unexpected creation. In interpretation neither the text nor the reader remains the same. Each new reading, new fusion, will bring about something different. Thus, for Gadamer, interpretation as the metaphorically described fusion of horizons is dependent upon our willingness (intention), the text (which we allow to interrogate us), and the structure of the experience itself (beyond our intention), in which we encounter the birth of new meaning and insight — if we are willing to risk our preconceptions and expectations in the refining fires of interpretation.

Gadamer's emphasis on our personal participation in every event of understanding excludes the possibility of the individual being a third-party objective observer, as if he or she is outside the hermeneutical event. It is the fusion itself that is the source of experience and understanding. We need not make an either/or decision between the subject (interpreter) or the object (text, etc.). Through the medium of our tradition (and language) and our concrete and practical mode of being-in-the-world, Gadamer argues that the world is encountered in such a way that our mere subjectivities alone cannot grasp it, nor the ideals of objectivism see it. Truth emerges only when our individual horizons and the horizons of the other (e.g., text, person, work of art) fuse, bringing different worlds together in surprising new ways.

Tradition, Effective-History, and Prejudice

Perhaps the two most radical claims in *Truth and Method* — certainly the most popular among early readers of Gadamer — are how language is the medium of understanding and how we are thoroughly conditioned by our traditions (many of us being conditioned by more than one tradition). According to Gadamer, each society has its traditions (rituals, beliefs, etc.) and each is found in and experienced through a language of some kind. In fact, tradition itself is linguistic for Gadamer, just as most understanding is linguistic. To understand a language means that one understands a tradition, at least in part. In this sense, we might think of tradition as the filter through which we see the world and how we see ourselves. In a stronger sense, as Gadamer claims, tradition is who or what we are, rather than just a filter through which we see the world. This does not mean that the tradition in which we are situated or the personal history each of us has prevents new experiences or holds us back from making genuine choices. Rather, our traditions and histories are what make all new discoveries and meanings possible. Understanding does not happen by writing on a blank slate but by building upon the experiences and understandings that have come before. The more experiences we have, the better our chances of seeing things correctly the first time around.

Thus, for Gadamer, prior to any experience of truth and act of interpretation, our biases and prejudices (prejudgments) will have given us a sense of how we are to approach a given subject matter. Gadamer sees tradition as something that grasps us far more than something we grasp. It is part of the self-understanding we bring to each new experience whether we recognize it or not. Still, as we have already discussed, Gadamer does not think that our participation in tradition means that we are limited to only the possibilities of our own contexts. While Gadamer's notion of tradition may seem deterministic — and to a certain degree it is — he is nevertheless very optimistic that we may transcend our limited horizons and self-understandings and become more than just the products of our previous histories.

For Gadamer, we are all "historically effected consciousnesses," and philosophical hermeneutics is his attempt at making what this means more structurally explicit. How much does prior experience influence us? How important is tradition and culture to interpretation? Does my language influence how and what I may know? To answer these questions Gadamer examines the nature of prejudice and tradition under the umbrella concept of "effective-history" *(Wirkungsgeschichte)*.

It is hardly surprising to claim that our personal histories are important influences in the formation of who we are — shaping our interests, beliefs, goals, desires, etc. The question Gadamer asks has to do with how deeply we are related to our traditions and what kind of relationship this manifests in the present. The nature of effective-history is of particular importance for Gadamer's overall description of how we come-to-understand, for if we are truly bound to it in hidden ways that we cannot fully recognize or discern, then this reality will surely influence what we mean when we say that we know something as true. If all truth is in some way prejudiced (prejudged), is any of it really true? Is genuine interpretation even possible? May I ask a question of a text that the text alone may answer, or will my own history condition whatever I may possibly hear?

We all have basic assumptions or intuitions that we believe to be self-evident truths, things that are correct and valid. In reality many of these often turn out to be preconceptions and prejudices that are dislodged as soon as our opinions are disrupted by our exposure to something new and unexpected. Only then do we become aware of our presuppositions as faulty and misleading. The frustrating reality is that while we may recognize certain prejudices or biases as groundless opinions and then work toward greater clarity of understanding, there will always be countless others that we are not yet conscious of waiting to emerge and many more developing all the time. Making prejudgments and assumptions about the truth or falsity of something is a necessary part of our everyday lives. Our effective historical consciousness is not an activity we perform intentionally, reflectively, or critically. It develops on its own as an ongoing process of dialogue and question-asking between the past, present, and an anticipated future, none of which may be fully controlled by our wills.

For Gadamer, while we may be somewhat confident in our ability to understand and work toward greater awareness — although we are fallible and sometimes wrong — we must also appreciate that our historically mediated intuitions and interests cannot all be made visible to us. We are in many important respects hidden from ourselves, unable to fully know who or what we are regardless of how closely we look. Between our horizon of historically shaped prejudices and our sincere attempts to gain clarity, there will always remain something undisclosed and outstanding — a hidden world behind all we think and do in our conscious lives. Philosophical hermeneutics recognizes that there is a fundamental mystery, unpredictability, and cloudiness in the act of interpretation, whether of texts, others, or even ourselves.

Not surprisingly, one of Gadamer's most controversial moves is his defense of the importance of prejudices in interpretation. For Gadamer, understanding requires presuppositions and assumptions that enable understanding as well as misunderstanding. We always bring our finite and conditioned awareness with us when we encounter something, for to make sense of something is to bring into play what is already known. However, to genuinely understand, for Gadamer, also means that we put what is known at risk, allowing our traditions and long-held assumptions to be challenged and tested. There may be no new experience of understanding otherwise. The hidden prejudices that are woven into the fabric of our understanding cannot blind us to the world indefinitely if we are prepared to be open and vulnerable to correction. If we are, Gadamer believes that we may refine and correct our prejudices and biases through exposure to other horizons, i.e., to the views and experiences of others. Over time new experiences and encounters with others will help disclose our initial judgments and beliefs, allowing for greater clarity of insight and even self-understanding. This, again, depends upon whether and to what degree we allow ourselves to be tested and questioned, i.e., whether we allow ourselves to be open to new experiences, thereby bringing our own assumptions and beliefs into the light so to speak.

Schleiermacher and Dilthey both assume that the historical and cultural distance of the interpreter from the phenomena being interpreted (or person encountered) creates misunderstanding. For Gadamer, historical and cultural distance is the productive grounds of interpretation. By accepting that the differences, disagreements, strangeness, and misunderstandings between horizons are the productive grounds for understanding and achieving a common accord, Gadamer presents a very controversial argument, but it is one that has helped many approach the Bible in new ways.

Gadamer's emphasis on the importance of being exposed to differences and on the role of the finite historicity of each interpreter's context provides the grounds for his argument that the meaning of a text always goes beyond its author's intended meaning. Interpretation in this sense is a productive as well as reproductive effort. Regardless of how small the gap created by differences between interpreter and interpreted may be, Gadamer believes that a text may never be fully understood within the interpreter's horizon because it is always somehow different than the author's horizon. However, while the meaning of a text goes beyond its author, this does not imply a necessarily relativistic interpretation. There is always a "givenness" or "fixed limit" within the horizon of the text that we must attempt to understand, according to Gadamer. That is, there is a limited range of what is possible to encounter or make sense of within the text at any one time, and no more. For instance, reading a comic book about robots cannot be interpreted meaningfully to be about gardening. Still, while we encounter a certain givenness within every text, we are also presented with a sense of otherness because the text is changing and evolving as we ask it new questions. Like tradition that is living and changing, the meaning of a given text (work of art, etc.) is never static. Meaning is always dynamic and unfinished, changing to meet the differences of those who participate in it.

To understand is to have an experience that is partially prior to our reflections and intentions, and determined by our ontological structure, i.e., the structure of who and what we are — our very being. Yet to understand at all we must be open to something more — something other than ourselves. It requires, for Gadamer, an openness to a question and a question's horizons in which we put ourselves at risk. Authentic experience shakes us awake and opens our eyes to the new and unexpected, that which is beyond our personal horizon. Again, within every event of understanding, truth is partially relative to the interpreter's own horizon though never entirely consumed by it. In this way Gadamer wants to guard against radically subjective and objective worldviews, while offering a sense of genuine progress in interpretation as we realize the limit and range of possibilities in the fusion of horizons.

Early hermeneutical philosophers such as Schleiermacher and Dilthey argue for the abandonment of one's own perspective when trying to understand a historical text. For example, Schleiermacher attempts to abandon his own perspective by placing himself in the position of the author so that he might overcome or remove problems created by differences. Gadamer argues to the contrary. If one grants the impossibility of overcoming and making explicit our finite historical conditionedness, then it follows that the best we may do is work outward from within our historical location with the prejudices and fore-conceptions at hand. Once we accept the role of our prejudiced and historical understanding, we may begin to reflect more critically in light of the inhibiting aspects we see, however vaguely and imperfectly we may see them, rather than remaining blind because we believe we have freed ourselves fully of all influences.

Play and the Work of Art

As we have seen, Gadamer is opposed to the separation of subjects from objects, e.g., the interpreter from what is interpreted, which has become the dominant way of thinking in the sciences. His protest reflects an overarching concern with the alienation of humanity that has become, to him, the foundation of Western philosophy and the Western world. Part of his strategy for overcoming alienation is a rekindling of the ignored sphere of art and the relevance of its truth claims to our lives. Art, for Gadamer, speaks to our lives and has a claim to truth that science does not and cannot understand. To that end, his recovery and development of ignored notions of truth and understanding through his metaphor of "play" or "game" (Spiel) has a very important descriptive role in his hermeneutics. This is the case because his analysis of the ontology of the experience of art — the hermeneutical description of the structure of our experience of art — is also an analysis of our experience of truth in general. According to Gadamer, what happens when we experience something meaningful in our encounters with art (a poem, painting, music composition, etc.) has the same basic structure as our other experiences of truth, whether those are scientific experiences or otherwise. Science, however, has failed to recognize its own way of understanding the world because of its emphasis on objectivity and method. Purposefully moving away from being only theoretical (thinking in terms of detachment and abstraction), Gadamer focuses his attention on describing the concrete "experience" of art. Like our other experiences, for Gadamer, the work of art is more than just an object we look at "out there." Art is something that occurs to us as an event of being, something in which we participate and invest our innermost selves in understanding. Thus, for Gadamer, if we are able to describe better the "play" of our encounter with art, we should be closer to appreciating how our other encounters with truth happen as well.

Gadamer argues that in play one commits to a transpersonal or extrapersonal understanding where dialogue between oneself and the work of art is not merely about one talking to oneself, but an existential leap that involves the testing and risking of belief within the give-and-take of a living dialogue. For Gadamer, in play we experience truth that overcomes the false subject/object dichotomy in which we do not confront the work of art as an object to be merely observed but participate in it — talk with it — as an event between partners, giving ourselves over to the rules and the structure of play. For Gadamer, when one participates in play, as a dialogue with art, one will often experience a strong sense of the altering power in art that dislocates pre-understandings and challenges us in an intimate fashion. If one believes one has encountered a genuine work of art but remains unchanged, Gadamer argues that one has not truly encountered the work at all. This is a very strange notion for many of us who are unaccustomed to thinking of art as having a contemporary voice. Indeed, for those who live in a culture convinced that objective and literal truth is far more valuable than the non-literal symbolism of art, Gadamer's claims are difficult to appreciate. Nevertheless, we must remember that he is trying to describe how we understand generally, namely, as a submission to something greater than ourselves — the structure of play we engage during dialogical understanding.

While it is a personal experience, play is more than just about the one who plays or the one who interprets. As we have seen in his structural description of dialogue, "play" has the same features in which there is reciprocal "being-played" of oneself as well as the "playing" one does — all play is also a being-played just as a dialogue is a saying and a hearing. Play is not merely a sequence of intentional activities in which the participant's actions become the source of truth. Real play is often counter to our intentionality as a negative experience in which one is grasped by the game in unexpected ways, for play and dialogue require our openness in terms of vulnerability and risk. To encounter another person's horizon through dialogue is to allow our own horizon to be potentially changed. In the same way, play is neither a passive subjective experience nor an external objective observation. It is a transformative process that requires our effort to maintain an open attitude, as well as our courage to hear the questions a work of art may ask. A neutral or indifferent engagement will not suffice to fulfill Gadamer's notion of understanding that occurs in play. To truly encounter the work of art, we must invest ourselves, but without pushing ourselves upon another (person or work of art) by asserting our demands (implicitly or explicitly). Hence, while neither the interpreter nor the work is passive in such an encounter, to experience truth one must be willing to engage the work like a game by becoming subject to its rules, which includes the possibility of somehow losing. For example, to read a biblical passage and allow the text to speak for itself may mean that the interpreter comes away from it frustrated and disappointed because what was said was not expected or desired. Such is an indication of a genuine play, dialogue, and an encounter with difference that offers new truth.

For Gadamer, the experience of art needs our voluntary participation and creative interpretation because meaning reveals or asserts itself in a manner akin to our "being played" rather than merely as a result of our playing. In play, truth is more than opinion in the personal and changing experience that transcends one's own immediate horizon and even one's ability to describe the event. After a genuine encounter, one may only be able to say there has been change and an unexpected dialogue with meaningfulness, without being able to specify what that change means — even though it means something. Gadamer argues that the sort of understanding associated with art is beyond reflection, theory, and observation. Hence, to describe in detail one's own sense of change from the experience is problematic if not impossible. Play is the essence of genuine art in which the experience goes beyond method and resists reduction of the problem of understanding to either the subjective consciousness of the interpreter or the originator of the work. Play is a disclosure of our ontology in the act of understanding beyond objective and subjective categories. Our relationship to art is an experience of truth where we engage it and become transformed.

To be clear, when Gadamer proposes that the work of art is similar to a game or structured like play he is not assuming an "I" and "thou" relation where a subject comes into contact with an object like a chessboard to be used by a player. The kind of game he has in mind involves both the subject and the object in a dialectical activity — a fusion. It is tempting to think in terms of an I and thou relationship and the division between the two, especially when one engages in a conversation with another person, yet Gadamer reminds us that while two distinct people may be in conversation there is a new voice created by them in the conversation that neither person could predict or control, for the conversation itself takes on a new life in response to the fusion. Moreover, in conversation there are no completely isolated individuals, for there is always a form of common understanding that makes the conversation possible, i.e., a sharing of a language and therefore at least a partially shared sense of tradition. There can be no radical severing of I and thou, subject or object, for such entities are always somehow able to understand one another because there exists some common ground. Unlike Schleiermacher's proposal that misunderstanding always precedes understanding, Gadamer argues that we experience the alien only upon the basis of something common. Every misunderstanding presupposes a common experience or understanding. Our everyday social interactions would be impossible without some form of commonality between members of society, however small.

Gadamer believes that the work of art speaks to us directly and without need for external verification to prove that what is experienced is authentic. However, in keeping with his desire to avoid falling into either subjectivism or objectivism, he maintains that the work of art does not allow for an entirely relative comprehension to be understood at the arbitrary fancy of the interpreter. An experience of art requires the application of a standard of appropriateness. Like a text, art speaks to us. In this way, the work of art can become an object of hermeneutical investigation because it has something to say, and in saying something it confronts us — speaking to every person's self-understanding if we are willing to hear it. However, in the refusal of the work of art to entertain certain interpretations (to exceed its given range of possible meanings) and in its excess of meaning (for there is no one unifying meaning but many), the work of art holds a transcendent status beyond itself (more than just a physical object) and beyond the realm of one's thinking. For example, one is not likely to come away from a painted scenic landscape with the impression that it was about the history of automobiles. The horizon of possibilities within the painting is limited even though there is an incredible excess of meaning preventing a complete impression or interpretation. In play, we encounter a hermeneutical sphere of understanding that takes place neither solely within us nor solely outside us.

Art has a language and a voice that we experience in a dialogical conversation, a fusion, as the creative communication between the interpreter and work. In this way, Gadamer's experience of art represents an avenue to truth beyond the radical subjectivism of art that he sees as harming many cultures. Moreover, as we have seen, the work of art is not merely an object for our pleasure or decorative display. Rather, the experience of art — like that of a text or person — keeps us attentive to its own meaning when we allow it to question our horizon, pulling us into a new relationship with our own truths and perceived meanings. Paradoxically, it allows us to encounter ourselves as we come-to-understand the meaning and truth of the experience, and our place within it. This is a living dialogue for Gadamer, one that is always relevant. How we understand in any given situation will be meaningful for that moment. How we understand a painting today speaks to our immediate concerns, ambitions, and experiences. Tomorrow we may see something in the same painting that is entirely different, though nevertheless real and relevant to our lives.

Gadamer's understanding of truth in the work of art is perhaps best represented in his thinking on poetry. In his essay "On the Contribution of Poetry to the Search for Truth" (in *The Relevance of the Beautiful and Other Essays*), Gadamer gives poetry a unique place because of its ability to remain separate from both the author and the interpreter, and by being separate it shows its relationship to truth. He argues that the poem is self-fulfilling and stands as its own verification that uniquely completes itself; that is, we do not need to argue its point by gathering data and evidence to support its meaning. Like all texts, the poem is detached from the origin and situation of its author. The language of the poetic expression is able to stand for itself while also being the same language as employed in ordinary speech. Gadamer maintains that ordinary or common language typically points beyond itself to something else. He illustrates this by describing someone who instructs another to look at a house and, in response, the other person must look beyond the expression (command) toward the house. In that way there must be something outside the language to verify or validate the expression. By contrast, the poetic expression is autonomous. The poem does not need to point outside itself because our experience of it is self-fulfilling and fully complete. So while the experience of art requires our participation and creative interpretation in order to make sense of what is being said, the poetic expression is able to reveal itself without external reference or appeal in order to be justified. An experience of truth, in the poem, is the relationship of a giving and accepting of what the poetic expression says, but only when we accept it and see through it to the world it is in itself. This autonomous fulfillment does not mean it is a closed sphere we cannot bring our unique questions to, as if the poem only speaks rather than responds. The work of art, as a world in itself, is continuous with our own world that we bring along with us while refusing to be an object at the mercy of an interpreter's whim.

The Question of Openness

Gadamer sees the logical structure of openness as uniquely characteristic of one's hermeneutical awareness or consciousness. Of particular importance to his notion of openness is the structure of the question. "The question" (or rather the nature of the question) plays an essential role in his ontological analysis. He believes that it is the question that has a priority in every genuine experience of meaning and truth. Without opening ourselves by asking questions, we cannot have new experiences. Hence, the openness Gadamer believes is essential to every experience has the structure of a question that takes priority over the answer. Following Socrates, Gadamer points out that asking a question — a good question — is often harder than answering it.

When one asks a question, its basic or core idea is rarely entirely open or aimless but often has a certain sense or pre-established motivation. We ask about specific things because we want to know specific things — we do not ask questions in a vacuum. And when we ask a question we expect a certain kind of answer, more or less. The internal sense or idea gives direction to the question, which, if it is to be answered or fulfilled, requires a number of activities on our part that, for Gadamer, must respond to the implicit range of possible directions within the question before it will make sense (unless we modify the question). That is, each question requires a unique resolution, for to fully answer a question we must work out its specific direction(s) and motivation(s). Thus, every question is limited by a horizon — its own range of (feasible) possibilities — just as we are also limited by our horizons. The hermeneutical goal (virtue), then, is to ask a question that is as open as possible, all the while recognizing that we are only capable of answering the question to the degree that it falls close to the acceptable purview of our own horizons. To sincerely ask and then try to answer a question is a difficult task, for we are all prone to a degree of selective listening (and asking), such that we unnecessarily limit the range of potential answers — a range of possibilities made available but also inhibited by our situatedness, our being-in-the-world.

All knowledge, for Gadamer, is mediated through the question. The openness in the question consists in that its subject matter is not yet answered; that is, an authentic question's topic must be at heart undetermined and unknown. To question genuinely cannot be the posing of an apparent question for which one already knows the answer or the asking of a question with a readily predictable resolution. Such would be the making of statements in disguise rather than the sincere exposure of one's horizon to the new and unpredictable. To ask a question appropriately is to have come into true openness without holding to persistent presuppositions and selfish motives we know to be false or misleading.

Further, we cannot expect to standardize the asking of questions because the basis for knowledge, according to Gadamer, is the dialectic between questions and answers that cannot have a methodic or formulaic structure. The dialectic is an organic activity in which new questions (and answers) will often arise suddenly and without planning. How often have you found yourself in a conversation with someone about a specific topic only to discover at the end of the conversation that the direction you first set out in has taken a number of surprising twists and turns, sparking entirely new and unexpected questions? We may plan questions and then hold them accountable to standardized rules and criteria, but these will not be responses to the current and emerging subject matters of our lives or products of genuine dialogue with new and strange horizons. Prearranged questions are typical of the sciences, which seek particular kinds of facts about things and the world. And while these kinds of questions are far from fruitless, they rarely offer much that contributes meaningfully to our lives such that they aid in making sense of practical demands. Scientific and hermeneutic questions are distinct in what they offer, the latter being too often overlooked and forgotten, according to Gadamer.

Part of the motivation behind an open question will be to confront popular opinions that are often arrogant and closed to the possibility of being wrong. To be open in the hermeneutical experience requires us to put aside and suspend our own opinions (to the extent possible), venturing into radical uncertainty by allowing sometimes uncomfortable questions to break through our preconceptions and take us in new directions. A real question will challenge our openness and willingness to encounter the unknown at every turn. For Gadamer, confronting opinion (one's own or another's) is less about arguing against it and more about searching for an open question(s) within. Even the most closed-minded of opinions may, at least in principle, be sufficiently disturbed such that it realizes the hidden but nevertheless real potential of the open question(s) inside. In effect, to confront opinions is to break them open to the uncertainty they are disguising, an uncertainty that exists, according to Gadamer, whenever we probe below the surface of our prejudices. In this way, hermeneutics is clearly not about glossing over differences of opinion (should two people simply agree to disagree), about naïvely accepting personal beliefs and biases (no matter how cherished they may be), or about avoiding difficult questions. Hermeneutics, as the art of understanding and interpretation, involves a high degree of honesty and a sincere attitude of openness — itself having the nature of a question.

Within the uncertainty of the question, Gadamer identifies a frustrating duality. On the one hand, he believes that we should avoid trying to question in a methodological and preplanned sense, which is unfortunate because such an approach would be helpful in a number of respects. On the other hand, he believes that we should never stop trying to break through to the unknown by asking questions that challenge our horizons, encouraging us to move beyond our individual isolations. This duality creates a difficult situation. If we cannot preplan the act of questioning or rely on methods to systematize it in a meaningful sense, what are we supposed to do? Gadamer believes that we should seek to foster a certain hermeneutical desire or attitude of question-asking. For him, questioning has more in common with a passion or a spirit that we kindle within ourselves than it does with strategies or procedures. Questioning is an art we perform when we are able to continue questioning, continually breaking through closed opinion and preconceptions. It is an attitude that seeks to sustain openness and vulnerability to the new and different.

Dialogue

Philosophical hermeneutics is phenomenological. For Gadamer, this means thinking about understanding in a descriptive, creative, intuitive, and concrete manner. Above all, this means looking at human understanding as a response to our lived experiences in which we allow things to reveal themselves in our everyday lives. As we have repeatedly seen, according to Gadamer when we have an objective or theoretical account then we have only a limited form of understanding that is disconnected from our life-

99

worlds. Throughout his philosophical hermeneutics, Gadamer defends the all-important role of communicative or dialogical rationality over the one-sidedness of calculative and instrumental rationality. Through dialogue, the things in themselves emerge and the subject matter reveals itself. The living dialogue we are and the questions we ask reflect our orientation to situations and practical affairs of life. We cannot hold a conversation with stale and abstracted facts that have little or no significance for our lives. Philosophical hermeneutics, as a phenomenology, describes a dialogical way of thought in which theory and practice are inseparable from our daily lives.

Gadamer's notion of dialogue and his description of the structure of the question and answer are distinct features of his hermeneutics. His views on dialogue further enforce his description of the experience of truth as neither explicitly subjective nor objective. For example, in conversation between two people who seek agreement, what is present between them — the emerging subject matter of the dialogue — is not a product that belongs to either person. It is a living truth and meaning that transcends them both without being fixed and permanent. The dialogue generates truth that transcends participants, bringing about questions and answers neither could have anticipated. Similarly, when in dialogue with a text, the interpreter may be presented with a question the author did not ask, yet a real question the text is able to answer nevertheless. This is experienced whenever one reads the Bible and appreciates what is said in regard to one's life even though someone living today is far removed from the context of a given author. In our dialogue with texts, every question brings about a modification or move of the text's horizon, and at the same time, all that is questioned is limited and directed by the interpreter's horizon. Both text and interpreter are changed in the act of interpretation — evolving with and adapting to one another in the playful experience of dialogue.

To question is to open up a dialogue that seeks the horizon of the question — a horizon that includes various possible answers determined by the horizon of the thing. Gadamer recognizes in the case of a text that it does not speak like a thou or question us like another person; rather, it is the interpreter who must make the text speak. We allow such speaking when we interject our anticipated answers. This forced speech is not arbitrary, as if it is entirely initiated by the reader, but is in response to the horizon implicit in the text itself.

In attempting to interpretively reconstruct the circumstances of a text, Gadamer holds a skeptical view of any naïve historical objectivity.

Coming-to-understand a text is not about merely peering into the historical past and reconstructing the intent and tradition of the author, summarizing meaning as it is constructed. On the contrary, we are perpetually attempting to reinterpret the question the text is possibly answering and doing so in response to a living question we have in mind. Understanding is more than merely re-creating another's meaning. It occurs when we appreciate questionableness and open-endedness, and when we begin working out available possibilities. It may be tempting to impose oneself too much by asserting opinions, but games cannot continue when participants refuse to be subject to the rules. The event of understanding occurs and happens to us in a dialogue that is not of our making.

In short, Gadamer's question-and-answer dialectic may be understood as a temporally and culturally contingent event of interpretation in which meaning evolves in relation to the rules of evolving horizons. It is not a disclosure of fixed and timeless truth but a living dialogue. His proposal is that we attend to the emerging subject matters, recognizing that they speak to real questions we have and possibilities implicit in the phenomena being interpreted. Truth is the hermeneutic experience of possession by means of which we are opened up for the new and the different. Through asking questions, we experience the world and bring texts to life.

A Critical Appraisal of Philosophical Hermeneutics

As will become more apparent in Chapter Six, Habermas is especially critical of Gadamer's relativist inclinations. According to Habermas, the pre-reflective conditions of understanding that Gadamer draws out in terms of tradition, history, and prejudice cannot be critically evaluated. Indeed, it seems problematic that we may not, in Gadamer's account, be able to clearly transcend our own history in order to hold it to critical evaluation. Is a critique of our historicity even possible? Or does such a critique belie the force of Gadamer's claims? The creation of universal norms and the prescribing of rules for clarifying understanding that Gadamer avoids are the very things many of his critics think he is too quick to dismiss. Yet while Gadamer denies that hermeneutics is a prescriptive or normative way of life — one in which there are critical-rational criteria of the sort Habermas desires — it is implicit that once we recognize the fuller sense in which understanding is possible we will attempt to foster it in our own lives, such as by questioning closed opinions and holding our prejudices open to revision.

As we shall also soon see, there has been a longstanding debate between Derrida and Gadamer. In the later Derrida chapter it will become clearer why Derrida considers Gadamer to be stuck in a metaphysical system that does not recognize radical difference in understanding. For Derrida, Gadamer's hermeneutics rests on the centrality of understanding and the possibility of agreement. Derrida is highly critical of this sense of understanding. Even so, Derrida and Gadamer eventually reconciled some of the philosophical differences between them, especially as Derrida came to understand Gadamer's position more clearly. Both Gadamer and Derrida are two of the strongest examples of Heideggerian scholars who have continued his legacy in unique ways.

Conclusion

Gadamer's use of Heidegger's event-structure or event-ontology in the revealing of truth, his arguments for reclaiming the important forms of truth in the experience of art, and his articulation of understanding as the fusion of horizons (including his notions of play, openness, and dialogue) represent significant steps toward conceptualizing truth and meaning beyond that described by modern science and epistemology. Philosophical hermeneutics describes ways of overcoming both artificial objective boundaries and the alienation of radical subjectivism as we learn to participate in the infinite possibilities of conversation. Like Heidegger, who stresses the linguisticality of the hermeneutical event in which language is at the heart of all understanding, Gadamer identifies language as the mediating basis for our experiences of truth. Unlike Heidegger, however, Gadamer emphasizes tradition in more radical ways. Within the hermeneutical experience language is the medium as we participate in our present historically situated reality and fuse with other horizons in a never-ending dialectical activity of question-asking and prejudice-considering.

Traditionally the hermeneutic act has been understood as offering insights that contribute to the understanding and application of various concepts of translation, methods of biblical exegesis, and virtually all methods of literary inquiry. However, the hermeneutical experience, as we have seen it with Gadamer, offers a turn that contributes to a fuller understanding not only of the hermeneutical act itself but of faith experiences as they relate to an understanding of ourselves in the world and to our articulation of belief. The timeless truths of faith derived from divine revelation are not understood by just taking a good look to see what is there. Gadamer's hermeneutics shows us that what matters most is our present involvement or relationship with the Bible and its living truth. Interpretation is a gradual, perpetual, and creative interplay between horizons. We must continually return to the Bible and enter into its excess of meaning and possibilities. Biblical interpretation is a matter of participation in which we attempt to remain open in dialogue with the text and allow it to speak on its own — pulling us into its world as we remain rooted in the present.

REFERENCE WORKS

Dostal, Robert J., ed. *The Cambridge Companion to Gadamer.* Cambridge: Cambridge University Press, 2002.

Gadamer, Hans-Georg. *The Beginning of Philosophy,* trans. Rod Coltman. New York: Continuum, 1998.

————. *The Enigma of Health: The Art of Healing in a Scientific Age,* trans. John Gaiger and Nicholas Walker. Oxford: Polity Press, 1996.

————. *Hermeneutics, Religion, and Ethics,* trans. Joel Weinsheimer. New Haven: Yale University Press, 1999.

————. *The Idea of the Good in Platonic-Aristotelian Philosophy,* trans. P. Christopher Smith. New Haven: Yale University Press, 1986.

————. *Philosophical Apprenticeships,* trans. Robert R. Sullivan. Cambridge, MA: MIT Press, 1985.

————. *Philosophical Hermeneutics,* ed. and trans. David E. Linge. Los Angeles: University of California Press, 1977.

————. *Plato's Dialectical Ethics: Phenomenological Interpretations Relating to the "Philebus,"* trans. R. M. Wallace. New Haven: Yale University Press, 1991.

————. *Praise of Theory: Speeches and Essays,* trans. Chris Dawson. New Haven: Yale University Press, 1983.

————. *Reason in the Age of Science,* trans. Frederick G. Lawrence. Cambridge, MA: MIT Press, 1981.

————. *The Relevance of the Beautiful and Other Essays,* trans. Nicholas Walker, ed. Robert Bernasconi. Cambridge: Cambridge University Press, 1986.

————. *Truth and Method,* trans. Joel Weinsheimer and Donald G. Marshall. 2nd rev. ed. New York: Continuum, 2002 (1960).

Grondin, Jean. *Hans-Georg Gadamer: A Biography,* trans. Joel Weinsheimer. New Haven: Yale University Press, 2003.

————. *Sources of Hermeneutics*. Albany: State University of New York Press, 1995.

Malpas, Jeff, Ulrich Arnswald, and Jens Kertscher, eds. *Gadamer's Century: Essays in Honor of Hans-Georg Gadamer*. Cambridge, MA: MIT Press, 2002.

Palmer, Richard E. *Hermeneutics: Interpretation Theory in Schleiermacher, Dilthey, Heidegger, and Gadamer*. Evanston, IL: Northwestern University Press, 1969.

Pearson, Brook W. R. *Corresponding Sense: Paul, Dialectic and Gadamer*. Leiden: E. J. Brill, 2001.

Thiselton, Anthony C. *The Two Horizons: New Testament Hermeneutics and Philosophical Description*. Grand Rapids: Eerdmans, 1980.

FIVE

Paul Ricoeur's Hermeneutic Phenomenology

Introduction

Paul Ricoeur (1913-2005), the French philosopher, has emerged in recent years as a major hermeneutical thinker whose extensive work has proved productive in a number of areas of interpretation. Ricoeur was a phenomenologist with wide-ranging interests, especially in hermeneutics and language, the human subject, psychoanalysis, and religion. His writings are also very wide-ranging, and his work in both North America and France has given him a unique perspective and platform for his philosophy. This broad platform has been enhanced in some circles by his Christian (Protestant) perspective, which aligned him with socialist and pacifist causes throughout his life, and also led to some biblical interpretation by him. However, it is only in relatively recent times that Ricoeur has begun to have the kind of influence that his writings deserve. In particular, his philosophy at a particular point took a decidedly hermeneutical turn, with the result that his work on language and hermeneutics has recently come into favor in a number of circles, and it merits serious consideration because of its linguistic grounding and literary application.

Ricoeur and Hermeneutic Phenomenology

Like a number of major European philosophers especially of the late twentieth century, Ricoeur's biography and his intellectual development and literary production are inextricably intertwined. The kinds of philosophical questions that he raises in his lengthy philosophical career are closely related to the circumstances around him, even though he shunned a romantic approach to philosophy and often appeared outwardly to live his life in firm separation from the various political and social developments around him. Nevertheless, one of the best ways to grasp the developing hermeneutical thought of Ricoeur is to trace the events of his life (found in Reagan's biography of him, *Paul Ricoeur*), before turning to his major works of hermeneutical and interpretive interest.

Life and Influences

Formative and Early Philosophical Years

Ricoeur was born in 1913 in a small town south of Lyons, France. Though born into an educated family and the son of a high school *(lycée)* teacher, Ricoeur's life was thrown into its first major life-crisis when his father went missing in action during World War I (his body was later found). As a result, Ricoeur, along with his sister, was reared by his great-grandparents with the help of his aunt and as an "orphan of the state," a status that provided some needed financial support. His upbringing was strict in most ways, including disciplined intellectual inquiry and devout religious piety, both of which influences are witnessed later in his life. Ricoeur received the undergraduate degree *(licence)* from the University of Rennes in 1933, a degree that qualified him as a school teacher. He had tried to gain admission to the *École normale supérieure,* the school known for training France's intellectual and political leaders, but, in a great irony that does not reflect on the person, he failed the philosophy examination and so was not admitted.

After a year of teaching, Ricoeur began studies in 1934 at the Sorbonne for the *agrégation* (advanced teacher qualification) in philosophy. There are a number of key events — both fortuitous and disheartening — that took place during this time of study. One was the death of his sister from tuberculosis. The second was his tremendous opportunity to meet and study with Gabriel Marcel (1889-1973), the Christian existentialist philosopher, who had enduring intellectual and personal influence on Ricoeur. The third was that Ricoeur, due to his keen mind and hard work, received the second highest mark in his *agrégation* studies, which qualified him for one of only ten available teaching positions requiring this qualification. The fourth important event was that he got married. Newly married, Ricoeur then took up a teaching position near Strasbourg as professor of philosophy in a high school.

After a year of compulsory military service, ending with his commission as a lieutenant in the reserves, Ricoeur returned to teaching, this time in Brittany, and began what would be a regular pattern of disciplined writing for publication that would endure for over sixty years. He began writing on issues of interest to him as a Christian socialist, and in 1940 published his first article in phenomenology. He also studied a short time in 1939 in Munich to improve his German, but this time of study was interrupted by the events leading up to World War II. In 1939, with the war upon him, Ricoeur was activated for military service. Despite his being an avowed pacifist, he was also a French patriot and in his ensuing service won a medal as a soldier, and he never seemed to find it inconsistent that he could and would defend his country. His time as an active soldier did not last long, as he was captured in 1940 and became a prisoner of war for five years, being held captive in three different camps during this time.

Phenomenology and Ricoeur's Philosophical Development

Ricoeur's time in the prison camps was foundational for his philosophical development, as during this time of incarceration he read important thinkers who helped to form his philosophical foundations. Life in the prison camps was hard, but despite the difficulties Ricoeur and his fellow prisoners made the most of their situation and were apparently treated less harshly than those in other camps. He and several other professors in the camp formed study groups and eventually offered university courses that were later recognized for degrees. This environment provided a place for Ricoeur to undertake some of his earliest serious philosophical scholarship in two major ways. The first was a regime of disciplined and extensive reading. During this time, he read the complete works of the existentialist and psychiatrist Karl Jaspers (1883-1969). More importantly, he also read the first volume of Edmund Husserl's (1859-1938) *Ideen zu einer reinen Phänomenologie und phänomenologischen Philosophie* (1913; most recently translated as *Ideas Pertaining to a Pure Phenomenology and to a Phenomenological Philosophy*; only the first volume was published in Husserl's lifetime). The second major intellectual achievement begun during this time was engagement in philosophical writing. During his imprisonment, once he received Husserl's *Ideas* in 1943, Ricoeur translated this entire volume from German into French. No doubt because of this important intellectually formative experience, Husserl's ideas figured largely in Ricoeur's intellectual and professional development throughout his extensive philosophical career. In another example of his writing during this time, Ricoeur's first major work in philosophy, *Freedom and Nature: The Voluntary and the Involuntary* (1950), was drafted during his time in the prison, and in some ways is patterned after Jaspers's *Philosophy of Existence* (3 vols., 1932). During his several years of imprisonment, Ricoeur also formed an important friendship with a fellow prisoner and existential philosopher, Mikel Dufrenne (1910-1995), with whom out of common interest he would later write a book on Jaspers.

Never expecting to be held captive for so long, Ricoeur and his fellow prisoners eventually were freed in 1945, and he made his way back to Paris and then to his home. He soon took up a new teaching position in a former Jewish refugee school, teaching there for three years before accepting the position as head of the history of philosophy department at the University of Strasbourg in 1948, a position he kept until 1957. During this postwar time, Ricoeur resumed the writing projects that he had begun during the war, and then began a very productive time of philosophical research and publication. Ricoeur first published the book with Dufrenne on Jaspers, titled *Karl Jaspers et la philosophie de l'existence* (1947; Karl Jaspers and the Philosophy of Existence). This work consisted primarily of an interpretation and commentary on the three volumes of Jaspers's work. Although never translated into English, this book discusses some of the major ideas that Ricoeur would pursue throughout his philosophical career, such as the question of existence. Ricoeur followed this work with another of the same type. This time he undertook a comparative study of Marcel and Jaspers, titled *Gabriel Marcel et Karl Jaspers: Philosophie du mystère et philosophie du paradoxe* (1948; Gabriel Marcel and Karl Jaspers: Philosophy of Mystery and Philosophy of Paradox). Like its predecessor, this work was never translated into English, but it too reflects Ricoeur dealing with phenomenological ideas that would occupy him subsequently. To meet the requirements for a doctoral degree at Strasbourg, and as was customary in France at the time, Ricoeur needed to submit two written theses, a minor and a major one. The minor one that he submitted in 1950 was his translation of Husserl's *Ideas*, translated into French for the first time, with an extensive introduction and commentary (the foundation for a later collection of essays on Husserl titled *Husserl: An Analysis of His Phenomenology* [1967]). The major thesis was Ricoeur's work on freedom and the will, which he had first drafted while a prisoner. This work, *Freedom and Nature*, the first volume of his *Philosophy of the Will*, was also published in 1950.

Of these four works (on Jaspers, Marcel and Jaspers, Husserl, and freedom and nature), the most important is generally deemed to be Ricoeur's work on the human will, as it reflects major themes of much of Ricoeur's subsequent philosophical research work. One of these interests is the role of the human subject, or what Reagan in his biography of Paul Ricoeur calls "philosophical anthropology" (19). Ricoeur frames this anthropology in the phenomenological categories of Husserl, in opposition to the unbridled freedom of the existentialist Jean-Paul Sartre (1905-1980). In this work on freedom and nature, Ricoeur is concerned with what it means for a human to will, i.e., the various types of human willing. He represents this as voluntary and involuntary actions, with the latter, involuntary actions, providing the constraint on absolute freedom. One's decision to will is based on involuntary bodily conditions that result in the decision to act. This decision leads to an action to do something, i.e., to move one's body in a certain way, but one that is resisted by the body as well. One gives consent for such a voluntary action, which is given in opposition to involuntary resistance provided by such things as the unconscious or character. The result is that there is a dialectic between the voluntary and involuntary, between freedom and nature. For every voluntary act, there is an involuntary act that counters it, and therefore dialectical mediation. One exercises voluntary acts in order to accomplish things — the definition of Ricoeur's philosophy of action, which he developed further in later work. Ricoeur opposes seeing the human as a mind-body dualism, and argues for a "lived body," a body that is also identified with the human being. Besides the work of Husserl, Ricoeur in his work on freedom and nature was influenced by a number of other important thinkers, including Marcel, Jaspers, and another phenomenologist, Maurice Merleau-Ponty (1908-1961). As a result of these early publications, especially *Freedom and Nature,* Ricoeur became recognized as a leading expert in the area of phenomenology, which based being not on scientific positivism but on the phenomena of experience and consciousness.

In the 1950s, a number of further important events occurred in Ricoeur's life and scholarly career that would affect his future and especially his philosophical development. In 1955, he traveled to North America and to China for the first time, and, from 1957 to 1965, he was professor of general philosophy at the Sorbonne in Paris, a very prestigious position especially for a philosopher who had come from a rural French educational background. During this time, Jacques Derrida (1930-2004), whose ideas Ricoeur would later seriously question, was one of Ricoeur's students. Ricoeur was also invited with his family to live together in a community where residents shared common political and religious beliefs. This community, called *Les murs blancs* (The White Walls), was located in a small village south of Paris. Ricoeur and his family took up residence there and became part of the community.

Ricoeur's time at the Sorbonne was very productive. Just before being appointed there, he published a collection of his essays in 1955, titled *History and Truth,* which brought together a number of papers on a variety of subjects, such as philosophy and history, and religion and God. In many ways, these individual papers were exploratory exercises that paved the way for his more substantial later works, such as the final essay on negation, which is reflected in his next major book.

Hermeneutical Turn

The 1960s-1970s marked another period of significant development in Ricoeur's philosophical thought and writing, the most noteworthy being the increased role of hermeneutics in general and its importance in his own philosophical development in particular. It is at this point that Ricoeur made what might well be termed his hermeneutical turn (see Reagan, *Paul Ricoeur,* 24). In 1960, Ricoeur published the second volume of his *Philosophy of the Will,* in two parts. The first was titled *Fallible Man.* Ricoeur explores the human person and the will, in particular the human who wills to choose evil. Exploring what it means to will to do evil, Ricoeur contends that the human will, bound by voluntary and involuntary constraints, has a tenuous disposition that includes its vulnerability to fallibility. The second part was titled *The Symbolism of Evil.* This study represents Ricoeur's first serious effort at dealing with the concept of symbols. He recognizes the importance of dealing with symbols because, following on from his discussion of evil, he believes that evil is always presented in metaphorical or symbolic language. He interprets cultural myths as important symbolic statements regarding evil that merit philosophical discussion. The publication of these two volumes marked an important hermeneutical shift in Ricoeur's philosophy. From this point forward, a central focus was the role of language in his philosophical thought. This marked Ricoeur's so-called hermeneutical turn.

In 1965, Ricoeur published his major treatment of Freud, titled in English *Freud and Philosophy: An Essay on Interpretation*. Ricoeur had become interested in Freud while he was researching his book on evil, and, from 1958 to 1961, he read all of Freud's works, and then gave lectures on the psychiatrist at Yale University and at Louvain University. His published lectures became his book on Freud. At this time, Freud was becoming a very popular figure among French intellectuals, including the highly controversial psychoanalyst and philosopher Jacques Lacan (1901-1981). Ricoeur approaches Freud as a philosopher, and so, as a phenomenologist, attacks Freud's entire philosophical program, as one of those who created the environment of a "hermeneutics of suspicion," as being partial, phenomenologically inaccessible, and not teleologically oriented. This essentially unsympathetic treatment of Freud aroused the ire of Lacan who, at that point, had not published a major work on Freud (and never did, as far as we can tell), though he was seen to be one of his leading proponents. The opposition between the two French intellectuals and philosophers became bitter, to the point that advocates for Lacan accused Ricoeur of stealing Lacan's ideas. This charge is generally regarded as completely unfounded, as Ricoeur takes what is obviously a very different approach from that of Lacan.

In 1955, Ricoeur had published an important article on the value and place of teaching, stating that teaching — contrary to popular belief in France at that time — does function in the real world. During the 1960s and early 1970s, there was much student unrest in European universities, and this was certainly the case in France. Admittedly, most European educational systems had serious deficiencies at that time. Some of the difficulties concerned class sizes, pedagogical styles, teacher contact and involvement, community building, and style and standardization of curricula, among others. In some ways, and as a result, it is no surprise that, in 1967, Ricoeur and two colleagues left the tradition-bound and inflexible Sorbonne to take up posts at new suburban universities, where there was the prospect of a different approach to French university education. Ricoeur was appointed to the University of Paris X in Nanterre, west of Paris. This new university was designed to address many of the difficulties raised by the more traditional Sorbonne. Nevertheless, despite such efforts, and no doubt because of the tenor of the times, students protested vigorously at

Nanterre, but without satisfactory immediate resolution. A year later, Ricoeur was appointed the Dean of the Faculty of Letters. A number of factors led to a terribly disappointing outcome for Ricoeur. First, the university was seen to be the weakest of the new French universities, and so was ripe as a place for demonstrations against what were said to be failed government policies. Second, French law restricted police presence on university campuses unless invited by the Dean, a request that was used sparingly to preserve the academic freedom of the university and to avoid confrontation with protesters. In 1969, student protests erupted again on the Nanterre campus, and in the midst of this Ricoeur took two weeks of stress leave. During this time, the situation deteriorated, until it was nearly impossible for the university to continue. During these events, Ricoeur himself was assaulted, which shook him up, as he considered himself to be a liberal-minded person sympathetic with the students' cause. Ricoeur made the decision to allow police on campus, but the riots got worse until finally the police took drastic measures to restore control, leaving the campus physically a wreck. During the course of this series of unfortunate events, Ricoeur decided to resign. This was a tremendous personal blow to him, as he had been a socialist and pacifist, and in many ways on the side of the students in their demands, but he had not been able to bring his philosophical position to bear on a situation exacerbated by any number of outside political and even criminal influences.

Ricoeur at first took a three-year leave of absence, before returning as a professor at Nanterre, from which he retired in 1980. During this leave of absence, Ricoeur taught at the University of Louvain. He also accepted an appointment as the philosopher and theologian Paul Tillich's (1886-1965) successor, as the second John Nuveen Professor at the Divinity School of the University of Chicago, a position he held from 1971 to 1991, when he became professor emeritus. There were many very appealing reasons for Ricoeur to consider taking up the appointment at Chicago. His friend, the religious historian Mircea Eliade (1907-1986), was a professor there, and so Ricoeur would have a suitable intellectual and personal contact upon his arrival. North America also promised freedom from the constrictions of the French educational system that had taken its direct toll on him. During this twenty-year period in Chicago, Ricoeur became a world-renowned philosopher, lecturing throughout the United States and around the world, and receiving honorary degrees from over fifteen institutions, on top of the several he had already received. Of special note were lectures and consultations that he was invited to give at Texas Christian University

(1973), Oxford (Zaharoff Lecture in 1979), Rome (1983, 1985, and 1994), and Edinburgh (Gifford Lectures 1986), the last of which unfortunately were followed by the suicide of one of his sons, which was a tremendously debilitating experience for Ricoeur.

Despite the travail at Nanterre, as well as a rigorous annual travel schedule as he moved among Paris, Chicago, and other sites for pleasure or lecturing, Ricoeur continued to develop and write about his major philosophical concepts. During his time as Dean at Nanterre, he published a collection of essays, *The Conflict of Interpretations: Essays in Hermeneutics* (1969). These essays reflect Ricoeur's hermeneutical development, as he engages more fully in discussion of various types and kinds of texts, and in his opposition to the form of structuralism that was making serious inroads in France in the 1960s. For example, in his essay on "Existence and Hermeneutics" (in *Conflict*, 3-24), Ricoeur introduces the notion of semantics into his concept of hermeneutics and further defines the symbol as a "structure of signification" in which there is a "direct, primary, literal meaning" that also indicates an "indirect, secondary, and figurative" meaning perceivable through the former (12). Interpretation also becomes the task of "deciphering the hidden meaning in the apparent meaning" (12). By means of semantic structures, Ricoeur states, the interpreter gains access to other levels of meaning as well. In responding to structuralism, Ricoeur objects to the rigorous forms found in such proponents as the Copenhagen school linguist Louis Hjelmslev (1899-1965) and his glossematics. Ricoeur challenges fundamental notions of such forms of structuralism as: language being treated as an item of scientific investigation; language as system *(langue)* being given priority over language as change *(parole)*; the sign system of the language being self-defining and without any absolute terms; and the sign system being autonomous and only self-referential. Many of these ideas were taken up further by Ricoeur in his major hermeneutical writings. Ricoeur further objects to structuralists such as Claude Lévi-Strauss (1908-2009) applying structural linguistics to other fields of investigation, such as kinship relations. Lastly, the structuralist system, according to Ricoeur, excludes the creativity that is found in speech or in history, or even the ability to say something through language about anything outside of language (summarized by Thompson, *Paul Ricoeur*, 8-9).

In light of his strong and rigorous critique of structuralism, it is not surprising that Ricoeur further pursued the important topic of metaphor. In 1972, he wrote a major essay titled "Metaphor and the Main Problem of Hermeneutics," where he sees metaphor in relation to a text as a word in relation to a work, with the idea that a metaphor is a "work in miniature" (Reagan and Stewart, *Philosophy of Paul Ricoeur,* 136). Building upon his structuralist critique, Ricoeur sees a discourse as an "event," not as an instance of *langue* but as *parole,* with the metaphor having "specific' structure" with "force" or "content" (here he draws on the speech-act theory of J. L. Austin [1911-1960]). In a very important insight for his hermeneutical program, Ricoeur also sees the metaphor as saying something about something and hence having reference (136-37). Ricoeur develops these ideas further in a collection of essays titled *The Rule of Metaphor: Multi-Disciplinary Studies of the Creation of Meaning in Language* (1975), which concludes with an essay that argues for the referential nature of metaphorical language.

Time and Narrative

While still continuing to refer to significant events in the life of Ricoeur, at this point we wish to discuss in more detail the first of two of his fundamental hermeneutical works. In the early 1970s, Ricoeur began pursuing topics that would lead to the last of his great philosophical works, those on time and narrative. Four necessary preliminary works paved the way for this culminative treatment of narratology. In these works, Ricoeur extends further a number of his major themes that he had previously discussed. These include an exploration of the nature of discourse as narrativity; a recognition of and appropriation of the place of creativity, appreciating Saussure's dimension of *parole;* extending his work on the human will by incorporating and modifying a conception of speech-act theory as part of his human action model; and exploration of the issue of time. The first of his works was an article published in 1971, "The Model of the Text" (repr. Thompson, *Paul Ricoeur,* 197-221), in which Ricoeur argues that problems in the human sciences are hermeneutical problems, insofar as objects and methods of these sciences resemble problems in the interpretation of texts. Besides offering a further critique of structuralism, Ricoeur defines human action as discourse, and uses the concept of discourse to comment on human action. In "Explanation and Understanding: On Some Remarkable Connections among the Theory of Text, Theory of Action, and Theory of History," published in French in 1977 (Reagan and Stewart, *Philosophy of Paul Ricoeur,* 149-66), Ricoeur argues on the basis of examining theories of the text, action, and history that explanation and understanding constitute a dialectic, not an opposition. The third work is his Zaharoff Lecture, delivered at Oxford in 1979, later published as *The Contribution of French Historiography to the Theory of History,* in which he discusses issues related to history and narrative. The fourth essay, published in 1980, is titled "Narrative Time," where Ricoeur attempts to find correlates between features of narrative and features of temporality. He notes what he calls "structural reciprocity" between temporality and narrativity.

Finally, in 1983, 1984, and 1985, Ricoeur published in three volumes the four parts of his massive philosophical and hermeneutical work *Time and Narrative.* Many of the themes adumbrated above find direct expansion and development in this important work on narratology. In part 1 (in vol. I), Ricoeur deals with the "Circle of Narrative and Temporality." The thesis of this entire work is that "what is ultimately at stake in the case of the structural identity of narrative function as well as in that of the truth claim of every narrative work, is the temporal character of human existence. The world unfolded by every narrative work is always a temporal world" (3), hence the title of his work, "time and narrative." The circularity of the idea that every narrative projects a temporal world is not vicious, but rather is at the heart of the notion of narrativity. Ricoeur first contrasts Augustine's (AD 354-430) and Aristotle's (384-322 BC) views of time, Augustine's to arrive at the idea that time is a distension of the mind, not an extension in space, and Aristotle's for the notion of emplotment. As a result, Ricoeur claims that *"time becomes human to the extent that it is articulated through a narrative mode, and narrative attains its full meaning when it becomes a condition of temporal existence"* (vol. I, 52; italics original). To mediate between time and narrative, Ricoeur introduces the useful notion of mimesis. He defines three types of mimesis, with mimesis2 as the mediating term by way of emplotment. This function of mimesis2 opens "up the plot and institutes . . . the literariness of the work of literature" (vol. I, 53). As Ricoeur states in support of this fundamental notion, "We are following therefore the destiny of a prefigured time that becomes a refigured time through the mediation of a configured time" (vol. I, 54). Mimesis1 is related to the traditional notion of plot, and mimesis3 relates to application to the listener or reader. Mimesis2, therefore, functions as the configuring force between these two types of mimesis, i.e., between "individual events or incidents and a story taken as a whole" (vol. I, 65), by configuring the whole, including its ending, and the various orderings of its events.

In part 2 (also in vol. I) of *Time and Narrative,* Ricoeur goes further and applies this theory of narrative and time to history. After dealing with

French historiography's rejection of narrative, he argues on behalf of both causal analysis and intentionality, with the result that he wishes to apply the concept of emplotment to history as well. In part 3 (vol. II), Ricoeur takes the notion of mimesis2 and emplotment and applies them to fiction. He is able to do this because he claims that they both perform what he calls "configurating operations" (vol. II, 3) that fall under mimesis2. The difference in fictional and historical works is in their relation to mimesis3 and the notion of truth claims, i.e., the relation of the individual events to the truth. The reasons for his treatment of fiction and history in this way include the fact that both occur in our daily lives, not just in restricted generic types, so that even new generic types end up assuming the same types of narrative emplotments. In part 4 (vol. III) of *Time and Narrative*, Ricoeur expands upon his previous analysis so as to provide "as complete an explication as possible of the hypothesis that governs our inquiry, namely, that the effort of thinking which is at work in every narrative configuration is completed in a reconfiguration of temporal experience" (vol. III, 3). Reaffirming Husserl's view of time, Ricoeur corrects Augustine by noting that time is an internal perception, and, following Heidegger, he notes that one cannot consider a given instant in time without also "appealing to phenomenological time and vice versa" (vol. III, 96). In finally tying treatment of history and fiction together, Ricoeur discusses a "poetics of narrative" in relation to "aporias of time brought to light by phenomenology" (vol. III, 99) as the key to issues regarding reconfiguration of time. Rejecting the literary critic Wayne Booth's (1921-2005) configuration of narrative categories, Ricoeur believes that the reader must utilize hermeneutics, rather than rhetoric, to develop a reading strategy. This requires that the reader be in dialectical response to the refiguration of narrative, in which reading is both a place and a process: "This twofold status of reading makes the confrontation between the world of the text and the world of the reader at once a stasis and impetus" (vol. III, 179). This interpretive framework of place and process, stasis and impetus, applies to both history and fiction, in which "the interweaving of history and fiction in the refiguration of time rests, in the final analysis, upon this reciprocal overlapping, the quasi-historical moment of fiction changing places with the quasi-fictive moment of history. In this interweaving, this reciprocal overlapping, this exchange of places, originates what is commonly called human time where the standing-for the past in history is united with the imaginative variations of fiction against the background of the aporias of the phenomenology of time" (vol. III, 192).

The publication of *Time and Narrative* secured Ricoeur's philosophical and especially his hermeneutical reputation in both North America and Europe, where he had unfortunately been overlooked since the educational and civil disaster at Nanterre. In the closing years of his career, Ricoeur published a number of further works. Two to note for their hermeneutical significance are his *From Text to Action: Essays in Hermeneutics*, II (1986), which, as a collection of recently written essays on hermeneutics, serves as a companion to his earlier *Conflict of Interpretations*. This volume includes further thoughts on the issue of human action. The other is *Oneself as Another* (1990), which includes essays on language, human action, personal identity, and ethics. In 1991, Ricoeur was awarded the philosophy prize from the Académie Française, a confirmation of the importance of his work in France. Then, in November 2004 in the United States, just six months before his death, Ricoeur was awarded the John W. Kluge Prize for Lifetime Achievement in the Human Sciences. Ricoeur died at home, in Châtenay-Malabry, in 2005.

Discourse and the Surplus of Meaning

Insofar as developing a workable hermeneutical model for the interpretation of texts, Ricoeur wrote a number of works that, while critical, provide a rebuttal to the "hermeneutics of suspicion" prevalent in contemporary hermeneutics. Those focused on the Bible include, among others, several lectures delivered and/or published in 1973-1975 on hermeneutics (repr. Bovon and Rouiller, *Exegesis*, 265-339), a major paper titled "Biblical Hermeneutics" published in 1975 in the experimental journal *Semeia*, a collection published in English of *Essays on Biblical Interpretation* (1980), and, with the biblical scholar and colleague from Chicago André LaCocque, *Thinking Biblically: Exegetical and Hermeneutical Studies* (1998).

The most focused exposition of his hermeneutical model for the interpretation of texts comes from lectures that Ricoeur gave in 1973 at Texas Christian University. These lectures outline the major configurations of his hermeneutical work and contain the seeds of the narratological thought he developed later in *Time and Narrative*. In that regard, this treatment constitutes close to an encompassing model of Ricoeurian hermeneutics by providing a workable and useful compendium of his thought regarding understanding the language of literary or other types of discourse. The overall framework of Ricoeur's hermeneutical approach is to identify the apparent conflict or dialectic between the concepts of explanation and understanding, and to argue that this dichotomy is more apparent than real. Ricoeur does this through two major hermeneutical moves. The first is to consider language as discourse, especially written language, and the second is to consider the notion of what he calls plurivocity, by which he means plural meaning at every level of language, from the word to the discourse.

Ricoeur begins his discussion with discourse. Ricoeur recognizes that the problem of language as discourse is as old as the ancients themselves. This problem stems from a fundamental distinction between language as code and language as it is used or functions. Linguistics concentrates on language as system or structure (i.e., code), rather than on language as it is used, which formulation relegates discourse to a marginalized or secondary position. The neglected situation of discourse is the result of Saussure's fundamental dichotomy between *langue* and *parole*. For Ricoeur, *parole* is to be equated with discourse, whereas Saussure emphasized and made the heart of his analysis *langue* as the synchronic analysis of language systems. This dichotomy of *langue* and *parole* was perpetuated in the work of the Russian Formalists and came to identify structural linguistics, which was distinguished by its synchronic and paradigmatic approach to language, in which every element is meaningful within language-immanent finite systems. Within this analysis, *langue* is seen to be a homogeneous entity, while *parole* is heterogeneous.

A further useful distinction, so Ricoeur believes, is to be made between semiotics and semantics as corresponding to the two language units of the sign and the sentence. The sentence is not simply an extension of the word, but is a new type of element. Whereas semiotics applies to the formal analysis of signs, semantics is concerned with sense, or what might be better called meaning. The concept of discourse, used instead of the term *parole,* is, in Ricoeur's analysis, what he calls "the" event of language and has ontological priority, whereas the language system has only virtual existence. Discourse is characterized by having propositional content, and this is directly related to its predicate structure. A subject identifies a singular item, while the predicate indicates a universal feature, such as the class or relation or action type involved. Thus, a discourse has its own structure. Discourse as a proposition is an abstract notion, dependent upon the structure of the sentence. This discourse, however, is actualized in time, as opposed to the virtuality of the language system that exists outside of time. Discourse, which is realized as an event, is therefore understood as having meaning. The notion of meaning may be differentiated between speaker meaning and sentence meaning. The language system does not produce meaning, as it is individual humans who speak and produce meaning. The speaker's meaning is found within the discourse, by means of the sentence structure. The meaning of this structure points to the speaker's meaning.

Ricoeur finds support for his analysis of discourse in two areas. The first is the speech-act theory of Austin, applied to what Ricoeur calls interlocutionary acts. Just as an illocutionary act has a grammar that expresses a particular intention, the interlocutionary act conveys the dialectic and the propositional content of an event. Ricoeur finds this more satisfying than Roman Jakobson's (1896-1982) communications model, because it directly describes discourse without treating it as a subsidiary function of language, because it treats discourse as a structure and not as an irrational event, and because it displaces the notion of language as code with the notion of communication. This discourse structure conveys several meaningful features: propositional content, in which polysemic words are constrained by context; and the locutionary act, which has the intention of being seen as a type of illocution. This concept of meaning is therefore related to the notions of sense and reference. Meaning is what both speakers and sentences do. Utterance meaning contained in the propositional content constitutes the objective dimension of meaning. Utterer meaning, contained in self-reference, illocution, and intention by hearers, constitutes the subjective dimension. Within the objective dimension, there is both a "what" and an "about what," as Ricoeur phrases it, of discourse. The "what" dimension constitutes the sense and the "about what" the reference. Only at the level of the sentence does reference have meaning, as individual words, such as those in a lexicon, only function in relation to other words in the lexicon of the language. Language, therefore, is only referential when it is being used; that is, a sentence only refers in a specific situation and use. In fact, Ricoeur contends that it is only by being referential that language can be said to be meaningful. Therefore, discourse mediates between the speaker and the world.

With regard to speaking and writing, the shift from speaking to writing results in meaning being detached from the event. Therefore, writing is the form in which discourse is fully expressed, not, as Derrida suggests, that the two have separate origins. To help understand the function of discourse, Ricoeur analyzes the main features of Jakobson's communications model. The first feature of that model concerns fixation of the message and medium. For language to be fixed it must be fixed as discourse, not as *langue.* Using speech-act theory to articulate the relation between event and meaning, Ricoeur believes that, to the degree that an illocution can be expressed by grammar and related procedures, its "force" can be written. Because of that, perlocutionary force is the least inscribable and more related to spoken language. The second feature of Jakobson's model concerns the message and the speaker. The transference of language from reading to writing affects the relationship between message and speaker, so that writing is not a specific case of speaking. Instead, the act of inscription is equated with the text's semantic autonomy. In response to objections to both the intentional fallacy and the "fallacy of the absolute text" (*Interpretation Theory*, 30), Ricoeur still posits and maintains that the text constitutes a discourse from someone to someone about something. Hence, what Ricoeur calls authorial meaning is a property of the text. The third feature of the communications model concerns the message and the hearer. A written text, as addressed to an unknown and unidentifiable audience, results in the audience's being universalized. Because the text has semantic autonomy, the potential readers are expanded. The fourth Jakobsonian feature concerns the message and the code, or, to state it differently, the issue of genre in textual production. Ricoeur draws an analogy between genre and discourse, and generative grammar and individual sentences. There is a close correlation, he believes, between the generic codes that govern writing and production of discourse. The fifth and final feature is message and reference. Whereas speech is located in dialogue, the same is not true for discourse. According to Ricoeur, discourse destroys the dialogue, and is always *about* something; that is, it is situated in a "world." The "world" is the set of references made possible by texts, and accessed by ostensive and non-ostensive reference. It is discourse, and not speaking, that, freed from its author and audience and their dialogical matrix, is therefore world-projecting. In response to the critique that writing exteriorizes discourse, Ricoeur invokes the notion of iconicity, in which writing is a reinscription or transcription of the world or reality. This analysis of writing as the exteriorizing of discourse establishes the proper framework for interpretation. The opposition of writing and reading can be viewed as an opposition between distanciation and appropriation. Distanciation is the inevitable result of writing, as it is the inevitable and natural outcome of the created distance between a discourse and its reader. Appropriation overcomes the issue of distanciation through appropriating what is alien, the discourse. Writing and reading are the means for this distanciation and appropriation, in which reading appropriates what is distanciated through writing.

For Ricoeur, as we noted above in tracing his hermeneutical development, metaphor and symbol are important parts of his hermeneutical understanding. To discuss the notions of explanation and understanding, Ricoeur notes that literary works have a "surplus of meaning" (45), but the question is where this surplus of meaning comes from. In other words, the question is whether such a surplus of meaning originates internal or external to the discourse. Ricoeur believes that the surplus of meaning is the meaning that goes beyond what is conveyed by the linguistic sign. This is what is meant by a symbol — that which has this meaning as both a sign and a second surplus meaning. This concept is what Ricoeur calls "double-meaning" (45, 46). Metaphor is related to the categories of structural semantics by means of the equation of denotation with the cognitive and connotation with the emotive in language, in which the cognitive is associated with semantic meaning and the emotive with figurative and non-cognitive meaning. Ricoeur uses metaphor as a means of exploring the type of surplus of meaning found in literature. He hence calls into question the traditional major assumptions regarding metaphor. Metaphor is not simply, as some posit, a displaced figure regarding word signification. Metaphor functions at the level of the sentence, not at the level of the word, and is part of the sentence predication, rather than the denomination of the subject. In that way, a metaphor is not word based but is utterance based, as its minimal unit is the two items, the tenor and the vehicle of the metaphor in tension. Further, metaphor requires an interpretation to see the absurdity of the contradiction being posed. Metaphor therefore is about mitigating the shock of the juxtaposition of incompatible ideas. The mere substitution of words, as in traditional metaphor theory, does not account for how metaphors create meaning, as does Ricoeur's "tension theory," in which the sentence produces a new meaning. Finally, a metaphor such as this is not translatable, only paraphrasable, as the meaning cannot be fully contained. Such a metaphor is substantial in that it both describes and gives new information about this created reality, and is not merely ornamental.

The study of metaphor provides access to the study of the concept of symbol, which, in Ricoeur's mind, is more complex because symbols involve more fields of study. They also unite the linguistic and the non-linguistic worlds in a way that metaphor does not. Analysis of a symbol involves for Ricoeur three steps: analyzing the "semantic kernel characteristic" (54), identifying the non-linguistic elements of the symbol, and appropriating further insights. Like a metaphor, a symbol provides an "excess of signification" (55) in the opposition between the literal and symbolic meanings, of which both are necessary (that is the difference between symbol and allegory, where the literal is not necessary). The notion of assimilation captures the complexity of the symbol, because its boundaries and relations to other things are not precise, and there is no means of capturing all of the possible semantic dimensions that a symbol provides. Whereas this is the semantic content of a symbol, the non-semantic part is also important. This non-semantic component of meaning is the part that is not linguistic or metaphorical, and occupies the space between the linguistic and non-linguistic worlds. Therefore, a symbol is a bound entity, as it does not have autonomy apart from experience. This boundedness also ties discourse to the sacred dimension, because it always stays outside of language and ties itself to the sacred. There is, therefore, always something powerful in a symbol that remains outside of language.

Having elaborated these various dimensions of meaning, including discourse, metaphor, and symbol, Ricoeur is in a position to discuss explanation and understanding. Ricoeur begins with some fundamental correlations — understanding is in relation to reading in the same way that the discourse event is in relation to the discourse utterance, and explanation is in relation to reading in the same way that autonomy of word and text is to objective discourse meaning. In other words, understanding relates to the discourse event and explanation to textual and verbal autonomy. There is a dialectical structure to both reading and discourse, whereas in traditional romantic hermeneutics they are treated in opposition to each other. The problem with this romantic hermeneutical model is the mediated nature of experience and knowledge. Instead, for Ricoeur, experience and knowledge are part of a process that moves from understanding to explanation and, finally, to comprehension. Each utterance begins with the generation of a new event in the text that objectifies the initial event. With the author's intention inaccessible, the first attempt at meaning must begin with a guess. In romantic hermeneutics there is a meeting of great minds that results in the notion that interpreters know authors' minds better than the authors themselves. Ricoeur disputes this romantic notion, because romantic hermeneutics has neglected to take into account the actual situation of the text in its written form, in which meaning surpasses intention in an environment where understanding is a semantic activity.

Even though understanding begins with a guess, for Ricoeur there are means of validating such guesses. The first is to realize that a text's meaning, as a part, is construed on the basis of the whole. A discourse is not a series of sentences, but a whole. These multiple sentences lead to a plurivocity of the discourse typical of complex discourses. These complex discourses consist of a complex hierarchy of elements — seen in the relation of the parts to the whole — that are recognized, so Ricoeur says, through a circular interpretive process. Further, understanding a text means that one must understand it as an individual text, not as a type. Any literary text also has a number of different potential meaning horizons. These are often posited through the metaphorical and symbolic extensions of meaning of the text. Ricoeur, in agreement at this point with the literary critic E. D. Hirsch (1928-), believes that it is logical probabilities that provide the validation of these potential horizons, rather than some kind of empirical proof, just as there are also, as per the philosopher Karl Popper (1902-1994), ways of falsifying interpretations and determining that some are more probable than others. Ricoeur sees all of this as part of the hermeneutical circle, in which there is a circular relationship between a guess and its validation. Thus, even though there may be several potential ways of understanding a text (the potential limited by the text itself), not all of the interpretations have equal validity. Validation procedures are designed to arbitrate these readings.

Concerning comprehension, Ricoeur posits a further important dialectic, in which explanation and comprehension find their counterparts in specific and abstract reference. The suspension or actualization of reference characterizes various types of reading. For example, structuralism, whether of the Geneva, Prague, or Danish school, chooses to suspend ostensive reference, and literature is correlated with *langue*. Examples may be found in the work of Lévi-Strauss and his analysis of myth, as well as in the narratological analyses of Vladimir Propp (1895-1970), Roland Barthes (1915-1980), and A.-J. Greimas (1917-1992). Ricoeur disputes this method of interpretation on several counts. He first believes that a text more resembles *parole* than it does *langue*. Even though structuralists reduce a myth to its constituents, this is not the end-point of interpretation. These individual constituents are themselves articulated in sentence form, and these sentences have meaning and make reference. The structure in which they are embedded does not neutralize their meaning. Further, the mythemes or smallest mythic units have fundamental or existential meaning. Such structural analysis presupposes that these myths have meaning in that they are narratives about the origins of fundamental things. In other words, structural analysis provides a necessary intermediate stage toward what Ricoeur calls "boundary situations" or "depth semantics" (87) to which the myths refer. The meaning of a text is thus turned around. The meaning does not exist behind or under the text but in front of it as something that the text discloses. In that way, a text moves from sense to reference, i.e., "from what it says, to what it talks about" (88).

This method of interpretation may be put within the larger framework of historicist and what Ricoeur calls "logicist" (90) hermeneutics, reflecting the notions of appropriation and distanciation. Historicism argues that a literary work is intelligible on the basis of its socio-cultural embeddedness. Logicists, such as Husserl and Gottlob Frege (1848-1925), argue that the text is not psychically dependent but objectively identifiable. Wilhelm Dilthey (1833-1911) took this category further by contending that a work of art could be understandable by others on the basis of its having sense. Some literary criticism has also come to realize the ahistorical nature of the text, whose idealized sense apart from historical context allows for a broadening of its communicative sphere. For Ricoeur, a written discourse has both semantic autonomy, in the same way that a literary work can have its own self-referentiality, and is based in oral discourse's objective meaning. The text becomes the point of mediation between the writer and the reader, in a dialectic of explanation and understanding. The notion of appropriation is also important for hermeneutics, in that interpretation depends upon an appropriation that results in an interpretive event. Appropriation is not based in personal appeal, but is instead a "fusion of horizons," as Hans-Georg Gadamer (1900-2002) would call it (*Truth and Method,* 306), that brings the reader and writer together with the text as the mediator. Appropriation is not governed by the original audience, but invites any and all readers on the basis of its universal sense. Appropriation is not interpretation by an actual reader, as the thing that is interpreted does not reside in the psyche of the reader but is in response to what is disclosed in the text. It is the text that has this power of disclosure.

Ricoeur, who began as a phenomenologist, developed into a significant hermeneutical thinker. His views encompassed most of the major issues in hermeneutical thought, including the relationship of the text to time, the nature of discourse, the role of metaphor and symbol, and the validation of meaning.

A Critical Appraisal of Hermeneutic Phenomenology

There are a number of important questions raised by Ricoeur's position. One of these is the relationship between Ricoeur and structuralism. Ricoeur maintains an ambiguous relationship with structuralism and a number of its major formulations. He rejects the emphasis upon *langue* and characterizes his analysis as focusing upon *parole*. He takes *langue* as abstract, while *parole* is instantiated in reality. On the other hand, he adopts the structuralist examination of myth as a means of liberating textual meaning from socio-cultural dependence. A privileging of *parole* might not provide the firm basis for several subsequent hermeneutical moves that Ricoeur makes toward textuality, stability of meaning, and especially reference.

A further question concerns idealized sense and context. Ricoeur is determined to preserve objective meaning. He does so by moving from sense to reference, in which every discourse is a text about something. That aboutness of the text is then objectivized, and construal of its meaning becomes the basis of objective meaning, even if there is a surplus of meaning as well. Ricoeur associates contextual meaning with subjectivity and, more than that, with the psychic interpretation he equates with romantic hermeneutics. Some would say that Ricoeur has made several logical missteps here. The first is his equation of aboutness with objectification. Another is the neglect of context, to the point that he may have fallen into the trap of mistaking his interpretive context for objectivization. A third is the relationship of individual elements to reference.

Speaking and writing are also important in Ricoeur's hermeneutics. Associated with the rejection of *langue* for *parole* is the move from speaking to writing. Whereas most linguists assert the primacy of spoken language on the basis of language learning and use, Ricoeur emphasizes written language. For him, written language may not have priority insofar as chronology is concerned, but it has priority in objectivity and meaning. Ricoeur again equates objectivization in written form with reference.

The surplus of meaning is an idea that has come to characterize Ricoeur. He believes that there is a surplus of meaning in a text, and that this surplus is related to the sentence as the minimal unit of meaning, because of predication. He does not provide a means of arbitrating the constraints on meaning of the sentence, nor does he provide a means of testing the surplus of meaning of a text. This surplus is often related to the metaphorical and symbolic capabilities of language. While recognizing their potential, Ricoeur invokes the discourse as the arbitrating factor on meaning.

Ricoeur also recognizes that understanding requires addressing the question of validity of interpretation. Validity of the various interpretive possibilities is seen by Ricoeur to be based not upon empirical evidence, but upon logical probabilities. This seems to establish a set of extratextual unvalidated criteria by which to determine textual intention and meaning. Related to validity is the intentionality of author and text. Ricoeur recognizes but minimizes the role of the author and especially authorial intention, as a means of freeing meaning from historicism and a particular author. However, he must also limit the possibilities of textual meaning, so he invokes the notion of textual intention. The notion of textual intention is predicated upon having a validation system by which various meanings can be scrutinized.

A further, related concept is that of sense and reference. Ricoeur adopts Frege's perspective on the notion of an idealized sense. However, Ricoeur also gives priority to reference. He adopts a realist view of language in which language has an inherent referent, and such language has external and hence objective reality. Ricoeur takes this tack because he wants to minimize the influence of authorial intention, and so he needs to have referentiality connected to language, rather than it being a linguistic capability created by language users. If language is not referential in its use, but simply denotes, i.e., indicates classes or types of items when it is not used referentially, then Ricoeur's connection to the outside world is rendered problematic.

One of the fundamental issues Ricoeur addresses is that of the relation of word and sentence. For Ricoeur the sentence is the minimal meaningful unit. He does not believe that lexical items have singular lexical meaning, in that a word must be either an indicator or a predicate and in relation to the other to have meaning. Even if words are not used in a sentence (say in a metaphor), the words must be in some sort of tension with each other to provide meaning. However, analysis of the sentence only provides constraints on meaning by means of certain types of relations. Sentence meaning is also dependent upon the individual elements having some form of meaning themselves, and the location of the sentence within the larger discourse.

Speech-act theory is one means by which Ricoeur attempts to move beyond the sentence. Ricoeur never explains how speech-act theory actually works in his *Interpretation Theory*. He adapts the idea of illocutionary acts and believes that this helps to break out of a narrowly constrictive view of language. Speech-act theory has encountered a number of fundamental problems. There is question in both philosophical and linguistic circles whether speech-act language rules can be formulated, whether a limited number of illocutions can be correlated with a seemingly unlimited number of perlocutions or language functions, what the relation of basic illocutions is to functions, and whether context can be described in such a way as to provide a meaningful test of the illocutionary or perlocutionary force.

Finally, Ricoeur formulates a theory of the text in terms of autonomy, distanciation, and appropriation. Ricoeur argues for the autonomy of the text as it is separated from its author. He also maintains distanciation between the text and the reader. This provides the hermeneutic problem of interpretation to be overcome, while at the same time providing an objective status to the text. Ricoeur tries to overcome this alienation by appropriation, without saying how it is that appropriation can overcome distanciation.

Conclusion

Ricoeur has made enormous contributions to interpretive theory and offered numerous insights into the nature and use of language. Relying on various elements of phenomenology, (post)structuralism, and speech-act theory, among others, Ricoeur's hermeneutics has had appeal in many interpretive circles, such as biblical and theological interpretation. Ricoeur's work on metaphor, symbol, narrative, and time — including the hermeneutical themes of tradition, authority, and critique that we have discussed in previous chapters — have proven to be of significant interest to hermeneuts in this regard. In addition, Ricoeur's belief that the central hermeneutical problem is the merely apparent conflict between explanation and understanding is both provocative and enlightening — if controversial. Indeed, perhaps Ricoeur's most significant hermeneutical contribution begins with his identification of what he sees as a dialectic between the concepts of explanation and understanding.

As a well-known poststructuralist, Ricoeur combines Anglo-American and European traditions in his work, thereby offering a rare breadth of philosophical insight into uncommonly difficult issues. Like other phenomenologists, Ricoeur agrees that language is at the heart of being, of self-understanding. In our experiences of the world, others, and texts, we are not merely reaching out to grasp the object of our study, but engaging it in a dialectic of evolving meaningfulness. Ricoeur does not attempt to cover over the tensions and ambiguities that we experience as human beings, but works to show that all knowledge, even self-knowledge, requires interpretation and is mediated by signs, symbols, and texts. Interpretation, such as that of texts, engages a surplus of meaning that surpasses the intention of the author — though this does not entail relativism according to Ricoeur. As a result, a number of biblical and theological interpreters have been attracted to various dimensions of Ricoeur's thought. These include the emphasis upon discourse, the stability of meaning, and the referentiality of language, among others. Many of these notions require further discussion.

Similar to Gadamer in many respects, Ricoeur is nevertheless skeptical of Gadamer's hermeneutics, which he views as insufficiently critical. While we may be interpretive beings, for Ricoeur this does not preclude the possibility of a more robust self-critical attitude that Gadamer's philosophical hermeneutics seems to ignore. We may, for Ricoeur, have a hermeneutical critique of tradition, even though we engage in it within tradition. As we shall see in the next chapter, Jürgen Habermas (1929-) agrees that a more critical hermeneutics than Gadamer's is possible, though he goes about describing one in terms quite unlike those of Gadamer and Ricoeur. The degree to which and manner in which a critique of tradition is possible continues to loom large among hermeneuts. We may take Gadamer, Ricoeur, and Habermas to represent three of the most important and influential positions in this regard — not as mutually exclusive theories, but with each representing many different points along a continuum that sometimes complement, sometimes contradict, and sometimes do not seem to relate to one another at all.

REFERENCE WORKS

Austin, J. L. *How to Do Things with Words.* Oxford: Clarendon, 1962.

Gadamer, Hans-Georg. *Truth and Method,* trans. Joel Weinsheimer and Donald G. Marshall. 2nd rev. ed. New York: Continuum, 2002 (1960).

Husserl, Edmund. *Ideas Pertaining to a Pure Phenomenology and to a Phenomenological Philosophy. First Book: General Introduction to a Pure Phenomenology,* trans. F. Kersten. The Hague: Nijhoff, 1982 (1913).

Jeanrond, Werner G. *Theological Hermeneutics: Development and Significance.* London: SCM Press, 1994.

LaCocque, André, and Paul Ricoeur. *Thinking Biblically: Exegetical and Hermeneutical Studies,* trans. David Pellauer. Chicago: University of Chicago Press, 1998.

Reagan, Charles E. *Paul Ricoeur: His Life and His Work.* Chicago: University of Chicago Press, 1996.

Reagan, Charles E., and David Stewart, eds. *The Philosophy of Paul Ricoeur: An Anthology of His Work*. Boston: Beacon Press, 1978.

Ricoeur, Paul. "Biblical Interpretation." *Semeia* 4 (1975): 27-148.

———. *The Conflict of Interpretations: Essays in Hermeneutics*, ed. D. Ihde. Evanston, IL: Northwestern University Press, 1974 (1969).

———. *The Contribution of French Historiography to the Theory of History*. Oxford: Clarendon, 1980.

———. *Essays on Biblical Interpretation*, ed. L. Mudge. Philadelphia: Fortress, 1980.

———. *Fallible Man*, trans. Charles Kelbley. Chicago: Henry Regnery, 1965 (1960).

———. *Freedom and Nature: The Voluntary and the Involuntary*, trans. Erazim V. Kohak. Evanston, IL: Northwestern University Press, 1966 (1950).

———. *Freud and Philosophy: An Essay on Interpretation*, trans. Dennis Savage. New Haven: Yale University Press, 1970 (1965).

———. *From Text to Action: Essays in Hermeneutics*, II, trans. Kathleen Blamey and John B. Thompson. Evanston, IL: Northwestern University Press, 1991 (1986).

———. *History and Truth*, trans. Charles Kelbley. Evanston, IL: Northwestern University Press, 1965 (1955).

———. *Husserl: An Analysis of His Phenomenology*, trans. Andrew Ballard and Lester Embree. Evanston, IL: Northwestern University Press, 1967.

———. *Interpretation Theory: Discourse and the Surplus of Meaning*. Fort Worth: Texas Christian University Press, 1976.

———. "Narrative Time." In *On Narrative*, ed. W. J. T. Mitchell, pp. 165-86. Chicago: University of Chicago Press, 1981 (1980).

———. *Oneself as Another*, trans. Kathleen Blamey. Chicago: University of Chicago Press, 1992 (1990).

———. *The Rule of Metaphor: Multi-Disciplinary Studies of the Creation of Meaning in Language*, trans. R. Czerny with K. McLaughlin and J. Costello. Toronto: University of Toronto Press, 1978 (1975).

———. *The Symbolism of Evil*, trans. Emerson Buchanan. New York: Harper & Row, 1967 (1960).

———. "The Task of Hermeneutics," "The Hermeneutical Function of Distanciation," "Philosophical Hermeneutics and Biblical Hermeneutics." In *Exegesis: Problems of Method and Exercises in Reading (Genesis 22 and Luke 15)*, ed. François Bovon and Grégoire Rouiller, trans. Donald G.

Miller, pp. 265-96, 297-320, 321-39. Pittsburgh: Pickwick Press, 1978 (1973-75).

————. *Time and Narrative,* trans. Kathleen McLaughlin, Kathleen Blamey, and David Pellauer, 3 vols. Chicago: University of Chicago Press, 1984, 1985, 1988 (1983-1985).

Thiselton, Anthony C. *New Horizons in Hermeneutics: The Theory and Practice of Transforming Biblical Reading.* Grand Rapids: Zondervan, 1992.

Thompson, John B., ed. *Paul Ricoeur: Hermeneutics and the Human Sciences. Essays on Language, Action and Interpretation.* Cambridge: Cambridge University Press; Paris: Editions de la Maison des Sciences de l'Homme, 1981.

Vanhoozer, Kevin J. *Biblical Narrative in the Philosophy of Paul Ricoeur: A Study in Hermeneutics and Theology.* Cambridge: Cambridge University Press, 1990.

————. "Ricoeur, Paul (1913-2005)." In *Dictionary of Biblical Criticism and Interpretation,* ed. Stanley E. Porter, pp. 327-28. London: Routledge, 2007.

six Jürgen Habermas's Critical Hermeneutics

Introduction

Jürgen Habermas (1929-) is one of the most influential of living philosophers and social theorists today. He is best known for the development of
"the theory of communicative action" and "universal pragmatics." With
universal pragmatics (or the more recent label "formal pragmatics"),
Habermas attempts to provide a foundation for the development of universal social norms made possible by the rationality he believes to be inherent in our communicative action, e.g., discourse, debate, cooperation.
His theory of communicative action is a complex combination of critical
theory, sociology, and philosophy, all areas in which Habermas has proven
himself thoroughly conversant. Through his work on communicative rationality and the related development of universal pragmatics, Habermas
has been involved with important and longstanding issues such as the nature of human agency, subjectivity, language, understanding, reason, and
ethics. The theory of communicative action is central to his philosophy
and forms the basis for his description of all social interactions, including
the nature of democracy and the formation of law. Habermas's unique perspective on the role and function of critical thought within hermeneutics
follows directly from his understanding of communicative rationality and
is meant largely to supplement what he sees as reflective deficiencies in
contemporary hermeneutics, especially Hans-Georg Gadamer's (1900-
2002) philosophical hermeneutics. Habermas's critical hermeneutics,
along with the philosophical hermeneutics of Gadamer and the herme-

neutic phenomenology of Paul Ricoeur (1913-2005), constitutes one of the three most important developments in recent hermeneutical thought.

Habermas and Critical Hermeneutics

The goals of critical hermeneutics are to develop the means of having a more thorough and rational understanding for the sake of enlightenment, social consensus, and fostering good will. As a result, it draws upon several of the major streams of hermeneutical thought.

Life and Influences

Habermas was born in Düsseldorf, Germany, in 1929. He started university in 1949 and studied subjects such as psychology, economics, literature, and philosophy. As a student he spent time at a number of universities including those of Göttingen, Zürich, and then Bonn, where he received a doctorate in 1954 with a dissertation on F. W. J. Schelling (1775-1854). In 1956, he went to the University of Frankfurt, where he was a research assistant to Theodor Adorno (1903-1969) at the Institute for Social Research until 1959. Habermas's studies in philosophy and sociology under Max Horkheimer (1895-1973) and Adorno, who were co-directors of the Institute at that time, were crucial to Habermas's intellectual development. Also during this time, roughly the mid-1950s, Habermas became more familiar with the Marxist tradition, which is evident, if mostly in a generalized way, in his later development of a critique of society. In 1961, he completed his *Habilitation* (necessary for teaching in a German university) in philosophy under Wolfgang Abendroth (1906-1985) at the University of Marburg with a book titled *The Structural Transformation of the Public Sphere.*

Habermas's first tenured position was as an associate professor at the University of Heidelberg (1961-1964), followed by a full professorship at Frankfurt (1964-1971), where he taught philosophy and sociology. In 1971, he became co-director of the Max Planck Institute for Research of Life Conditions in the Scientific-Technological World, where he remained for twelve years until he returned to Frankfurt to become a professor in philosophy and sociology. Retired from Frankfurt since 1994, Habermas continues to lecture, write, publish, and actively engage in discourse concerning important social, political, and philosophical issues around the world. In 2004, he was awarded the Kyoto Prize for Arts and Philosophy, which, next to the Nobel Prize, is widely held to be one of the highest intellectual honors.

To appreciate Habermas's unique philosophical approach, it is important to recognize certain key events of his formative years. When Germany lost the war in 1945, Habermas was only fifteen. His father had been a National Socialist sympathizer and Habermas himself had served in the Hitler Youth. During the last months of the war, Habermas had even been sent out to the western defenses despite his young age. Yet, as difficult and life-changing as these times may have been, it was after the Nazis fell and Germany began its postwar reconstruction that Habermas experienced one of his most significant awakenings, which would shape the trajectory of his intellectual life including his later interests in politics, social justice, and ethics. Gradual revelations coming from radio broadcasts of the Nuremberg trials and released documentary films on the concentration camps came as troubling disclosures to Habermas. He was deeply struck by both the horrors committed by the Nazis and the political illusions under which the German people seemed to have lived. As the postwar efforts continued, Habermas became increasingly dissatisfied with what he saw as persisting social elites and cultural prejudices, including the relative ease with which various prominent Nazis reintegrated into society without any serious political accountability for their actions. Had Germany (or the world) learned anything from the war? Were the German people too quick to move forward without more reflective accountability, or moral and political renewal? If so, could it all happen again? Habermas was too young to have participated in the criminal practices of the Nazi regime, yet he was old enough to understand the dramatic social and political changes around him. This sensitivity opened the way for his interest in Germany's rich intellectual tradition, much of which fosters reason, freedom, and justice — ideals that Adolf Hitler (1889-1945) seemed to have too easily corrupted. Today, Habermas continues to work vigilantly for the practical goal of emancipation from corruption and domination through achieving more robust forms of social justice, individual rights, and political freedom.

Habermas is notorious for being indifferent to religion. However, while he is clearly a secular thinker without any religious inclinations of his own, he is not anti-religion *per se.* What minimal interest he does have in religion is indirect and routed through his sociological and philosophical preoccupations with what he considers to be fundamental elements in everyday lived experience. In short, this amounts to his recognition that while religion has a powerful and persistent voice that cannot be ignored in the development of an adequate social critique or a philosophy of language, it does not have any genuine transcendental or supernatural insight and merit. His approach to religion has often been described as "methodological atheism." According to Habermas, this is the best approach for a postmetaphysical philosophy that neither embraces religion nor attempts to eliminate the religious perspective. His somewhat indifferent views notwithstanding, Habermas is committed to the ongoing task of recognizing and fostering critical thought that generates free dialogue and the coexistence of faith and reason in a postsecular atmosphere of tolerance.

Habermas became well known in 1953 when he reviewed Martin Heidegger's (1889-1976) *Introduction to Metaphysics* (1935) and criticized its implicit political stance, most notably Heidegger's lack of moral and political responsibility for the atrocities committed by the National Socialists. Habermas's public visibility was secured with the 1962 publication of *The Structural Transformation of the Public Sphere*. Since that time, he has continued to find a worldwide audience and, at home, growing acceptance as one of Germany's leading philosophers and public intellectuals. It was during largely the 1980s and 1990s that Habermas became known to English-speaking audiences, though his reception has often been difficult for those who try to come to terms with his complex and highly intellectual writings. Besides having large audiences in German-, English-, and French-speaking countries, many of his works have also been translated into Japanese. His ongoing commitments to public debate and dialogue have further contributed to his stature as a visible and outspoken intellectual, and encouraged the reception of his thought in areas often deaf to philosophy and social theory.

Habermas's Place in Contemporary Thought

Habermas follows in the tradition of those such as Immanuel Kant (1724-1804), G. W. F. Hegel (1770-1831), and Karl Marx (1818-1883), and combines elements of both the Continental (e.g., Edmund Husserl [1859-1938], Heidegger) and the Analytic (e.g., Ludwig Wittgenstein [1889-1951], J. L. Austin [1911-1960], John R. Searle [1932-]) traditions. Indeed, Habermas's unique melding of views presents us with a very challenging and controversial project, incorporating an incredible breadth of contemporary scholarship. And while Habermas's educational and intellectual developments are deeply rooted in the complex web of Germany's traditions, including phenomenology and hermeneutics, he cannot be identified solely with any of them or with any one of his contemporaries. He shares many concerns with those such as Heidegger and Gadamer, including that of the all-important role of language and dialogue, and the impact of instrumental and technological rationality within the organization of social life — e.g., in bureaucracies, laws, policies — but with many differences. Habermas is deeply indebted to Heidegger — once his most important influence — although, over time, his work has developed along much different lines and addressed much different questions. Whereas Heidegger's philosophical starting point is the being question, i.e., the question of what it means "to be," Habermas's philosophical reflection begins with the social and intersubjective nature of human beings: What does it mean to live as a political animal in a public space, a polity?

Habermas's clearest contrast is with "postmodern" or "poststructuralist" sentiments. Unlike postmodernists who have abandoned the Enlightenment era's defense of the all-important nature of human reason, Habermas views Enlightenment rationality as an unfinished though far more worthy project. He argues that through communicative rationality (the universal rationality inherent in communication) one may make epistemological claims that are, at least to some degree, objectively real and defensible. This is not a claim concerning the objectivity of natural language, which has universal features such as phonetics and semantics. Rather, Habermas argues that when language is acted out or in use it has universally rational structures. From a hermeneutical perspective, Habermas's insistence on a quasi-objective form of rationality raises a number of important questions about the nature of interpretation, and the role of reason and tradition in it, none of which have simple answers.

There are important similarities between Habermas's philosophical genesis and that of the Enlightenment, which began in large part as a response to tyranny, superstition, and inequality. Habermas's appeal to universal rationality, however, should not be viewed as merely a repetition of the Enlightenment rationalist tradition, as if one must be committed to the whole when committed to a part. There can be little doubt, even for Habermas, that much of what has come out of the Enlightenment — or the Age of Reason, as it is sometimes called — has been fruitless, incomplete, and sometimes just simply misguided and wrong. Many of the commitments and values of seventeenth- and eighteenth-century rationalism resulted in the opposite of what was intended, including further inequality through oppression. Nevertheless, Habermas is able to acknowledge many of its failures while remaining optimistic about his own commitments to rationality, which, he argues, are far more promising than those held by postmodernists. Their commitments, he believes, result in hopeless relativism, pessimism, and irrationalism. Hence, rather than accepting what he sees as the undermining of Enlightenment rationality with postmodern cynicism, Habermas hopes to achieve a new Age of Reason through the rational organization of everyday life. This new age requires critical hermeneutics.

Habermas has become well known for his controversial positions, most notably for his insistence on universalism and his outspoken opposition to poststructuralism and postmodernism. Many scholars have been quick to condemn Habermas for remaining devoted to ideals of reason that they believe have almost superstitious qualities. Reason according to Habermas, such critics argue, is just not possible given the limitations of the human mind. Indeed, he is something of an enigma to those who recognize his outstanding intellectual abilities and his persistent defense of positions that the current intellectual climate often dismisses as untenable. Regardless of whether one finds oneself in agreement with Habermas, his views and challenges are more often than not relevant to many academic questions being discussed today — whether philosophical, sociological, or literary.

The Public Sphere, Rationality, and Discourse

Generally speaking, many of us tend to assume that the enforcement of law is one of the most fundamental goals necessary for the successful administration of our communities and industrialized nations. This widely held assumption is hardly surprising, for civil societies function daily through implicit and explicit appeals to the legal principles of those societies. Knowing the legally acceptable ways of acting in a given society is paramount to successfully living within it. When these principles are challenged, perhaps when someone breaks a law or when individuals' rights seem to conflict, legal arbitrators such as judges and lawyers are needed to clarify the law and judicially resolve issues. It often seems to be the case that within such legal arbitrations, even widely shared moral standards are secondary considerations next to the formal consistency of the law. This is part of the reason laws are in need of revision, such that they might "catch up," so to speak, with the current moral standards of society. Habermas finds the appeal to the formal consistency of laws lacking in important ways. He argues that we need a more fundamental activity that displaces appeals to abstract legal dictates, constitutions, policies, and the like. Rather than emphasizing the consistency and formality of a given legal system, he argues that we should be concerned with creating conditions for the "ideal speech situation." Habermas believes that creating and maintaining free, rational, and democratic societies depends ultimately upon our ability to have relatively clear and critical communication with one another. Therefore, the proper foundation needed to develop the best laws and to maintain civil order should be rational communication that is connected to and reflective of the changing needs of a given society.

Through his discourse theory, grounded in his theory of communicative action, Habermas develops what he believes to be minimal and universal standards of critical-rationality necessary for organizing just and free social frameworks. One of the preeminent themes found throughout Habermas's philosophy is the legitimization of the public sphere or public space that he believes has been eroded by various twentieth-century developments. The public sphere is the realm or arena in which citizens organize themselves, express opinions and desires, and argue different points of view. Along with his concern for the legitimacy of the public sphere, Habermas continually returns to two other themes, namely, discourse and, as we have seen, critical-rationality. These three interrelated issues are present in all his major philosophical and sociological endeavors.

In his first major historical-sociological work, *The Transformation of the Public Sphere* (1962), Habermas examines what it means to have a "bourgeois public sphere." Through his analysis of the historical emergence of the public sphere and its structural changes in the contemporary era, he questions the increased hegemony of economic and governmental organizations. Habermas believes that many people have resigned themselves to being primarily consumers of goods and services, rather than active participants in the fostering of public consensus, opinion, and good. One of his main questions concerns what it means to have an opinion that is not only private, but public. More specifically, he is interested in fostering public opinion that is free of dominating ideologies and monopolizing interests or prejudices. Habermas desires a democratic public sphere in which members may freely, without any form of compulsion, enter into rational discourse so as to debate the legitimacy of given assertions, laws, and policies. All of this is possible, according to Habermas, because rationality is universally present in communication and not, therefore, merely a matter of what some select individuals possess or something to be used solely as an instrument to meet given goals. Communication in the public sphere is most meaningful and unbiased when rational agreement is sought and legitimate consensus forms the basis for moral and political activities.

To be clear, Habermas does not think that the public sphere encompasses the whole of society. Nor does he think that every society has a public sphere. Also, for those societies that do have such a sphere, there will be varying degrees of legitimacy or illegitimacy, for each society will express itself uniquely and with varying degrees of success. One of the persistent problems in this regard is that the current nature of mass media in many industrialized societies often causes the public sphere to be dominated by those who wish to make themselves and their own desires most visible. It has become common for politicians to enter the public sphere as a platform for self-presentation, enabling themselves to be the continued focus of attention. In response to this self-aggrandizing, many of us allow ourselves to become little more than passive spectators. By contrast, those who enter the public sphere with the intention of participating in scholarly or political debates do so ideally with the intention of actively adding to critical-rational discourse rather than their own visibility. In this sense, for Habermas, the public sphere serves as a credible and legitimizing force for the active engagement and exchange of questions and answers on a shared subject.

Since the 1970s, Habermas has focused most of his efforts on a philosophical analysis of language, the intersubjective nature of communication, and working out the implications of his argument that, in order to realize a truly democratic society, we must have a discursive (discourse-oriented) democracy. According to Habermas, while democratization requires the recognition and fostering of communicative rationality and discourse, this does not mean adopting the sort of combative or silver-tongued communication typical of many political forums in which the louder or more eloquent opinion is victorious. A legitimate public sphere must always be aimed at achieving public opinion or common accord rather than the presentation of selfish and private desires, interests, prejudices, and the like. Through his discourse theory, Habermas believes we may overcome monopolizing interests and desires formed by socially accepted prejudices and ideologies. To bring about this kind of free interaction aimed at mutual understanding, his discourse theory is meant to act as a critical and reflective stance within the hermeneutical event of understanding by finding something that is universally rational and objectifiable. This, Habermas argues, cannot be attained by either Heidegger's or

Gadamer's hermeneutics because of their radical commitments to pre-conscious and pre-reflective conditions of understanding, i.e., our historical finitude.

Critical Theory, System, and Life-World

Since his early philosophical studies, Habermas has been aligned with the critical theory coming out of the Frankfurt School (which refers to members of the Institute for Social Research). He is currently the most significant advocate of the second-generation Frankfurt School of neo-Marxist critical theorists, himself more of a post-Marxist. While Habermas is clearly an important representative of critical theory that overlaps significantly with his own interests, he stands outside the tradition in important ways. Most visibly he parts with many critical theorists because of his favorable approach to Enlightenment rationality.

The Institute was founded in Frankfurt in 1923. It was the first Marxist-oriented research center to be associated with a major German university. Initially the Institute tended toward empirical and historical concerns that included problems of the working class. During the 1930s, under Horkheimer, the Institute began developing an interdisciplinary social theory that combined cultural theory, political theory, sociology, and philosophy for the purpose of social transformation. When Hitler came to power key members of the still relatively unknown school left Germany. The Institute was then associated primarily with Columbia University in the United States, until Horkheimer and Adorno returned to Germany after the war.

After the war the Frankfurt School continued to gain popularity, and critical theory increasingly came to represent a wide range of concepts throughout disciplines and fields of research. Indeed, critical theorists differ significantly in their views. For the most part, the critical theory coming out of the Frankfurt School may be characterized as an interdisciplinary approach focused on social critique and change. One of the continuing preoccupations of the Frankfurt School has been with the Western conception of instrumental rationality and the Enlightenment heritage, which they view as inherently destructive and leading to various forms of pervasive domination. The social theory of the Frankfurt School is distinguished from other social theories mainly because of its more theoretical orientation, in contrast to those that are strictly empirical. Many critical theorists, including Habermas, are adamant in their opposition to positivist dispositions interested solely in verifiable and quantifiable facts. The positivist movement has been credited by many theorists as having severely limited our understanding of the social and natural world by too narrowly defining genuine knowledge claims. True knowledge, for the positivists, is that which comes from uninterpreted and value-neutral observations; that is, genuine knowledge is observed fact, not interpreted meaning.

Habermas offers a new version of critical theory that combines philosophy and various forms of social theory in order to develop an ideal form of democratic capitalism. Like the neo-Marxists of the Frankfurt School, Habermas believes that modern societies are facing a very real crisis in which possible progress is far from guaranteed. In particular, he believes that the legitimacy of many social institutions is at risk. Habermas argues that as capitalist and democratic societies have developed, the public sphere and communication within the public sphere have become "colonized" by systems that are not based in rational evaluation or public accord. This colonizing has undermined legitimacy and the belief by members of society that social institutions are benevolent, worthy of their loyalty and support, and operated in the best interests of members. He believes that citizens who are unable to achieve a meaningful sense of public opinion or rational discussion but find themselves governed by formal systems divorced from their concrete lives and practical concerns will, in due course, begin to question the credibility of those institutions.

In his social theorizing, Habermas distinguishes between two major paradigms that comprise the whole of social existence, namely, the life-world (*Lebenswelt*, borrowed from Husserl) and system. The life-world or social world is created and sustained through the intuited social skills and knowledge of its members. It is the world we live every day through relationships with others and it includes all the norms, values, and traditions of a community. The life-world represents the intersubjective nature of human existence through which we recognize the world as meaningful in our relationships with other members of society. Social systems manifest themselves through structured and institutionalized relations, and are controlled primarily by instrumental rationality that exerts a regulatory or institutional force on its members, thereby limiting communicative action and critical-rationality.

For Habermas, perhaps the most important of controlling social institutions are those responsible for the distribution of power and money, most notably governments and commercial enterprises, i.e., corporations.

However, when these institutions become dominated by money, power, and bureaucracy, and further separated from the life-world, they subdue and colonize it at the expense of communicative rationality. The ever-present danger for any life-world is to become colonized and turned into a further extension of the system. It then ceases to reflect genuine public accord and legitimacy. One of the main characteristics of a dominating social system is the demand for efficiency in achieving given goals or objectives over and above critical debate, discourse, and public reasoning or consensus building.

According to Habermas, during the early stages of modernity numerous people were able to engage in interactive debate and discourse within the public sphere. The public sphere emerged, he proposes, during the eighteenth and early nineteenth century with the rise of a politically active and informed public. This was made possible by free society and democratic forums such as the free press, newspapers, coffeehouses, and other social gathering places such as salons. People were able to interact with one another and formulate public opinion, which then influenced political decisions. Informed citizens were able to engage in critical-rational discourse concerning socio-political issues and have a say once reserved for male property owners, nobility, the state, and the church.

However, Habermas argues, by the late nineteenth century, communication and discourse had begun to degrade as the public sphere experienced a "refeudalization." With the emergence of modern social welfare states in which the state assumes comprehensive responsibility for its citizens, the public sphere lost the legitimacy it had in the early stages of modernity. Even in democratic societies that afforded everyone the opportunity to engage in public debate, including those who were simply unprepared for such responsibility, the public sphere has continued to degenerate into mere formalities of institutionalized rights, laws, policies, etc., rather than being a free and open forum for genuine discourse. Habermas is convinced that democratic nations are no longer controlled by a public sphere that could rationally mediate between the interests and private lives of the people and of the state. His conclusion is that much of what we think of as contemporary democracy is really only disguised as rational consensus, when in fact it is dominated by wealthy elites and corporations.

Habermas deeply criticizes commercialized mass media, which, he claims, have seriously damaged legitimacy in the public sphere. When the press and other forms of public media began defending particular ideologies and privatized interests, they became tools for swaying opinion and controlling the public consensus. Due to the powerful influence of contemporary mass media, the public sphere has continued to deteriorate as a place for people to attempt common agreement through critical-rational discussions of their differences. The public sphere has become a place where the dominant voice presents itself over the weaker, that is, where the dominant voice is that of media controlled by power and money. Rational-critical discourse has given way to dominating interests (private or corporate) in money and power, themselves valued above open and free discussion aimed toward the most reasonable argument and the public good.

According to Habermas, the corruptive power of social systems, i.e., the administered welfare society, has permeated down to the individual or personal level. Added to this concern is his belief that even personal creativity and imagination seem to have become colonized through the rapid technologizing of our lives. In response to often very subtle though nonetheless intense forms of domination, Habermas argues for a form of critical hermeneutics through which we may realize freedom and autonomy by overcoming distortions that limit communication and social interaction — communication itself being essential to interaction. It is at the level of the public sphere that Habermas sees possible change occurring as an effective restructuring force, even to the point of reorienting the nature of mass media such that they too become rational and socially responsible.

Communicative Action and Universal Pragmatics

Habermas's most significant work, especially for social theorists and philosophers, is *The Theory of Communicative Action* (2 vols. [1981]). In it, Habermas weaves together the different strands of his prior research as he continues to incorporate an incredible breadth of scholarship including that of Kant, Hegel, Dilthey, Husserl, Marx, Wittgenstein, Stephen Toulmin (1922-), Austin, and earlier critical theorists (i.e., Adorno, Horkheimer, and Herbert Marcuse [1898-1979]). His theory, which is largely the combination of elements from leading sociological theories, is meant to provide a critical understanding of the whole social world (including both the social system and life-world) in an account that is objective and rational yet explicitly avoids either extreme of scientific-analytic objectivism, e.g., positivism, or historical-hermeneutical relativism, e.g., Gadamer. Habermas argues that it is possible to identify universal norms in communication and to be objective and rational while remaining open to the fluidity, plurality, and complexity of the life-world, thereby offering a hermeneutical position between that of Heidegger, Gadamer, and more scientific accounts of human knowledge.

Unlike some philosophers and linguists who study language exclusively as the medium of representation in which language conveys reality between what is in the world (in itself) and our minds, Habermas highlights a concept of rational language as first and foremost that which allows us access to the world and enables us to reach agreement with others about what is in the world. The study of language, he claims, should be less about its parts or elements and more about how it functions as a whole in our lives. To that end, Habermas makes a basic distinction between purpose-rational action (including strategic and instrumental action) and communicative action that is intersubjectively formed. He recognizes that there are different forms of rational action within society, such as those oriented toward success in business and science. These forms of rational action are often competitive and governed by principles of efficiency. By contrast he proposes communicative action, which is about more than employing words as instruments to achieve specific utilities, more than analyzing the validity of propositional statements as if "truth" exists fully in propositions, and certainly more than trying to manipulate others into doing something. Although in reality it is not expected to always attain complete accord, communicative action is action oriented toward achieving mutual understanding and genuine or rational consensus. It is the action of participating with others in ways that foster mutual reciprocity, respect, and autonomy. Habermas recognizes that communication is always goal oriented in a general sense, aiming at various ends, yet with communicative action every goal is subordinate to that of achieving mutual understanding or consensus through critical-rational discourse.

Like Gadamer, Habermas recognizes that language is imbued with meaning that cannot be separated from one's worldview. Language is something we participate in regardless of how simple or complex the social interaction. And like Gadamer, Habermas argues that it is the medium of dominating ideologies. Hence, critical reflectivity, guided by an interest in freeing oneself from ideologies, plays a central part in Habermas's critical hermeneutics that is meant to create an ideal speech situation. In an ideal speech situation, made possible by the freedom generated by critical-reason, he believes that we may identify and overcome hidden and dangerous elements that are implicit in our traditions. Through open, free, and rational discourse, we may achieve an ideal speech situation, in which everyone may have equal opportunity to argue and question. In an ideal speech situation one is freed of all distortions and constraints so that the better argument prevails. The force of critical-reason, and one's obedience to critical discourse, will move one beyond mere opinion, no matter how cherished a belief or desire may be.

While Habermas accepts language as the medium of understanding and that tradition is woven into the fabric of language, he does not believe meaning is fixed in language and non-negotiable or that we must naïvely participate in our linguistic traditions without recourse to rational standards and criteria. To that end, Habermas proposes a reconstructive science or "universal pragmatics" of the assumptions present in our communicative actions and implicit in all our intersubjective understandings. However, even if we accept his proposal that in communication there are guiding universal norms that we may appeal to in order to make our discourse genuinely rational, the goal of critical-rational dialogue and mutual understanding must remain an ongoing task. Critical-rational discourse is only possible to relative degrees of success and failure. It is not an all-or-nothing situation. Moreover, the ideal speech situation does not demand specific conclusions or prescribe specific outcomes. How critical-rational discourse is actualized will remain unknown until it is achieved in the moment.

Habermas's ideal speech situation is based on his argument that utterances presuppose underlying claims and that every communicative act oriented toward mutual understanding has a structure (universal conditions, norms, or rules) that may be reconstructed and made explicit. Within an ideal speech situation, the speaker and listener establish an interpersonal or intersubjective relationship and become bound to the other in ways that raise specific obligations or "validity claims." For there to be communicative competence in any situation, Habermas posits the need for four universal and necessary claims that must be open to being challenged and defended, even if they are not immediately contested or criticized by one's dialogue partner. First, an utterance must be meaningful. This is a commonsense claim. If an utterance is incomprehensible or unintelligible, then there can be no basis upon which we can begin to generate common agreement. Second, the utterance must be true. A speaker must provide what he or she believes to be reliable facts about the social or natural world. Third, the speaker must be sincere. Is the speaker reliable or is he or she lying, joking, etc.? Finally, the speaker must have a right to say what he or she says. Does the speaker offer something that seems appropriate in light of given norms and values shared with the hearer?

Communicative action is action guided by consensual norms, i.e., things that bind speakers and hearers, and exists wherever communicative competence or mutual understanding is achieved because specific obligations are assumed and met. If it is not already apparent, Habermas's proposal is rather utopian in nature. Many of his critics and supporters alike have noted that there has probably never been a completely ideal speech situation as he envisions it. Nevertheless, as a regulative ideal for us to at least try to achieve, universal pragmatics offers an intriguing notion of truthfulness, for it does not emphasize what is found in consensus itself, i.e., what is agreed upon, but the means of securing that which undergirds the process of arriving at consensus, namely, validity claims in the form of binding consensual norms.

Habermas's view that there are universal norms or principles within communication has often been met with severe criticism. What about the radical differences among cultures and historical periods? Surely what is meant by reason and rationality, the very things Habermas claims are universal and normative, has differed significantly among times and places. Indeed, we must be cautious in our consideration of Habermas's insistence on the universal nature of communicative action, for it has often been misunderstood by his detractors. While Habermas describes the rationality inherent in the hermeneutical event in procedural terms, i.e., a rationality we may achieve if we adhere to certain key ideals, this does not mean it manifests itself in the same manner each time — only that the "basis for the result" is a reasonable one each time. It is a rationality we may work out or realize in any culture or situation, while simultaneously being responsive to our culture and situation. Critical-rational discourse is not, for Habermas, merely a "one size fits all" rationality. He accepts that we must be cautious of any so-called "rational action" that subdues the dynamic character of our life-world. Hermeneutics is not about unnecessarily simplifying things or reducing complexities to their lowest common denominator. Thus, whatever rationality is achieved in communication must be an open-ended one.

Habermas's insistence on universalism is meant to be a regulative ideal rather than a truthfulness guarantee. Communicative rationality is not like a formal argument that will result in a completely logical, e.g., valid and sound, conclusion each time. Rather, it is meant to guide us in our unending dialogical search for understanding. So, to be clear, Habermas argues that critical discourse supports only the rational basis of the relative outcome. Even if the criteria for communicative competence are universally assumed and intersubjective consensus and accord are achieved, his universal pragmatics cannot be responsible for the outcomes people accept.

In summary then, Habermas's universal pragmatics is a reconstruction of general presuppositions of consensual speech acts and is meant to foster autonomous and responsible speakers. By developing his universal pragmatics in these ways, Habermas hopes, among other things, to offer a project that will be both freeing (from harmful beliefs or ideologies) and enabling (by fostering critical-rational discourse). This is possible when speakers begin to recognize the mutual demands of reciprocity and trust, i.e., fair play guided by reason in the public sphere.

A Critical Appraisal of Critical Hermeneutics

The now famous debate between Habermas and Gadamer began in the late 1960s after Habermas's critical review of Gadamer's *Truth and Method* (1960). Since then the somewhat bipolar character of the initial debate has softened, even though differences remain firm. From the very beginning of the debate, Habermas supported Gadamer's philosophical hermeneutics for its usefulness in the historical-hermeneutical sciences, especially its ability to reveal the historical conditions of knowledge and to offer a critique of the positivistic sciences, while simultaneously criticizing it as incomplete and ultimately inadequate for a critique of society. Gadamer, on the other hand, tended to look upon Habermas's project as delusionary and an impossible means to securing a kind of truth that is unavailable, and even counter to our actual experiences of reality.

Despite the seriousness of the debate and the obvious disagreements, there are a number of strong similarities between the two hermeneutical projects. These similarities have led many scholars to view the differences between philosophical hermeneutics and critical hermeneutics as tensions rather than abrupt breaks or schisms. As already noted, Gadamer and Habermas both agree on the historicity of human existence and the view that language is a universal medium of intersubjective understanding. Further, they share a common concern for the undue narrowness of the dominant conceptions of knowledge and rationality, especially those that manifest as instrumental and technological, with detrimental effects on the life-world or everyday life of individuals and societies. Truth, for Habermas and Gadamer, is not something absolute and valid in the same way for all people at all times. Truth in understanding is mediated through the pre-understandings of the interpreter's situation and evolving historical contexts. And while they both believe the health of modern societies is in jeopardy because of very limited allowances for what should count as legitimate truth claims, neither is willing to downplay the importance of the empirical or analytic sciences. Rather, Habermas and Gadamer want to show why it is that these dominant forms are not the only legitimate ways to truth and understanding, and how it is that we may live in societies that are not organized in primarily instrumental ways. For all of these similarities, however, their differences are not cosmetic but fundamental to how each approaches the problem of understanding. For instance, Gadamer maintains an ontological approach whereas Habermas moves into methodological and epistemological areas with his normatively based theory. And whereas Gadamer perceives the subjective and objective dichotomy to be a misguided ideal, Habermas reintroduces a quasi-objectivity into his critical hermeneutics.

One of the best ways to capture the character of the debate is to ask, What kind (or degree) of rational reflection is possible in dialogue (Gadamer) or discourse (Habermas)? By asking what passes as rational in dialogue and discourse, we raise the two major issues of universality and rationality to which Gadamer and Habermas return time and again. How rational may we be if we are all historically affected beings? May we add something to the hermeneutical experience to make it more critical and therefore truthful? Both Habermas and Gadamer agree that dialogue must be more or less free and open, yet they differ significantly on what free and open mean. Is it the play of dialogue that remains open to the priority of the question within the circularity of the hermeneutical experience, or the communicative competence of the ideal speech situation that offers idealized conditions for unrestrained and critical discourse?

We saw in Heidegger's existential analytic the proposal that all knowledge is interpretive. Interpretation is the only fact we may know, for all facts are in some ways interpretations. The more we attempt to reflect upon the nature of human understanding the more it reveals itself as a response to historically determined contexts and interests. Gadamer continues Heidegger's emphasis on a hermeneutics of facticity in which our finitude is preeminent. Understanding is possible because we are being-in-the-world. We understand through events of meaning and experiences of truth, which are, themselves, mediated through language, tradition, and the concreteness of our everyday experiences. Gadamer's argument for the hermeneutical claim to universality is that interpretive understanding is always already happening — we are always already being-in-the-world, in language and in tradition, which we cannot step out of through method or technique. Our pre-understandings are both the limiting and enabling conditions of understanding that make possible our awareness of the world and ourselves. Gadamer is unwavering in his view that we belong to tradition and that tradition makes experience possible. Further, if the prejudices of our tradition are both the possibility and the limits of our experiences, then they must always, at least partially, escape our control or methodological reflection. Thus, for Gadamer, the hermeneutical experience transcends method and reflection. After all, how might one step outside the event of understanding (through methods and procedures) in order to understand more clearly? This does not seem possible for Gadamer. Critical reflection and rationality must always happen within the possibilities and limits of language and historicity. The problem Habermas has is that this position seems to allow prejudice and tradition to have too much power over our thinking.

Like Gadamer, Habermas rejects infallible foundations upon which to base interpretation and understanding. For him also, understanding is achieved through the ongoing task of interpretation, for we are all caught up in the infinite play of hiddenness and disclosure. Yet Habermas does insist on a foundational approach that he believes makes it possible to subject our traditions and our prejudices to critical, even quasi-objective, examination. He insists that the only way to liberate ourselves from distortions and ideologies, and to recover legitimacy in the public sphere, is through critical reflection. He argues that Gadamer's hermeneutics cannot offer us this. In Gadamer's account, such a foundational approach is impossible, for it too would be conditioned by pre-understandings.

Habermas has two main concerns with Gadamer's philosophical hermeneutics. First, he does not like the supposed universal validity of pre-understandings, which he sees as similar to the universal claims of positivism. Second, he does not like what he sees as Gadamer's inability to verify or check pre-understandings for corrupt ideologies and prejudices. Habermas agrees with Gadamer that statements and their meaning are understood within a tradition, yet he desires to go further by judging the tradition within which meaning arises. He therefore accepts the hermeneutical circle as the starting point for all understanding while simultaneously proposing a way to step out of the circle. What is prior to the hermeneutical priority of the question, for Habermas, is the claim to universally valid groundings. Indeed, Habermas adamantly opposes the full force of historicism implicit in Gadamer's thought and argues that Gadamer is unable to justify or make sense of understanding and interpretation because he cannot critically evaluate the validity claims of others in a given context or tradition. Whereas Gadamer describes the interpretive act as a fusion of horizons, Habermas argues that the horizon of reason is always already implicit, and to ignore implicit validity claims is manifestly absurd, for they are necessarily a part of every fusion of horizons.

Habermas believes Gadamer has ignored and, even worse, fostered problems encountered in dialogue. By describing dialogical experience without going below the surface to examine the underlying structures, Gadamer has not adequately addressed dangerous ideologies, corruptive powers, etc. For Habermas, Gadamer has abandoned any possible procedural reflectivity that is necessary for a rational-critical public sphere. Habermas's emancipatory and theoretical stance runs directly against what he sees as Gadamer's abandonment of the individual to his or her own tradition. Habermas believes that all that is passed on through tradition and all that we know in the web of meanings in which we live is open to question and challenge. If these conditions on our understanding are beyond critique, how may we ever be confident in the correctness and just character of our beliefs and traditions? How may we have free communication that is not manipulated or dominated unless we are able to reflect upon and ultimately reject tradition?

From Habermas's position, Gadamer seems lost within tradition without the conceptual tools needed to work his way beyond distorting forces. Though he agrees with Gadamer that tradition belongs to the pre-reflective sphere, this in no way negates our ability to suspend and judge it critically and rationally. In this sense, Habermas's critical hermeneutics is a meta-hermeneutic that allows us to break out of the hermeneutical circle and gain a vantage point over what Gadamer believes we cannot escape but must always live through. By pulling truth and method closer together, Habermas works out methodical criteria for the successful analysis of communication, and thereby overcomes what he sees as the limited Gadamerian view that lacks the necessary application of judgment.

We must ask, how, if at all, one might overcome Habermas's antithesis between reason and tradition in Gadamer's hermeneutics. First, it should be noted that Gadamer himself does not accept the view that there is an explicit tension between tradition and reason. He does not think tradition and reason are antithetical or that philosophical hermeneutics is irrational.

Rather, reason is always "practically reason" and something we know by virtue of tradition, not in spite of tradition. We may very well ask what sorts of things require reflection that is necessary for legitimization or we may argue that some things are simply beyond reflection, but all this supposes that there is a possible reflective stance outside the hermeneutical experience capable of legitimizing tradition. Hence, the view of reason as in opposition to tradition is something that has a givenness or direction foreign to philosophical hermeneutics. Second, contrary to Habermas's depiction, Gadamer's hermeneutics offers critical correctives within our dialogical encounters that allow for the distinction between blinding prejudices and enabling prejudices. There is an implicit move within the fusion of horizons to question the truth claims a tradition makes upon us as we seek deeper levels of understanding. And although we cannot objectively arbitrate between which prejudices or interpretations we wish to take up or discard, as if they are laid out before us for our discretionary choice, this does not mean we are left without any critical movement within the hermeneutical experience, only that any self-critical stance will be internal to the dialogical process of questioning and answering that takes place in the perpetual to and fro we have with tradition and emerging possibilities. Even the judgment that a given dialogue has been successful or not, which we all invariably make, will come from within the hermeneutical experience itself, rather than an externally verifying procedure or method.

Philosophical hermeneutics recognizes the power of pre-understandings over us, while simultaneously affirming dialogue as a means of moving, at least in part, beyond them. Through dialogue, we make explicit the prejudices that were once only implicit and, consequently, bring to light many false and dogmatic devotions. However, we must make an effort within dialogue to continue it, for it is not something we may passively participate in. Dialogue interrupts the ongoing conversation we are born into; that is, it interrupts the prejudices and opinions we accept by breaking them open through question-asking. According to Gadamer, tradition may be the background to which we appeal for judging our understanding, but this does not mean we must take up tradition in a robot-like manner. In our dialogical relation to our tradition, we wrestle with our pre-understandings in order to arrive at new horizons of meaning, all the while doing our best to maintain an openness to the unknown and even to that which may be against us. This theme of "openness" is comparable in both Habermas's notion of genuine discourse that is transpersonal consensus, and Gadamer's notion of "play" that emerges in dialogue. In both discourse and dialogue, one must refrain from blindly as-serting one's opinion over another's and allow meaning to emerge of its own accord. That is, we must do our utmost to remain open so as to allow the subject matter *(die Sache)* to reveal itself. As we saw earlier, Gadamer proposes that as we project upon our initial prejudices we come to new un-derstandings that were not previously evident or contained in our pre-understandings — we attend to the emerging subject matter while recog-nizing it is a response to real questions we have as well as possibilities im-plicit in the phenomena being interpreted. Hence, the truth of the dialogue will vary to the degree that the subject matter is not forced or dominated. Both discourse and dialogue require this openness to the other. Still, this is nowhere near the level of concrete, universal, and systematic verification Habermas is looking for. At most, for Habermas, Gadamer has offered only a description of the change within self-understanding in the dia-logical encounter with tradition. Gadamer has failed to provide a way to interject critical-rational change into our worldviews and traditions.

Conclusion

Throughout his career, Habermas has repeatedly returned to three key concepts, the public sphere, discourse, and reason. Around these, he devel-ops a comprehensive social theory meant to free us from oppressive ideol-ogies, prejudices, and biases. Habermas's critical hermeneutics is meant, among other things, to displace distortions within communication and understanding, and to open the way to the rationality inherent in interper-sonal linguistic communication. Again, this is important for Habermas because through it we may come closer to freeing our societies from domi-nation, violence, coercion, and ignorance. His focus on distorted commu-nication and interaction, evident both by his theorizing about the condi-tions of legitimacy crises, e.g., colonization, and also by his theorizing about the conditions necessary for restoring legitimacy, e.g., the ideal speech situation, reflects his persistent emancipatory interest.

Habermas rekindles the Enlightenment project of rationality and, as a consequence, opens the door to what he sees as the way toward achieving public spaces for discourse, laws, and even democracy. Indeed, Habermas has spent considerable effort in trying to overcome what he sees as one-dimensional forms of rationality. Through his elaboration of an intersubjec-tive theory of communication, critical hermeneutics promises us ways of being objective while we work toward achieving the public good, made possible through our rationality that exists beyond the reign of regional biases and prejudices. For Habermas, universal pragmatics may be performed generally, consistently, and without contradiction, even though we may accept that the hermeneutical circle is the starting-point for all understanding.

Like Gadamer, Habermas avoids prescribing specific ways of acting, interpreting, thinking, etc., as if these could guarantee specific outcomes. Unlike Gadamer, Habermas prescribes procedural norms and practices for arriving at genuine and rational consensus. In this sense, Habermas's transcendental pragmatics, ideal speech situation, etc., represent, for many, the same misguided foundationalism found in Husserl's phenomenological reduction and the historical foundationalism of Dilthey. By attempting to reflect objectively on our pre-understandings, one might argue that Habermas has merely reinstated a form of objectivity and universalism that led Heidegger and Gadamer to emphasize facticity in the first place. It is not surprising that many find his regulative principles to be far too idealistic, ahistorical, and unrelated to experience, especially given that many of his distinctions seem arbitrary and rigid, e.g., between system and life-world.

REFERENCE WORKS

Bernstein, Richard, ed. *Habermas and Modernity*. Cambridge, MA: MIT Press, 1985.

Gadamer, Hans-Georg. *Truth and Method*, trans. Joel Weinsheimer and Donald G. Marshall. 2nd rev. ed. New York: Continuum, 2002 (1960).

Geuss, Raymond. *The Idea of a Critical Theory: Habermas and the Frankfurt School*. Cambridge: Cambridge University Press, 1981.

Habermas, Jürgen. *Between Facts and Norms: Contributions to a Discourse Theory of Law and Democracy*, trans. W. Rehg. Cambridge, MA: MIT Press, 1997 (1992).

———. *Communication and the Evolution of Society*, trans. T. McCarthy. Boston: Beacon Press, 1979 (1976).

———. *Justification and Application: Remarks on Discourse Ethics*, trans. C. Cronin. Cambridge, MA: MIT Press, 1993 (1991).

———. *Knowledge and Human Interests*, trans. J. Shapiro. Boston: Beacon Press, 1971.

———. *Legitimation Crisis*, trans. T. McCarthy. Boston: Beacon Press, 1975.

———. *Moral Consciousness and Communicative Action*, trans. C. Lenhardt and S. Nicholsen. Cambridge, MA: MIT Press, 1990 (1983).

————. *On the Logic of the Social Sciences,* trans. S. Nicholsen and J. Stark. Cambridge, MA: MIT Press, 1988 (1967).

————. *Postmetaphysical Thinking: Philosophical Essays,* trans. W. Hohengarten. Cambridge, MA: MIT Press, 1992 (1988).

————. "A Review of Gadamer's Truth and Method." In *Understanding and Social Inquiry,* ed. F. Dallmayr and T. McCarthy, pp. 335-63. Notre Dame: University of Notre Dame Press, 1977.

————. *The Structural Transformation of the Public Sphere: An Inquiry into a Category of Bourgeois Society,* trans. T. Burger with the assistance of F. Lawrence. Cambridge, MA: MIT Press, 1989 (1962).

————. *Theory and Practice,* trans. J. Viertel. Boston: Beacon Press, 1973 (1963).

————. *The Theory of Communicative Action,* Volume 1: *Reason and the Rationalization of Society,* trans. T. McCarthy. Boston: Beacon Press, 1984 (1981).

————. *The Theory of Communicative Action,* Volume 2: *Lifeworld and System, A Critique of Functionalist Reason,* trans. T. McCarthy. Boston: Beacon Press, 1987 (1981).

Held, David. *Introduction to Critical Theory: Horkheimer to Habermas.* Berkeley: University of California Press, 1980.

Ingram, David. *Habermas and the Dialectic of Reason.* New Haven: Yale University Press, 1987.

McCarthy, Thomas. *The Critical Theory of Jürgen Habermas.* Cambridge, MA: MIT Press, 1978.

Thompson, John, and David Held, eds. *Habermas: Critical Debates.* London: Macmillan, 1982.

White, Stephen, ed. *The Cambridge Companion to Habermas.* Cambridge: Cambridge University Press, 1995.

SEVEN   Structuralism and Daniel Patte

Introduction

Structuralism is a multivariate and multifaceted area of study that has had significant influence over a wide range of academic and intellectual inquiry, including both the sciences and the arts. Structuralism emerged during the early years of the twentieth century in Europe in linguistic and anthropological circles, and developed in a number of different and not always compatible ways according to physical location and focus of interest. After World War II, there were efforts made to consolidate some of the diverse branches of structuralism, as they had developed in some considerably divergent ways. Structuralism made its major migration to North America in the 1920s, where it was popular for several decades as a hermeneutical model in a number of fields, such as linguistics, literary criticism, biblical studies, and anthropology, among others. Structuralism continues to be a major force in some fields of study, such as anthropology and linguistics, but it has lost its influence or become transformed into various other, including poststructural, forms of inquiry in such fields as literary and biblical studies. The complexity and breadth of the field makes it impossible to describe all of its dimensions, and so some significant people and movements will be passed over quickly in an attempt to deal with major movements and people as they are related to its significance for hermeneutics.

154

The Development of Structuralism

As an intellectual enterprise, structuralism has reached widely into many areas of contemporary thought, to the point that there are structuralist approaches to most major academic disciplines. As a result, there are a number of key figures and movements in its development that have a significant relationship to hermeneutical questions and practices.

Ferdinand de Saussure

The origins of structuralism are — at least in part — in the linguistic theories of the Swiss scholar Ferdinand de Saussure (1857-1913) and the so-called Geneva school of linguistics (see Godel, *Reader*). Saussure was trained as a Neogrammarian in the late nineteenth century, and made his mark in that field, dominated by fixed laws of language change and development. At the age of twenty-one, he published an important work on the vowel system of Indo-European (1879), and received his doctorate two years later for research on the genitive case in Sanskrit. However, when he was given the opportunity to lecture on general linguistics in Geneva, he unveiled a series of concepts that radically shifted linguistic and related thought. Saussure lectured three times in alternate years (1906-1911) on questions of general linguistics that had occupied his interest during his career. After his untimely death, several of Saussure's students — linguists in their own rights (Charles Bally [1865-1947] and Albert Sechehaye [1870-1946]) — created from their several sets of notes a composite and harmonized volume that became the formative document for modern linguistics and the development of structuralism, published as the *Course in General Linguistics* (French orig., 1916; ET, 1959).

Several of the key notions in Saussure's thought that form the basis of structuralism include: (1) the arbitrary nature of the sign: Saussure distinguishes between the *signifié* (thing signified) and the *significant* (signifier), and he sees their relationship as unmotivated; that is, there is no necessary correlation between the concept and the sounds used to speak of it. (Saussure addresses both onomatopoeic words and partially motivated words, seeing them as not part of the language system, and somewhat arbitrary.) They — sound and concept — are joined together into a unit that he calls the sign. The arbitrary relation of sound and concept was an idea that Saussure probably got from the Neogrammarians, who insisted upon consistently regular sound changes (only possible if the relation between sign and concept is entirely arbitrary). (2) *Langue* versus *parole:* Saussure sees *langue* as the sign system held in common by the users of a language, while *parole* is each user's personal and idiosyncratic use of that *langue.* Saussure distinguishes the social from the individual, and the essential from the incidental, with priority clearly upon *langue. Langue* is the primary object of linguistic investigation. (3) Synchrony versus diachrony: Saussure defines synchrony as concerned with the grammatical form and the sound of a given language at a point in time, and diachrony as the changes that affect any language over time. Since Saussure, many have wanted to recognize a close relation between the diachronic and synchronic dimensions of language, with the latter contingent upon the former. However, the historical nature of language, and the way it had been studied previously, are what drove Saussure to this important distinction. He wanted to divorce analysis of the language from any necessary influence from the historical. (4) Language as difference: Saussure maintains that in language there are only differences; in other words, language is based upon differences among its elements. (5) Language as system: Saussure, drawing further upon the arbitrary nature of the sign, indicates that individual languages establish their own sets of arbitrary relations. Hence, each language divides the world up according to its own system, not as isolated and independent entities, which were the object of previous language study. (6) Syntagmatic versus paradigmatic relations: Saussure believes that language functions in the single dimension of time, in which individual elements exist in this one sphere (paradigmatically), but appear in a succession in relation to each other (syntagmatically). (7) Language as social entity: Saussure emphasizes that language exists as a social phenomenon, in which the society establishes the norms for usage, and the use of language reflects a set of social conventions. Saussure envisioned linguistics as part of the larger field of semiology, concerning theories of signs other than those in language.

Saussure's thought was the primary basis of what we now label as structuralism, although structuralism has taken many different forms since them. We will discuss development of structuralism in Europe, including its roles in anthropology and linguistics, and then American structuralism, before turning to literary structuralism. We conclude by examining the work of the major proponent of biblical structuralism.

Structuralism in Europe

Structuralism had a significant impact upon anthropology — which we will not discuss at length, as it is not at the heart of hermeneutical questions — influencing at least three major anthropological schools of thought: French, British, and American. French structural anthropology, whose origins were in the work of Émile Durkheim (1858-1917) and others, is arguably best represented by Claude Lévi-Strauss (1909-2009). Lévi-Strauss, like most anthropologists, is concerned with human systems found within their cultural contexts (e.g., the use of color or kinship terms), especially as these reflect the way the human brain consistently processes information, from ancient to modern times, on the analogy of language use. Lévi-Strauss is known for three major areas of exploration: kinship theory (e.g., terms for various relations, and the pairings that people groups use), the logic of mythology (e.g., oppositions such as light vs. dark, noise vs. silence, and sacred vs. profane), and theories regarding the ways primitive societies classify things. Lévi-Strauss was influenced by the linguist Roman Jakobson (1896-1982) when they taught together in New York (they co-wrote a famous essay on Baudelaire's "Les Chats" [reprinted in DeGeorge and DeGeorge, *Structuralists*, 124-46]), and Lévi-Strauss has had a significant influence upon semiological theories and the development of the field of semiotics, especially French semiotics (see below). However, his emphasis is upon universal structures, rather than social instantiation. Lévi-Strauss is interested in unconscious universal systems of structures that can be deduced from the observational data. Structural anthropology in Britain had a structuralist-functionalist orientation ever since the work of Bronislaw Malinowski (1884-1942). Malinowski, less a theorist than a field observer, had a significant influence on structural and functional linguistics, in particular upon the first British professor of general linguistics, J. R. Firth (1890-1960), whose work has a structuralist framework. Perhaps better known today as British structural anthropologists are Edmund Leach (1910-1989) and Mary Douglas (1921-2007). A student of Malinowski, Leach utilized a more overt structuralism, in part through introducing Lévi-Strauss to the English-speaking world, and in doing his own research on political systems. He also published on the mythology of Genesis, and wrote a small study on John the Baptist that emphasized his mythological characteristics. Douglas studied cultural behavior with regard to pollution and taboos using Leviticus as one of her examples, but applied her categories to other areas as well. In her work, she attempted to see cultural practices within a classificatory system, rather than as ad hoc phenomena. The American school of structural an-thropology takes its inspiration from the work of the linguist Franz Boas, and is treated below.

Linguistic Structuralism: Prague and Copenhagen

Linguistic structuralism, usually depicted as the direct result of the thought of Saussure, developed in at least two different forms, with some significant crossover after World War II. Linguistic structuralism first de-veloped on the continent, as seen in two schools of thought: the Prague school, and the Copenhagen school.

The Prague school of linguistics occupies a place of much greater sig-nificance in the development of structuralism than is often recognized. The Prague school of linguistics was formally very short-lived, from its found-ing in 1926 to its dissolution in 1948. However, the movement has been long-lived in its often-unrecognized influence. Today, this movement, while sometimes mentioned, is little understood or appreciated for its abid-ing significance in a number of areas of intellectual inquiry, including pro-mulgating various forms of non-linguistic structuralism. The relationship of Saussure's thought to that of the Prague school is vague, as some of the major assumptions of structural linguistics, especially in opposition to the Neogrammarians, seem to have emerged concurrently. In fact, the founder of the Prague school, Vilém Mathesius (1882-1945), delivered a paper in 1911 that argued for the synchronic study of languages. In 1926, Mathesius and a small group of scholars held the first meeting of what was to become, for-mally, the Prague Linguistic Circle, an organization that lasted until it was disbanded because of communist totalitarianism, which restricted non-Marxist methods. The organization welcomed scholars from all over Eu-rope to give papers at their small, exclusive gatherings, they published their own journal and monograph series, and they participated in the wider lin-guistics world of the time. The basic orientation of the Prague school was laid out in nine theses that they developed for presentation in 1928 to the First Linguistics Congress in The Hague, the Netherlands. Many see this as the formal beginning of the school. Among other things, the theses articu-lated a view of the relation of synchrony and diachrony that attempts to overcome the stringent separation of the two by Saussure (the statement was written by Jakobson). Many believe that it is to the credit of Prague school linguistics, especially in phonology, that the disjunction was mitigated. Further, they articulated that the sounds of a language are part of a system governed by oppositions. The goals of the school were further articulated in a subsequent Manifesto (found in M. Johnson, *Recycling*) prepared for the 1929 First International Congress of Slavists, held in Prague. The theses of this manifesto extended the scope of the Prague school in numerous ways. They can be summarized in their concern with two major concepts: the structure of language and its function. By this they meant that languages constitute structured systems of usage that are employed for various communicative purposes or functions within given language communities, and hence in various types of contexts, in which diachronic and comparative perspectives are also important.

The accomplishments of the Prague school are conveniently divided into two parts, roughly corresponding to the first and second decades of its existence. The first decade's major contribution was in the area of phonology and phonetics, and the second decade in more general communicative topics, including semiotics. Two of the earliest and most important members of the Prague school were not, in fact, Czech, but were the Russians Nikolai Trubetzkoy (1890-1938) and Jakobson. These two Russians, who had become acquainted with Saussure's thought, brought with them interests in literature from the Russian Formalist school, which also had influence on the Prague school. Trubetzkoy was a member of the Russian nobility who had fled after the revolution, and had become a professor at the University of Vienna. Trubetzkoy, who coined the term *phoneme,* was influenced not only by Saussure but by the work of his Vienna colleague Karl Bühler (1879-1963), the psychiatrist and linguist, who distinguished among three functions of language: representative, expressive, and appelative. Phonology applied to the representative plane, where sound features can be examined with regard to their accumulation, delimitation, or distinctiveness. Regarding distinctiveness, Trubetzkoy analyzed sounds for their oppositions, either as distinctive or non-distinctive. A phoneme is a minimal distinctive sound (or phonological) unit. These phonemes can further be distinguished by their oppositions as to whether they are privative, graduate, or equipollent, according to their marked feature. Although there were other accomplishments in the area of phonology by members of the school, especially Jakobson, Trubetzkoy's work has had abiding significance in structural thought.

The second period of Prague linguistics made many useful contributions to various views of semiotics. One of these developments was in the area of syntax. Although he had been working on his ideas regarding syntax for some time, during the 1940s Mathesius, who was responsible for the terminology that came to be translated as theme and rheme (or, sometimes, topic and comment following Charles Hockett [1916-2000]; originally nucleus and peripheral), developed what is called the "Functional Sentence Perspective" by those working in the Prague school tradition. Mathesius, in some ways also recognizing the distinctions made by Bühler, takes a functional view of the sentence, in which he makes a number of observations: that sentences are not used individually or in isolation, that sentences convey more than simply factual information, and that they have ways of being organized to facilitate communication. As a result, he observes that the theme of a sentence is the part that repeats information that is already known, while the rheme includes new information. In some ways, there is a correlation of these semantic notions with the subject and predicate of a sentence, but this is not always the case, and the theme precedes the rheme. However, the ordering of elements may be changed to alter the functional significance of the sentence. Important to Mathesius's notion of the "Functional Sentence Perspective" is an appreciation of context, because it is the immediate context that is responsible for the various permutations that are made to the fundamental sentence configuration. Mathesius's observations had implications for the recognition that sentences are parts of larger wholes or discourses.

A second development in the area of semiotics actually dates back to at least the original Manifesto, and is concerned with literary structuralism. Jan Mukarovsky (1891-1975) was responsible for the statement on poetics in the Manifesto, although the statement also shows the influence of the Russian formalism of Jakobson and Trubetzkoy, both of whom were accomplished literary critics interested in such things as folklore (see below), and the phenomenology of Edmund Husserl (1859-1938). The Prague school linguists were intent on overcoming a general neglect of poetic language by linguists, and they contended that synchronically based descriptive principles should be developed that are appropriate for analysis of the language of art, without falling victim to the fallacy of thinking of poetic language simply as communicative language. They drew upon the terminology of *langue* and *parole* to distinguish poetic language as *parole* used against the backdrop of *langue*. Mukarovsky emphasizes the role of linguistic features in analysis of the structure of literary works. Another scholar who worked in the field of literary structuralism in Prague was René Wellek (1903-1995), a student of Mathesius who became one of the leaders of the literary-critical movement in North America called the New Criticism. Other important scholars who had meaningful contact with the

Prague linguistic school, such as giving lectures in Prague or publishing with them, include Otto Jespersen (1860-1943), Viggo Brøndal (1887-1942), Louis Hjelmslev (1899-1965), Emile Benveniste (1902-1976), André Martinet (1903-1999), and Leonard Bloomfield (1887-1949). All are well-known structuralist linguists. The field of semiotics, however, expanded beyond the confines of linguistics into a general theory of signs, on the basis of the work not only of Saussure and Charles Sanders Peirce (1839-1914), but especially of Jakobson and several French structuralists (see below). Due to a variety of reasons, semiotics at first developed along two independent tracks, an Eastern and a Western form. The Eastern form, sometimes called Soviet Semiotics, shows the distinct influence of Jakobson, and includes the work of such semioticians as Boris Uspensky (1937-) and Umberto Eco (1932-). The Western form, which developed in many ways independently of the Eastern form, was highly influenced by the work of Thomas Sebeok (1920-2001), and can be seen in the work of the literary critic Robert Scholes. More recently, as social and political boundaries have changed, semiotics has become much more eclectic and integrative, with crossing of previously untraversed boundaries.

The Copenhagen school of structural linguistics is not as well known as the Prague school, but was nevertheless a significant school of structuralism and has also had influence on subsequent semiological developments. Linguists such as Jespersen, Brøndal, and Hjelmslev are associated with the Copenhagen school. The most innovative and clearly structuralist in orientation are Brøndal and Hjelmslev. Brøndal is not well known today, although his attempt to find universal linguistic categories across all languages resonates with much more contemporary linguistic thinking. The seminal Copenhagen school linguist was Hjelmslev, who formally instigated the Copenhagen Linguistic Circle in 1931 and was the co-founder, with Brøndal, of its leading journal. Hjelmslev's contribution to structuralism is what he called glossematics, explicated in his *Prolegomena to a Theory of Language* (1943). In some ways following the logically instigated analysis of Brøndal, Hjelmslev is concerned with the internal relations of linguistic phenomena of a given language and the system that unifies them. According to Lepschy (*Survey,* 68-69), Hjelmslev thought that a descriptive linguistic theory must be immanent (based upon language only), arbitrary (deductive in nature), and appropriate (empirical). Hjelmslev posited two sets of oppositions that result in four layers of analysis: form and substance, and expression and content. Each can be broken down into its individual elements. Though they are not directly correlative, Hjelmslev thought they could be viewed coordinately. The formal rigor of Hjelmslev's glossematics took Saussure's principles of system and autonomy to new levels of formalization. Firth, who founded the functionalist London school of linguistics with its major proponent Michael A. K. Halliday (1925-), was also influenced by Hjelmslev. Halliday himself has contributed to structuralist linguistics through his early scale and category grammar, which posited a hierarchy of language, in which increasingly higher units are composed of units from the next level down, from the sentence down to the morpheme.

The work of Saussure, along with that of other early seminal thinkers, laid the groundwork for structuralist linguistic thought. This thought was developed in several major ways, especially in the work of the Prague school of linguistics, with its resultant developments in anthropology and semiotics, and the Copenhagen school. The effects of the fundamental ideas of Saussure continue to resonate in linguistic, anthropological, and semiotic circles.

Structuralism in America

Structuralism in linguistics also made its way to the United States, where it was inspired by the work of Franz Boas (1858-1942). Boas noted that there were varieties of classification systems that could be used to describe the structures of languages (seeing that American Indian languages could be analyzed along different lines than those traditionally used for European languages), and that there was a relationship between language and thought patterns. This observation was extended to the idea that speakers might be forced to think according to the strictures of linguistic categories. The notion of linguistic determinism was developed much further by Boas's student, Edward Sapir (1884-1939), and Benjamin Lee Whorf (1897-1941). The major American structuralist, however, was Leonard Bloomfield (1887-1949), who came to be identified with the American form of structuralism. Two features of Bloomfield's structuralism are important. The first is that he was a mechanistic behaviorist, by which he means that language is based upon stimulus and response, by the speaker and hearer. Bloomfield thus distanced himself from any sort of mentalism in linguistics, as he did not want to be influenced by non-mechanistic factors that came from outside of language, e.g., by psychology. The second feature of Bloomfieldian linguistics — one that had a far greater impact on linguis-

tics from the 1930s to the 1950s and in some circles beyond, and that reflects his structuralist orientation — is his notion of immediate constituent
analysis. Bloomfield posits that a linguistic construction, such as a sentence or phrase, consists of constituents. A construction can be composed
of any number of constituents, which are made of smaller constituents. His
immediate constituent analysis begins with the smallest constituents of a
larger constituent and hence their being immediate, such as the phoneme,
which then composes larger and more complex units, such as the morpheme. These are displayed by a form of tree diagram, from immediate
constituents to the entire construction. The elements of such constituents
can be analyzed according to their distribution and relationships to each
other. Post-Bloomfieldian thought is reflected by such linguists as Hockett,
Henry Gleason (1917-2007), and Eugene Nida (1914-).

Two major structuralist-inspired departures from standard post-
Bloomfieldian structuralism may be noted here. One of these is the tag-
memics of Kenneth Pike (1912-2000). Bloomfield had already laid out a
theory of *-emes,* such as phonemes and morphemes and taxemes (units of
syntax). Pike developed Bloomfield's thought further in several ways. He
abandoned mechanistic behaviorism and tried to create a unified theory of
human behavior. He also posited the tagmeme as the fundamental structural unit, as both a functional and a formal unit filling the slots that com-
pose larger units. Historically more significant is the influence Bloomfield
had on Zellig Harris (1909-1992), who published his *Methods in Structural
Linguistics* in 1947 (republished in 1951 simply as *Structural Linguistics*).
Harris took Bloomfield's notions of distribution and formal description of
linguistic elements to their furthest lengths, reducing syntax simply to a
matter of elemental distribution. In the end, Harris realized that such analysis had insuperable constraints on understanding, which led him to his
development of string analysis and a form of transformational analysis not
based upon syntactical function, besides doing elementary work on discourse analysis. This transformational analysis was picked up and developed by his student, Noam Chomsky (1928-), whom he thanks in the preface to *Methods.* The rise of Chomskyanism marks in many ways the end of
structuralist linguistics for North America and much of the rest of the
Western world, with his development of transformational and generative
grammar based upon a mentalistic approach to language that some have
seen as a reduction of the study of language to only its "psychological
structures" (Kristeva, *Language,* 260).

Literary Structuralism

Literary structuralism was a logical and anticipated development from linguistic structuralism. Literary structuralism has two major foci of development, Russia and France. The Russian Formalist school, though short-lived, was highly influential. This movement, which arose around the turn of the nineteenth and twentieth centuries, refers to a group of scholars located in (then) Petrograd (now St. Petersburg) and Moscow, who after 1916 came to be called the Russian Formalists. In 1928, two of their members, Iurii Tynianov (1894-1943) and the above-mentioned Roman Jakobson, published eight theses that defined the movement (in DeGeorge, *Structuralists,* 81-83). This group of scholars, who included linguists, literary critics, and folklorists, were labeled formalists because of their emphasis upon form and formal elements (the term was originally a pejorative one, accusing them of separating form from content). The goal of these scholars was to bring scientific rigor to the analysis of literature by developing a scientifically robust methodology. The major tenet of Russian Formalism was to find the synchronous ordering principle or structure of a literary work, whether narrative or poetry, and then to study the "morphology" of this work, i.e., to break it down into its smallest segments. Jakobson, who had been a member of the Moscow Linguistics Circle, was one of the leaders of the Russian Formalist movement, and he probably introduced Saussure's thought to the group. Trubetzkoy was an early member and literary interpreter who wrote a number of articles from this perspective, many of which focused upon segmentation. Today, perhaps the best known of the members was folklorist Vladimir Propp (1895-1970). His *Morphology of the Folk Tale* (1928) is a study of an entire genre, the Russian folktale. He concentrated on studying the plots of these individual folktales, and thereby was able to develop a theory of their general structural rules. He believed that all folktales could be described by means of thirty-one functions and seven character-types. As Milne states, Propp was trying to "demonstrate that the plot of the fairly tale is syntactically ordered and that the pattern of its component elements is governed by rules" (*Vladimir Propp,* 28). Propp wrote near the end of the existence of the Russian Formalists, who were disbanded in about 1930 for failing to heed Marxist doctrine. (The Russian Formalist school has had significant influence, and continued a somewhat tumultuous existence in the work of such scholars as Mikhail Bakhtin [1895-1975].) When Jakobson first went to Prague and then to the United States, he took Russian Formalism, and with it the work of Propp, with him, and this was a significant influence on the development of structuralism.

French literary structuralism was the result of the confluence of a variety of linguistic and other factors, although it was never a unified and singular phenomenon (see, for example, the papers in Macksey and Donato, *Structuralist Controversy*). Lévi-Strauss is often heralded as the primary force in the development of French literary structuralism, but the relationship of Lévi-Strauss's thought to subsequent French structuralism is not entirely clear. Another influence was the thought of Peirce, who stands as the founder of semiology (and was later an important source for the development of semiotics) with his threefold distinction between a sign, its object, and its interpretation. Other influences on French structuralism were Jakobson and Propp. Many consider French structuralism as the beginning of literary structuralism, but it was in France that structuralism as a recognizable literary movement came to a fairly abrupt end in about 1967, under the influence of a complex of philosophical, political, and intellectual upheavals that destabilized belief in the kinds of structures so central to structuralism. The notion that structures have a quasi-ontological status — or at least a permanence that is not subject to epiphenomenal change — met with strong resistance in an era in which all stable authorities were subject to critique. A number of those who at one time had been positively influenced by structuralism came to reject such a claim for it, as a reimposition of dogmatic truth. The result was that French structuralism as a coherent belief system disintegrated, and was dispersed in at least two major directions.

The first direction was development from structuralism as a broad, though reasonably coherent, intellectual movement into poststructuralism, as a catchall term to describe those who had moved beyond structuralism by rejecting its ontological proclivities — while still apparently embracing and expanding upon many of its fundamental assumptions regarding the sign and signification. Roland Barthes (1915-1980) is emblematic of this development. Jackson (*Poverty of Structuralism*, 124-67) has identified four periods in Barthes's intellectual journey. The first, influenced by Sartre and the French new novel, illustrates Barthes as the journalistic critic of contemporary society, as seen in such a work as *Writing Degree Zero* (1953). The second stage, influenced by Barthes's reading of a number of linguists, such as Benveniste, Halliday, and Harris, is his structuralist phase. Concerned with structuralist taxonomies, Barthes wrote his short and basic *Elements of Semiology* (1964) and his arguably more important though strangely sterile *Système de la Mode* (1967), a lengthy and involved analysis of fashion. These works both exemplify a very strong structuralist perspective, and resulted in his significant influence upon the development of semiotics. Then, in the late 1960s, Barthes came into direct contact with the work of Jacques Derrida (1930-2004) and Jacques Lacan (1901-1981), who undermined Barthes's structuralist principles. Others to reflect this disintegrative trajectory were Michel Foucault (1926-1984) and Louis Althusser (1918-1990). At this point, especially under the influence of Derrida, who became the notional representative of poststructuralism with his advocacy of deconstruction and severing of sign and signified (to which we devote an entire chapter), Barthes abandoned structuralism *per se* and entered his poststructuralist phase, writing *S/Z* (1970). His final stage marked a return to a concern with literature, but without his earlier political agenda. Barthes thus took up many of the interests of those such as Derrida, Lacan, Foucault, and Althusser, among others, and became strongly identified with what has come to be called poststructuralism.

The second direction in which French structuralism developed was into what is called narratology. The earlier structural research of Propp had a significant influence upon the development of French narratology, as seen in the work of two of its major figures, A.-J. Greimas (1917-1992) and Tzvetan Todorov (1939-), both of whom have had significant impact upon hermeneutics. Other important French narratologists include Claude Bremond (1929-), with his own attempt at a narrative syntax, and Gérard Genette (1930-), who is concerned with narrative organization. There are many who have followed in their wake, including Mieke Bal (1946-), who, motivated by Genette, has written extensively on biblical texts, and Seymour Chatman (1928-), the best-known American narratologist, who has had a profound influence on literary criticism (see Chapter Eleven). The best known and probably most influential of these narratologists is Greimas, especially through his major work, *Structural Semantics* (1966). Showing his dependence upon Propp, as well as a number of other structuralists, Greimas attempts to create a complete structural (even syntactic) theory of meaning (semantics), beginning with the lexeme and ending with the discourse. In a departure from concurrent work in semiotics, his framework is firmly placed within the sphere of semiology, i.e., the concern for human meaning (although it has implications for semiotics, or systems or signs of meaning; see his semiotic square). He therefore relies upon a number of fundamental structuralist distinctions, such as the difference between signification and signifier. His developed description of signification leads directly to his actantial model of discourse. Rather than making use of Propp's thirty-one functions, Greimas develops a set of six major actants, not to be equated with characters in narrative but with actantial roles. These six actants are: Subject versus Object, Sender versus Receiver, and Helper versus Opponent. There have been many critiques offered of Greimas's work, most finding fault not with the rigor but with the applicability of his taxonomy of meaning. In any case, his attempt at a structural semantics stands as a landmark in structuralism. Less well known, although also very important, is Todorov, who builds on the work of Greimas. Todorov, tracing the roots of his work in ambivalent ways to Russian Formalism and Prague school linguistics, is concerned to develop a grammar of narrative. He has applied this grammar especially to fantasy literature, as in his *The Fantastic* (1970), and in a variety of works that attempt to define a narrative syntax, as well as pursuing such topics as poetics and symbol, where he deals with matters of signification. More recently, there have been narratologists who have announced a "postmodern narratology" (Moore, "Afterword," 256).

This climate of developments in French structuralism was one of intellectual excitement as the foundations of the discipline were reconfigured in a variety of poststructural expressions. The situation led to a creative ferment and intense intellectual debate as various interpreters sorted through their philosophical and hermeneutical stances.

Daniel Patte

Daniel Patte (1939-) is probably the best-known, most productive, and most rigorous biblical structuralist. There have been two major approaches to the Bible from a structuralist perspective. One is the approach of confirmed structuralists who have written on the Bible. These include, for example, Roland Barthes, Jean Starobinski (1920-), Louis Marin (1931-1992), Claude Chabrol (1930-), and Mieke Bal, among others. In 1971, Barthes and Starobinski gave lectures along with biblical scholars at a conference sponsored by the faculty of theology of the University of Geneva. These essays were translated into English and were important introductions to structuralism for those in biblical studies (Barthes et al., *Structural Analysis*, 1974). Unfortunately, at least in the case of Barthes according to Jackson's analysis, Barthes had already moved on from structuralism into his poststructuralist phase — although, as indicated above, poststructuralism is in fundamental ways a continuation of structuralism, or at least heavily dependent upon it. The other approach to the Bible is that of biblical scholars who engage in structuralist analysis. These include such scholars as John Dominic Crossan, Dan Otto Via, Robert Polzin, Robert Funk, Robert Detweiler, and Elizabeth Struthers Malbon, among others, who evidence a range of structuralist approaches and concerns. Particularly influential among biblical scholars has been the narratological model of Greimas. His narrative analysis has provided the theoretical framework for work by Jean Calloud, Richard Hays (who in the second edition of his book moves away from his Greimasian structuralism [*Faith*, xxvii], even though his narrative analysis and hence conclusions are predicated upon it), Hendrikus Boers, and Ole Davidsen. The one who has been the most rigorous and productive in structural analysis, including the use of Greimas, however, is clearly Patte.

Life and Influences

Patte, born in France in 1939, was educated at the University of Grenoble, the faculty of Protestant theology at Montpellier, and the University of Geneva. He did his Th.D. at Chicago Theological Seminary, finishing the degree in 1971. After earning his *licence* (roughly equivalent to an undergraduate degree) in theology at Geneva, Patte taught French literature in the Congo for two years. After that and throughout the rest of his scholarly career — which is still active — he has taught religious studies and especially New Testament, mostly at Vanderbilt University in Nashville, Tennessee.

Patte's career can be divided into three deliberate periods, reflecting the major emphases of his research and writing. Although only the second of these is clearly focused upon structuralism, structuralism has had a decided influence on all of the major work by Patte in each of the three periods.

Despite his having attended the University of Geneva, the first period is Patte's prestructuralist time. His first major book was *Early Jewish Hermeneutic in Palestine* (1975; the published form of his Th.D. dissertation), in most ways a straightforward exposition of Palestinian Jewish interpretive practice. As he notes in an article written nearly twenty-five years after the book's publication, Patte was writing his dissertation in Chantilly when he was exposed to structuralism and his work took what he calls a "semiotic twist" (Patte, "Critical Biblical Studies," 4). At the beginning of his work on Jewish hermeneutics, Patte notes the influence of French structuralism upon his thinking, and he appended a final chapter when the work was published in 1975 in which he proposes a normalization of terminology for Jewish interpretive practice along structuralist lines. The second period of Patte's career is devoted primarily to structuralism, to which we will turn in more detail below. During this period he wrote numerous structurally motivated volumes, edited and contributed to several collections of essays in the experimental journal *Semeia*, and translated the Greimasian-influenced biblical scholar Jean Calloud's *Structural Analysis of Narrative* (1976). The final period of Patte's publishing career (to date) is concerned with cultural issues in exegesis, and includes a number of works on what might best be described as the culturally located exemplification of Christianity. In this area, Patte has published books on the ethics of interpretation and especially discipleship, as well as editing volumes on reading New Testament books within various historical and cultural frameworks.

Structural Hermeneutics in Theory and Practice

Patte's major publications in structuralism are of two types: theoretical works on the nature of structuralism, and what amount to pedagogical handbooks on structural exegesis of the New Testament. What is clear in most of his major works is the influence of structuralism, and not just structuralism in a variety of its forms but in particular the structuralism of Greimas — to the point of especially developing Greimas's method into a tool for analysis of religious thought. Soon after completing his dissertation, Patte published in 1974 his first major article using a structural exegetical model, an analysis of the narrative structure of the parable of the Good Samaritan, and then published his first major volume in structuralism, *What Is Structural Exegesis?* (1976), an introductory guide to the subject for students of the New Testament. This volume was followed by a number of structuralist analyses of discourse and narrative (e.g., 1978, 1980, 1983, 1988), and then two further programmatic works, *Structural Exegesis from Theory to Practice* (1978; with Aline Patte) and *Structural Exegesis for New Testament Critics* (1990), both exemplifying and developing his approach to structural exegesis. In 1990, Patte also published probably his most important full-length theoretical treatment of structuralism, and in particular analysis of the structuralism of Greimas: *The Religious Dimensions of Biblical Texts*. His method has also been thoroughly though less overtly applied in two major volumes, *Paul's Faith and the Power of the Gospel* (1983) and *The Gospel according to Matthew* (1987), along with a number of further articles.

Throughout these works, especially in his major monographs, Patte makes clear that his structuralism has three primary goals: to make structural semiotics and in particular the structural model of Greimas accessible to others; to be able to describe the semantics or meaning of religious dimensions of biblical texts; and to provide a serviceable exegetical tool, in contrast but not necessarily in opposition to other tools, such as the historical-critical method. Patte's burden is to define and situate within the wider field of biblical exegesis a clear structuralist exegetical method that can be employed to examine the texts of the New Testament, with the particular purpose of elucidating their faith dimension. When Patte wrote his first volume on structural exegesis, structuralism for the most part had only been known to New Testament scholars for a little over five years (dating from the time of French structuralism). By the time he wrote his final major works on the topic in 1990, there had been many practical applications of the method, and Patte himself had certainly led the way in development of Greimasian structural semiotics as a potential tool for biblical exegesis. To understand Patte's structural hermeneutics, we must examine his major theoretical work on Greimas, and his two most important structural exegetical handbooks.

Greimas's Structural Semiotics and the Religious Dimensions of Biblical Texts

Patte's 1990 monograph on Greimas and the religious dimensions of biblical texts, in many ways like his earlier work (Patte and Patte, *Structural Exegesis*), attempts to reach all of the major goals of his structuralist program, with emphasis upon defining the theory and practical implications of what he labels Greimas's structural semiotics. Revealing its structuralist and more particular Saussurian foundations, Greimas's theory is grounded in the notion of "difference." Greimas's semiotic square is organized around three types of relational differences that form a square of oppositions connecting the corners: contrariety, contradiction, and implication. Around this semiotic square, much of Greimas's generative semiotics is organized.

Apparently in response to historical critics who fail to appreciate an alternative exegetical method, Patte defends what he calls "semio-structural exegesis" as a general and comprehensive theory of meaning that can complement other methods of exegesis, such as historical criticism on the one hand and literary criticism on the other. Meaning, according to Patte, is multidimensional and relational, and is concerned with the "meaning-effect" (31), i.e., the meaning that comes about as the product of the inter-relational features of meaning. In this sense, semio-structural exegesis is one of several types of structural research, which are preoccupied with various types of structures — either universal or text-specific — and can be applied to various types of textual structures. Greimas's structural semiotics is one form of structuralism that concentrates upon "systems of signification" (50) for the production of meaning-effecting texts. The signification systems of semio-structural exegesis consist of two types: syntagmatic and paradigmatic. Syntagmatic systems are "chain-like series of actions that form a narrative development, or plot" (54), whose action is a "transformation" (55). These transformations are found in Greimas's actantial analysis, in which he characterizes the participants in the narrative by their roles (sender, object, receiver, helper, subject, opponent), arranged in opposed pairs (this is attributed by Patte to the early stage of Greimas's thought, superseded by what Patte is now presenting). Paradigmatic systems consist of sets of "textual features organized by the repeated application of the same pattern or paradigm" (62), and are constituted by the codes of the social systems and the symbols found in the text.

In order to make these notions more concrete, Patte turns to Greimas's generative trajectory in his semiotic theory. As opposed to other theories of meaning that begin with the communicative act, Greimas begins with the system of significations and their attendant structures, by which the meaning-effect is produced. The notion of a generative trajectory is an attempt to define the ways in which the various components that produce meaning are organized and interrelated in hierarchical fashion. There are three fundamental distinctions that are maintained in outlining the generative trajectory. These include the distinction between syntactic and semantic components, the distinction between what are called "semio-narrative structures" and "discursive structures" (77), i.e., those structures within the narrative and those outside the narrative as part of the communicative process, and the distinction between deep or fundamental and surface structures.

The six components of Greimas's generative trajectory consist of the following. (1) Fundamental and Narrative Semantics. The first, and in order of hierarchy, primary trajectory is the recognition of fundamental and narrative semantics. Any semiotic system, including a discourse, "presupposes a *semantic universe*" (78). This semantic universe is the product of perceptions of the world, which have either verdictory (i.e., whether they exist or are illusory) or thymic (i.e., whether they are thought to be pleasant or painful) characters. (2) Fundamental Semantics. At this point Patte disagrees with Greimas, who wishes to posit structural universals for fundamental semantics, whereas Patte wants to characterize them not as universals but as culturally bound oppositions within a given semantic universe, but not based upon a given discourse. (3) Narrative Semantics. Narrative semantics are what Patte characterizes as "a great number of microsemantic universes or narrative semantic systems" (84), each one concerned with various areas of human life, and each one the possible basis for a different story. Thus, using the three categories above, the semantic universe consists of the fundamental and narrative semantics, and these provide the semantic basis for the construction of a discourse. (4) Fundamental Syntax. As Patte states, "a discourse . . . is progressively generated by transforming this semantic framework into 'syntactic systems'" (89). The semantic systems are not as dynamic as the syntactic systems, and various "syntactic operations" (89) are performed that enable the generation of the discourse. This begins with the fundamental syntax. Fundamental syntax includes basic operators, such as assertion and negation, by which the "semantic universe is transformed into a 'universe of ideas'" (92), in which the notion of "ideas" is the realization of various syntactical arguments. (5) Narrative Syntax. It is at this point that the notion of actants comes into play. The fundamental syntax is transformed into a set of interactions within the narrative, such as Subjects, Objects, and Receivers. This set of transformations constitutes the fundamental compositional units of any narrative, and the narrative syntax itself becomes a relational set of transformations that are interrelated to each other, just as a chain is linked together. The result is a narrative, but not yet a discourse, as the various interactions are present, but could result in a number of different stories. (6) Discursive Syntax. At the level or stage of the discursive syntax, the story becomes recognizable because the set of compositional units is "brought into the realm of the interactions between enunciator and enunciatee" (97); in other words, it becomes a discourse within a context of potential speakers and hearers. (7) Discursive Semantics. At this stage the story now makes sense as an actual discourse that is communicating a particular message. Discursive semantics involves two major dimensions: thematization and figurativization. Thematization involves the representation of the narrative semantics in particular actors. Figurativization is concerned with the views that are represented within the discourse and that will be recognized by the hearers.

Thus Patte attempts to provide, using the work of Greimas, a comprehensive semiotic model that encompasses both fundamental and surface representations through a process of transformations. These transformations involve various semiotic oppositions and their realizations in various levels and types of semantic and syntactic structures, so that the move from a semantic universe is able to generate a discourse syntax and a discourse semantics, in which the fundamental semantics are transformed from actants in narrative syntax into specific characters within a context of speaker and hearer.

Patte recognizes, however, that this presentation has a noticeable sterility to it unless it is mobilized in service of his larger project of discussing the religious dimensions of biblical texts. This is based around the notion of belief or conviction providing the semantic universe of the text. This notion of belief has various dimensions to it, including that of belief on the basis of authority and belief as being sure of a truth, and belief as thinking that something is true. With this system of convictions determining one's semantic universe, Patte then is concerned to show how this defines the religious dimensions of biblical texts, including how such a semantic universe affects the various components of the generative trajectory and has implications for examination of the biblical text. However, this discussion remains recognizably theoretical. For more concrete and extended instances of the use of a semio-structural hermeneutic in biblical exegesis, one must turn to the exegetical applications of Patte's interpretation of Greimasian theory.

Structural Exegesis Defined and Exemplified

Whereas Patte gives his most extensive definition of Greimasian structuralism in his 1990 monograph, he had already begun to exemplify how such a structural hermeneutic constituted a ground for exegesis in his 1976 work, *What Is Structural Exegesis?* The method of structural exegesis that Patte defines is clearly dependent upon French structuralism, in particular the form passed down from Saussure, exemplified by the anthropologist Lévi-

Strauss, and then systematized in the semiotic framework of Greimas. Patte contends that the modern interpretive context with its manifest cultural transformation demands a new form of exegesis concerned with humanity. He sees structuralism as providing the means by which one can bring both exegesis and hermeneutic — a distinction that Patte makes — into meaningful relation, whereby exegesis (the analysis of text) leads to hermeneutic (what the text means for the modern reader). He contrasts structural exegesis with "traditional historical exegesis" (a diachronic form of exegesis; 9), because its attention to origins does not explain how one moves from exegesis to hermeneutic. Instead, Patte endorses a synchronic exegetical approach that "uncovers" the various structures of the text, i.e., its linguistic, narrative, or mythological underlying structures. These complex underlying structures — arguably unknown by the author — are what determine the meaning of the text, not the author's intention.

For Patte, as noted above, there are a recognizable number of different structural approaches, but they all have a number of common features that are important for interpreting a text. These include: the meaningfulness of structures, differentiation of syntagmatic and paradigmatic relations, and a linguistic model that realizes the arbitrary relation between the signifier (expression) and the signified (content) for both form and substance (a distinctly Saussurian concept). This orientation leads Patte again (or rather, from the start) to adopt the narrative structural model of Greimas as the basis of his structural exegetical method.

Patte is not concerned to defend his choice of Greimas here (as he appears to have been in his later work), nor to articulate the foundation for Greimas's own exegetical framework. He is instead concerned to break the model down into its structural components and then to apply it to biblical texts. Patte defines six components of Greimas's narratological model: sequences, narrative syntagms, narrative statements, canonical narrative functions, actants, and the actantial model (Patte is utilizing an earlier form of Greimas's structural hermeneutical program). Sequences are patterns of narrative events, described as being either correlated, topical, or subsequent. The sequence is what provides the basic narrative framework or deep structure of the narrative, and is the basis for the further analysis. The individual sequences within a narrative can be broken down into syntagmatic units. These syntagmatic units can be classified as contract, disjunction/conjunction, and performance syntagms. These syntagms establish the basic action of the narrative as the contract of a sequence and the subsequent actions in relation to this contract. Individual syntagms are made up of narrative statements. According to Patte, a narrative statement is a technical term for a unit of structure that consists of two further units, labeled as functions and actants. These narrative statements function on two levels, one the deep structure of the narrative itself and the other at the level of manifestation of actions or actors within the surface story. There are a number of what Patte calls "canonical functions," i.e., functions that are part of the narrative deep structure, rather than being manifestations in the surface text. Of all of the possible structural functions, following Calloud, Patte reduces these to a fixed set. These include: arrival versus departure and departure versus return; conjunction versus disjunction; mandating versus acceptance or refusal; confrontation or affrontment; domination versus submission; communication versus reception; and attribution versus derivation. One notes that most of these canonical functions are conceptualized as binary oppositions. Finally, in relation to the functions, there are a number of actants and the roles that they play. Following Greimas, Patte defines the standard six actants in the actantial model: sender, object, and receiver on the axis of communication; subject and object on the axis of volition; and helper, subject, and opponent on the axis of power.

Reflective of his more inclusive structural model in his earlier work, Patte goes on to define a form of mythical structural exegesis based upon the work of Lévi-Strauss (something he apparently later rejected when he rejected Greimas's dependence upon structural universals). Lévi-Strauss, also using the work of Greimas, defines the deep structure of myths in his work, and Patte applies this framework to Galatians 1:1-10, along with an actantial analysis. Despite what Patte then saw as the potential of such a method for discovering the mythical structures of Hellenism and Judaism, he does not develop this mythical method here, although he attempts a further development of it in his *Structural Exegesis* (1978, with Patte). In this volume, Patte also demonstrates his model of actantial analysis within a Greimasian framework in a number of different studies. These include a study of the parable of the Good Samaritan that exemplifies actantial analysis. In Patte's analysis, the traveler is the receiver, and the object is health. The subject is the Samaritan, and the helper is what he provides for the traveler, as opposed to the opponent robbers.

In attempting to go beyond structural hermeneutical theory and answer the question of what actually constitutes structural exegesis, Patte presents a mixed model of Greimas and Lévi-Strauss that he later pulled back from, but he does engage in several important exegetical exercises, using the work of both.

Steps to Structural Exegesis

Apparently responding to those who did not think that the semio-structural model was as explicit as it needed to be to become an accepted and widespread method of structural exegesis, Patte returns to the model in one of his last major works in the area, *Structural Exegesis*. He acknowledges that the method is theoretically derived and theory-bound in its application. As a result, he outlines a six-step hermeneutical method of applied structural exegesis. He claims that this method in various forms lies behind both of his major structural commentaries, those on Matthew and Paul's letters. The six steps include the following: (1) identifying a complete discourse unit; (2) identifying the explicit oppositions of actions; (3) identifying the qualifications of the contrasted opposed subjects; (4) identifying the effects on the receivers that exemplify the opposed actions; (5) drawing conclusions regarding the author's faith characteristics; and (6) elucidating the specific features of the given discourse unit.

These six steps provide the basis for Patte's structural exegetical work. (1) Apparently, though not explicitly, reflecting later influence from discourse analysis (an inclusive method that examines language use above the sentence), Patte's criteria for identifying a formal unit consist of two major features: thematic change at the beginning and end of the unit, and inverted parallelism between the beginning and end of the unit. This mix of semantic and formal criteria is seen, first, in how the reader perceives the thematic cohesiveness of the unit, and second, in how the reader grasps the formal unity of the unit when the introduction recurs in the conclusion.

(2) The second step, identifying explicit opposed actions, is stated by Patte to be a formally based exercise, and it encompasses three important subsidiary principles. The first is to identify the opposed actions by means of use of two explicit verbs of doing. The second principle is that the two opposed actions must be genuinely opposed; that is, one of the actions must be positive and the other negative. The third principle is that these two opposed actions must be actions of a comparable sort, so that there is genuine opposition. In other words, the action may be opposed in manner, person, or polemical force.

(3) The third step involves identification of the qualifications that oppose the subjects involved. Each person involved in the action can be identified by qualifications that differentiate that person from any other persons involved in the discourse unit. Identifiers include such things as

names, although names are potentially not as informative as identifiers of the forces that influence the will of the subject and that indicate the subject's abilities. For any given set of opposed characters, there will be contrastive or negative and correlative or positive comparisons made. Within any set of actions, there will also be qualifications that one might identify but that are extraneous to characterization of the subject.

(4) The fourth step identifies the effects on the opposed characters by their opposite actions, especially the resulting convictions that are identified and exemplified by a character. Patte notes that characters in opposition will have a modifying effect on each other, and the goal of this step is to identify the change that then transpires. This is especially true of the convictions or qualifications of the individual characters involved in the opposition. This particular step often occurs at the same time as step three, as the characters oppose each other.

(5) The fifth step, drawing conclusions regarding the author's faith convictions, begins the process of drawing together the convictions expressed by the various characters in their relations and formulating a pattern of characteristic behavior that is related to the entire discourse. The subsidiary steps necessary for this to happen involve identifying the categories that the discourse utilizes in characterizing and calibrating convictions of the characters, and then noting the organization of the convictions within each of the categories. The types of convictions that one may find within a religious discourse are related to convictions about the divine, the mediator, religious leaders, and believers. Whereas Patte envisions these steps as applicable to a variety of religious texts, his descriptions are especially geared toward the New Testament.

(6) The sixth and final step is that of identifying the features that specify the given discourse unit. Within the context of dealing with religious texts, Patte notes that the goal of such texts is the communication of a faith to the readers of the text. This faith involves the perception of what he characterizes as "meaningful human experience" (62). This is done with specific examples that demonstrate this faith. However, Patte also draws two further conclusions regarding characterizing the discourse. The first is that what a discourse unit appears to be concerned with, characterized at the outset as its theme, is in reality the means of conveying a "faith-pattern" (63). The second is that the theme that is chosen by the author, despite its ultimate purpose of conveying a faith-pattern, is the one used nevertheless because the author considers it the most suitable within the discourse situation. The implied author, in this sense, is seen to be trust-

worthy. Readers, furthermore, are challenged by such a set of convictions to modify their views when confronted by the new point of view of the implied author.

This method is applied by Patte in his two major commentaries on Matthew and Romans, although he admits that he applies the method in different ways and not in an obvious fashion that all will recognize. In this book, however, the method is explicitly used in two significant studies of John 4:4-42 and Luke 10:21-42 that allow him to compare the results of Johannine and Lukan perspectives from a structuralist perspective. For both passages, Patte utilizes the six steps. The major results that one observes are his identification of the major oppositions between characters, and the resulting opposed beliefs. For example, in the Johannine passage, he identifies the opposition between Jesus and the Samaritan woman, knowledge of Jesus' identity and lack of knowledge, living water and literal water, etc. In the Lukan passage, Patte identifies the opposition between divine and human knowledge regarding Jesus, the son as knowing the father and human lack of knowledge, the disciples and the prophets, etc. After analyzing these oppositions and their qualifications and effects, Patte compares what he calls the hierarchies of convictions about believers in John and Luke. For example, he describes John as depicting humans as having "preliminary knowledge" about Jesus, in contrast to Luke depicting humans as having "preliminary knowledge" of the law and of tangible divine manifestations; humans in John as willing to come and interact with Jesus, in contrast to simply existing during Jesus' ministry; and being exposed in one's deeds in contrast to having a close relationship to Jesus; etc. Thus, Patte sees a number of similarities and differences in the two Gospels' depictions of their faith-patterns.

Patte and the Implications of a Structural Hermeneutics

Though the major proponent of structuralism in New Testament studies, Patte has since moved to a form of cultural criticism that is concerned to realize the cultural positioning of any exegetical position, including structuralism. The fact that Patte has moved in this direction is enlightening when one considers his use of structuralism as a hermeneutic. Several observations can be made regarding Patte's form of structuralist hermeneutics. One is that his use of structuralism is narrow in scope, and for the most part confined to several versions of Greimasian structural analysis. The second is that Patte presents a mixed picture of Greimasian structuralism. His monograph devoted to Greimas is highly technical, and engages in a complex analysis that is heavily reliant upon technical vocabulary and complex concepts. However, while outwardly utilizing many of the features of Greimas's structural semantics in his exegetical works, he presents a simplified and much less-technical form of structuralism that is more readily compatible with other forms of criticism. A third observation is that Patte's structuralism — it has this feature in common with some other forms of structuralism — appears to be, at the end of the day, a literary and phenomenological method primarily concerned with the surface phenomena of the text. Even when Patte claims to have identified the qualifications of the characters, these are identifications of surface phenomena. A fourth observation is that Patte's structuralism, although identifying the notion of a deep or fundamental structure, does not seem to explore or develop this concept as fully as he might, especially where he departs significantly from Greimas or Lévi-Strauss. It appears that he develops his own position to culturally locate even deep structure, and to clearly distance himself from what he sees as the universalist perspective of Greimas. Discussion of deep structure is not a major feature of his exegetical treatments, where his analysis of deep structure is confined to the faith-patterns that he observes in religious texts, a cultural-anthropological conceptualization. A fifth observation is that Patte's structuralist hermeneutic has a high contextual groundedness to it, in which the structures that are identified are not functions or actants but categories established by the surface text. Sixth and finally, Patte retains the category of religious literature, and sees structural exegesis functioning as an exegetical method especially designed to aid in the recovery of the faith that underlies these religious narratives. This is Patte's distinctive contribution to structural hermeneutics.

A Critical Appraisal of Structuralism

There are at least seven significant hermeneutical questions raised by structuralism. A number of these questions have already been broached along the way in our discussion above. They merit repetition here.

What is the ontological status of deep structures? Structuralism's major claim is to identify "deep structures" that underlie surface phenomena. These structures have been identified in a range of phenomena, including anthropological, linguistic, and even religious structures. The question concerns the status of these supposed deep structures. Some see them as identifying the fundamental compositional structures that in some way generate or at the least ground surface phenomena. Others see them as simply prototypical abstractions that provide useful categories for discussion of a wide range of otherwise intractable surface phenomena.

Is structuralism ideologically neutral? Structuralism's major claim is to identify fundamental structures, whether these have ontological status or not. The question then becomes whether the identification is ideologically or theoretically neutral, or whether there is an ideology that attaches to such an exercise, and even to the deep structures themselves. Some have made a distinction between the kind of structuralism found in linguistics that attempts to describe a circumscribed set of language phenomena and a more universalistic structuralism that purports to describe fundamental structures of human cognition. There has been a tendency over time for structuralism to become increasingly ideological, especially in French structuralism, as it is used as a means of describing the world — until its collapse in poststructuralism. The tendency is for structuralism to be used to describe the world as non-contextual, deterministic, and even materialistic.

Is the notion of structure used in the same way in all types of structuralism? The notion of structure is used in a variety of ways in various forms of structuralism. In some forms of linguistics, for example, linguistic structure is a means of identifying sets of relationships between linguistic units, whereas in some forms of anthropology, structures are a means of describing fundamental oppositions that are found within the universe, such as day and night, etc. These are then sometimes extrapolated to universal oppositions, such as those of life and death, good and evil, human and nonhuman, and male and female.

What is the relationship of deep structures to surface structures? The relationship between the deep structure and surface structure remains problematic and enigmatic in structuralism. For some, such as Patte and some narratologists, the emphasis is clearly upon the surface structure, as a means of speaking about the way humans can and should think, even about such things as faith. For other structuralists, however, the surface structure is secondary, it being derived from or simply reflective of the underlying deep structure. In either case, it is not clear what the relationship is between the two, and whether there is a generative or recursive function from one to the other.

How does structuralism move beyond generalization or reductionism? A common criticism of structuralism is that it has a tendency to overgeneralize and to be reductionistic. That is, in an effort to find a common descriptive language, complex surface phenomena are overgeneralized or reduced to less complex and simple, even simplistic, equivalents. If we examine Greimas as seen through the work of Patte, we see that a complex narrative, involving a number of complex characters, is reduced to a set of oppositions and posited qualifications or characterizations. No matter how accurate such analyses may be, there is always the chance, if not the likelihood, that other features of the text that are not capable of being captured through such oppositional analysis are overlooked and lost. Further, even if one can say, with Propp and his followers, that there are only so many ways a story can be told, the fact is that there are many individual stories, even if they reflect similar underlying frameworks.

What is the relationship between mind and culture in structuralism? There is a distinct sense in which structuralism is a cognitive model, in that the deep structures may be posited to reflect the ways that humans conceptualize and categorize the world. In many instances, it is difficult to say where the deep structures are located apart from the minds of those who find the mental constructs informative. There is also a sense in which structuralism reflects cultural phenomena and attempts to categorize them by means of specific cultural features, such as kinship terms or color terms that are unique to a particular culture. It is unclear what the nature of the relationship is between the individual mind and the collective framework.

What is the test for the validity of structuralism? If some of the questions raised above have validity, especially concerning the status of deep structures and their relationship to surface structures, a further question is raised regarding how such a method is tested. Some structuralists have simply refused to describe their method or to say how such a method might be tested. They are content to let the interpretive insights speak for themselves. Others, however, have used the available data as a point of comparison, while recognizing that the method itself to some extent dictates the nature and interpretation of the data.

Conclusion

Structuralism has been one of the most important intellectual movements of the twentieth century. Its influence has been immense, and has extended to a wide range of intellectual disciplines, including hermeneutics.

As a result, structuralism is also a diverse field of study, as it has influenced different fields of academic and intellectual inquiry, which include both the natural sciences and the arts. Structuralism made its major migration to North America in the 1920s, where it was popular for several decades as a hermeneutical model in fields including linguistics, literary criticism, biblical studies, and anthropology, among others. Structuralism continues to be a major force in such fields as anthropology and linguistics, but it has lost its influence or become transformed or at least shifted into various poststructural forms of inquiry in fields such as literary and biblical studies.

Daniel Patte is concerned to define and situate within the wider field of biblical exegesis a definable structuralist hermeneutic and exegetical method that can be used to examine the texts of the New Testament, with the particular purpose of elucidating their faith dimensions. He sees structuralism as providing the means by which one can bring both exegesis and this socio-semiotic hermeneutic into meaningful relation, whereby exegesis (the analysis of text) leads to hermeneutic (what the text means for the modern reader). Patte endorses a synchronic exegetical approach that "uncovers" the various linguistic, narrative, or mythological underlying structures. These complex underlying structures — arguably unknown by the author — are what determine the meaning of the text.

For Patte, there are a recognizable number of different structural approaches, but they all have common features that are important for interpreting a text. These include: the meaningfulness of structures, differentiation of syntagmatic and paradigmatic relations, and a linguistic model that realizes the arbitrary relation between the signifier (expression) and the signified (content) in both form and substance. This orientation leads Patte to adopt the narrative structural model of Greimas as his structural exegetical method, which he has developed like no other biblical scholar into a theory of generative significance.

REFERENCE WORKS

Bakhtin, Mikhail. *The Formal Method in Literary Scholarship: A Critical Introduction to Sociological Poetics,* with P. N. Medvedev, trans. A. J. Wehrle. Baltimore: Johns Hopkins University Press, 1978 (1928).

———. *The Dialogic Imagination: Four Essays,* ed. M. Holquist, trans. C. Emerson and M. Holquist. Austin: University of Texas Press, 1981.

Bal, Mieke. *Murder and Difference: Gender, Genre, and Scholarship on Sisera's*

Death, trans. Matthew Gumpert. Bloomington: Indiana University Press, 1988.

———. *Narratology: Introduction to the Theory of Narrative,* trans. Christine van Boheemen. Toronto: University of Toronto Press, 1985; 3rd ed. 2009.

———. *On Meaning-Making: Essays in Semiotics.* Sonoma, CA: Polebridge, 1994.

———. *On Story-Telling: Essays in Narratology,* ed. David Jobling. Sonoma, CA: Polebridge, 1991.

Barthes, Roland. *Elements of Semiology,* trans. Annette Lavers and Colin Smith. London: Cape, 1967 (1964).

———. *The Rustle of Language,* trans. Richard Howard. New York: Hill & Wang, 1986.

———. *The Semiotic Challenge,* trans. Richard Howard. New York: Hill & Wang, 1988.

———. *Système de la mode.* Paris: Seuil, 1967.

———. *S/Z,* trans. Richard Miller. New York: Hill & Wang, 1974 (1970).

———. *Writing Degree Zero,* trans. Annette Lavers and Colin Smith. New York: Hill & Wang, 1968 (1953).

Barthes, Roland, et al. *Structural Analysis and Biblical Exegesis: Interpretational Essays,* trans. Alfred M. Johnson, Jr. Pittsburgh: Pickwick, 1974 (essays by Barthes and Jean Starobinski, among others).

The Bible and Culture Collective. *The Postmodern Bible.* New Haven: Yale University Press, 1995 (esp. ch. 2 on "Structuralist and Narratological Criticism").

Bloomfield, Leonard. *Language.* London: George Allen & Unwin, 1933.

Boas, Franz. *Handbook of American Indian Languages,* I. Washington, DC: Government Printing Office, 1911.

Boers, Hendrikus. *Neither on This Mountain nor in Jerusalem: A Study of John 4.* SBL Monograph Series. Atlanta: Scholars Press, 1988.

Bremond, Claude. "The Narrative Message." *Semeia* 10 (1978): 5-55.

Bühler, Karl. *Theory of Language: The Representational Function of Language,* trans. Donald Fraser Goodwin. Amsterdam: John Benjamins, 1990 (1934).

Calloud, Jean. *Structural Analysis of Narrative,* trans. Daniel Patte. Philadelphia: Fortress, 1976.

Chatman, Seymour. *Story and Discourse: Narrative Structure in Fiction and Film.* Ithaca, NY: Cornell University Press, 1978.

Crossan, John Dominic. "A Structuralist Analysis of John 6." In *Orientation by*

Disorientation: Studies in Literary Criticism and Biblical Literary Criticism, ed. Richard A. Spencer, 235-49. Pittsburgh: Pickwick, 1980.

Crossan, John Dominic, ed. *Narrative Syntax: Translations and Reviews. Semeia* 10 (1978).

Culler, Jonathan. *Saussure.* London: Fontana/Collins, 1976.

————. *Structuralist Poetics: Structuralism, Linguistics, and the Study of Literature.* Ithaca, NY: Cornell University Press, 1975.

Davidsen, Ole. *The Narrative Jesus: A Semiotic Reading of Mark's Gospel.* Aarhus: Aarhus University Press, 1993.

DeGeorge, Richard, and Fernande DeGeorge, eds. *The Structuralists from Marx to Lévi-Strauss.* New York: Doubleday, 1972 (with essays by Ferdinand de Saussure, Roman Jakobson, Claude Lévi-Strauss, Roland Barthes, Louis Althusser, Michel Foucault, Jacques Lacan, among others).

Detweiler, Robert. *Story, Sign, and Self: Phenomenology and Structuralism as Literary-Critical Methods.* Philadelphia: Fortress, 1978.

Douglas, Mary. *Purity and Danger: An Analysis of Concepts of Pollution and Taboo.* London: Routledge, 2002 (1966).

Eco, Umberto. *A Theory of Semiotics.* Bloomington: Indiana University Press, 1976.

Ehrman, Jacques, ed. *Structuralism.* New York: Doubleday, 1970 (with essays by André Martinet, Claude Lévi-Strauss, Jacques Lacan, and Michael Riffaterre, among others).

Firth, J. R. *Papers in Linguistics 1934-1951.* Oxford: Oxford University Press, 1957.

Funk, Robert W. *Parables and Presence: Forms of the New Testament Tradition.* Philadelphia: Fortress, 1982.

Genette, Gérard. *Narrative Discourse: An Essay in Method,* trans. Jane E. Lewin. Ithaca, NY: Cornell University Press, 1980.

————. *Narrative Discourse Revisited,* trans. Jane E. Lewin. Ithaca, NY: Cornell University Press, 1988.

Godel, Robert, ed. *A Geneva School Reader in Linguistics.* Bloomington: Indiana University Press, 1969.

Greimas, A.-J. *On Meaning: Selected Writings in Semiotic Theory,* trans. Paul J. Perron and Frank H. Collins. Minneapolis: University of Minnesota Press, 1987 (1970, 1976).

————. *Structural Semantics: An Attempt at a Method,* trans. Daniele McDowell, Ronald Schleifer, and Alan Velie. Lincoln: University of Nebraska Press, 1983 (1966).

Grenholm, Cristina, and Daniel Patte, eds. *Reading Israel in Romans: Legitimacy and Plausibility of Divergent Interpretations.* Harrisburg, PA: Trinity Press International, 2000.

Halliday, Michael A. K. *Halliday: System and Function in Language,* ed. Gunther Kress. Oxford: Oxford University Press, 1976.

Harris, Zellig S. *String Analysis of Sentence Structure.* The Hague: Mouton, 1962.

————. *Structural Linguistics.* Chicago: University of Chicago Press, 1951.

Hawkes, Terence. *Structuralism and Semiotics.* Berkeley: University of California Press, 1977.

Hays, Richard. *The Faith of Jesus Christ: An Investigation of the Narrative Substructure of Galatians 3:1–4:11.* Chico, CA: Scholars Press, 1983; 2nd ed. Grand Rapids: Eerdmans, 2002.

Hjelmslev, Louis. *Prolegomena to a Theory of Language,* trans. Francis J. Whitfield. 2nd ed. Madison: University of Wisconsin Press, 1961.

Jackson, Leonard. *The Poverty of Structuralism: Literature and Structuralist Theory.* London: Longman, 1991.

Jakobson, Roman. *On Language,* ed. Linda R. Waugh and Monique Monville-Burston. Cambridge, MA: Harvard University Press, 1990.

Jameson, Fredric. *The Prison-House of Language: A Critical Account of Structuralism and Russian Formalism.* Princeton: Princeton University Press, 1972.

Jankowsky, Kurt R. *The Neogrammarians.* Janua Linguarum Series Minor 16. The Hague: Mouton, 1972.

Johnson, Alfred M., Jr., ed. and trans. *The New Testament and Structuralism: A Collection of Essays by Corina Galland, Claude Chabrol, Guy Vuillod, Louis Marin, and Edgar Haulotte.* Pittsburgh Theological Monograph Series 11. Pittsburgh: Pickwick, 1976.

————. ed. *Structuralism and Biblical Hermeneutics: A Collection of Essays.* Pittsburgh Theological Monograph Series 22. Pittsburgh: Pickwick, 1979 (with essays by Roland Barthes and Louis Marin).

Johnson, Marta K., ed. and trans. *Recycling the Prague Linguistic Circle.* Linguistica Extranea 6. N.p.: Karoma, 1978.

Kristeva, Julia. *Language: The Unknown. An Initiation into Linguistics,* trans. Anne M. Menke. New York: Columbia University Press, 1989.

Leach, Edmund. *Lévi-Strauss.* Rev. ed. London: Fontana/Collins, 1973.

————. "Structuralism in Social Anthropology." In *Structuralism: An Introduction,* ed. David Robey, pp. 37-56. Oxford: Clarendon, 1973.

Lepschy, Giulio C. *A Survey of Structural Linguistics.* London: Andre Deutsch, 1982.

Leroy, Maurice. *The Main Trends in Modern Linguistics.* Oxford: Blackwell, 1967.

Leska, Oldrich. "Prague Circle Linguistics." *Linguistica Pragensia* 8, no. 2 (1998): 57-72.

Lévi-Strauss, Claude. *The Savage Mind.* Chicago: University of Chicago Press, 1966 (1962).

————. *Structural Anthropology,* trans. Claire Jacobson and Brooke Grundfest Schoepf. Garden City, NY: Doubleday, 1967 (1958).

Lucid, Daniel P., ed. *Soviet Semiotics: An Anthology.* Baltimore: Johns Hopkins University Press, 1977.

McKnight, Edgar V. *Meaning in Texts: The Historical Shaping of a Narrative Hermeneutics.* Philadelphia: Fortress, 1978.

Macksey, Richard, and Eugenio Donato, eds.. *The Structuralist Controversy: The Languages of Criticism and the Sciences of Man.* Baltimore: Johns Hopkins University Press, 1970 (with contributions from René Girard, Tzvetan Todorov, Roland Barthes, Jacques Lacan, Jacques Derrida, and Jean-Pierre Vernant, among others).

Malbon, Elizabeth Struthers. *Narrative Space and Mythic Meaning in Mark.* San Francisco: Harper & Row, 1986.

Malinowski, Bronislaw. *Magic, Science and Religion and Other Essays.* New York: Doubleday, 1948.

Martin, Wallace. *Recent Theories of Narrative.* Ithaca, NY: Cornell University Press, 1986.

Matejka, Ladislav, ed. *Sound, Sign and Meaning: Quinquagenary of the Prague Linguistic Circle.* Michigan Slavic Contributions 6. Ann Arbor: University of Michigan, 1976.

Milne, Pamela J. *Vladimir Propp and the Study of Structure in Hebrew Biblical Narrative.* Sheffield: Sheffield Academic Press, 1988.

Moore, Stephen D. "Afterword: Things Not Written in This Book." In *Anatomies of Narrative Criticism: The Past, Present, and Future of the Fourth Gospel as Literature,* ed. Tom Thatcher and Stephen D. Moore, 253-58. Resources for Biblical Study 55. Atlanta: Society of Biblical Literature, 2008.

Palmer, Gary B. *Toward a Theory of Cultural Linguistics.* Austin: University of Texas Press, 1996.

Patte, Daniel. "An Analysis of Narrative Structure and the Good Samaritan." *Semeia* 2 (1974): 1-26.

————. *Aspects of a Semiotics of Didactic Discourse: Analysis of 1 Thessalonians.* Working Papers and Pre-Publications, Centro Internazionale di Semiotica e di Linguistica, Università di Urbino, Italy, 97-98-99, Series B (1980): 1-59.

————. *The Challenge of Discipleship: A Critical Study of the Sermon on the Mount as Scripture.* Harrisburg, PA: Trinity Press International, 1999.

————. "Critical Biblical Studies from a Semiotic Perspective." *Semeia* 81 (1998): 3-26.

————. *Discipleship According to the Sermon on the Mount: Four Legitimate Readings, Four Plausible Views of Discipleship, and Their Relative Values.* Valley Forge, PA: Trinity Press International, 1996.

————. *Early Jewish Hermeneutic in Palestine.* SBL Dissertation Series 22. Missoula, MT: Scholars Press, 1975.

————. *Ethics of Biblical Interpretation: A Reevaluation.* Louisville: Westminster/John Knox, 1995.

————. *The Gospel According to Matthew: A Structural Commentary on Matthew's Faith.* Philadelphia: Fortress, 1987.

————. "Method for a Structural Exegesis of Didactic Discourses: Analysis of 1 Thessalonians." *Semeia* 26 (1983): 85-129.

————. *Paul's Faith and the Power of the Gospel: A Structural Introduction to the Pauline Letters.* Philadelphia: Fortress, 1983.

————. *The Religious Dimensions of Biblical Texts: Greimas's Structural Semiotics and Biblical Exegesis.* Semeia Studies 19. Atlanta: Scholars Press, 1990.

————. "Speech Act Theory and Biblical Exegesis." *Semeia* 41 (1988): 85-102.

————. "Structural Criticism." In *To Each Its Own Meaning: Biblical Criticisms and Their Application,* ed. Steven L. McKenzie and Stephen R. Haynes, 183-200. Louisville: Westminster/John Knox, 1999.

————. *Structural Exegesis for New Testament Critics.* Guides to Biblical Scholarship. Minneapolis: Fortress, 1990.

————. "Textual Constraints, Ordinary Readings, and Critical Exegesis: An Androcritical Perspective." *Semeia* 62 (1993): 59-79.

————. "Universal Narrative Structures and Semantic Frameworks." *Semeia* 10 (1978): 123-35.

————. *What Is Structural Exegesis?* Guides to Biblical Scholarship. Philadelphia: Fortress, 1976.

Patte, Daniel, ed. *Semiology and Parables: Exploration of the Possibilities Offered by Structuralism for Exegesis.* Pittsburgh: Pickwick, 1976.

————, ed. *Thinking in Signs: Semiotics and Biblical Studies . . . Thirty Years After. Semeia* 81 (1998).

Patte, Daniel, and Aline Patte. *Structural Exegesis: From Theory to Practice. Exegesis of Mark 15 and 16.* Philadelphia: Fortress, 1978.

Pavel, Thomas. *The Feud of Language: A History of Structuralist Thought.* Oxford: Blackwell, 1989.

Peirce, Charles Sanders. *Collected Papers of Charles Sanders Peirce,* ed. Charles Hartshorne, Paul Weiss, and Arthur W. Burks. Cambridge, MA: Harvard University Press, 1931-1958.

Piaget, Jean. *Structuralism,* trans. and ed. Chaninah Maschler. London: Routledge & Kegan Paul, 1971.

Pike, Kenneth L. *Language in Relation to a Unified Theory of the Structure of Human Behavior.* 2nd ed. The Hague: Mouton, 1967.

Polzin, Robert. *Biblical Structuralism: Method and Subjectivity in the Study of Ancient Texts.* Semeia Supplements. Philadelphia: Fortress, 1977.

Preminger, Alex, and T. V. F. Brogan, eds. *The New Princeton Encyclopedia of Poetry and Poetics.* Princeton: Princeton University Press, 1993.

Propp, Vladimir. *The Morphology of the Folk Tale,* trans. L. Scott. Austin: University of Texas Press, 1968 (1928).

Robey, David, ed. *Structuralism: An Introduction.* Oxford: Clarendon, 1973.

Robins, R. H. *A Short History of Linguistics.* 2nd ed. London: Longman, 1979.

Salzmann, Zdenek. *Language, Culture and Society: An Introduction to Linguistic Anthropology.* 2nd ed. Boulder, CO: Westview, 1998.

Sampson, Geoffrey. *Schools of Linguistics.* Stanford, CA: Stanford University Press, 1980.

Saussure, Ferdinand de. *Course in General Linguistics,* ed. Charles Bally and Albert Sechehaye, trans. Wade Baskin. London: Fontana/Collins, 1959 (1916).

————. *Mémoire sur le système primitif des voyelles dans les langues indo-européennes.* Leipzig: Teubner, 1879.

Schleifer, Ronald. *A. J. Greimas and the Nature of Meaning: Linguistics, Semiotics and Discourse Theory.* Lincoln: University of Nebraska Press, 1987.

Scholes, Robert. *Semiotics and Interpretation.* New Haven: Yale University Press, 1982.

————. *Structuralism in Literature.* New Haven: Yale University Press, 1974.

Sebeok, Thomas A. *Semiotics in the United States.* Bloomington: Indiana University Press, 1991.

————. *Signs: An Introduction to Semiotics.* Toronto: University of Toronto Press, 1994.

Silverman, Kaja. *The Subject of Semiotics.* New York: Oxford University Press, 1983.

Todorov, Tzvetan. *The Fantastic: A Structural Approach to a Literary Genre,* trans. Richard Howard. Ithaca, NY: Cornell University Press, 1973 (1970).

————. *Introduction to Poetics,* trans. Richard Howard. Minneapolis: University of Minnesota Press, 1981 (1968).

————. *The Poetics of Prose,* trans. Richard Howard. Oxford: Blackwell, 1977.

Trubetzkoy, N. S. *Principles of Phonology,* trans. C. A. M. Baltaxe. Berkeley: University of California Press, 1969.

————. *Writings on Literature,* ed. and trans. Anatoly Liberman. Minneapolis: University of Minnesota Press, 1990.

Uspensky, Boris. *A Poetics of Composition: The Structure of the Artistic Text and Typology of a Compositional Form,* trans. Valentina Zavarin and Susan Wittig. Berkeley: University of California Press, 1973.

Vachek, Josef. *The Linguistic School of Prague: An Introduction to Its Theory and Practice.* Bloomington: Indiana University Press, 1966.

————, ed. *A Prague School Reader in Linguistics.* Bloomington: Indiana University Press, 1967.

Via, Dan O., Jr. *Kerygma and Comedy in the New Testament: A Structuralist Approach to Hermeneutic.* Philadelphia: Fortress, 1975.

Vitz, Evelyn Birge. *Medieval Narrative and Modern Narratology: Subjects and Objects of Desire.* New York: New York University Press, 1989.

EIGHT Jacques Derrida and Deconstruction

Introduction

The French philosopher Jacques Derrida (1930-2004) is the most famous of deconstructive writers and one of the most controversial of contemporary European thinkers. Friedrich W. Nietzsche (1844-1900) is often regarded as the first deconstructionist, followed by deconstruction in its modern form beginning in the late 1960s with Derrida's criticisms of structuralism and the Western metaphysical tradition. His wild and difficult writings are some of the most mystifying in recent times, perhaps even more so than Martin Heidegger's (1889-1976), and bear witness to his refusal to be boxed in or understood in any unilateral fashion. Many have complained that Derrida seems to be difficult for difficulty's sake, but these assessments are often guided by the assumption that a description of human understanding may be reduced or simplified into something that is more or less straightforward. Derrida is difficult to understand precisely because he is trying to open up his readers to what is, in his account, by nature incredibly complicated and turbulent. He does this by affirming the surpassing openness of meaning (whether written, spoken, or thought) and its infinite undecidability and deferral. What for some is often regarded as direct and transparent truth (X *is* Y, this *is* that) is always already irreducibly composite and fluid according to Derrida. His persistent efforts to expose what he sees as the ambiguous and complex nature of language, writing, reading — indeed life in its totality — has led skeptics and admirers alike to label him a nihilist, pessimist, skeptic, hopeless relativist, and so on. Yet he never understood himself as such and found these charges absurd. For him the task of the thinker is to break human thought open to the elusive, indefinable, excluded, marginalized, and subverted. It is not to prove that anything may pass for truth, as the relativist does, or that nothing at all may pass for truth, as the radical skeptic does. According to Derrida, we may speak meaningfully and truthfully, though never absolutely or with complete certainty.

Derrida and Deconstruction

Although the roots of deconstruction go back to earlier reactions against Western philosophical thought, the work of Derrida has come to distinguish the movement; and his own reactions against Western metaphysics, and especially against structuralism, are crucial factors in his hermeneutical thought.

Life and Influences

For most of his life Derrida embraced the credo that the only thing that should be said biographically about a philosopher was that he was born, he thought, and then he died. Derrida believed that a philosopher's life should always fade into the background of his or her philosophy as an anecdote or something accidental. In keeping with this belief we will say only a little here about his personal history. Derrida was born into an Algerian Jewish family in 1930. He left Algeria as a teen in 1949 for France. After failing the entrance exam twice, Derrida began his studies at one of France's most prestigious schools in 1952, the *École normale supérieure*. He later taught there from 1965 to 1984. From 1957 to 1959 he taught French and English in Kolea (near Algiers) to children of soldiers in the Algerian war for independence as an alternative to military service. From 1960 to 1964, he taught philosophy and logic at the Sorbonne in Paris.

During the late 1950s Derrida began his doctoral thesis on Edmund Husserl (1859-1938) titled "The Identity of the Literary Object." However, completing a doctorate would prove frustrating for many years. Even so, this early work, though never finished, signals the beginning of what would remain a privileged place for literature and textuality in Derrida's thinking. In 1962, he produced his first publication, a translation of and lengthy introduction to Husserl's *Foundations of Geometry*, titled "The Origin of Geometry." In 1967, Derrida's coinciding major publications, *Speech and Phenomena, Of Grammatology*, and *Writing and Difference*, earned him significant notice as a scholar. His stature as an important thinker was further established, and for many solidified, in 1972 with the publication of two collections of his essays, *Dissemination* and *Margins of Philosophy*, and a third publication of collected interviews with Derrida titled *Positions*. In 1980, he successfully defended as his doctoral thesis a collected selection of some of his prior publications. The introductory comments of this thesis were later published in English as "The Time of a Thesis: Punctuations" (1983). All told, Derrida published an enormous amount during his lifetime, including a seemingly endless number of articles and an incredible number of books, over sixty of which have already been translated into English. Today there is still a significant portion of unpublished and untranslated material from Derrida's prolific literary career. Just a few of his other major works include *Glas* (1986), *The Post Card: From Socrates to Freud and Beyond* (1987), *Spectres of Marx* (1994), and *The Gift of Death* (1995).

Throughout his career Derrida's role as a scholar and academic rarely strayed far from controversy. His work earned him honorary degrees from many universities including Essex, Louvain, and Columbia, yet in 1992 disagreement over whether or not he was a worthy scholar raised serious doubts for some as to his receiving an honorary degree from Cambridge University. His status as a rigorous and serious philosopher was debated by various members of the philosophical (mostly "analytic") community, including the celebrated logician Willard Van Orman Quine (1908-2000), who, along with many others, signed a letter of objection to his receiving of the degree. Derrida's place as a legitimate philosopher was so strongly debated that he almost did not receive the degree. To this day, Derrida's name still prompts strong opposition and antagonism from prominent scholars who think of him as little more than a dangerous intellectual prankster.

Derrida's relationship — or lack thereof — with religion and theology is far from clear-cut or forthright. On the one hand, he grew up with a strong awareness but ultimately a rejection of the religious practices of his family, which he saw as thoughtless, filled with misunderstandings, and mostly blind repetition. Moreover, it should come as no surprise to those already a bit familiar with his philosophy that, at least on the surface, it seems obvious that his deconstructive way-of-life would be at odds with any kind of religious belief that makes ultimate truth claims, the very thing deconstruction undermines. Yet, on the other hand, Derrida, who was rightly understood to be an atheist, repeatedly showed strong interests in religious concepts and motifs, especially in his later writings. In fact, Derrida's path often parallels significantly — and is often indistinguishable from — negative theology, although he is emphatic that his way of thinking is not really that of negative theology.

One of the main problems with religion and theology that Derrida returns to time and again is his belief that even the most negative of negative theologies — including those that make explicit denials of divine "presence" or "Being" (as if God were a created "thing" among other things) — still affirm some form of hyper-essentiality, i.e., being. They thereby remain caught up in "the metaphysics of presence" that Derrida harshly criticizes. If God is a being like others insofar as he has a presence, surely such a creature is less perfect than a God that is fully beyond creation, i.e., one not limited by presence. His approach to religion, then, is something that may be awkwardly characterized as a non-metaphysical theology wherein he speaks of faith, the messianic promise, and other overt religious motifs, but in ways that kept him from ever arriving at a divine being or belief in God in the customary sense. His is paradoxically "a religion without a religion" and definitely, at least for Derrida, a religion without dogma.

During his career Derrida traveled widely and lectured around the world. For the most part he divided his time between Paris and various American universities such as Johns Hopkins, Yale, and the University of California at Irvine, the last two centers for deconstruction. In 2003, Derrida was diagnosed with an aggressive form of cancer and had to cut back on his many engagements. He died in October of the following year.

The Non-Philosophy-Philosophy Deconstruction

Through his deconstructive approach, Derrida responds to three important twentieth-century movements, namely, phenomenology, structuralism, and psychoanalysis. And while his early scholarship focused mostly on Edmund Husserl (1859-1938) and his phenomenological method, it would be a mistake to privilege Husserl's influence above Nietzsche, G. W. F. Hegel (1770-1831), Sigmund Freud (1856-1939), Karl Marx (1818-1883), Emmanuel Levinas (1906-1995), and especially Heidegger's deconstruction of the Western metaphysical tradition, i.e., his "de-structuring" *(Destruktion)* and "unbuilding" *(Abbau),* which Derrida embraced in his own unique way.

Derrida's now famous essay, "Structure, Sign, and Play in the Discourse of the Human Sciences" (see *Writing and Difference*), originally a 1966 lecture delivered at Johns Hopkins University, marks what many consider to be the birth of deconstruction in America and the death of French structuralism. Along with Derrida's 1967 coinciding publications of *Speech and Phenomena, Of Grammatology,* and *Writing and Difference,* deconstruction quickly grew into an unmistakable movement with a dominant voice in American universities, only later to become better known in France and elsewhere. Since the height of its popularity in the 1970s and early 1980s, deconstruction has lost most of its initial momentum, especially in America, yet it still continues to find an audience globally. At first, Derrida's influence was felt primarily among literary theorists, but deconstruction has since then had great influence in shaping philosophy, religious studies, theology, art criticism, psychoanalysis, politics, legal studies, architecture, and many other areas. It is one of the major driving forces behind what is generally known as "postmodernity."

Deconstruction has been especially important for philosophy and literary criticism as the theory, method, or hermeneutics for reading that seeks to uncover hidden assumptions (not necessarily meaning) and contradictions that shape texts. However, because deconstruction has no specific thesis, argument, or simple definition, it is often misunderstood and misapplied. Strictly speaking, deconstruction is not a philosophy, theory, or set of beliefs. It is often described as a literary method for reading texts, especially philosophical texts, but calling it a method implies too much, for it is not reducible to instrumentality, sets of rules and techniques, or even language. The challenge of trying to define it is further complicated by the fact that there are many forms and offshoots of deconstruction that vary significantly from Derrida's own views.

Contrary to what the name implies, Derrida does not believe deconstruction is negative but affirmative (thus not really positive either). Similar to Heidegger's existential analysis, which is critical of traditional ontology without destroying the possibility of an ontological investigation, Derrida's deconstruction is not an annihilation or demolition but a practice or attitude of double reading that, while often textually based, goes beyond texts. His deconstruction is most often described as a way of critique, but it is, for him, something else, an irreducible experience. According to Derrida, to do deconstruction is not even hermeneutics, whether phenomenological, philosophical, critical, or otherwise. In fact, there can be no proper name with any specific properties that we might use as a label for this non-philosophy-philosophy. Whatever defining concepts are used are themselves subject to further de-structuring, dismantling, and re-arranging to expose something else, something different. The term "de-construction," which has worked its way into popular culture, is only one of many words Derrida employs to de-center traditional metaphysics. Other popular terms include *différance,* margin, trace, supplement, dissemination, and logocentrism. None of these are fixed or final but are used tentatively and contingently within his writings. "Deconstruction" is something he considers merely one of the least of ill-fitting names for something without definition. While seemingly paradoxical, deconstruction may best be defined as an attitude toward the "wholly other" and an "experience of the impossible." Derrida continually returns to the question of the otherness of the other and, especially in his later works, the political and ethical responsibility that the "other" requires of us all.

As a quasi-poststructural and quasi-postmodern approach, Derrida's deconstruction radically criticizes accepted notions of the referentiality of language and the objectivity of structures as the false assumptions of traditional Western metaphysics. Yet deconstruction is not only poststructural and postfoundational but also antifoundational, for it critically undermines conventional notions of truth, reality, and knowledge. According to Derrida there is no transcendentally signified, e.g., transcultural, transhistorical truth, or fundamental grounding (whether principles, laws, meaning, etc.) of the sort traditional metaphysics has attempted to disclose. There is only an endless "play" that connects signs to other signs. Meaning is always contextual, deferred, provisional, and incomplete because it is structurally unstable. Texts do not have final and perfect meanings that we must grasp but are full of internal tensions and contradictions that make their truth claims, and even an author's intended meaning, no more than reflections of the free play of language — an infinite play of signs. However, while words do not refer to fixed truth or meaning, only to other words, Derrida accepts that there is still meaning and understanding, although often undecidable and at all times open to further play. What philosophers, theologians, and the like take to be coherent and unified Derrida describes as always already imbued with radical otherness and difference. For instance, in contrast to Husserl, Derrida proposes that the things themselves always escape us. And in contrast to Hans Georg Gadamer (1900-2002), he proposes that dialogue is always in some way interrupted and ruptured.

Structuralism

In order to better appreciate Derrida's work, it is important to understand his relation and reaction to French structuralism, and the larger metaphysical tradition to which he believes it belongs. As we recall from the previous chapter, structuralism does not refer to any specific school or program. It is a multivariate and multifaceted approach to human knowledge that, as the name implies, argues that there are structures underlying all communication. Meaning is the product of underlying and hidden structures. It does not come from above, e.g., God, revelation, or from within, e.g., subjective self, one's being, consciousness, but from deep and preconscious structures, i.e., socio-economical, cultural, psychological.

One of the best examples of structure and one of the most important of systems is language. In the structuralist account, language, both spoken and written, is the product of structures that shape, or even determine, our thinking. Language is not something we create or determine on our own. We learn how to think within structures of language, religion, culture, etc. Those are forces we cannot control and for the most part do not recognize as determining our thought. In this way the study of structure becomes a kind of supralanguage of intelligibility or understanding, for language itself is a product of these forces. Whether theology, philosophy, literature, etc., all meaningful phenomena are believed to fall under a thoroughly logical and material account. All meaning emerges from structures that are believed to be suitable to scientific explanation even though they are deeper than and constrained by thought. In order to expose these structures, structuralists have examined phenomena as diverse as games, entertainment, religious activities, and sometimes rituals in food preparation.

One of the central proposals of structuralist thought is that meaning only emerges within systems of difference. For instance, words are said to be meaningful only in relationships to other words. That is, a word by itself does not mean anything except in relationship to other words in a system of difference and contrast. Structuralism rejects the popular notion that meaning comes from things in themselves or as something intentionally produced and reproduced by human beings. Words do not refer to a reality outside language, objects in the world or fixed and transcendental truth. Meaning emerges only from out of differential, arbitrary (without natural connection), and binary relations, e.g., right versus wrong, presence versus absence, good versus evil, soul versus body, none of which are linked to any definite and final meaning.

Structuralism claims that a word or sign is composed of a concept or meaning (signified) together with a sound or image (signifier). The relationship between signified and signifier is always arbitrary, for words and signs are concepts with nothing behind them, i.e., no essences. After all, if the relation between signified and signifier were static and absolute it would be very difficult, if not impossible, to account for the many different and changing languages of the world. Focused on concepts such as signified and signifier, the structuralist attempts to explain the internal constitution of signs and how linguistic elements function within the structural system. A major implication of this theory in the case of reading a text is that most structuralists will not approach a book with the purpose of locating authorial intent or desire, but as the study of deep and unconscious structures that produced the text and its author. One of the major moves of structuralism has been to shift the focus from objects and things in and of themselves toward relationships. Thus, structuralism represents a coherence theory of truth in which truth relates to the internal coherency of signs, rather than a correspondence theory of truth in which truth is a matter of the relation of signs to actual things.

Structuralism is supposed to be a way of finding out how things work without following what structuralists argue are the mistaken avenues to truth and meaning of metaphysics, ontology, epistemology, etc. Derrida argues, although one would be hard-pressed to locate any typical argumentative style in which reasoned premises lead to a clear conclusion, not that structuralism is an examination of the function of structure or phenomena, but that it actually goes much further and becomes another way of making metaphysical truth claims and putting a center, order, and ground (structure) where there is none. For example, whereas structuralists view binary oppositions as stable in a more or less formal and logical structure, Derrida sees them as always unstable and imbalanced. Despite the structuralist argument, Derrida finds that structure is merely a concept among other metaphysical concepts that refer to presence and an originary nature — the logos.

Logocentrism

Derrida sees the history of Western thought since Plato as a prolonged search for the logos. He describes the Western way of understanding as caught up in what he calls "logocentrism" and a "metaphysics of presence," i.e., the persistent belief in and search for a pure and unchanging origin of meaning and truth. This origin or ground has been described by various philosophers and theologians in many ways, e.g., as the presence of pure intelligibility, true forms or ideas, essences, the ego, the divine/eternal law as belonging to a spiritual realm, and so on. One of the primary examples of the logos as physical and material manifestation is the incarnation of Christ. Yet even in non-religious contexts, many logocentrists refer to the logos as manifesting or as having effects that are physically real. However the logos may be described, whether as emanating from a divine mind or as something internal to our being, etc., the logocentric point of view remains basically the same. It is the belief in a pure and undefiled origin and source against which we may judge the rest of the world. Why study theology, biblical interpretation, philosophy, and the like? The answer from a logocentric perspective is that they bring us closer to the ground of meaning and truth. They are our means to an end where the end is the logos, capitalized Truth and Meaning.

Logocentrism is most visible in the use of binary oppositions where there is a logical and ontological priority of a given term or metaphysical concept over another, e.g., positive over negative, nature over culture, soul over body, center over margin, rational over irrational, *ad infinitum*. In a set of related concepts, the closer of the two to the unchanging and eternal is privileged over the other, which is believed to be contingent, inferior, and even negative. This privileging of one ideal or concept above another is a hierarchical ordering and exclusivity of either/or, one or the other, such as in natural science where objectivity has priority to the extent that it excludes subjectivity. One of the most common examples of metaphysical subordination and the favoring of one side over another is the common privileging of speech over writing (sometimes referred to as "phonocentrism"), in which speech is believed to be purer than writing. Speech is the most transparent medium, it is argued, for its meaning is associated with the immediacy of thought, presentness to consciousness, presence-to-itself, etc., which cannot be said of writing. Writing is something that may be carried over great historical and geographic distances to various unknown recipients, despite the intention and even death of the author. Speech, unlike writing, does not suffer the same erosion of meaning caused by these transfers and distances.

Attempts to find an inherent, self-same, or self-sufficient meaning are part of what Derrida pejoratively views as the "metaphysics of presence," i.e., a universal and transcendental signified or meaning by which all other signifiers and meanings may be grounded in or pointed back toward, i.e., through our being, reason, identity, authenticity, etc. When Derrida refers to metaphysics in this sense, he is not identifying a subdiscipline of philosophy or merely one branch among many for theoretical and abstract inquiry. Metaphysics is something much broader for Derrida because it is the background that conditions our thinking, knowing, and experience, whether we believe we are participating in it or not. Metaphysical presuppositions are apparent everywhere. According to Derrida, they are neither rightly accepted nor possibly escaped. The metaphysics of presence is one's belief in a transcendental signified and "full presence" behind everything, offering incorruptible meaning, grounding, and thus purpose, to a messy and "seemingly" ambiguous world. In Derrida's account, even the most neutral and seemingly modest of metaphysical assumptions reveals dogmatic and violent hierarchies in the form of binary descriptions and oppositions, i.e., one world sensible and perishable, the other world eternal and incorruptible — one always correct truth and one always false.

In response, Derrida's deconstructive approach attempts to first expose, then reverse, and finally subvert the use of binary systems and hidden centers. For Derrida, what is needed is a rigorous rethinking and rereading of the conceptual dilemmas inherent to the metaphysical tradition of the West. Even in his early work of 1967, *Of Grammatology* (perhaps his most famous work), Derrida attempts to undermine the speech/writing opposition. He has no interest in reincorporating the binary language of metaphysics in something more critical or somehow more accurate. He is interested in exposing then subverting its either/or, showing that the "either" and "or" are always part of each other. Many had attempted to break with traditional metaphysics already, but, according to Derrida, they unintentionally continued to incorporate its language and binary approach. Even in Heidegger, Derrida finds what he believes is a failure to recognize the subtle and persistent lure of metaphysical presence in his existential search for a more fundamental experience. In fact, Derrida considers all phenomenology, whether transcendental, existential, or hermeneutical, to be caught up in metaphysics and an obsession with presence.

In contrast to structuralism and traditional metaphysics, Derrida argues that we are not forced to make extreme choices between one concept or ideal over another more corrupted and distorted, as is so often presented as the case. Derrida argues that difference and deferral in meaning infects and prevents any possible claim to presence or original meaning. Thus it is an unjustifiable opposition to give a "self-evident" or "natural" priority to one concept or term, treating the other as accidental and marginal. From his deconstructive point of view there can be no absolute self-identity or binary difference, so priorities such as speech over writing, like all binary oppositions, are baseless and misleading ideals. Derrida understands speech to be intrinsically a kind of writing, and the spoken word to be an impure sign already imbued with differences and absence. There is no absolute, eternal, and clear rational over irrational, right over wrong, good over evil, and so forth. Even if there were a full presence, logos, or ground, we cannot possibly reach it, for we can never escape the chain of signifiers to gain sight of a transcendental signified. We are caught up in an endless play, ambiguity, and process of infinite deferral that keeps us from a pure undifferentiated presence, norm, or center by which the world may be judged or measured. There is a clear irony here, namely, that insomuch as we accept metaphysical ideals we are really pushing aside and ignoring the world that we are trying to describe. That is, by trying to find a metaphysical grounding in order to come to terms with existence, we are actually preventing ourselves from being able to affirm life as it is.

The deconstructive declaration of the closure of the metaphysical era is not an outright rejection of metaphysics so much as a new work within its tradition, language, texts, and margins, with the purpose of revealing its blind-spots and conceptual problems. As insistent as Derrida is that there are inconsistencies and problems in traditional metaphysics that make it a misguided failure, he is also insistent that one cannot simply float above it. We must work within its discourse. After all, like everyone else, Derrida and his deconstructive activity that disrupts and destabilizes prevailing positions depends on the language of metaphysics and its concepts and categories. One cannot do deconstruction unless doing so in conjunction with the history and tradition of metaphysics. What would there be to deconstruct without it? Again, to be clear, Derrida is not seeking a way of imposing a new or purer philosophy from the outside to supersede the old. Deconstruction is not a replacement theory of knowledge or a superior way of discerning the being of beings. It exposes what already deconstructs itself as the free play of understanding. Deconstruction is parasitic inasmuch as it lives within traditions and texts themselves, disclosing what is overlooked and subverted, while never appealing to an external rule, criterion, or standard upon which to base judgment and understanding.

Différance *and Trace: Conditions of the (Im)possible*

Derrida's essay "Différance" (see *Margins of Philosophy*) introduces one of his most famous terms. The quasi-transcendental word *"différance"* is often counted as one of Derrida's many neologisms (new words brought into use), but it is (he would cross out the word "is") neither a concept nor a word. It represents the play that comes before words and concepts. It is hardly surprising, then, that this word that is not a word is somewhat difficult to understand, if it can be understood at all. And it is not surprising that this concept that is not a concept has a history of confusion surrounding it. While it may not be a concept or a word, after reading his essay one knows more about *différance* than he or she did before. Even so, this does not constitute "understanding" or "knowing" in the typical sense, for Derrida argues that *différance* has no fixed definition or observable properties. This makes deconstruction all the more difficult to appreciate, for *différance* is one of Derrida's crucial recurring motifs. Set largely against the backdrop of Heidegger's existential analysis, the notion of *différance* reflects elements from many thinkers including Levinas, Freud, Nietzsche, and Ferdinand de Saussure (1857-1913). In a very basic sense, *différance* is one of the ways in which Derrida tries to understand our experiences of the other, i.e., text, person, which is never wholly present (transparent or obvious) or fully absent (hidden and mysterious) when we encounter it/them.

This cryptic non-word often receives a privileged place among Derridaean scholars even though Derrida does not use it on its own, as if it could stand as the name for something proper. *Différance* is always supplemented by and supplementary to other terms and motifs that, while overlapping, do not replace one another. A pronounced example of this overlapping is Derrida's *"différance"* and "trace," which often seem indistinguishable from each other. And while it is true that either may be replaced by an entirely new name or word, they are not so fluid as to be totally interchangeable. Like all of his terms, they are complementary and interdependent.

According to Derrida, *différance* is the condition for the possibility of knowing. As a sort of catch-all term, it both describes and provides the encompassing term under which all meaning, identity, and presence occur. It is also that which disrupts, de-stabilizes, de-centers binary oppositions, undermines the notion of logos, and dispels the myth of "full" presence. *Différance* drastically undermines foundationalist thinking, for there is no start, level, or point at which to interject *différance* as a beginning. It is what is always already although never actually present. *Différance* is not a logos, center, ground, or fixed structure, yet Derrida views it as a kind of ground and structure, for it is the "nonsimple origin" of differences that all discourse and thought depend upon. Inasmuch as it is that which thinking and signification depend upon, it is a movement and play that is itself unthinkable. *Différance* is, in a rather opaque and ill-defined sense, too convulsive and turbulent to be examined in any straightforward manner, so much so that it can never appear as itself (there is no "itself") or as a thing. *Différance* is nothing, not even a name, yet Derrida believes it is the condition of all appearing.

The graphical representation of *différance* instead of the commonly used "difference," without the exchanged "a," may only be read because there is little audible distinction in French between the English word *difference* and the non-word *différance*. This subtle twist serves to emphasize Derrida's argument that writing is not secondary to speech. Yet what is happening in *différance* is just as invisible as it is silent. *Différance* draws our attention to the play of traces and differences as a spacing and a temporalizing that are not reducible to binary oppositions like negative or positive, active or passive, present or absent, etc. With this non-word/non-concept, Derrida is arguing for what he sees as the conditions that make experience possible and impossible. In many ways similar to Heidegger's ontic-ontological difference that works toward a more authentic experience, Derrida believes *différance* represents an even more primal description of thinking. What is it that makes Heidegger's difference (between Being and beings) possible? What allows a word to mean? What makes possible the presentation of the being-present? We may begin to answer these questions with *différance*. Still, while we may ask questions such as, What are the conditions for the possibility of experience? and we may find that notions like *différance* help make sense of experience, we will never have a sense of closure to our questions or a perfect and complete interpretation, for deconstruction never arrives at an end or an answer.

Like the structuralists, Derrida favors difference over sameness and offers his key non-concept *différance* as the condition for the possibility of difference and deferral, i.e., differentiality. *Différance* refers to the simultaneous "differing," the space of a sign from that which it represents (distinction), and "deferring," a temporalization that is to delay, postpone, or put off until later. Characteristic of all signification, for Derrida, is spatial difference and temporal deferral. *Différance* is what allows signs to function and what constitutes them as signs, i.e., to differ from something and to defer full identity and presence. Moreover, this play of differentiality is not strictly linguistic, for all that we know, perceive, and are conscious of is by virtue of differing-deferring.

Following Saussure's now famous proposal that meaning emerges in systems of difference and arbitrariness rather than from sure and given terms of signification, i.e., transcendental signified, Derrida argues that there is always an excess of signification that remains unsignified and that only within the sphere of differentiation and postponement is meaning generated. There is, for Derrida, an always undecidable and unpresentable aspect necessary for the conception of meaning. The condition for the possibility of meaning, presence, and identity is the unidentifiable "trace," which is neither present (here and now) nor absent, but nevertheless necessary for any reference to occur. The trace is also the condition of impossibility. Texts, indeed all experiences, are made up of traces with nothing before them or behind them. In this way, he follows the structuralist account (and perhaps more closely Nietzsche's) wherein language is not so much referential as rhetorical.

Derrida argues that meaning emerges through a relation with what it is not, e.g., the "yet to be determined," an unpresentable absence, i.e., something always missing, and an elusive mark or element, i.e., a trace. If we grant that words are traces of other words that depend upon one another for their meaning, then we are granting that meaning, which is by virtue of the web of traces, has no original or grounding trace (a word by itself, referring directly to something in the world) but is by virtue of the play of words and their differences. In this way, we experience indirectly a given transitory element or meaning in the here-and-now as something present that is simultaneously related to something other than itself and therefore somehow always already not here and therefore absent. Paradoxically, presence depends upon absence that we cannot know, i.e., the unknowable and simultaneous absent and present trace. This trace that is both absent and present, though never simply present "or" absent, makes presence both possible and impossible at the same time. Derrida understands this mysterious sense of trace to be something (really no-thing) that always erases itself in presenting itself — where something present is the trace of the erasure of the trace, i.e., where presence blots out or covers over *différance*.

Again, to be clear, to be conscious of something is by virtue of the differing-deferring trace which is always already ungrounded, decentered, unfixed, etc. A word or sign is never itself, i.e., self-same or self-identical, but is always a substitution and a "stand-in" for another sign with nothing before it except that there is differentiality and, also, repeatability. It is the sign's nature to be a repeatable self-erasing trace that can signify over and over again in new contexts *ad infinitum*. Derrida uses the word "iterability" for a sign's nature as a repeatable/differentiating trace that has neither an inherent and specific authorial intention nor final contextual determination. Any sign may live on in different ways in different contexts, but never alone or even as itself. The sign not only means by difference from other signs, but by difference from itself. Iterability is the possibility of meaning beyond a fixed number of intentions or possibilities, where a sign's repeatable and self-erasing trace may have all sorts of intentions depending on given contexts. In this way, the deconstructive account of our understanding in general, and texts in particular, is initially and originally anchored in the violent condition *différance*.

Textuality and Aporias

Derrida's strategies for reading are far too complex to deal with in detail here, but a number of things may be said without trying to summarize his summary-resistant approach. As already noted, Derrida's way through the philosophical tradition is text-oriented and his deconstruction is very much a matter of translation. In fact, he sees all things as texts and everything we are conscious of as a play of differences always deferring, never fully present, and never reaching closure. A text is never simply composed of the graphical marks on pages but is something far more generalized. Life can be read the same way one reads a text, i.e., as signifiers referring to other signifiers for meaning without any ideal signified. In this sense, translation is not a secondary activity done to texts but understanding in the first place. Again, Derrida's claim is that there is no absolute distinction between written and spoken language, for even spoken language is written in some sense. His emphasis on textuality has led to a frequent and mistaken belief that he is prioritizing writing over speech, which seems to be the case in his most famous statement, "There is nothing outside the text." However, his argument is not that there are only texts or that writing is more important than speech, only that we should not privilege one over the other, opposing one to the other in an either/or schema. Nor should we attempt to view their relative importance in a more "balanced" or "fair" manner, as if we could possibly weigh their worth independently of each other or achieve something like balance.

As we have seen, deconstruction is not a way of finding the only authentic or accurate meaning hidden within a text. Deconstruction is not meant to arrive at "the truth" but highlights what is already revealed in a text and that which has been subverted, marginalized, and excluded. A deconstructive reading does not ask, What did the author intend? but, What do these signs mean? And it does so while being aware that there will never be a final reading or closure on interpretation. Indeed, perhaps the most stinging attack on authorial intention belongs to Derrida, for a deconstructive reading will often show not only that a text in question means something other than what it seems to say, but also that it does not even mean what the author intended for it to say. Through deconstructive readings, we may discern true and false statements in given contexts and judge what is more or less appropriate, yet such deconstructive experiences will also expose the necessary incompleteness of given texts and their structural undecidability.

Derrida refers to structural undecidability using the word "aporia." Aporia represents "non-passage" or that which is "impassable" and is, for Derrida, an irreducible experience of not knowing what path to follow or even where the path may be found. When we encounter an aporia within a text we experience an impossibility that cannot be overcome, for we are unable to decide where or how to carry on. Aporias are part of the deconstructive experience as fundamental doubts and unavoidable moments that cannot be solved or subdued, and yet they are necessary for experience. In *différance*, we see the persistent differing/deferring in every supposed opposition that is infected with aporias. To deconstruct a text is to show meaning as both affirmed and postponed, such as when one uses figures of speech, metaphors, and analogies. Hence, according to Derrida, we may never take the reading of any text as straightforward, for it will always be filled with unavoidable aporias that undermine stability, resulting in impassable positions that cannot be resolved no matter how stringent our analysis or exegesis.

Another word Derrida is famous for using in relation to texts is "dissemination." Dissemination has no meaning or definition of its own but brings together the non-word/non-concept *différance* and trace. Derrida claims that texts are constantly in the process of disseminating themselves whereby they undergo an un-semination of dispersal or scattering (though never absolute scattering or dispersion). Dissemination, like *différance* and trace, is the name of that by virtue of which meaning is generated within the web of differentiations that grapple and struggle with one another in the context of sentences, paragraphs, and pages.

Derrida's exercise of these disruptive and dismantling terms and ideas may seem to undermine our reading of texts, perhaps even to the point of making reading pointless and arbitrary, but his use of them may also be seen as necessary conditions for undermining arrogant opinion and posturing that attempts to marginalize and subvert what a text may be saying. Caught up in the ceaseless ebb and flow of the play of traces, one may very well think it useless to try to find any semblance of meaning in which we may be confident, but the play of differentiality comes to a partial halt because there are determining contexts. While interpretation will always be swept up in the play of differing/deferring meaning, it will also be in a context that engenders a limited set of possibilities and finite, though incomplete, determinations. Therefore, even though a text's meaning may be undecided, context reduces inescapable ambiguity. A deconstructive reading is not about stopping at the indeterminacy of meaning, as if there are no specific possibilities given. It is about living with undecidability as a perpetual movement between given possibilities. Deconstructive readings must work within and from out of given contexts while never trying to totally break free of them.

Derrida and Gadamer: Interpretations of Interpretation

The best-known dialogue between Derrida and Gadamer, which was unfortunately a failed dialogue from the start, took place at the Goethe Institute in Paris in April 1981 (see further, *Dialogue and Deconstruction: The Gadamer-Derrida Encounter* [1989]). This meeting is significant for a number of reasons, perhaps the most important of which is that it revealed just how difficult it was for two leading figures of two of the most important movements in contemporary thought to overcome linguistic and conceptual barriers for the sake of meaningful interaction and debate. One has only to reference the diversity of interpretations from other scholars concerning the significance of what took place to see how complex the issues are, not only about what actually happened at the debate itself, but also about how we should appreciate the overall relationship, or perhaps nonrelationship, between hermeneutics and deconstruction.

Derrida and Gadamer clearly have different views of interpretation, writing, and language, yet their perspectives are perhaps not as dissimilar as some scholars tend to emphasize. The differences are certainly not as dissimilar as Derrida initially believed them to be. For instance, that they share common concerns for language and texts (which are independent of their authors) offers strong grounds for making a comparison and contrast of their views. Also, both Gadamer and Derrida share a concern for the metaphysical bias of presence. We have seen their respective challenges to the metaphysical tradition through their distinct notions of "play," wherein both place an emphasis on the experience of otherness and difference in every event of understanding. Both agree that, in play, we experience a movement of infinite deferral of any absolute affirmation of meaning, as well as of determining boundaries and contexts that prevent a nihilistic sense of relativity. Further, Derrida and Gadamer agree that there is neither a transcendental vantage point from which to understand nor any language-dominating position to be enjoyed. We are the ones controlled by language, subject to its ceaseless play and endless generations of meaning. Yet, while both agree that meaning is ambiguous and that every event of understanding must remain open-ended toward further change and exposure to the unknown (unknowable), Derrida believes Gadamer fails to go far enough, for he seems to rely on a continuous sense of mutuality and appropriation of the other, i.e., a dialogical bridge between self-understanding (not to be confused with self-consciousness) and the other. To understand, according to Derrida, Gadamer tries to reduce or cover over the otherness of the other, and thus he overlooks the radical and inherent differences that cannot be bridged.

Derrida is pessimistic to say the least about any kind of hermeneutics, whether philosophical, critical, or otherwise. For him, Heidegger, Gadamer, Jürgen Habermas (1929-), and the like have all plotted mistaken avenues of inquiry that fail to recognize and work beyond their logocentric tendencies. In the case of philosophical hermeneutics, Derrida believes it is aimed toward uncovering and making present the hidden meaning and truth of texts, and therefore reflects what he argues is Gadamer's belief in the possibility of complete and ideal understanding that the interpreter is charged with realizing. What is hermeneutics working toward except that it is some kind of presence or common ground? Moreover, Gadamer's notion of tradition and effective-historical consciousness appears to be precisely the sort of misleading framework characteristic of the larger metaphysical tradition Derrida earnestly opposes. Is not effective history some kind of metaphysical concept against which or by which we may judge the world? While Derrida agrees that tradition and cultural context are always relevant and necessary for interpretation, Gadamer's proposal goes too far and becomes a ground that offers a premature sense of closure, thus simply another metaphysical misstep in the wrong direction.

Derrida is also skeptical of dialogue as a shared experience of understanding, for it mistakenly assumes an ideal, unfolding meaning and continuity of understanding. Instead of continuity, Derrida sees rupture. Instead of a fusion of horizons, he emphasizes undecidability. And instead of dialogue, he returns time and again to his radical views on difference and otherness. Unlike Gadamer, who seems to naïvely wait upon the guiding subject matter to emerge and show itself, such as when one allows texts to speak, Derrida is much more guarded and expects at any time to run up against the impossibility of deciding where and how to move forward. Instead of placing emphasis on the possibility of mutual agreement and reciprocity, Derrida believes we should be willing to appreciate the other and let it remain in its otherness.

Where Gadamer's fusion of horizons seems to be an ever-expanding horizon of meaning and intelligibility wherein we give ourselves over to be played by the subject matter at hand, Derrida wants to interject the reality of discontinuous re-structuring, constant interruption, absence, and ruptures — thus frustrating what he sees as any possible continuity of understanding assumed by hermeneutics. At this point one may justifiably ask if Derrida has arrived at a place where deep and meaningful interaction is impossible. Indeed, at times he seems to be saying precisely that, yet, as we have already made clear, there is more to deconstruction than the concern for what is disrupted and absent. What Derrida is claiming is that hermeneutical exchange with another is based upon a center or ground of continuity and is therefore something susceptible to further deconstructing. He does not mean that interaction must necessarily be trivial or fleeting.

So we must ask, May hermeneutics be as deconstructive as deconstruction, or is Gadamerian dialogue merely a logocentric spinoff? Gadamer does not believe dialogue with a text or person is a simple and straightforward phenomenon of uncovering truth or that achieving understanding will occur ideally with every attempt. Dialogue and understanding require a never-ending commitment without guaranteed outcomes, for the other is always still other. Further, Gadamer understands that the challenge presented by an experience of the other is a challenge present in every event of understanding. To experience at all, one is faced with foreignness and the risk of being wrong. For example, the transformative experience of the work of art is not a continuous development and change for Gadamer, but every bit a rupture or break that Derrida argues is evident "before" every experience (dialogue).

For hermeneutics, coming-to-understand does not begin with broken conversation or end with total otherness, although it recognizes them as essential elements to experience, for there is always more to come in the way of dialogical interaction. Where Derrida steps into hermeneutics so that he may deconstruct it, showing that what is really happening in understanding is often non-understanding, incompleteness, and so on, there Gadamer already stands. In the hermeneutical experience, we are confronted by otherness in even its most radical forms. Indeed, hermeneutics always openly embraces the challenge presented by otherness. A sizeable portion of the unnecessary complications involved in understanding the relationship between hermeneutics and deconstruction comes from the unfair and misleading characterization of the main issues as "differences and undecidability" over/against "dialogue." Gadamer also argues that to understand is to understand differently each time. And while it is true that in our hermeneutical encounter with the other we implicitly seek a fusion of horizons that attempts to critically appropriate the truth of the experience, such attempts are always open to rupture, failure, and the frustrating reality that understanding is structurally unstable. Thus, Gadamer also recognizes elements and conditions similar to Derrida's, even though he is optimistic that we may fruitfully attempt to bridge them for the sake of dialogue, however incomplete and limited. Just how or where hermeneutics becomes a metaphysics of presence, as Derrida claims, is simply unclear. In the end, rather than bipolar opposites, deconstruction and hermeneutics respond to one another as correctives — one a reminder of inherent differences that guard against simple appropriations, and, in response, the other a corrective to an overly pessimistic view of the frustrations of understanding.

A Critical Appraisal of Deconstruction

The harshest criticisms of deconstruction, and along with it of Derrida, have come from the British and American analytic philosophers, for whom his name still holds ominous connotations. In the name of deconstruction, some see Derrida as giving himself an antinomian (lawless) privilege of interpreting however he feels, without any sense of responsibility or accountability. At best, his detractors see him as advocating an irresponsibility that results in a dis-associative and apathetic attitude toward those he might otherwise engage in critical-rational dialogue. At worst, they see his illogical style as so entirely disengaged from common sense and reason that it reduces his deconstructive project to the level of childish gibberish. Indeed, most of Derrida's work fails to satisfy current standards of clarity and, because of this, his non-philosophy-philosophy is treated as a joke by many. Even so, this does not change the reality that deconstruction has and continues to have a sizeable impact on postmodern thought. No doubt there is much that remains contested concerning the merits of deconstruction. Of what little can be agreed upon, it is clear that by its very nature his is a difficult and frustrating project. By insisting on the arbitrariness of play and the pervasiveness of *différance*, Derrida often seems to succumb to pointless relativism wherein anything goes. While this may have some modest merit, as a prolific writer he clearly meant to have his works read. In the very least, this implies a hope that readers would find hints of his intended meaning despite all the inherent difficulties of doing so. As many have already questioned, Why write except that one wants to be understood?

Inspired for the most part by Nietzsche, Freud, and Heidegger, Derrida is one of the most original of recent thinkers. With his playful style of writing packed full of word-games and puns, Derrida composed his works in such a way that he guaranteed a break with orthodox academia in his attempt to expose the contingency of our understanding and the inconsistencies so many seem to blindly cling to in the name of philosophy, theology, and so on. There can be little doubt that he is responsible for fostering another step in the history of philosophy toward the unbuilding of metaphysics. Even so, one must pause to ask if there is anything left to do after doing deconstruction. Is there anything left to have or say that is undeconstructable?

As an attitude of openness to the other and an experience of the impossible, deconstruction is far from a method or science for disclosing truth, whether of texts or life. We do not have truth after doing deconstruction. Further, deconstruction is not a kind of higher language, for we are never able to go beyond or above language with some trans-technique aimed toward a non-linguistic, stable, transpersonal, and transhistorical meaning, logos, and ground. Hence, not only does deconstruction refuse to offer truth, it also refuses a way of finding truth. Nevertheless, Derrida claims that what we do have after deconstruction is an awareness that truth and (metaphysical) presence are illusions generated by the violent power structures and binary activities of the Western metaphysical tradition. Then, once we have arrived at this awareness, we will be able to affirm the world that remains, however vague and incomplete.

It has probably become obvious by this point that speaking negatively about deconstruction (what it is not) is easier than speaking positively (what it is). Unfortunately, this way of describing makes it more difficult to see how Derrida can properly argue that deconstruction is an affirmative movement that can affirm "something" in the flux and transience of play, and our experience of the impassable (and, perhaps, impossible). However, for Derrida, that we all must face undecidabilities and aporias is not a negative experience even though we get caught up in them and cannot find our way out. Rather, it becomes negative when we fail to recognize our own waylessness and the incomplete nature of the path we are on. What is truly "destructive" is our ignorance of our own contingent understanding.

Nonetheless, one might rightly object that this tells us nothing. If Derrida is correct, then what? What does informing us of such frustrations accomplish? Derrida's response is that to talk of aporias is to affirm the world and its becoming, which frees us from our mistaken dogmas and misplaced confidence in capitalized Truth. The affirmation of undecidability and radical differentiality does not make life meaningless or our choices irrelevant. Rather, the affirmation of free play reminds us of our responsibility to make correct choices and to follow through with the ones we make. As with Heidegger, to take up our decision making in this way is an act of making our possibilities our own. To affirm life deconstructively is to begin to appreciate the other in its otherness, rather than try to make the other fit a limited horizon not its own. To affirm the ambiguity of meaning and the perpetual movement between possibilities is not so much to embrace nothingness, as it is to embrace an attitude of openness to the other.

Conclusion

Poststructural, postfoundational, and similar postmodern movements have, for better or for worse, brought light to bear on the continuing epistemological crisis in hermeneutics. Like the hermeneutical phenomenologists, hermeneutical deconstructionists are dissatisfied with the idea that interpretation should be seen as an epistemological or methodological activity. Derrida's radical style of philosophy has in many ways both helped and harmed the efforts of those wishing to bring much-needed attention to projects that rethink the nature of understanding non-foundationally. While some may and do object to Derrida's style of thinking and his personal response to transcendental groundings, credit is due him for disrupting and de-stabilizing many otherwise closed opinions about the nature of interpretation — which is seen by most hermeneuts to be far more fluid and relative than many are comfortable admitting. What remains for those who wish to appropriate the insights of Derrida's deconstruction is to decide how and in what manner we might think deconstructively in a helpful and hermeneutically beneficial manner, e.g., by taking it up as a conceptual tool to help guard against our own instinctive reliance on historical, linguistic, and social foundations, to the detriment of open and interactive interpretation.

REFERENCE WORKS

Bennington, Geoffrey. *Interrupting Derrida.* London: Routledge, 2000.

————. *Jacques Derrida.* Chicago: University of Chicago Press, 1993.

Caputo, John, ed. *Deconstruction in a Nutshell: A Conversation with Jacques Derrida.* New York: Fordham University Press, 1997.

————. *The Prayers and Tears of Jacques Derrida: Religion without Religion.* Bloomington: Indiana University Press, 1997.

Cohen, Tom, ed. *Jacques Derrida and the Humanities.* Cambridge: Cambridge University Press, 2001.

Derrida, Jacques. *Acts of Literature,* ed. Derek Attridge. New York: Routledge, 1992.

————. *Aporias,* trans. Thomas Dutoit. Palo Alto, CA: Stanford University Press, 1993.

————. *Dissemination,* trans. Barbara Johnson. Chicago: University of Chicago Press, 1976.

————. *Given Time: I. Counterfeit Money,* trans. Peggy Kamuf. Chicago: University of Chicago Press, 1991.

————. *The Gift of Death,* trans. David Wills. Chicago: University of Chicago Press, 1995.

————. *Glas,* trans. John Leavey and Richard Rand. Lincoln: University of Nebraska Press, 1986.

————. *Margins of Philosophy,* trans. Alan Bass. Chicago: University of Chicago Press, 1982.

————. *Of Grammatology,* trans. Gayatri Spivak. Baltimore: Johns Hopkins University Press, 1982.

————. *Positions,* trans. Alan Bass. Chicago: University of Chicago Press, 1972.

————. *The Post Card: From Socrates to Freud and Beyond,* trans. Alan Bass. Chicago: University of Chicago Press, 1987.

————. *Spectres of Marx: The State of Debt, the Work of Mourning, and the New International,* trans. Peggy Kamuf. New York: Routledge, 1994.

————. *Speech and Phenomena and Other Essays on Husserl's Theory of Signs,* trans. David B. Allison. Evanston, IL: Northwestern University Press, 1973.

————. *Writing and Difference,* trans. Alan Bass. Chicago: University of Chicago Press, 1978.

Kamuf, Peggy, ed. *A Derrida Reader: Between the Blinds.* New York: Columbia University Press, 1991.

Michelfelder, Diane P., and Richard E. Palmer, eds. *Dialogue and Deconstruction: The Gadamer-Derrida Encounter.* Albany: State University of New York Press, 1989.

Moore, Stephen D. *Poststructuralism and the New Testament: Derrida and Foucault at the Foot of the Cross.* Minneapolis: Fortress, 1994.

Silverman, Hugh, ed. *Derrida and Deconstruction.* New York: Routledge, 1989.

Williams, James. *Understanding Poststructuralism.* Stocksfield, UK: Acumen, 2005.

Wood, David, ed. *Derrida: A Critical Reader.* Cambridge, MA: Blackwell, 1992.

NINE

Dialectical Theology and Exegesis:
Karl Barth and Rudolf Bultmann

Introduction

Dialectical theology and its related exegesis, often referred to as neo-orthodox theology, is a hermeneutical method associated with a number of major figures in early to mid twentieth-century theology. These theologians, led by Karl Barth and Rudolf Bultmann, but also including such people as Paul Tillich (1886-1965), Emil Brunner (1899-1966), and Dietrich Bonhoeffer (1906-1945), among others, emerged on the theological and interpretive scene with the demise of theological liberalism and the events surrounding World War I. The development of dialectical theology was in large part an attempt to formulate a constructive theological reaction to the loss of confidence in the predominant hermeneutical model of the day, theological liberalism, and provide a new means of bringing modernism into creative theological and interpretive dialogue with the traditions of orthodoxy. The result was a dialectical interplay between many of the tenets of theological orthodoxy and the modernist worldview. Because of its dialectical nature, this new form of theology interacted not only with higher criticism but with other philosophical and hermeneutical thought of the time, such as existentialism.

Karl Barth

Karl Barth (1886-1968) is considered by many to be the most significant Protestant theologian since at least Friedrich Schleiermacher (1768-1834), and the most prolific since Martin Luther (1483-1546). He certainly stands out as the most significant theologian of the twentieth century, and his influence has continued, perhaps even recently increased, since his death after nearly fifty years of writing and teaching. His theological work encompassed and responded to the major events and theological movements of the twentieth century, including the fall of theological liberalism, two world wars, the rise and fall of German National Socialism, and the postwar transformation of Western life. In many ways, his theology is a direct, personal, and fulsome response to these issues and events. The dialectical theology that he championed throughout his intellectual career — a theology full of existential tensions and paradoxes — became the most significant response to the fall of liberal theology and attempted to address these many issues.

Life and Influences

Barth was born on May 10, 1886, and died on December 10, 1968, in Basel, Switzerland. Between these two dates, Barth had a huge impact on the theological world, especially of Europe. Barth came from a family closely tied to Basel and Reformed theology. His father and grandfathers on both sides had studied theology and been ministers, being greatly influenced by pietism. Barth's father, like his grandfather, had studied with Johan Tobias Beck (1804-1878), who had been a teacher of the theologian and exegete Adolf Schlatter (1852-1938). In 1889, Barth's family moved to Bern, when his father, Johann Friedrich Barth, accepted a position at the University of Bern, succeeding Schlatter and becoming professor of early and medieval church history. It was in Bern that Barth grew up and received his primary and secondary education.

Barth's life is conveniently divided into four influential periods that help to explain the development of his dialectical theological hermeneutics.

Theological Formation

The first period in Barth's life, from 1904 to 1911, involves his university education and early work before taking a pastorate in Safenwil, Switzerland. Barth attended four universities in the course of completing his formal studies and completing the theological examinations that qualified him to become a pastor. He first studied at Bern, where he attended his own father's lectures, learned historical criticism — although he seems not to have readily or fully accepted it in theory or in his later exegesis — and became familiar with Immanuel Kant's (1724-1804) *Critique of Practical Reason,* a book that would have significant later influence on him. Rather than going to the University of Marburg at that time, which was considered too liberal, Barth went to the University of Berlin, where he heard lectures by the Old Testament scholar Hermann Gunkel (1862-1932), the history-of-religions scholar and pioneer form critic; the theologian Julius Kaftan (1848-1926); and Adolf von Harnack (1851-1930), the leading liberal scholar of his day (and successor to the originator of theological liberalism Albrecht Ritschl, 1822-1889), and one to whom Barth was greatly attracted. Barth returned to Bern, and then went to the University of Tübingen, where he was taught by the conservative scholar Schlatter and theologian Theodor Häring (1848-1928). He finished his education in Marburg, where he studied with the liberal theologian and ethicist Wilhelm Herrmann (1846-1922), the newly arrived New Testament scholar Wilhelm Heitmüller (1869-1926), and the neo-Kantian philosophers Hermann Cohen (1842-1918) and Paul Natorp (1854-1924), among others. After his exams, Barth served for a short time as a pastoral trainee near Bern and as an editor for the journal *Die Christliche Welt* (The Christian World) edited by the Marburg liberal pastoral theologian Martin Rade (1857-1940), and then became a probationary pastor in Geneva for two years. Barth's education shows that he studied with some of the most influential theologians and biblical scholars of his time, both conservative and liberal, but that he was especially drawn to the liberals such as Harnack and Herrmann. His early years as a pastor reflected his endorsement of the liberal theology of the time, including the view that Jesus was not God but an exemplary man.

Commentary on Romans

The second stage of Barth's career surrounds his writing of his commentary on Romans. Barth began his time as pastor in Safenwil in 1911. Safenwil was a small industrial village where the local people were traditionally controlled by the factory owners in the area. In sympathy, Barth joined the Social Democratic Party in 1915, believing that the kingdom of God would be brought by means of socialism. However, three major factors in his life led him to begin rethinking his theological positions. The first was a series of events that surrounded the beginning of World War I. In 1914, as the war was beginning, a number of Germans with whom Barth had sympathy signed a statement endorsing the war effort as a means of preserving civilization. The list of signees included leaders of the Social Democratic Party, and, perhaps more importantly, several of his most influential teachers, including Harnack and Herrmann. The second factor was his coming under the influence of a number of other important thinkers and writers. Barth was strongly influenced by the philosophy of the Danish existentialist Søren Kierkegaard (1813-1855), the novels of Fyodor Dostoevsky (1821-1881), the writings of the philosopher Franz Overbeck (1837-1905), the eschatological character of the New Testament as described in the works of Johannes Weiss (1863-1914) and Albert Schweitzer (1875-1965), and the preaching of J. C. Blumhardt (1827-1891). By all accounts, the third factor was Barth's rediscovery of the Bible. In 1916, he delivered a lecture on "The New World of the Bible," which records a significant change in his thoughts regarding the relationship of God to humanity. This led Barth to undertake further serious theological investigation of the Bible, including an intense study of Paul's letter to the Romans.

Barth began work on his commentary to Romans in 1916, and delivered the manuscript to the publisher in December 1918. Through this combination of factors, Barth came to what many have seen as a radical departure from theological liberalism, as he discovered that the Bible was not about the person's thoughts about God, but about what God as wholly other thinks about human beings. Barth's commentary on Romans was published in 1919 with financial help from friends, but attracted very little attention outside of his immediate sphere in Switzerland. Barth almost immediately undertook to produce a second edition of the commentary. The reception of the commentary, and with it Barth's theological position, was greatly aided by recognition Barth gained for writing a pamphlet on "The Christian in Society." Suddenly there was great interest in Barth and his views. He delivered the second edition of the commentary to the publisher in 1921 (published in 1922). The second edition uses the phrase "God is God," for which Barth is now so well known. By this, he indicates a move away from the human-centeredness of liberal theology to a position where God is not an object knowable and controllable and explainable by humans. Instead, as Barth attempts to show in the commentary, God as wholly other chooses to reveal himself to humanity, who in faith are open to the Word of God rather than relying on themselves or any other human means, including religion. The commentary is less an exegesis of the book of Romans — even though Barth complains in the preface of being accused of being a Biblicist — than it is a work of dramatic and "extraordinary rhetorical force" (Riches, *A Century of New Testament Study,* 53). It presents what has come to be seen as Barth's dialectical theology — the expression of extreme paradoxes in which God is wholly other from humanity. The three major planks of dialectical theology — which does not resolve the dialectic as in Hegel, but leaves them in tension as in Kierkegaard — are that God is God, the Word of God is expressed in Jesus Christ, and there is no other foundation for theology (Heron, *A Century of Protestant Theology,* 79). These concepts not only are fundamental to Barth's dialectical theology, but also constitute the basis of his dialectical hermeneutic.

Barth in Germany

The third period in Barth's development came about as a direct result of the notoriety of his commentary on Romans, and encompasses his teaching in German universities before his deportation. Even though he had no earned doctorate or *Habilitation* (the second published work required for German university teaching), in 1921 Barth was, on the strength of his Romans commentary, invited to a new teaching position in Reformed theology that was being established through support of the American Presbyterian Church at the University of Göttingen. Though not a member of the faculty and supposedly prohibited from giving lectures in systematic theology, Barth gained a significant following for his lectures, and had major influence throughout Germany during his three years there. While in Göttingen, Barth co-founded and co-edited a journal, *Zwischen den Zeiten* (Between the Times), which gave a voice to dialectical theology. Barth was then invited to a position at the University of Münster in 1925, where he became professor of dogmatics and New Testament, until 1930, when he became professor of systematic theology at the University of Bonn. He remained in Bonn until 1935, when he left for Switzerland as a result of his stance toward National Socialism.

In 1934, one year after the rise to power of National Socialism, Barth was the primary author of the so-called Barmen Declaration. This document affirmed, not Hitler as leader, but Jesus Christ as the "one Word of God," and established the Confessing Church in opposition to the German Evangelical Church with its sympathies for Nazism. This document stands as an important reflection of opposition to Nazism and as a significant development in Barth's own thought. Barth himself came to realize that, as opposed to traditional Lutheran theology, the law of God and the state cannot be equated, but obedience is to God, with Christ the center of the church. Barth also realized that the Jews and Christians were in an "indissoluble bond" on the basis of covenant (Busch, *Barth,* 10). Not all in the Confessing Church accepted Barth's position, with some contending that there could be more common ground between the church and state. Barth's outspoken comments on these issues, as well as his refusal to sign a loyalty oath to Hitler, led to his being dismissed from his academic position. He was successful in appealing this decision, but was then pensioned off and forced to leave Germany.

Barth's thought also developed during this time through significant publications. In 1927, besides publishing a commentary on Philippians, Barth began an ambitious project that he called *Christian Dogmatics,* but he only published the first volume on the doctrine of God as a prolegomena to the topic. This was designed to be a complete systematic theology, elucidating his dialectical approach. However, Barth abandoned this project and restarted it in 1931 with the *Church Dogmatics* (*CD*; see below), apparently because of his analysis of Anselm which convinced him that theology should originate in the church with no philosophical or other presuppositions (as he states at the outset of *CD* 1/1).

Church Dogmatics

The fourth and final stage of Barth's life and development actually begins before his return to Basel in 1935. When he arrived in Basel, he took up a position arranged by supporters, and then was officially welcomed into the theological faculty in 1938. He held his position at the University of Basel until his retirement in 1962, except for one year when he lectured in Bonn and throughout Germany (1947-1948), followed by his death in 1968. Lectures that he gave in 1946 were published in 1947 as *Dogmatics in Outline,* and Barth's final major work was his *Evangelical Theology,* published in 1963 from lectures given in 1961-1962. Barth actually began work on his *Church Dogmatics,* for which he is best known, while he was at Bonn. He began to lecture in 1931 on the topic of church doctrine, and this pattern of lecturing and publishing instigated the thirteen published volumes of his *Church Dogmatics.* The work was originally conceived in five volumes, in many parts: Word of God, God, Creation, Reconciliation, and Redemption. The last volume, Redemption, was never attempted. Reconciliation ends with the publication of a fragmentary fourth part on baptism. Nevertheless, Barth published individual volumes from 1932 to 1967 (with English translation occurring from 1936 to 1969, with a volume of indexes in 1975). After World War II, Barth tended to isolate himself from the politics of his day, eschewing especially the anti-communist movement and efforts to rebuild Germany politically. Instead, Barth was much more active in ecumenical movements, including the World Council of Churches, where he delivered a major lecture ("The Church") in 1948 at its founding and again in 1954, and in Roman Catholic dialogue.

A cursory survey of the *Church Dogmatics* illustrates that many of the conventional topics for a systematic theology are not treated by Barth. Further, some of the usual topics are treated several different times, as he returns to them. This is part of his method, in which his dialectical approach is exemplified. There are numerous summaries of the major significant points made in the *Church Dogmatics,* but most scholars agree that the following are some of the most important. (1) The Word of God. Central to the foundation of Barth's dialectical hermeneutic is the claim that the biblical testimony is that "God has spoken." The revealed, written, and proclaimed Word is the threefold form of the Word that God has revealed. The Word of God is not to be equated with the Bible, but transcends it, as God transcends humanity. (2) The Triune God. The Trinity *per se* is not part of revelation, but is what the church affirms about God. God is the wholly other one but who as revealer chooses to reveal himself in divine self-disclosure as Creator, Reconciler, and Redeemer. (3) Scripture. The Bible is not to be equated with the Word of God, but is a witness to revelation of what it means that the word was made flesh. The Bible, though the fallible product of human beings, has authority as a witness to God in Christ.

The Hermeneutics of Barth

The hermeneutics of Karl Barth grows out of the same platform of thought found in his *Church Dogmatics,* and is based upon the fundamental notions of his dialectical theology. The following hermeneutical approach has been gleaned from volume 1, part 1 of the *Church Dogmatics,* which outlines Barth's approach to Scripture (what follows is directly dependent upon Provence, "Sovereign Subject Matter"). Barth makes some strong claims for hermeneutics, especially the relationship of biblical hermeneutics to general hermeneutics. He asserts that the common task of hermeneutics is to understand the words of the writers or speakers, using the tools of literary-historical exegesis. Biblical hermeneutics has an advantage over general hermeneutics in that it must restrict its knowledge of the text to what is found in the text, rather than importing ideas from outside the text. In light of this, the following hermeneutical principles have been identified by Provence in Barth.

(1) The Nature of Language. Barth takes a referential view of language, in which an author's words are meant to create an image or picture of the thing written about, and thereby to guide the reader to the object itself. Barth rejects views that give words ontological status or make them reflective of their author's feelings or thoughts. Instead, they point beyond themselves to what the particular text is about, its subject. Communication through words occurs not only when those words perform their referential function but when the reader by means of the medium of human words catches a glimpse of the referent in some sense. Barth's general hermeneutical rule is that "a text can be read, understood, and expounded *only with reference* to and in the light of its object" (*CD* 1/2: 493; trans. Provence, 244), which object or subject regulates meaning and understanding of the text.

(2) Dispute with General Hermeneutics. Barth distinguishes biblical hermeneutics from general hermeneutics along two lines. The first is that he believes that general hermeneutics introduces beliefs from outside the text regarding what things they believe can and cannot happen, and he rejects this principle. The second is that he believes the Bible itself imposes the principle that the subject of a text itself must determine its own parameters for understanding of that text.

(3) Peculiar Character of the Biblical Object. Barth develops the notion of the significance of the word in the Bible from his perception of the centrality and, in fact, the overwhelming presence of the word in the Bible itself. Barth says that the object of this quantity of words is Jesus Christ. As Provence states, "Jesus, the living word of God, is the subject matter of the Bible, and if one is to understand the Bible, he must understand it because he has perceived the image of the Word of God about whom it speaks" (246). This reflects what has often been called Barth's "christocentric" approach, in which even language itself is not understandable apart from Jesus Christ. This has implications for understanding not only the text of the Bible, but any text, as Jesus Christ as Creator becomes the necessary presupposition for understanding.

(4) Freedom of the Subject Matter. The peculiar character of the biblical object leads directly to the fourth hermeneutical principle. The process of understanding, according to Barth, requires that the interpreter understand the words used, but that is not sufficient if the interpreter does not understand the subject. For Barth, it is the subject that determines meaning. For routine objects, this poses no significant problem. However, for understanding the Bible and what is meant by the Word of God, one is dependent upon God making his Word known. By this, Barth warns interpreters away from overconfidence in understanding, and toward humility in the use of various interpretive tools as a means to genuine understanding.

(5) Limitation of the Interpreter. In light of the above hermeneutical principles, it comes as no surprise that Barth believes that the interpreter is clearly limited in ability to understand the Bible as God's revelation of Jesus Christ. The major limitation concerns the nature of the object of the Bible. The object is Jesus Christ, who may or may not choose to reveal himself to the interpreter. He stands as wholly other to the subjective interpreter. A second limitation is that of the interpreter. Barth does not believe that the human has any intrinsic capabilities or qualities that would enable the human to be an interpreter of the Word. In other words, Barth sees an unbridgeable divide between God and humanity, one that can only be bridged by God in his willingness to be known through his Word.

(6) Limitations of Exegesis. Barth rejects any defined method for knowing the Word of God. He eschews such methods for several reasons. One is that he does not believe that such methods can accomplish what they purport to be able to do. That is, they cannot penetrate the text and get behind it to understand the events that lie behind the text. A second is that he believes that such an approach runs the risk, certainly, of misinterpretation of the Bible, and, quite possibly, of attempting to dominate the text itself and subject it to the church, rather than the church being confronted by the Word. A third reason is that attention to understanding the words of the text misses Jesus Christ as the Word. This was the peculiar problem of theological liberalism, with its subjective emphasis.

(7) Necessity of the Text. There is an inextricable relationship between the text and the subject of the text, in this instance, the subject of the Bible being Jesus Christ. In some ways, the relationship is circular, as one must know the subject to understand the words, while the subject is only knowable through the words of the Bible. For Barth, however, this is a necessity, because one cannot seek understanding of the subject of the Bible from outside of the Bible. As a result, the Bible is indispensable for the

church, as it alone provides access to the subject, and in a restricted way to the Word of God. God reveals himself through the words of Scripture of his own volition.

(8) Need for Methodology. Barth himself embraces a paradox regarding interpretation when he asserts that the interpreter must be subordinate to Scripture, while acknowledging that our interpretive methods are our *only* means of understanding Scripture. What this indicates is that human interpretive methods are subservient to the subject matter of Scripture, while these methods are used to understand the words of the text concerning this subject. This ensures that our interpretive methods are subordinate to the Word of God, rather than attempting to dominate it, and enables us to have at least some means of understanding the text.

(9) History and Understanding. Barth underwent a significant shift from his earlier approach to history as found in his commentary on Romans to that of his *Church Dogmatics*. Part of what it meant to rid himself of all philosophical presuppositions was to rid himself of his existential approach by which the past and present are seen to be simultaneous. Instead, in direct address of Gotthold Lessing's (1729-1781) "ugly ditch," Barth believed that the church's beliefs were true not because of their being grounded in history, but because they reflected universal truth. God did act in history in Jesus Christ, but this has contemporary relevance because of the act of God through such things as election and revelation.

(10) Inspiration and Understanding. Concerning the concept of inspiration, Barth believes in three key moments. The first is revelation itself; the second is inspiration of the biblical authors, by which he means that human authors were obedient to revelation; and the third is inspiration of the biblical reader, who as a spiritual person by the Holy Spirit understands what the authors say.

(11) Prayer and Understanding. Interpretation of Scripture is not based upon interpretive methods, but simply upon Jesus Christ through the Holy Spirit. The one avenue available to the human interpreter is prayer. By prayer, Barth means the human confessional stance of recognition of creaturely dependence upon God for interpretive understanding.

Admittedly much more could be said about Barth's dialectical thought, and in particular his hermeneutical position, especially as he wrote so much and engaged in so much theological interpretation. Nevertheless, these eleven theses give a clear indication of his hermeneutical stance.

A Critical Appraisal of Barth's Hermeneutics

It is hard to overstate the influence of Barth on Christian theology. Barth has had a significant impact on continental theology, to the point where much German-language and related theology functions in a post-Barthian context, recognizing his contribution and building upon it in various ways. Recognition in Anglo-American circles has been more diverse, ranging from wholesale dismissal to welcome embrace. After a period of relative neglect, it appears that there is increased interest across a range of theological perspectives in the theology of Barth. Though he himself showed little to no awareness of contemporary philosophy, there is some thought that Barth and Ludwig Wittgenstein (1889-1951) have some philosophical affinities (MacDonald, *Karl Barth*). In any case, his work raises significant questions on a number of issues.

Neo-orthodoxy. One of the major issues regarding Barth has been whether or not he is one of the "neo-orthodox" theologians. Anglo-American scholarship has tended to see him in this light. Whereas some recent scholarship has rejected this label for him (e.g., McCormack, *Karl Barth's Critically Realistic Dialectical Theology*), the term is still appropriate. One of the major challenges in understanding Barth is the often finely nuanced disjunction between traditional theological terminology and his meaning of such terms. These include any number of terms and concepts, such as the Word of God, the Trinity and its modes of being, inspiration, election, and reconciliation, among others. As a result, Barth has given the impression that he is much more orthodox in his understanding of these terms than he actually is. Recent theological discussion of such areas as the inspiration of Scripture has been heavily influenced by a Barthian hermeneutic, in which a disjunction is drawn between the Bible and the Word of God, and therefore has raised questions regarding such issues as scriptural authority and fallibility. In some sense, Barth, while distancing himself from the liberal theology of his upbringing, in vacating the terms of orthodoxy, as well as accepting the historical judgments of liberal theology, did not move far from theological liberalism.

Hermeneutical Principles. The hermeneutical principles that Barth tacitly developed caused a significant reaction especially among theological liberals, because his efforts to distinguish interpretation as method, text, and history seemed to run contrary to the Enlightenment development of historical criticism. There are certainly a number of perplexing paradoxes in his thought, especially as he attempts to assert the priority of the object of interpretation over understanding. His desire to counter subjectivity with an objectivity in which God is wholly other poses an interpretive dilemma, when the sources of understanding are confined to Scripture. Further, his word-based method that seems to function only within a theological framework seems to minimize the immediacy of historical context for his christological interpretation. The results of his interpretive framework are subject to the Word of God, but in a way that cannot be verified — which Barth would (unfortunately) probably consider one of the strengths of his method.

Biblical Interpretation. When one examines some of the results of Barth's biblical interpretation, a number of his well-known interpretive positions are called into question, on the basis of either his own hermeneutical methods or those of historical criticism. For example (see Busch, *Barth*), Barth, drawing upon a long tradition of biblical interpretation including Jewish exegesis, interprets Genesis 1 and 2 as utilizing not historical accounts but two different sagas, the first reflecting creation as the external basis of the covenant and the second reflecting creation as the internal basis of the covenant (*CD* III/1: 81-82, 97-99, 231-38). Here Barth is clearly dependent upon more than the biblical text for his understanding, with direct implications for his views of covenant and natural theology. His discussion of covenant (see Jeremiah 31:31-34), and whether there is replacement of the first covenant by a second of the heart, is based upon a strained view of what replacement means. He ends up wishing to assert that replacement is a positive term that means fulfillment. The new covenant is taken to mean that none of the human race is excluded (*CD* IV/1: 32-34). Elsewhere Barth speaks of election "on behalf of the world" (*CD* II/2: 423). These kinds of statements leave him open to the oft-repeated charge and probably correct implication of holding to some form of universalism. Barth interprets Mark 3:34 as the model of the true church, because of Christ being in the midst of a community (*CD* IV/4: 37), a theological but not a defensible exegetical interpretation. Barth interprets the prodigal in the parable of the prodigal son (Luke 15:11-32) as Jesus Christ, who goes to the "distant country" and returns as a servant to be exalted (*CD* IV/1: 772; 2: 21-25) — an allegorical rather than strictly exegetical conclusion. Barth is apparently intentionally ambiguous regarding the historicity of the resurrection, rejecting assessment of the event by historical methods but suggesting that it be seen as "saga," "legend" (*CD* III/2: 446, 452, 453; IV/1: 336), or "'pre-historical' happening" (*CD* IV/1). In other words, the resurrection was for Barth a different kind of history than the life of Jesus up to his death. O'Neill goes so far as to say that, on such issues as the resurrection and miracles, Barth remained firmly with the liberal theologians who denied such events as historical (in the generally accepted sense), with Barth using the term *Wunder* rather than *Mirakel* for such things as the virgin birth (*Bible's Authority*, 273-77). Further, Barth takes the Easter event not as a singular event but as one that includes all time, and equates this with three movements of Jesus Christ — Easter, the presence of the Spirit, and his return in judgment (*CD* IV/2: 622; 3: 290ff.; Busch, *Barth*, 81-82). In his discussion of reconciliation, Barth interprets 2 Corinthians 5 in a mix of literalistic and analogical statements, by which he endorses reconciliation of the world and sees a type of corporate identification with sinful humanity (*CD* IV/1: 75-76). His interpretation of Colossians 3:3 — "your life is hidden with Christ in God" — as a justification for one not being cognizant of one's status in Christ is exegetically strained at best (*CD* IV/3: 317-18). Barth is clearly an interesting but not always satisfying interpreter of the Bible, whether judged by historical-critical criteria or, in some instances, even by his own hermeneutical standards.

Despite these observations, Barth remains one of the most influential theologians and biblical interpreters in the contemporary theological scene, as new generations of readers encounter his dialectical hermeneutic.

Rudolf Bultmann

Rudolf Bultmann (1884-1976) is considered by many to be the most important New Testament interpreter and theologian of the twentieth century. He certainly loomed large over more than fifty years of New Testament interpretation in both Europe and North America. Bultmann was clearly a product of nineteenth-century scientism including German historicism and liberal theology, forces from which he was never able to fully extricate himself. Like Barth, he too confronted the major events of German history in the twentieth century, including World War I, the rise and fall of National Socialism, World War II, and the years after. Whereas Barth approached these matters as a dialectical theologian, Bultmann approached them as a dialectical thinker more heavily influenced by contemporary philosophy and historical-critically based exegesis of the Bible.

Life and Influences

Bultmann was born August 20, 1884, in Wiefelstede, near the northern German city of Oldenburg, as the oldest son of a Lutheran pastor who was the son of a missionary to Sierra Leone. He died in Marburg on July 30, 1976, where he had been professor of New Testament from 1921 to 1951. He studied at the local *Gymnasium,* the equivalent of secondary school, from 1895 to 1903, where he studied Latin, Greek, Hebrew, religion, and German literature.

Bultmann's life can also be conveniently divided into several major periods. These help to reveal the various influences upon his hermeneutical thought.

Bultmann and University

The first period includes Bultmann's studies at university. As was the European custom, he attended a number of universities, including those in Tübingen, Berlin, and Marburg. Because of his similarity in age to Barth, he studied with some of the same people. At the University of Tübingen, Bultmann heard lectures from the newly arrived church historian Karl Müller (1852-1940) and the conservative scholar Theodor Häring. At the University of Berlin, Bultmann heard lectures by Harnack, Gunkel (who had a strong influence upon him), and the theologian Julius Kaftan (1848-1926) — although Bultmann identified much more with the personal and private religion of Schleiermacher than with that of Harnack. At the University of Marburg, Bultmann heard lectures by the New Testament scholar Johannes Weiss, the theologian Herrmann, the New Testament scholar Heitmüller (who replaced Weiss when he went to Heidelberg), and the New Testament and church history scholar Adolf Jülicher (1857-1938). After three years of university study, while preparing for his theological examinations, Bultmann returned to Oldenburg to teach in the local *Gymnasium*. After passing his examinations in 1907, he continued as a graduate student in Marburg. The subject for his dissertation was suggested to him by Weiss, although Bultmann finished the dissertation under Heitmüller when Weiss left in 1908. This piece of research, *Der Stil der paulinischen Predigt und die kynisch-stoische Diatribe* (The Style of the Pauline Preaching and the Cynic-Stoic Diatribe), was accepted (and published) in 1910, and Bultmann received his licentiate of theology degree. He then went on under Jülicher to write his *Habilitationsschrift*, titled *Die Exegese des Theodor von Mopsuestia* (The Exegesis of Theodore of Mopsuestia), which was accepted in 1912 (though not published until 1984). The predominant influence upon Bultmann was exercised by scholars who were liberal theologians, and their influence upon him continued throughout his career. The two most important, insofar as his later theology was concerned, according to O'Neill (*Bible's Authority*, 286-87), were probably Herrmann and Weiss. Herrmann, who also had a significant influence upon Barth, was a liberal who no longer believed in liberalism, resulting in a vacuous concept of faith, in which all of the tenets of orthodoxy had been eroded. Weiss was known for his eschatological view, made more well known by Albert Schweitzer, that Jesus taught that there was a future kingdom of God with a coming Messiah other than himself. This perspective became one of the central tenets of Bultmann's belief regarding Jesus and the kingdom — that Jesus the proclaimer of the kingdom had become the proclaimed by the early church.

Early Career

The second period in Bultmann's life reflects the time when he was establishing his career. In 1912, upon successful completion of his *Habilitation*, he was appointed as a *Privatdozent* (lecturer without salary) in New Testament at Marburg. During this time, Bultmann was heavily involved with proponents of liberal theology. Like Barth, he became a member of the society, *Freunde der Christlichen Welt* (Friends of the Christian World), and attended its weekly meetings sponsored by the pastoral theologian Rade, who was the editor of the companion journal *Die Christliche Welt* (The Christian World). Bultmann continued to be associated with Rade and this outspoken liberal journal until after World War I, although Bultmann came to critically reject many of its fundamental positions. He did not take the usual liberal theological view towards miracles, i.e., either denying or explaining them naturalistically, and, on the basis of his belief in revelation, he did not accept that Christianity was simply one religion among many, nor accept belief in scientism or historicism. In 1916, Bultmann was appointed to a position as associate professor in the University of Breslau, where he stayed until 1920. During this time, he wrote his now classic work on the synoptic Gospels, *The History of the Synoptic Tradition* (1921). In 1920, Bultmann became professor of New Testament at the University of

Giessen, succeeding Wilhelm Bousset (1865-1920), a position he held for only one year, leaving in 1921 to return to Marburg to take the position of Heitmüller, who moved to Bonn.

Professor at Marburg

The third and final period of Bultmann's life, the longest and in many ways the most important, was his time as professor of New Testament at Marburg, from 1921 until his retirement in 1951. However, he continued to live in the city until his death in 1976. During his time in Marburg, Bultmann had wide-ranging and significant influence on those with whom he came into contact either as his students or as colleagues, and through his writings (which will be treated below). Concerning his involvement with National Socialism, Bultmann was a member of the Confessing Church since 1934 when it was founded. Although his profile is not large with respect to his public posture on Nazism, he was instrumental in Marburg's rejecting the "Aryan paragraph" regarding the hiring and retention of Jews in positions of church leadership, and in condemning other universities, such as Erlangen, which had endorsed this policy. However, Bultmann's influence and ideas are much more clearly seen in his personal contacts. As a professor, he had great influence over a number of significant students, including Heinrich Schlier (1900-1978), Ernst Käsemann (1906-1998), Günther Bornkamm (1905-1990), Hans Jonas (1903-1993), Ernst Fuchs (1903-1983), Gerhard Ebeling (1912-2001), Erich Dinkler, and Helmut Koester, among many others.

Bultmann's most important personal and intellectual developments, however, occurred in relation to his contemporary colleagues. When Herrmann died in 1922, Rudolf Otto (1869-1937), who had been a colleague at Breslau, came to Marburg as well. Although there was potential for continuing mutually beneficial dialogue between Bultmann and the history-of-religions professor Otto, by this time Bultmann had joined the ranks of the dialectical theologians, and they found that they had little in common. Instead, during the period from around 1920 to 1927, dialectical theologians such as Barth, Friedrich Gogarten (1887-1968), and Barth's close associate Eduard Thurneysen (1888-1977) had a significant influence on Bultmann's developing theological thought. Bultmann, Barth, and others attended the meetings of the "Friends" society, Bultmann read some of Barth's early writings, and Bultmann published a very positive review of the second edition of Barth's commentary on Romans, in which he sided with Barth against theological liberalism in the need for revelation to be perceived by faith. Bultmann's dialectical stance was reflected in statements he made at this time to the effect that talk about God had no sense, as in talking about God he loses his wholly otherness. The most important professional relationship, however, developed between Martin Heidegger (1889-1976) and Bultmann. Heidegger came to Marburg as professor in 1922 to succeed Natorp as professor of philosophy. They worked collaboratively, with each attending seminars of the other, from 1923 to 1928, when Heidegger left to become a professor at Freiburg.

Already during Bultmann's lifetime, evaluation of his voluminous work had begun, so that the closing years of his life were engaged in a number of interpretive and hermeneutical disputes with colleagues and even former students. Many of these are at the heart of his hermeneutical program.

Dialectical Theology and Hermeneutics

There is much that could be profitably said about Bultmann's biblical exegesis and theology, as he is enduringly known as a New Testament scholar. However, in this section we will deal with his various hermeneutical positions, many of which make their way into his exegetical and theological work. These positions are all grounded to varying degrees in Bultmann's form of dialectical theology.

Exegesis and the Problems of Hermeneutics

Bultmann wrote two important essays that summarize his views on hermeneutics, which had been clearly developing since his student days and in his early publications. The first essay is "The Problem of Hermeneutics" (1950; in *Essays Philosophical* and *New Testament and Mythology*) and the second is "Is Exegesis without Presuppositions Possible?" (1957; in *New Testament and Mythology* and *Existence and Faith*). In these essays, Bultmann recognizes the growth and development of what he calls "hermeneutical rules" from the time of Aristotle (384-322 BC) to the present. These hermeneutical rules were related to the formal study of a literary work, including attending to its grammatical rules, the particular language usage of an author, and its historical location. In other words, Bultmann recognizes the role of philology and believes that it should be done in as objective a manner as possible, while avoiding and eliminating prejudices that might interfere with one's exegesis. However, Bultmann goes further and criticizes this kind of rule-based hermeneutic for failing to grasp the importance of arriving at understanding of the text. Understanding is not based on these hermeneutical rules, but upon other factors, which he believes that Schleiermacher, Wilhelm Dilthey (1833-1911), R. G. Collingwood (1889-1943), and Heidegger grasped. Bultmann did not embrace all that Schleiermacher, Heidegger, and the others proposed, but he was especially sympathetic to the notion of a personal relationship between text and interpreter.

On the basis of this perspective, Bultmann proposes instead that understanding is based upon a number of factors. These include: (1) Preunderstanding. Bultmann believes that understanding of a text is always determined by a prior understanding of the text and what it is about. This involves a sympathetic understanding or what Bultmann calls a "living relationship" with the subject matter of the text. This is well illustrated in the process of translation, which is predicated upon the translator having a familiarity with the text and its environment. (2) Existential Encounter. More to the point, Bultmann believes that the interpreter needs to have an open rather than closed pre-understanding, so that one can have an existential encounter with the text. This existential dimension involves asking fundamental questions about the nature of oneself and of human existence. One who is able to understand, according to Bultmann, must be existentially alive and concerned. One must be further open to what the text has to say about the possibilities for human existence, including one's own existence. (3) Questioning the Text. It follows from one's pre-understanding of the text, a point that Bultmann seems to have learned from the philosopher and historian Collingwood and passed on to Hans-Georg Gadamer (1900-2002), that the interpreter must formulate a particular question, with a specific objective for understanding the text in mind. Bultmann realizes that there are wide varieties of types of texts, ranging from scientific texts to historical texts to philosophical texts to poetry. Each requires different objectives and hence that different questions be posed in order to arrive at understanding. Literary texts, and here Bultmann also includes the Bible, are those that are most amenable to answering questions about the nature of human existence. (4) The Hermeneutical Circle. Fergusson (*Rudolf Bultmann*, 52-59) notes that Bultmann formulates a hermeneutical circle, in which there is a reciprocal spiral of growing understanding as the interpreter brings a pre-understanding to interpretation of the text and then that pre-understanding is confirmed, denied, or modified in dialogue with the text, as one goes through the process of critical interpretation.

Existential Hermeneutics

There has been repeated question about the influence of Heidegger on Bultmann's existential hermeneutics, especially after Heidegger's involvement with National Socialism. Some have seen a large influence of Heidegger on Bultmann's intellectual development, while recent interpreters, such as Thiselton (*Two Horizons,* 275-83) and Fergusson (*Rudolf Bultmann,* 64-69), have seen Heidegger as helping Bultmann to find the language that helped him deal with questions that had already been raised in his own mind regarding human existence. In either case, there are a number of points that have been identified (especially by Fergusson, 65-66) where Heidegger had direct influence upon Bultmann's thought. The first is in the area of pre-understanding. Bultmann's prior questioning of the relation of God to humanity, in which he came to believe that questions about God are really questions about what it means to be human, is reinforced by Heidegger's belief that there is an innate awareness of Being in the human that philosophy (or, in Bultmann's instance, theology) can help to articulate. Bultmann too believes that humans have some inherent understanding of God (Bultmann's form of natural theology). The second concerns the life of faith. Bultmann speaks of life before faith and life under faith. This formulation correlates with Heidegger's assessment of the human dilemma as the question of what it means to live an authentic versus an inauthentic existence. The third area involves differentiation between *existential* and *existentiell. Existential* questions are concerned with questions of Being, whereas *existentiell* ones are concerned with lived experience. Bultmann uses these categories as a way of showing the importance of theology, which tells how one should live when philosophy identifies that one should live an authentic life.

In many ways, Bultmann exemplifies his principles of existential hermeneutics most readily in his understanding of Paul, as found in the second volume of his *New Testament Theology.* This part of the theology is divided into two parts: man prior to the revelation of faith, and man under faith — i.e., inauthentic and authentic existence. Whereas Bultmann did not consider Paul a systematic or philosophical thinker, he characterizes Paul in terms that create a philosophical understanding of him. He describes Paul as one who is concerned with knowledge of both God and humanity, in which faith and knowing are reciprocal. As a result, Paul is not concerned with an abstract notion of God but one in relationship with humanity. As Bultmann states, "Every assertion about God is simultaneously an assertion about man and vice versa. For this reason and in this sense Paul's theology is, at the same time, anthropology" (*New Testament Theology*, vol. I, 191). Thus, statements about God relate to his relations with humanity and statements about humanity are about God. Therefore, Bultmann states, "Paul's theology can best be treated as his doctrine of man: first, of man prior to the revelation of faith, and second, of man under faith, for in this way the anthropological and soteriological orientation of Paul's theology is brought out" (vol. I, 190). Bultmann then goes on to describe Paul's terminology for speaking of human existence, "body" *(soma),* and what it means to lead a life of existence prior to faith. This is opposed to what it means to be justified. For Bultmann, who remained a Lutheran in his theology as well, justification is the condition of being under faith and having life, the essence of salvation.

History of Religions

The history-of-religions school of thought had an important influence upon Bultmann's hermeneutics. In light of his development as a dialectical and existential thinker, some scholars are inclined to minimize the influence of the history of religions upon Bultmann's development and subsequent career. However, recent discussion, especially by his former student, Helmut Koester, has made it clear that Bultmann was formed in the spirit of the history of religions. Koester outlines six general perspectives of characteristic work done in history-of-religions research: (1) Biblical concepts are mythical and eschatological, not moral and intellectual; (2) Christianity is syncretistic; (3) the center of religious experience is cult; (4) transmission of religious knowledge is by means of folklore and oral traditions; (5) religious experience is irrational; and (6) the understanding of religion must go beyond any one religion ("Early Christianity," 271).

The trajectory of Bultmann's development as a history-of-religions scholar illustrates some of the major interpretive trends in his thought. As noted above, Bultmann began his dissertation under Weiss and completed it under Heitmüller. Both were members of the history-of-religions school. There were a number of others who were part of the history-of-religions movement who also influenced Bultmann. The primary ones include Gunkel, William Wrede (1859-1906), Bousset, and Ernst Troeltsch (1865-1923), all of whom were at one time together in Göttingen, the seat of this methodological movement. Others were drawn into this framework of understanding, including the classicist Ulrich von Wilamowitz-Moellendorff (1848-1931), the biblical scholar Julius Wellhausen (1844-1918), and Otto, all of whom were in Göttingen at one time, and others including the classicists Albrecht Dieterich (1866-1908), Hermann Usener (1834-1905), Richard Reitzenstein (1861-1931), and Eduard Norden (1868-1941). During his career, Bultmann also supervised research theses in this area, by such students as Schlier, Käsemann, Bornkamm, and Jonas. Bultmann's own publications began in the area of history of religions. His dissertation on common elements between cynic-stoic diatribe and Pauline preaching is concerned with literary patterns that cross religious boundaries, and he followed this with two articles on ethics in the stoic philosopher Epictetus (AD 55-135) in 1912. His work on form criticism in the synoptic Gospels, published in 1921 and dedicated to Heitmüller, is a major work in the history of religions, as it again is concerned with literary transmission according to patterns that cross religious boundaries. He also published a major article on Gospel form criticism in the second edition of *Die Religion in Geschichte und Gegenwart (RGG)* in 1927-1932. This stream of interest culminated in his small book titled *Jesus,* which appeared in a German series called (in English translation) "The Immortals: The Spiritual Heroes of Humanity in Their Life and Work," published in 1926. Bultmann continued his interest in history of religions by undertaking to investigate myth in the New Testament. This resulted in an article on the religious background of the New Testament in 1923, on Mandaean and Manichean sources for John's Gospel, especially that of a redeemer myth in 1925, and a major two-part article on John's Gospel that explored a number of topics in 1928-1930. Part of this article was the basis for Bultmann's article on "truth" (*alētheia;* ἀλήθεια) in the *Theological Dictionary of the New Testament* (1933), which Koester thinks may have determined the course by which articles in subsequent volumes of this work were composed ("Early Christianity," 276). Then Bultmann published his commentary on John's Gospel in 1941, showing its dependence upon Gnosticism. His final work in this area was his 1949 book titled "Early Christianity in the Setting of Ancient Religions" (ET *Primitive Christianity*).

By Koester's account, many, if not most, of the major textual and exegetical works that Bultmann wrote were heavily influenced by history-of-religions thought — even if he departed from the major tenets of the school on occasion ("Early Christianity," 272-75). Bultmann did not apparently believe in the irrationality of religion, and did not try to discover a universal pattern of religious belief, but he did explore a number of the major tenets of the history of religions. These include his examination of the Bible from a mythological and eschatological viewpoint. Bultmann was heavily influenced by the eschatological perspectives of Weiss and Wrede, and especially by Martin Kähler (1835-1912), who minimized the ability to find the historical Jesus. Much of Bultmann's writing explores the syncretistic nature of Christianity, even if on occasion Bultmann also distinguishes Christianity from other religions, for example on the question of a redeemer myth. Bultmann's exploration of form criticism is a direct examination of how oral traditions were transmitted within early Christianity, on the basis of parallels found in other religious groups. Bultmann also explores various areas of folklore in both Christianity and other religions. Even though Bultmann did not discover, or even appear to make a huge effort toward discovering, a general notion of religion, the fact that he willingly and on numerous occasions undertook to examine the relationship of Christian texts to those of other religions indicates that he saw some common basis that would allow and even encourage such intellectual inquiry. A number of these works, especially those on form criticism and the synoptic tradition, continue to have influence.

Demythologization

The final hermeneutical position of Bultmann to discuss is his concept of demythologization, a position that is inextricably related to his existential hermeneutics. In 1941, Bultmann read a paper, titled "New Testament and Mythology," to a conference of pastors of the Confessing Church. When published, the essay made Bultmann famous, or infamous, depending upon one's perspective. In this essay, Bultmann begins simply by stating that New Testament cosmology is mythical, in which the world is depicted as a three-storied building. God and heavenly beings are on top, earth is in the middle, and the underworld or hell is underneath. This world is occupied by supernatural beings, miracles occur, and humans do not control their fate. When the New Testament speaks of redemption, it assumes this worldview. However, Bultmann continues, all of this is mythological, and its origins can be traced to other contemporary sources. As a result, the proclamation of the Bible cannot be believed by modern people, as no one holds to this worldview anymore. What are we to do so that modern people will respond to the preaching of the gospel? Bultmann's goal is not to eliminate Christian proclamation, but neither is he interested in saving it through selective means. Instead, one must understand myth. Myth is not designed to offer an objective view of the world but to "express man's understanding of himself in the world in which he lives" ("New Testament and Mythology," 10). In other words, myth should be interpreted anthropologically, or, better, existentially. The New Testament itself, Bultmann believes, encourages this kind of an interpretation. Rather than dismissing myth as did liberal theology or simply treating it as a depiction of religious life as did the history of religions, Bultmann believes that an existentialist interpretation is not just the best but the only way forward. Bultmann then engages in demythologizing the major tenets of Christianity, including human existence and faith as authentic existence, redemption as self-commitment and love, and the death and resurrection of Jesus Christ not as involving a physical resurrection (who can understand such a thing as other than myth, Bultmann asks) but as one cosmic redemptive event.

Strong reactions to Bultmann's paper on demythologization were to be expected, and they prompted a number of significant responses to his work in the 1950s and 1960s. Some condemned him, while others recognized that he was not saying anything new in this paper that he had not already articulated in the course of his research. Some even claimed he had not gone far enough (see Jaspers and Bultmann, *Myth*). Since then, the responses have continued, although, whereas once demythologization defined Bultmann, now he is heralded more for his New Testament research. There were a number of volumes titled *Kerygma and Myth* that contained continuing responses and discussion of the topic, and a number of well-known books that either praised or condemned Bultmann's program. Some criticized him for taking something essential away from religion by eliminating every element of myth, while others believed that he had taken something essential away from Christianity by eliminating its historical groundedness. Bultmann's view of the death and resurrection of Jesus Christ garnered major criticism, because of its ambiguity regarding the meaning, significance, and linkage of these two important notions. One trenchant criticism was that Bultmann had failed to eliminate the myth of the exclusivity of Christian revelation (Ogden, *Christ without Myth*).

One sees in Bultmann's demythologization a number of correlations among Heidegger's philosophical thought (the desire to address the situation of contemporary humanity), liberal theology of the nineteenth century (the anti-supernatural presupposition based upon scientific naturalism), and the history-of-religions school of thought (the attempt to find common religious origins and explanations).

Bultmann's Hermeneutical Legacy: The New Hermeneutic

Bultmann has not had the enduring hermeneutical legacy that Barth has had. Whereas Bultmann continues to be known and recognized as a biblical interpreter, few are as concerned with his hermeneutical agenda. In some ways, the issues that Bultmann faced appear dated and distinctly temporally located. Nevertheless, Bultmann had an appreciable hermeneutical legacy in the New Hermeneutic. The New Hermeneutic is associated with the writings of two of Bultmann's students already mentioned above, Ernst Fuchs, his successor at the University of Marburg, and Gerhard Ebeling. The New Hermeneutic, a distinctly theological hermeneutical model derived from but intent on building upon the philosophical and especially the existential thinking of Bultmann, was developed and promoted not only by Ebeling and Fuchs but by such scholars as Robert Funk (1926-2005) and Carl Braaten (1929-), and had its time of greatest interpretive significance in the 1950s and 1960s. Ebeling and Fuchs, independently though with common interests, each took up the challenge of Bultmann's existential hermeneutics in a practical attempt to show how the familiar biblical text could be seen to speak in a new way for the modern interpreter. In his definitive essay on the New Hermeneutic ("The New Hermeneutic"; repr. in *Thiselton on Hermeneutics;* cf. *Hermeneutics*, 190-95), Thiselton notes that the New Hermeneutic was concerned with asking questions of language not just existence, developing a theory of understanding, recognizing the role of empathetic common understanding, and characterizing the role of language as performative, or what Fuchs and Ebeling called word-events. The New Hermeneutic was popular because of its attempt to dissolve the subject-object divide in interpretation and to be transparent to the text, which was seen to be experiential and not propositional. The New Hermeneutic, though it raised important hermeneutical questions, has now largely faded from the hermeneutical scene as a hermeneutical stance to be consciously embraced.

A Critical Appraisal of Bultmann's Hermeneutics

Bultmann continues to exercise significant influence over New Testament studies, but less directly in hermeneutical circles. His adoption of dialectical theology and his powerful biblical scholarship provided a strong impetus for the dialectical movement. However, questions remain about his contribution to hermeneutics and interpretation.

Neo-orthodoxy. Bultmann is often categorized as a neo-orthodox thinker, along with Barth and others. However, insofar as such a term has validity, it is perhaps most questionable for Bultmann. On the one hand, there is a distinct line of thought in Bultmann that identifies with the use of orthodox theological terminology, even though he wishes to redefine it. His emphasis upon demythologization clearly wishes to retain the kerygma or proclamation of the early church while reinterpreting such notions as the cross, redemption, and resurrection in anthropological or existential terms. In this sense, Bultmann is unquestionably a neo-orthodox thinker. On the other hand, there is much in Bultmann's work that never moves very far away from theological liberalism, including its relationship with the history-of-religions school. Much of Bultmann's exegetical work, including some of his enduring contributions to scholarship, emerge from this ideological framework.

Bultmann and Heidegger. Bultmann's relationship to Heidegger raises questions about the significance of his own hermeneutical thought. Bultmann seems to have adopted and adapted many of his fundamental interpretive concepts from Heidegger. These would include the notions of existentialism such as authentic and inauthentic existence, attention to being, and the importance of pre-understanding, among others. However, Bultmann does not develop Heidegger's thoughts in significant ways. Instead, he appears simply to transport them into the framework of Christianity, so that Paul's encounter with the risen Christ becomes an experience of authentic existence in moving from the law to being under faith.

Bultmann and Hermeneutics. A third and final criticism — and perhaps the most important one — is to question whether Bultmann actually developed a hermeneutical framework or whether he was more concerned about negotiating the difficult road between theological liberalism and modernism and the orthodox language of German Lutheranism. Such a position can be neither verified nor falsified. In the end, as O'Neill states, according to Bultmann, "Christianity's uniqueness consists then . . . in its preaching a God who has no existence and in promulgating an ethics with no content save obedience" (*Bible's Authority*, 306). It does not appear that Bultmann developed significantly in his thought. The notions and concepts that he developed in the 1920s as a student and young teacher of New Testament — including his dialectical theology, his still liberal theologically inclined history-of-religions approach, his appeal to existential categories from Heidegger, and his anti-supernaturalism that emerged more openly in his demythologization — even if they form an uncomfortable mix, became the platform for his continuing scholarship and work.

Conclusion

Dialectical theology is both a product of its theological environment, and a theological system of continuing constructive influence. On the one hand, dialectical theology and its resulting hermeneutics is a reaction against theological liberalism, with its reliance upon higher criticism, and therefore a product of its own cultural, historical, and theological times. Nevertheless, as we have seen above, both Barth and Bultmann reacted in different ways to the hermeneutics of liberalism. Even though dialectical theology is clearly an attempt to find a new theological and hermeneutical language in light of the demise of liberal theology, its dialectical synthesis is dependent upon other competing philosophical modes of thought, such as existentialism. On the other hand, dialectical theology demonstrates by its dialectical method a hermeneutical robustness as it attempts to find a common language of neo-orthodoxy to encompass the results of modernism within an orthodox framework. Some of the results of this continual mediation are the recognition that dialectical hermeneutics has more than passing resemblance to postmodern thought as it attempts to transcend foundationalism and to propose means of interpreting the Bible in a modern, postliberal context.

REFERENCE WORKS

Baird, William. *History of New Testament Research*. II. *From Jonathan Edwards to Rudolf Bultmann*. Minneapolis: Fortress, 2003.

Barth, Karl. *Anselm: Fides Quaerens Intellectum. Anselm's Proof of the Existence of God in the Context of His Theological Scheme*, trans. Ian W. Robertson of 2nd ed. of 1958. Richmond, VA: John Knox, 1960 (1931).

————. *Church Dogmatics*, ed. Geoffrey W. Bromiley and T. F. Torrance. Edinburgh: T. & T. Clark, 1936-1969, 1975.

————. *Dogmatics in Outline*, trans. G. T. Thompson. New York: Harper & Brothers, 1959 (1948).

————. *The Epistle to the Philippians*, trans. James W. Leitch. London: SCM Press, 1962 (1927).

————. *The Epistle to the Romans*, trans. Edwyn C. Hoskyns from the 6th German edition. London: Oxford University Press, 1933 (1919; 2nd ed. 1922).

————. *Evangelical Theology: An Introduction*, trans. Grover Foley. Grand Rapids: Eerdmans, 1963 (1962).

————. *God Here and Now*, ed. Ruth Nanda Anshen. New York: Harper & Row, 1964 (including "The Church: The Living Congregation of the Living Lord Jesus Christ").

————. *Protestant Theology in the Nineteenth Century*. Valley Forge, PA: Judson, 1973.

Braaten, Carl E. *History and Hermeneutics*. New Directions in Theology Today, vol. 2. London: Lutterworth, 1968.

Braaten, Carl E., and Roy A. Harrisville, eds. *Kerygma and History: A Symposium on the Theology of Rudolf Bultmann*. Nashville: Abingdon, 1962.

Bultmann, Rudolf. "ἀλήθεια." In *Theological Dictionary of the New Testament*, ed. Gerhard Kittel and Gerhard Friedrich, trans. and ed. Geoffrey W. Bromiley, vol. 1, pp. 232-51. Grand Rapids: Eerdmans, 1964 (1933).

————. *Essays Philosophical and Theological*, trans. James C. G. Greig. London: SCM Press, 1955.

————. *Existence and Faith: Shorter Writings of Rudolf Bultmann*, ed. Schubert M. Ogden. New York: Meridian, 1960.

————. "General Truths and Christian Proclamation." *History and Hermeneutic*, ed. Robert W. Funk, pp. 153-62. New York: Harper & Row, 1967.

————. *The Gospel of John: A Commentary*, trans. G. R. Beasley-Murray. Oxford: Blackwell, 1971 (1941).

————. "The Gospels (Form)." In *Twentieth Century Theology in the Making*, ed. Jaroslav Pelikan, vol. 1, pp. 86-92. London: Fontana, 1969 (1927-1932).

————. *History and Eschatology*. Edinburgh: Edinburgh University Press, 1957.

————. *The History of the Synoptic Tradition*, trans. John Marsh. Oxford: Blackwell, 1963 (1921).

————. *Jesus and the Word*, trans. Louise Pettibone Smith and Erminie Huntress. London: Ivor Nicholson & Watson, 1935 (1926).

————. *Jesus Christ and Mythology.* New York: Scribner's, 1958.

————. "New Testament and Mythology." In *Kerygma and Myth: A Theological Debate,* ed. Hans Werner Bartsch, trans. Reginald H. Fuller, pp. 1-44. London: SPCK, 1953 (1941).

————. *New Testament and Mythology and Other Basic Writings,* ed. and trans. Schubert M. Ogden. Philadelphia: Fortress, 1984.

————. *Primitive Christianity in Its Contemporary Setting,* trans. Reginald H. Fuller. Philadelphia: Fortress, 1956 (1949).

————. "Das religiöse Moment in der ethischen Unterweisung Epiktets und das Neue Testament." *Zeitschrift für die neutestamentliche Wissenschaft* 1 (1912): 97-110, 177-91.

————. "Der religionsgeschichtliche Hintergrund des Prologs zum Johannes-Evangelium." In EUXARISTHRION: *Hermann Gunkel zum 60. Geburtstag,* 2.3-26. 2 vols. Göttingen: Vandenhoeck & Ruprecht, 1923.

————. *Der Stil der paulinischen Predigt und die Kynisch-stoische Diatribe.* Göttingen: Vandenhoeck & Ruprecht, 1910.

————. *Theology of the New Testament,* 2 vols., trans. Kendrick Grobel. London: SCM Press, 1951, 1955 (1948-1951).

————. "Untersuchungen zum Johannesevangelium." *Zeitschrift für die neutestamentliche Wissenschaft* 27 (1928): 113-63; 29 (1930): 169-92.

————. *What Is Theology?,* ed. Eberhard Jüngel and Klaus W. Müller, trans. Roy A. Harrisville. Minneapolis: Fortress, 1997 (1984).

Busch, Eberhard. *Barth.* Abingdon Pillars of Theology. Nashville: Abingdon, 2008.

————. *Karl Barth: His Life from Letters and Autobiographical Texts,* trans. John Bowden. Philadelphia: Fortress, 1976.

Cochrane, Arthur C. *The Existentialists and God.* Dubuque, IA: University of Dubuque Press, n.d.

Come, A. B. *An Introduction to Barth's Dogmatics for Preachers.* London: SCM Press, 1963.

Davis, George W. *Existentialism and Theology: An Investigation of the Contribution of Rudolf Bultmann to Theological Thought.* New York: Philosophical Library, 1957.

Dawes, Gregory W. *The Historical Jesus Question: The Challenge of History to Religious Authority.* Louisville: Westminster/John Knox, 2001.

Ebeling, Gerhard. "Theology and the Evidentness of the Ethical." In *Translating Theology into the Modern Age,* ed. Robert W. Funk, pp. 96-129. New York: Harper & Row, 1965.

————. "Time and Word." In *The Future of Our Religious Past: Essays in Hon-*

our of Rudolf Bultmann, ed. James M. Robinson, pp. 247-66. London: SCM Press, 1971 (1964).

―――. *Word and Faith,* trans. James W. Leitch. Philadelphia: Fortress, 1963 (1960) (including "Word of God and Hermeneutics" and "Dietrich Bonhoeffer").

Fergusson, David. "Bultmann, Rudolf (1884-1976)." In *Historical Handbook of Major Biblical Interpreters,* ed. Donald K. McKim, pp. 449-56. Downers Grove, IL: InterVarsity Press, 1998.

―――. *Rudolf Bultmann.* London: Continuum, 1992.

Franke, John R. *Barth for Armchair Theologians.* Louisville: Westminster John Knox Press, 2006.

Fuchs, Ernst. "The Hermeneutical Problem." In *The Future of Our Religious Past: Essays in Honour of Rudolf Bultmann,* ed. James M. Robinson, pp. 267-78. London: SCM Press, 1971 (1964).

―――. "Must One Believe in Jesus if He Wants to Believe in God?" In *The Bultmann School of Biblical Interpretation: New Directions?,* ed. Robert W. Funk, pp. 147-68. New York: Harper & Row, 1965.

―――. *Studies of the Historical Jesus,* trans. Andrew Scobie. Studies in Biblical Theology 42. London: SCM, 1964 (1960) (with essays on theology and historical criticism, translation and proclamation, and two on language-event).

Funk, Robert W. *Language, Hermeneutic, and Word of God: The Problem of Language in the New Testament and Contemporary Theology.* New York: Harper & Row, 1966.

Harrisville, Roy A., and Walter Sundberg. *The Bible in Modern Culture: Baruch Spinoza to Brevard Childs.* 2nd ed. Grand Rapids: Eerdmans, 2002.

Henderson, Ian. *Rudolf Bultmann.* The Makers of Contemporary Theology. Richmond, VA: John Knox, 1965.

Heron, Alasdair I. C. *A Century of Protestant Theology.* Philadelphia: Westminster, 1980.

Hordern, William E. *A Layman's Guide to Protestant Theology.* Rev. ed. New York: Macmillan, 1968.

Hunsinger, George. *How to Read Karl Barth: The Shape of His Theology.* Oxford: Oxford University Press, 1991.

Jaspers, Karl, and Rudolph Bultmann. *Myth and Christianity: An Inquiry into the Possibility of Religion without Myth,* ed. Norbert Guterman. New York: Noonday, 1958.

Johnson, William Stacey. "Barth, Karl (1886-1968)." In *Historical Handbook of*

Major Biblical Interpreters, ed. Donald K. McKim, pp. 433-39. Downers Grove, IL: InterVarsity Press, 1998.

————. *The Mystery of God: Karl Barth and the Postmodern Foundations of Theology.* Louisville: Westminster/John Knox, 1997.

Jones, Geraint Vaughan. *Christology and Myth in the New Testament.* London: George Allen & Unwin, 1956.

Jüngel, Eberhard. *Karl Barth: A Theological Legacy,* trans. Garrett E. Paul. Philadelphia: Westminster, 1986.

Kegley, Charles W., ed. *The Theology of Rudolf Bultmann.* New York: Harper & Row, 1966.

Koester, Helmut. "Early Christianity from the Perspective of the History of Religions: Rudolf Bultmann's Contribution." In his *Paul and His World: Interpreting the New Testament in Its Context,* pp. 267-78. Minneapolis: Fortress, 2007.

McCormack, Bruce L. *Karl Barth's Critically Realistic Dialectical Theology.* Oxford: Clarendon, 1995.

MacDonald, Neil B. *Karl Barth and the Strange New World within the Bible: Barth, Wittgenstein, and the Metadilemmas of the Enlightenment.* Bletchley, UK: Paternoster, 2000.

McKnight, Edgar V. *Meaning in Texts: The Historical Shaping of a Narrative Hermeneutics.* Philadelphia: Fortress, 1978.

Macquarrie, John. *The Scope of Demythologizing: Bultmann and His Critics.* London: SCM Press, 1960.

Malet, André. *The Thought of Rudolf Bultmann,* trans. Richard Strachan. Garden City, NY: Doubleday, 1969 (1962).

Miegge, Giovanni. *Gospel and Myth in the Thought of Rudolf Bultmann,* trans. Stephen Neill. Richmond, VA: John Knox Press, 1960 (1956).

Morgan, Robert. "Rudolf Bultmann." In *The Modern Theologians: An Introduction to Christian Theology in the Twentieth Century,* ed. David F. Ford, pp. 108-33. 2 vols. Oxford: Blackwell, 1989.

Morgan, Robert, with John Barton. *Biblical Interpretation.* Oxford: Oxford University Press, 1988.

Ogden, Schubert M. *Christ without Myth.* New York: Harper & Row, 1961.

O'Neill, J. C. *The Bible's Authority: A Portrait Gallery of Thinkers from Lessing to Bultmann.* Edinburgh: T. & T. Clark, 1991.

Perrin, Norman. *The Promise of Bultmann.* Philadelphia: Fortress, 1969.

Porter, Stanley E. "What Difference Does Hermeneutics Make? Hermeneutical Theory Applied." *Jian Dao* 34/*Pastoral Journal* 27 (July 2010): 1-50.

Provence, Thomas E. "The Sovereign Subject Matter: Hermeneutics in the

Church Dogmatics." In *A Guide to Contemporary Hermeneutics: Major Trends in Biblical Interpretation,* ed. Donald K. McKim, pp. 241-62. Grand Rapids: Eerdmans, 1986.

Riches, John K. *A Century of New Testament Study.* Cambridge: Lutterworth, 1993.

Robinson, James M., ed. *The Future of Our Religious Past: Essays in Honour of Rudolf Bultmann,* trans. Charles E. Carlston and Robert P. Scharlemann. London: SCM Press, 1971 (1964) (see Robinson's "Introduction").

Thiselton, Anthony C. *Hermeneutics: An Introduction.* Grand Rapids: Eerdmans, 2009.

―――. "The New Hermeneutic." In *New Testament Interpretation: Essays in Principles and Methods,* ed. I. Howard Marshall, pp. 308-33. Grand Rapids: Eerdmans, 1977.

―――. *The Two Horizons: New Testament Hermeneutics and Philosophical Description with Special Reference to Heidegger, Bultmann, Gadamer, and Wittgenstein.* Grand Rapids: Eerdmans, 1980.

Ward, Graham. "Barth, Modernity, and Postmodernity." In *The Cambridge Companion to Karl Barth,* ed. John Webster, pp. 274-95. Cambridge: Cambridge University Press, 2000.

Watson, Francis. "The Bible." In *The Cambridge Companion to Karl Barth,* ed. John Webster, pp. 52-71. Cambridge: Cambridge University Press, 2000.

Weber, Otto. *Karl Barth's Church Dogmatics: An Introductory Report on Volumes I:I to III:4,* trans. Arthur C. Cochrane. Philadelphia: Westminster, 1953.

Webster, John. *Karl Barth.* Outstanding Christian Thinkers. London: Continuum, 2000.

TEN

Theological Hermeneutics:
Anthony Thiselton and Kevin Vanhoozer

Introduction

Theological hermeneutics is a broadly conceived category that encompasses a variety of interpretive models and practices. They have in common the desire to find an appropriate hermeneutic that is faithful to the Christian theological tradition. In some ways, theological hermeneutics is a very recent development in hermeneutical and biblical interpretive thought, having been developed within the last quarter of the twentieth century as an attempt to bring philosophical interests to bear on theology and related biblical interpretation. In other ways, however, theological hermeneutics — or approaching the Bible first and foremost, if not exclusively, as a theological document — is an interpretive method that is as old as the early church itself, which performed all biblical interpretation in light of the church's understanding of the coming of Jesus Christ. Theological hermeneutics is thus seen as harking back to an ancient, established, and biblically grounded form of theological exegesis, and reacting against what is often seen to be the sterile readings of the Bible generated by those dependent upon historical criticism. Such an approach is today often given the more specific label of theological interpretation. There has been a significant groundswell of interest in theological readings of the Bible that clearly fall within the scope of and are dependent upon the varied approach that has come to be labeled as theological hermeneutics, including forms of theological interpretation. Two of the most important foundational advocates of theological hermeneutics are Anthony Thiselton and

Kevin Vanhoozer. Even though they approach the question of theological hermeneutics from differing initial perspectives, their common interest in philosophy and hermeneutics leads them in a number of similar directions. These hermeneutical tenets are made clear in a variety of major works on theological hermeneutics from these authors and others.

Anthony Thiselton

Anthony ("Tony") C. Thiselton (1937-) is a significant figure in biblical hermeneutics for a number of reasons. For many students of the Bible, both academic and otherwise, he has provided their first, and sometimes only, significant introduction to philosophically influenced hermeneutics. His work in hermeneutics is characterized by thorough examinations of the writings of the major philosophers, especially from Friedrich Schleiermacher (1768-1834) to the present, and detailed analysis of their arguments as he appropriates them for his theological hermeneutical stance. Besides his major works in hermeneutics, he is an accomplished New Testament scholar and has also profitably investigated the field of modern linguistics. As an active churchman throughout his life and professional career, Thiselton has also brought his theological interests to all areas of his scholarship. As a result, Thiselton pioneered theologically informed hermeneutics that focused upon the biblical text, and has exemplified this in works that show detailed and insightful exegesis.

Life and Influences

Thiselton was born in Surrey in the U.K. in 1937, and was a student at King's College London, where he received his B.D. and M.Th. degrees. His teaching career began at Bristol University, but after a year as the Stephenson Fellow at the University of Sheffield, he joined the Department of Biblical Studies there, where he taught from 1971 to 1985, reaching the rank of senior lecturer. During his time in Sheffield, he completed the Ph.D. at the University. He later became principal of St. John's College Nottingham and then St. John's College, Durham, two Anglican theological colleges, before becoming professor of Christian theology in 1992 at the University of Nottingham, from which he retired as professor emeritus in 2000. Upon retirement, he became research professor in Christian theology at University College Chester. Besides fulfilling various pastoral charges, Thiselton was also a Canon Theologian at Leicester Cathedral and Southwell Minster, as well as serving on various important committees of the Anglican Church. Thiselton suffered a major stroke in 2007, while his major book on hermeneutics and doctrine was in the final stages of editing for publication. He has since recovered and returned to active scholarship.

Thiselton's hermeneutically based theological interpretation of the Bible can be traced in his major written works. His first major work, a revision of his doctoral thesis, was *The Two Horizons: New Testament Hermeneutics and Philosophical Description* (1980), which treats in significant detail the work of Martin Heidegger (1889-1976), Rudolf Bultmann (1884-1976), Hans-Georg Gadamer (1900-2002), and Ludwig Wittgenstein (1889-1951). This was followed by *The Responsibility of Hermeneutics* (1992), co-authored with two literary scholars (Roger Lundin and Clarence Walhout) as a result of a year as visiting professor at Calvin College in Grand Rapids, Michigan, and later expanded as *The Promise of Hermeneutics* (1999). Thiselton continued his exploration of major hermeneutical developments from a theological standpoint in his *New Horizons in Hermeneutics* (1992), which attempts to develop a new model of reading the Bible. In *Interpreting God and the Postmodern Self* (1995), Thiselton applies Trinitarian theology to a critique of postmodernism. His only major work devoted entirely to biblical studies, a major commentary on the Greek text of 1 Corinthians, was published in 2000, with a revised and shortened version for pastoral use published in 2006. Thiselton issued a *Concise Encyclopedia of the Philosophy of Religion* in 2002. His last major constructive work of hermeneutics is *The Hermeneutics of Doctrine* (2007), although he has since then published a historically based introduction to hermeneutics that synthesizes and further develops some of his previous work (2009), a brief introduction to Paul (2009), and a reception-history commentary on 1 and 2 Thessalonians (2011). In 2006, he published *Thiselton on Hermeneutics,* a collection of mostly previously published articles and chapters along with excerpts from several of his books, and some new essays. On his retirement, Thiselton was honored with a volume of essays titled *After Pentecost: Language and Biblical Interpretation* being dedicated to him in 2001. Thiselton's works are characterized by a detailed taxonomic approach to any issue that he tackles, including extensive quotation to offer direct evidence of the person or topic being covered.

Theological Hermeneutics

Thiselton's ongoing project has been, first, the incorporation and critique of philosophical hermeneutics for biblical studies, and second, the development of a robust multidisciplinary theological hermeneutics that retains the integrity of both hermeneutical thought and biblical and theological studies. In several essays, Thiselton has retrospectively charted the development of his thought in both of these major areas, and he clearly believes that all of his major publications — encapsulated to a large extent in the collection *Thiselton on Hermeneutics* — have contributed to this progressive development. As a result, the first major portion of his scholarly career was devoted to providing the analysis that allowed him to develop his own major proposals in the second half. The progress of his thought can be divided into three major periods, according to three major questions that lie behind his thought.

What Is the Scope of Theological Hermeneutics?

Although trained as a theologian and New Testament scholar, early on Thiselton began to explore both practical and theoretical issues in hermeneutics. The practical issue was raised by the fact that there was little accessible hermeneutical scholarship available in English for students interested in the topic. The theoretical issue was raised by his own exploration of theological hermeneutics. The first major question that Thiselton seems to have raised is that of "What is the scope of theological hermeneutics?" He at first attempted to answer this question by examining traditional hermeneutics. He discovered that traditional hermeneutics, as found for example in the Protestant Reformers, was not unaware of problems of context and other interpretive difficulties, but that it was in a pre-theoretical period so far as rigorous and philosophically informed hermeneutical thought was concerned. He consequently rejected the common notion of hermeneutics as traditional exegesis or simply technique. Instead, Thiselton's theoretical entrance into hermeneutical thought came by way of offering a critique of the New Hermeneutic. The New Hermeneutic — associated in particular with the writings of Ernst Fuchs (1903-1983) and Gerhard Ebeling (1912-2001) — was a practical attempt to see how the familiar biblical text could be seen to speak in a new way for the modern interpreter. In his incisive essay on the New Hermeneutic ("The New Hermeneutic"; repr. in *Thiselton on Hermeneutics*), Thiselton notes that the interpretive movement was concerned with raising questions of language, developing a theory of understanding, recognizing the role of empathetic common understanding, and describing the role of language as performative.

Whereas Thiselton has much sympathy with many of the tenets of the New Hermeneutic, his critical dialogue with it led to the development of major platforms of much of his later hermeneutical theory. Thiselton, in an affirmation of Cartesian thought, argues against the loss of the subject-object divide in the New Hermeneutic. He believes there is a place for the active subject, but that the object of interpretation is not dissolved. Thiselton wishes to assert that hermeneutics is about more than simply reading the Bible anew but actually correctly interpreting it. This means that theology must be more than simply language about the individual person and must not devolve into anthropology or the doctrine of humanity. Thiselton further pulls back from the dissolution of the space between interpretive horizons and instead endorses Gadamer's notion of two horizons. Thiselton is especially appreciative of the language-oriented emphasis of the New Hermeneutic, in recognizing that interpretation takes place "through" language. Thus, as Thiselton recognizes along with the New Hermeneutic, language is performative. However, Thiselton disputes the linguistic basis of the New Hermeneutic and its view of performative language. The New Hermeneutic wants to see language as reality, whereas Thiselton appropriates the performative language perspective of the ordinary language philosophers J. L. Austin (1911-1960) and John R. Searle (1932-). For Thiselton, language is performative according to institutionalized conditions and specific conventions. The New Hermeneutic tended to favor the pictorial, existential, and kerygmatic language of the parables, whereas there is cognitive and factual language in the Bible as well, some of it addressed to those who are already part of the community of faith. In this sense, an adequate hermeneutic must be able to be multifaceted, and not only deal with one type of performative language. Thiselton draws upon Ferdinand de Saussure's (1857-1913) structuralism, especially the arbitrary relation of the sign and signification, in which the word is not the thing, to dissolve this realist tendency. Finally, rather than emphasizing imperatival language over descriptive language, Thiselton emphasizes the various performative possibilities of language within institutionalized contexts that make such language meaningful.

One sees in Thiselton's attempt to define the scope of theological hermeneutics several important characteristics of his work. One is wide exposure to the thought of other philosophers who might contribute to his theoretical understanding. Already at this stage, he benefits from the work of Heidegger, Gadamer, Bultmann, Wittgenstein, Austin, and Searle, among others. Another is that his exposure to the work of Austin and Searle leads to his adoption of speech-act theory as one of the most important elements of his hermeneutics.

What Is the Major Hermeneutical Question?

Once he had defined the scope of hermeneutics, Thiselton undertook to inquire about and describe a way forward in asking and answering the major hermeneutical question. His *Two Horizons* was instrumental in introducing philosophical hermeneutics to many biblical scholars who knew virtually nothing of its major thinkers. This work in many ways helped to clear the ground for a major movement forward in theological hermeneutics within biblical scholarship, because it clarified the central issues in hermeneutics and provided a foundation in the thought of several of the major thinkers so that a constructive hermeneutic could be developed.

The fundamental question that Thiselton asks is, "How do the two horizons of the ancient text and of modern readers actively *engage with each other creatively without merely bland, passive, domesticating assimilation?*" (*Thiselton on Hermeneutics*, 7; italics original). One can see his concern that both essential elements of the two horizons, the ancient and the modern, are respected. In order to provide a means of answering such a question, Thiselton examines the sweep of hermeneutics from Schleiermacher to the present. He builds on his previous insight that hermeneutics in the post-Schleiermacher tradition must be concerned with more than simply rules or technique, and focuses upon the philosophical systems of four major thinkers, Heidegger, Bultmann, Gadamer, and Wittgenstein. At the time, Thiselton did not think that Gadamer occupied the same position in philosophical circles as did the other three (*Two Horizons*, 24-25). In part perhaps through his own work, such is not the case today. Further, Thiselton believed that his major constructive insights came from his analysis of Wittgenstein (*Two Horizons*, xx).

In *Two Horizons,* Thiselton lays the foundation for his own "philosophical description" of these major thinkers by laying a firm and situated foundation for the wider field of philosophical hermeneutical thought, thus continuing the work of his first period. He notes the pastness of history (as opposed to those of the New Hermeneutic) but without wishing to exaggerate the concept of historical distance (against Dennis Nineham [1921-]). The study of the New Testament, and therefore theological hermeneutics, becomes a difficult but not insuperable problem to address. The difficulty can be addressed in part by first recognizing the importance of pre-understanding, and the role of the hermeneutical circle or spiral. From the time of Schleiermacher, there has been the recognition that there is some element of pre-understanding that is required in order to make understanding possible. One cannot say that one has genuinely understood or experienced something without having had some previous idea of what it is to experience such a thing. Regretting in part the use of the term "hermeneutical circle," Thiselton notes that there are two major ways that this metaphor is understood — the idea of interrogating the text, or the reciprocal relationship between the parts and the whole that serve to create mutual understanding, hence the better term "hermeneutical spiral." It is the hermeneutical spiral that provides for progressive understanding as the individual elements inform understanding of the larger entity, and the larger entity provides the interpretive context for the individual parts. Lastly, in moving away from traditional objectivist types of interpretation, Thiselton rejects the notion of a non-theological understanding of the New Testament and wishes to affirm that interpretation of the New Testament demands a theological pre-understanding.

Thiselton's interest in the four major philosophers noted above indicates further his interest in issues of language in hermeneutics (we will discuss speech-act theory, which does not materially enter into this stage of his thought, below). Thiselton positions his inquiry upon the foundation of Saussure's linguistics in two key ways. The first is that of affirming Saussure's basic principles regarding the conventionality of language, the priority of synchrony over diachrony, and the structured and systematic nature of language. The study of the New Testament, while also being a theological task, must be grounded in a proper view of language. This means that the kinds of exegetical exercises that have relied upon etymologizing or equating of words and concepts (the kinds of criticisms that have been levied by James Barr [1924-2006] against much biblical criticism) and have overlooked the interpretive impact of translation must be eliminated, even if they are found in some of the philosophical thinkers that are considered as foundational for understanding modern hermeneutics. Referring to his article on "The Supposed Power of Words in the Biblical Writings" (repr. in *Thiselton on Hermeneutics*), Thiselton notes that the attempt to see thought as dictated by language is misguided. Only a soft form of linguistic determinism can explain the relationship between language and thought, not a hard form of determinism that limits thinking on the basis of linguistic structure.

Thiselton's approach to philosophical hermeneutics is bolstered by the thinking of several major philosophers or hermeneuts, upon whom he draws in various tangible ways. Several of the major ideas of these thinkers are clearly foundational for hermeneutics and have had significant influence upon Thiselton's own thinking. His appraisal of their major contributions also provides insight into Thiselton's view of the major task of hermeneutics. Heidegger's notion of being, which is central to his philosophical program, and his concept of "horizon for understanding" are fundamental hermeneutical insights, because they reveal the situatedness of human existence *(Dasein)* and that there are constraints or horizons placed on understanding. Human situated existence is existence within a world, i.e., what Heidegger calls "Being-in-the world," a precognitive human existence before separation from the world. In a number of ways, Bultmann illustrates for Thiselton the inadequacy of pursuing Heideggerian thought. Bultmann, in his reaction against theological liberalism, ended up adopting a neo-Kantian philosophical Lutheranism, in which he affirmed a faith that was based on nothing objective or external. The resulting radical dualism differentiates between objective description such as "law" and the address of God in grace. This dualism pervades Bultmann's thought. One of its most obvious implications is for Bultmann's understanding of "myth." Bultmann, therefore, affirms the place of pre-understanding in interpretation, as seen in the numerous influences upon his thought (liberalism, neo-Kantianism, Lutheranism, history of religions, Heidegger, and the historian-philosopher R. G. Collingwood [1889-1943], among others). Bultmann's dualism, while subject to criticism, at least retains attention upon God rather than the human being, as had been the case in liberal theology. However, Bultmann's view of myth, which in some ways appears to be a theory of metaphor, ends up becoming a language about humanity, not God. To a large extent, the dualism of Bultmann is attributable to Heidegger, and results in insufficient language to talk about the issues he raises. In contrast to Bultmann, and in a major step forward from Thiselton's perspective, Gadamer brings a more positive view of history and tradition (tradition history; *Wirkungsgeschichte*) through his understanding of the recognition of the horizon of what is being interpreted. One enters into a dialogue of listening and questioning of the other. This interpretation is communal and results in stable interpretation on the basis of shared communal judgments. Finally, Wittgenstein, in Thiselton's scheme in *Two Horizons,* helps to focus these ideas with his concept of meaning. The earlier Wittgenstein was characterized by a positivistic attention to logic and propositions. The later Wittgenstein is concerned with meaning within the context of language situations and language games (similar to Heidegger's notion of worlds). In other words, Wittgenstein endorses the notion that meaning resides in given contexts, which may change and develop. Further, these language games indicate that human language use is fundamental to meaning, even if the concepts of meaning and use are not to be equated.

Thiselton illustrates his widespread endorsement of Wittgenstein in two major hermeneutical exercises. The first involves his extrapolating three classes of linguistic utterances from the thought of Wittgenstein, and then attempting to classify statements in the New Testament according to this theme. The idea is that if we can determine the type of statement found in the New Testament, we can be sure of its correct interpretation; that is, the classification of utterance indicates its language use (picture language is important here). Though Wittgenstein never engages in such an exercise, Thiselton does so as a means of classifying the types of statements found in the New Testament and hence offering a practical means for hermeneutical analysis. He can thus differentiate theological statements from each other. He further applies the notion of language games to the problem of justification by faith in Paul, and concludes that one is either justified or a sinner on the basis of the language game in which one is involved.

What Constitutes a Constructive Philosophical Theological Hermeneutics?

Thiselton's detailed description of philosophical theological hermeneutics and its possible implications for New Testament study led to calls for him to articulate and apply his own hermeneutical stance in more detail. The result was his *New Horizons in Hermeneutics,* where the major insights he gained from his previous analysis and his ongoing development of speech-act theory come together in a monumental way. Thiselton's hermeneutical stance can be summarized, as he does, along the lines that "biblical texts can transform readers, but readers also transform texts" (*Thiselton on Hermeneutics,* 11). In other words, he wishes to address "*what effects biblical texts produce* on thought and on life, and especially *on what basis these effects come about"* (*New Horizons,* 2; italics original). Thiselton is positioning himself in this work to provide both a hermeneutical theory and exemplification of how such a theory is to work.

Thiselton essentially wants to make two significant points regarding hermeneutics. The first is that one of the major preoccupations of hermeneutics is the place of the subject. He sees the kind of pre-critical understanding that assumed a subject and object as having been displaced during the Enlightenment era. The subject-object divide was prevalent in post-Cartesian thought, until the rise of so-called postmodernism. The rise of postmodernism did not necessarily lead to the exaltation of the subject apart from the object. Thiselton surveys a range of hermeneutical theories and their proponents — including various forms of semiotic theory, socio-critical theory, liberation hermeneutics, structuralism and post-structuralism, reader-response criticism, and deconstruction, among others — and concludes two things. The first is that some of these models offer suggestive interpretive frameworks, while others offer little promise. A moderate form of reader-response criticism includes the important insight that the reader has a role to play in interpretation, while extreme forms of reader-response criticism that appeal only to socio-pragmatic bases of meaning offer no substantial platform for hermeneutical development. Reception theory, however, because of its Gadamerian grounding, can be useful for understanding the relation of the two horizons of the text and reader. Likewise, Paul Ricoeur (1913-2005), with his interdisciplinary approach that engages in both a hermeneutical suspicion and a willingness to believe, posits a hermeneutic that is concerned with what happens in front of the text. The second conclusion is that the models that are not linguistically grounded lack a firm basis for hermeneutics, and that there is nothing inherent in the structure of the arguments or context that indicates that a relativistic worldview is the necessary result of postmodernism. Thiselton's major criticism of most recent hermeneutics is that it reflects socio-pragmatic interests, by which pragmatism alone becomes the criterion for evaluation of any theory. In one sense, postmodernism raises awareness of the role of the subject, including the role that it plays in the construction of meaning and the history of interpretation, i.e., self-involvement, which Thiselton sees as necessary to formalize in a hermeneutical model. However, postmodernism itself, as Thiselton makes clear in his *Interpreting God and the Postmodern Self,* becomes simply another attempt to grab power, the very thing that postmodernism is purporting to be arguing against, when it loses its groundedness. Thiselton suggests instead that the way forward in interpretive thought is a linguistically well-grounded theory of hermeneutics.

It is at this point in *New Horizons* that Thiselton turns to speech-act theory as the second important point for both hermeneutical theory and practice. Thiselton's interest in speech-act theory began with his critique of the New Hermeneutic, and continued through a number of his works, including *The Two Horizons* and *The Responsibility of Hermeneutics* (where it is called an action model) and the more recent *The Promise of Hermeneutics* and *New Horizons in Hermeneutics,* as well as a number of important articles. Tracing the roots of speech-act theory back to the later Wittgenstein (an origin some would dispute), Thiselton believes that speech-act theory, while not necessarily the only hermeneutical framework, can articulate the significance of meaning within a conventionalized speech community. Speech-act theory makes a distinction between the propositional content of a statement and the illocutionary force of such a statement. Drawing on the work of the philosopher Searle, Thiselton notes the three categories of speech-acts: a locutionary act of speaking; an illocutionary act, which would include such actions as commanding, warning, or informing; and a perlocutionary act, which is concerned with what is achieved by speaking, such as deterring, convincing, or persuading (*New Horizons,* 293). The notion (from Searle) of "directions of fit" between "words" and the "world" provides the framework in which Thiselton sees speech-acts functioning. When one makes an assertion, the direction of it moves from the words to the world, in the sense that it is the words that must be conformed to the world. When one makes a promise, by contrast, the direction of fit moves from the world to the words, in that it is the world that must be conformed to the words ("Jesus the Christ," 465-66; repr. in *Thiselton on Hermeneutics*). Such speech-actions therefore function in interpersonal, situational, and especially institutional contexts, which are the contexts that give them performative significance. Thiselton's analysis of a number of New Testament texts in light of this interpretive framework illustrates that New Testament scholars often confuse the operative contexts in which biblical utterances are made. This framework provides a means of extending the functional significance of a given text, in the sense that interpreters may use a text in ways not envisioned by the original author, so long as the text is used responsibly and appropriately (Lundin, Thiselton, and Walhout, *Responsibility of Hermeneutics,* 107).

Hermeneutics of Doctrine

In many if not all fundamental ways, the climax of Thiselton's work is seeing how his theological hermeneutics unites a number of horizons — between the Bible and theology, and between hermeneutical method and doctrinal practice. As Thiselton indicates, hermeneutics is an applied activity, in which understanding is seen in formative practice that is communal and public in nature and presuppositional in orientation. The culmination of his attempt in this direction is seen in his *Hermeneutics of Doctrine,* which provides both a hermeneutical model and doctrinal discussions that grow from such a theological hermeneutics.

Thiselton believes that hermeneutics is fundamental to the establishment of doctrine that is not simply abstract, theoretical, and overly general. Returning to and relying upon Gadamer, Thiselton approaches doctrine instead from the standpoint of asking hermeneutical questions from life. This is appropriate, because Christian confessions, such as the early creeds, reflect a life-context in which they are used. That life-context (as speech-act theory indicates) can result in truth claims, because confessional statements presuppose certain states of affairs. Moving from the biblical statements to first-person utterances, such as "I believe" statements, Thiselton argues that belief "is *action-orientated, situation-related,* and embedded in the *particularities and contingencies* of everyday living" (*Hermeneutics of Doctrine,* 21; italics original). By this, he means that traditional Christian belief, as illustrated in the Bible, the early church writers, and historic Christian doctrine, is itself reflective of faith that is "embedded in action and life," and reflects both "individual belief and communal doctrine" (*Hermeneutics of Doctrine,* 52).

Thiselton then turns to the origins of doctrine itself. Not only for Karl Barth (1886-1968) but for others as well, such as Wolfhart Pannenberg (1928-) and Karl Rahner (1904-1984), God is the source of all Christian doctrine. The God of Christian doctrine is a living and acting God, so this implies a living and dynamic doctrine — hence the need for hermeneutical investigation to appropriately investigate its particular and contingent nature. This involves recognition of the temporal and narrative character of doctrine, i.e., doctrine as narrative or drama. Drawing directly upon Ricoeur's *Time and Narrative,* an investigation of hermeneutics and narrative, Thiselton endorses the notion of narrative as temporally conditioned and open to the future. As a result, he adopts the notion of plot, whether on large or small scale, within narrative as providing the conditioned and embodied means by which God's actions may be revealed in particularized ways. Doctrine formulated in this way contains the potential for inspiring creative action and thought — as opposed to stultifying such constructive thinking as has occurred in much doctrinal discussion. The communal context of doctrinal development provides necessary safeguards against idiosyncratic developments and for opening up and exploring new horizons. Thiselton believes that the balance between change and development and a stable set of shared communal beliefs can, and should, be provided by Christian doctrine.

A position such as this, Thiselton realizes, is bound to result in some response by those who find it difficult to hold the notions of both coherence and contingency. Responding to scholars who question such a formulation, such as the contemporary scholar Jens Zimmermann, Thiselton notes that there is a widespread formulation of the problem of hermeneutics and doctrine, from Schleiermacher to Pannenberg, that finds the coherence theory of truth compatible with provisional certainty within developing doctrine. Further, a communal and contingent hermeneutic does not exclude having a rightly understood epistemology. Such an epistemology represents a soft foundationalism based upon an empiricism that responds to questions that arise from contexts of life, in which there are many voices in dialogue that have formative effect upon those concerned with doctrine. Drawing on the work of the philosopher of science Imre Lakatos (1922-1974), in his debate with fellow philosopher-scientists Thomas Kuhn (1922-1996) and Karl Popper (1902-1994), Thiselton notes that Lakatos's view of fallibilism is a means of affirming that theories must have explanatory power but be open to being modified in the process. Such a process, while not affirming traditional foundationalism, need not fall victim to simply community-affirming or power-imposing postmodernism.

In his latest work specifically on hermeneutics (2009), in many ways a compendium of Thiselton's thought on the major figures and movements in hermeneutics, he returns to many of the themes and ideas that he has raised throughout the course of his career, and that often appear in his various articles. These include the questions of what constitutes hermeneutics, both historically and contemporaneously, and of how one goes about constructing a hermeneutics that brings the horizons of text and interpreter together, while being faithful to the Christian tradition.

Kevin Vanhoozer

Kevin J. Vanhoozer (1957-) has become a popular scholarly figure in the field of theological hermeneutics in North America. Along with other contemporary writers such as Stephen Fowl, A. K. M. Adam, Francis Watson, and Daniel Treier, Vanhoozer has raised the popular profile of theological hermeneutics especially as it relates to interpretation within the church. As a result, he is closely associated with theological interpretation, a more narrowly constrained form of theological hermeneutics that interprets the Bible in light of the theological traditions of the church. His theological hermeneutics is identifiable as postconservative and postfoundationalist, though affirming the canon as the basis of belief.

Life and Influences

Vanhoozer was educated at Westmont College in Santa Barbara, California, Westminster Theological Seminary in Philadelphia, and then Cambridge University, where he wrote his Ph.D. dissertation under the direction of the Roman Catholic scholar Nicholas Lash (1934-) on the narrative work of Paul Ricoeur. Vanhoozer has taught at three institutions, first and again at Trinity Evangelical Divinity School in Deerfield, Illinois (1986-90, 1998-2009), where he was Research Professor in Systematic Theology, and in between at Edinburgh University, where he was senior lecturer in systematic theology. Vanhoozer took up a position in theology at Wheaton College in Illinois in 2009.

Vanhoozer has written four major volumes, as well as edited several important works, and written a number of significant essays. Vanhoozer's first major work was the publication of his revised dissertation, *Biblical Narrative in the Philosophy of Paul Ricoeur* (1990). This volume was first an analysis of Ricoeur's thought on narrative in a form that would be accessible to those in theological studies, and then an attempt to place him in recent hermeneutical discussion and demonstrate his significance for interpretation of the Gospels. This was followed by Vanhoozer's defense of authorial intention in *Is There a Meaning in This Text?* (1998), based in Reformed theology and using speech-act theory (which he calls speech-act philosophy, because he relies heavily upon the philosopher Nicholas Wolterstorff [1932-]). His *First Theology* (2002) brought together a number of his essays. In 2005, he published *The Drama of Doctrine,* in which he introduced his canonical-linguistic approach to theology (as distinct from the cultural-linguistic approach of the Yale school theologian George Lindbeck [1923-]). Also in 2006, Vanhoozer teamed up with several other authors to write one of the four sections in *Reading Scripture with the Church*. Vanhoozer's work is characterized by widespread accessibility, and he writes as a systematic theologian with a consistent focus upon matters of theological hermeneutics for the life of the postmodern church.

There Is a Meaning in This Text

Vanhoozer addresses two major questions in the bulk of his scholarly work. The first question he attempts to answer is, "What are the principles of general hermeneutics?" Beginning with ideas developed in his first major essay ("The Semantics of Biblical Literature"), and in some ways reflected in his book on Ricoeur, he answers this question in *Is There a Meaning in This Text?* with a general hermeneutic in which he "argued that readers have a mandate to do justice to the authors not only of the Bible but also of *all* texts" ("Imprisoned or Free?", 59). The second question he asks is, "What is particular about interpretation of the Bible?" In an essay from 2000 ("The Voice and the Actor"), Vanhoozer attempts to answer this question in *The Drama of Doctrine* with a theological special hermeneutic that reads the Bible unlike any other book.

Drawing upon what he identifies as the three ages of criticism, in *Is There a Meaning in This Text?* Vanhoozer notes these as the ages of the author, text, and reader. He equates each of these with an orientation and several different periods in literary (including biblical) interpretation: the age of the author with Reformation interpretation to the time of Schleiermacher and a modern resurgence in the work of Jacques Derrida (1930-2004) and Stanley Fish (1938-); the age of the text with the New Criticism and structuralism of the mid-twentieth century; and the age of the reader with various reader-oriented criticisms that emerged in the 1970s and 1980s. Beginning with three important interpretive beliefs — hermeneutic realism, hermeneutic rationality, and hermeneutic responsibility — his major effort is directed toward analyzing what has happened to all three of these for determining meaning in a text, and then reanalyzing them for constructing a general literary hermeneutic that is Trinitarian in orientation and basis.

Although Vanhoozer's analysis of the interpretive predicament is separated from his constructive proposal regarding creating a general hermeneutic, the issues that he tackles are indicative of those that he believes a general hermeneutics must address.

We begin with his analysis of the interpretive predicament. Concerning the author, there are several major movements to note. The first is to accept the importance of the author, to the point of equating God and the author in theological circles. However, a number of movements, including various forms of non-realism, such as deconstruction represented by Derrida and neo-pragmatism represented by Richard Rorty (1931-2007), have dissolved confidence in not only the author but anything outside of the text. In some circles, this was heralded as the death of the author, and with it came the undoing of the author's intention. Those who attempt to ground meaning in intention, and use it as the goal and guide to interpretation, as does the literary critic E. D. Hirsch (1928-), are seen to be merely asserting a preference. Instead, the intentional fallacy is seen to encompass any number of other fallacies, such as those of relevancy, transparency, identity, and objectivity. The result of this is the death of the author in interpreting the Bible, and with it a loss of grounded meaning in texts.

Concerning the text, the same kind of derogation of meaning occurs. The demeaning of the status of the text occurs along with the demotion of metaphysics and method that occurred in the twentieth century. There is a loss of the sense of objectivity and even of interpretation, to the point where there are questions raised regarding whether there is such a thing as a text. The text becomes a much more open concept, in which the reader is involved in the interpretation and even shaping of the text. The result is a variety of notions of meaning that may or may not be found in texts, to the point of textual indeterminacy becoming paramount, and texts being seen as entirely metaphorical and hence unstable in meaning. This leads also to biblical indeterminacy and canonical indeterminacy, with the resulting inability of interpreters to make claims about textual meaning.

Concerning the reader, there is more to be said, in that the age of the reader has come into its own. In one sense, the reader becomes a writer and is engaged in some actual way in constructing meaning. Readers' interests are governed by any number of factors. Vanhoozer identifies several of them: the critical goal of description, the ethical goal of evaluation, and the utilitarian aim of using the text. There are various possible ways that readers can read, not all of them resulting in the kinds of results that some hope for. The result can be violence done to the text on the basis of various political and ideological reading agendas. In all of these, there is a social construction of meaning of the text that subverts the meaning of the text.

In response to these central interpretive transformations, Vanhoozer proposes a revitalization of each of these three areas. Concerning the author, from the outset Vanhoozer transforms the discussion by positing a view of meaning as something that people do, i.e., an action model of communication. Moving beyond seeing language as individual words and as sign systems, Vanhoozer looks to semantics and the functions of sentences. Turning to ordinary language philosophy, as found in the work of Wittgenstein, Austin, and Searle, Vanhoozer invokes speech-act theory. He uses the example of making a promise, in which, for the promise to be actualized, certain conditions about the statement and the context in which it is used must pertain. Whereas this pragmatic use of language, contrary to deconstruction, would seem to apply to ordinary use, does it apply to literary texts? Invoking Ricoeur (despite Ricoeur's denial of authorial intention, which he equates with a psychological intention), Vanhoozer claims that the author of a literary text is an agent in the same way as one "doing" through the use of language. By this avenue, Vanhoozer is able to bring back a revived sense of authorial intention through speech-act theory. Intentions are communicated by means of linguistic conventions, which he takes to be a corporate intention. These intentions function within a context of institutional facts that operate within a system of constitutive rules. It is these rules that determine what counts for something within that system. With this system of meaning in place, the notion can be extended, following Hirsch's distinction between meaning and significance, to posit what Hirsch calls "transhistorical intentions," i.e., significances that extend beyond an author's immediate meaning. Finally, Vanhoozer addresses the question of a fuller sense of meaning within the Bible, and argues for divine intentionality and authorship that stands behind the biblical text, realized through the whole canon as the communicative act. This has come to be called double agency discourse, on the basis of work on intentionality by Wolterstorff ("Authorial Discourse Interpretation").

Concerning the redeemed text, Vanhoozer extends his analysis of the author. He positions his view of the text on four major planks: a Reformed hermeneutic, critical hermeneutical realism, literal but not literalistic or historical reading, and the role of genre and canon. Vanhoozer adopts the notion of testimony in the New Reformed hermeneutic, as the basis of interpretive belief. He recognizes that there appears to be interpretive diversity, but believes that what he calls a "regulative hermeneutic realism" (*Is*

There a Meaning in This Text?, 302), with meaning recognized as a regulative notion, prevails. Reading the Bible literally does not mean imposing a literalistic reading, but recognizing all of the dimensions of the communicative act, such as its propositional content, literary form, teaching function, and, ultimately, its witness to Jesus Christ. Finally, types of language knowledge may be seen by means of how they relate to levels of understanding, with genre regulative for individual works and canon for the entirety of the Bible, each following communicative covenants.

Concerning the reader, who may be a user, critic, or follower, Vanhoozer endorses following the illocutionary and perlocutionary force of the text. The perlocutionary force of a statement encompasses its effects, and raises the question of the ethics of reading. Rather than the reader creating meaning, the reader should be responsible in responding to meaning. For the Bible, this means the reader stands under the text as servant, rather than "overstanding" and attempting to dominate the text.

Drama of Doctrine

In answering the question of "What is special about reading the Bible?", Vanhoozer develops a theological special hermeneutic that reads the Bible unlike any other book. In one sense, his work on *The Drama of Doctrine* is a continuation of the speech-act theory that he develops in *Is There a Meaning in This Text?*, in which he sees the "Bible as a set of divine communicative acts" ("Voice and the Actor," 76) analyzed as what he calls a canonical-linguistic approach to Christian theology. He goes further, however, and adopts the notion of Scripture as drama, in which the Christian message is seen to be essentially dramatic in character. (This approach to divine action, as well as the dramatic element of theology, is developed further in his latest work, *Remythologizing Theology*.)

Vanhoozer adopts the canonical-linguistic approach in direct response to the cultural-linguistic "turn" of postliberal theology. As a result of the kinds of debates over theological authority that characterized modernism, the cultural-linguistic turn in theology was bound to come. The movement includes such Yale-school figures as Lindbeck, Hans Frei (1922-1988), and David Kelsey. Lindbeck's work, *The Nature of Doctrine*, signaled the beginning of the cultural-linguistic turn. Influenced by Wittgenstein and his emphasis upon meaning as a function of use, Lindbeck grounds theological authority in the church. Similarly, Frei shows that interpretation of the Bible was dominated by extrabiblical conceptual frameworks. Later he came to endorse a communal understanding of the Bible. Kelsey shows how the Bible was used as a means of bolstering various theological programs. As a result, Vanhoozer posits his canonical-linguistic approach "to correct (without overreacting to) this cultural-linguistic misstep by locating authority not in the use of Scripture by the believing community but in what Nicholas Wolterstorff calls divine authorial discourse" (*Drama of Doctrine*, 11). Further, he argues that "the normative use [of the Bible] is ultimately not that of ecclesial *culture* but of the biblical *canon*" (*Drama of Doctrine*, 16).

Vanhoozer constructs his drama of doctrine around four main important moments. The first outlines the drama as a whole. The theo-drama, as he calls it (admittedly using the same term as Hans Urs von Balthasar [1905-1988]), stands behind all theology, and consists of its major players and elements. This includes the role that God plays in an economic Trinity in relation to humanity. God is the one who speaks and acts, and humans respond. The job of theology is to enable this interaction, so that humans are followers of God and "perform" as disciples. The purpose of doctrine is to "direct" the right participation of the church in this theo-drama. One is able to participate through knowing God, which comes through knowing Jesus. This is understood through the narrative of Scripture, as guided by the Holy Spirit. Thus doctrine provides the necessary information and direction for a Spirit-guided performance that is both propositional and personal, cognitive and participatory.

The second part describes the script of the drama. Scripture as canon is a covenant document, which reflects the relationship between the church and God, as God communicates through the Holy Spirit, apostolic tradition, the church, and the text in its canonical form. This embodies what Vanhoozer wishes to call a revised Scripture principle. Canon is a means for understanding and locating the authority of Scripture and ensuring that a common identity as the church is maintained. The canon provides the norm by which performances of the gospel are assessed. Regarding tradition, rather than the interpretive community being the author and director of the theological performance, God is the divine author who, through his illocutionary acts, directs the church in its faithful performance. This is what Vanhoozer wishes to call his canonical-linguistic approach, in which theological normativity is based in the divine discourse. Vanhoozer further defines roles for the Holy Spirit and the rule of faith. The Holy Spirit serves as the one who testifies to Jesus Christ through prompting the authors of Scripture and enabling the church to respond to Scripture. The rule of faith is itself governed by the Scriptures, and serves as a distilled guide to interpreting the canon. Vanhoozer wishes to affirm the role of Scripture as canon, along with a role for tradition and the Holy Spirit. The canon not only serves as the norm for the church but issues in canonical practices. Canonical-linguistic theology calls for participation in scriptural practices, such as understanding of Scripture according to their genres as forms of social action, i.e., guides for participation in the story of Scripture. The canon also establishes canonical practices for members of the church regarding their covenantal behavior in the community of believers.

The theologian becomes the one who studies the script, i.e., Scripture, and makes it understandable by others so that they can enact its drama. There is both a scientific (exegetical) and a practical (performative) dimension to this task, in that the theologian is dealing with the reality of God's communicative action and guiding participation that is consistent, coherent, and in correspondence with the canonical norm. The result, Vanhoozer believes, is a postpropositionalist theology that moves beyond monologue and homogenization and appreciates canonical-linguistic plurality by listening to the polyphony of Scripture in its pluriform texts and theological fullness. Postpropositional theology is, therefore, a theology that goes beyond propositional revelation. This theology is also postconservative in that it recognizes the authority of Scripture but is not bound to a merely referential or propositional theology. This theology is also postfoundationalist, not non-foundationalist. Postfoundationalism believes in the notions of truth and objectivity, while at the same time acknowledging that human perception, because it is always contextualized, may itself be provisional and fallible. Concerning its practical character, theology is to be contextualized in ways that reflect the practices of Scripture. This theology is thus phronetic in its concern for what we ought to say and do, and prophetic in that it results in action in both speech and behavior, sometimes behavior that speaks against its culture and always as a witness to the resurrection.

A canonical-linguistic theology is ultimately concerned with performance, i.e., the behavior of the individual and the community. The call is for the individual not to be a hypocrite (playing on the ancient Greek term for actor) but to be one heading toward spiritual formation, as a person in union with Christ. Similarly, the church, like the theater, is to enact the body of Christ as sacrament and celebration (worship), as an interactive community concerned for right practice and demonstrating a readiness for martyrdom and reconciliation.

Vanhoozer's place within theological hermeneutics, and more particularly theological interpretation, is seen in the recent book that he co-authored with Adam, Fowl, and Watson, *Reading Scripture with the Church*, a title that captures much that characterizes the movement. Even though Vanhoozer was trained as a systematic theologian, and the other three as New Testament scholars, they have much in common in their attempt to arrive at a suitable theological hermeneutic. Their hermeneutical commonalities include their view of the significance of the church, Christian theology, postmodern thought, and ethical consequences of interpretation. However, they also have important distinctives. Adam, perhaps the most postmodern in his approach to theological interpretation, wishes to move what he calls "biblical theology" away from a verbal hermeneutic to one of "signifying practice" that encompasses a "way of living" (28). Fowl, basing his analysis upon Thomas Aquinas, argues that Aquinas presents a "multifaceted literal sense of Scripture" (36) that "provides a bounded plurality of meanings" (11). Fowl has also written a commentary on Philippians bringing the two horizons of biblical and systematic theology together (2005). Watson, in a more biblically centered treatment that appreciates the interpretive influence of the early church than the other essays (apart possibly from Fowl), argues that the fourfold Gospel, which mediates the church's view of Jesus, limits the bounds of plurality.

The major work of Francis Watson (1956-), arguably more than many others, is characterized by a robust, critical, and exegetically rigorous form of what is often thought of and represented as theological interpretation of the Bible. In some ways, he can be seen as a mediating figure between Thiselton and Vanhoozer, while in another he represents a much less philosophical and theological and more biblical-exegetical version of theological interpretation. Although not as conservative in his method or conclusions as some other recent theological interpreters (he is clearly a practitioner of historical criticism), Watson has come to approach the text as a biblical theologian; more so, as one who wishes to revitalize biblical theology dependent upon critical interpretation of the text. Whereas Thiselton and Vanhoozer approach theological interpretation by way of theological hermeneutics, with reliance upon major philosophical and systematic-theological writers, Watson approaches theological interpretation by way of biblical theology grounded in exegesis — although he acknowledges his debt to a number of philosophical and literary interpreters (and to a limited extent Thiselton and Vanhoozer). His commitment to traditional historical criticism is seen in his first book on Paul and Judaism

(1984), which he thoroughly revised (and partially recanted, by attempting to limit the implications of his original results) in 2007 apparently after his turn to theological interpretation. The progressive development of his theological interpretive method is evidenced in his major works that articulate and utilize this form of theological hermeneutics. In his *Text, Church, and World,* Watson develops his theological hermeneutics. He offers a response to postmodern and feminist critiques of the Bible, and arrives at a hermeneutic that is grounded in a theologically informed and (insofar as study of Jesus is concerned) narratively sensitive critical examination of the final form of the text within its canonical context, what he calls a "trinitarian hermeneutic." In his *Text and Truth,* Watson attempts to redefine and reinvigorate biblical theology (and dispute the trenchant critique of the biblical theology movement by James Barr). To do so, he draws upon such concepts as the Gospels as narrated history (with debts to Gadamer on effective history and Ricoeur on narrative and history), and the importance of the single sense of a text and its authorial intention as indicated by speech-acts (with recognition of Thiselton) and the importance of differentiating meaning from significance (based upon Hirsch). These basic notions, along with his advocacy of the singular gospel within multiple texts, set the stage for his defining biblical theology as an interdisciplinary approach integrating exegesis, theology, and hermeneutics (with emphasis upon theology) that brings study of both the Old and New Testaments together with systematic theology. Watson has applied his interdisciplinary theological hermeneutics in two further monographs. The first, *Agape, Eros, Gender,* is a discussion of sexual ethics in Paul. He critically engages three major texts, 1 Corinthians 11, Romans 7, and Ephesians 5, from a theological (Trinitarian) interpretive standpoint. The last, *Paul and the Hermeneutics of Faith,* is a theological examination of how the Old Testament was read by various Jewish readers, especially Paul the apostle. In a statement reflecting Thiselton's perspective cited above, Watson states that, in reading as an interactive activity between text and reader, "we must take seriously the agency not only of the reader but also of the text" (x).

A Critical Appraisal of Theological Hermeneutics

Theological hermeneutics has had increasing importance in recent theological investigation, in no small part because of the writing of Thiselton and Vanhoozer and their influence upon other scholars. Nevertheless, despite the popularity of their approach, there are several fundamental questions that can be asked of Thiselton's and Vanhoozer's hermeneutical approaches, because their approach is foundational for much that is defined as theological hermeneutics and theological interpretation.

Is the heavy reliance upon speech-act theory justified? Speech-act theory has two major forms, one linguistic and the other philosophical. Although Wolterstorff's philosophical form is drawn upon especially by Vanhoozer in a number of places to establish the idea of double intentionality, the linguistic form is the one that provides the major foundation for both Thiselton's and Vanhoozer's utilization (and Watson's). Speech-act theory, which has parallels with the Wittgensteinian reaction to logical positivism (though the formal connections are debated), is a cognitive pragmatic theory that attempts to formulate communicative rules for contextually based expressions. There is much question in both philosophical and linguistic circles whether such rules can be formulated, whether a limited number of illocutions can be correlated with a seemingly unlimited number of perlocutions or language functions, what the relation of basic illocutions is to functions, and whether context can be described in such a way as to provide a meaningful test of the illocutionary or perlocutionary force. Within the discussions of Thiselton and Vanhoozer, there appear to be problems related to use of the term "speech act," with it indicating sometimes a particular type of linguistic expression (rarely examined for its function) and sometimes a general notion used as a defense of intentionality, divine or otherwise. Thiselton seems to recognize functional models of language (e.g., Karl Bühler [1879-1963]), but rejects them, while Vanhoozer does not introduce them at all.

What is the linguistic turn in theological hermeneutics? Both Thiselton and Vanhoozer make appeal to developments in modern linguistics. Thiselton appeals in several places to Saussure's suppositions regarding the arbitrary nature of the sign and distinctions between *langue* and *parole*, and Vanhoozer labels his method as canonical-linguistic. However, it is unclear what the relation of these ideas is to the development of their hermeneutical theory. Thiselton seems to want to set the stage for Wittgenstein's thought regarding "language in use," but that is not what Saussure was emphasizing in his analysis of *langue*. Vanhoozer's canonical-linguistic approach has even less apparently to do with linguistics, apart from his use of speech-act theory. In fact, Thiselton himself, in a detailed critique of Vanhoozer's work in his *Hermeneutics of Doctrine* (79), raises the question of whether Vanhoozer has effectively moved beyond the cultural-linguistic method of Lindbeck, especially in its rejection of cognitive and propositional approaches to doctrine.

Have we recovered a meaningful notion of intentionality? Vanhoozer, as well as Watson, has invested heavily in the recovery of intentionality, and ends up with an approach that reinstates a modified form of Hirsch's distinction between meaning and significance. However, Vanhoozer goes a major step further and grounds this intention in divine intentionality. This is crucial to his initial and subsequent program of theological method, as it provides the basis for a normative canonical Scripture. However, there is a question of whether invoking this concept on the basis that he does actually accomplishes his purposes, especially as this is not tested in detailed exegesis. With his postfoundationalist stance, there are many implications for his entire theological agenda if the divine intentionality cannot be sustained. To his credit, Thiselton takes on some very difficult biblical passages in his exegesis, such as the topic of faith in Paul and James, and does not need to appeal to divine intentionality.

What exactly is the relationship between philosophy, theology, exegesis, and criticism? Thiselton and Vanhoozer in different ways and in varying degrees, along with Watson, raise the question of how these various elements can be integrated into a single hermeneutic, especially one that is labeled theological hermeneutics. A reification of the concept of theological hermeneutics has already occurred in the notion of theological interpretation, where some of the philosophical underpinnings of the hermeneutical approach are subsumed to the overriding theological interests. The history of criticism illustrates that it is not self-evident how these various elements speak with one voice, or can be made to speak univocally, as part of a common hermeneutical enterprise. In fact, the history of criticism shows how they have tended to fragment under pressures from various assertive critical orthodoxies. It would appear that one of the methods must take precedence, possibly at the expense of others. For theological hermeneuts, theology appears to be the governing interpretive framework, on the basis of a variety of arguments or assumptions about the place of the Bible in relation to the church and the history of interpretive tradition. The consequences for the other elements of the hermeneutical model are not entirely clear.

Can a metaphor be overextended? Vanhoozer uses the metaphor of theo-drama to develop his theological hermeneutic. As a result, the entire work is organized around extensions of this fundamental metaphor. However, it is possible that the metaphor is stretched too far, especially when such topics as genre and the use of story and narrative are also brought into the formulation.

Conclusion

Both Thiselton and Vanhoozer are advocates of theological hermeneutics, and they have much in common in their appeal to philosophy and the doctrine of the church. However, there are also a number of interesting and obvious points of contrast in their approaches. Thiselton is biblically oriented and exegetically grounded, whereas Vanhoozer approaches the topic as a systematic theologian. Thiselton is thus able to write commentaries on 1 Corinthians and 1 and 2 Thessalonians, including perspectives that fit within his hermeneutical framework, while Vanhoozer rarely focuses on extended passages of Scripture, but instead relies upon categories from systematic theology. The result is that their work approaches the topic of hermeneutics differently, with biblical exegesis providing the point of entry and evaluation for Thiselton, while Vanhoozer's major point of contact is theology. Thiselton's knowledge and documentation of philosophical writers is encyclopedic and exhaustive, while Vanhoozer tends to focus upon key thinkers, such as Gadamer, Ricoeur, and Wolterstorff, who provide the framework for his thinking. Thiselton goes so far as to point out that, as helpful and insightful as Vanhoozer's work is, it does not clearly indicate a consistent and robust use of some of the major philosophical thinkers (*Hermeneutics of Doctrine*, 103-4). Thiselton has paved the way at least in evangelical theological circles for developing the notion of theological hermeneutics, including such concepts as the use of speech-act theory, which others such as Vanhoozer have now appropriated. Thiselton seems to be disappointed that Vanhoozer has not clearly recognized or fully appreciated his previous ground-laying work (*Hermeneutics of Doctrine*, 78-80). Thiselton is uncompromising in his attention to the sources compared to Vanhoozer, whose language is more engaging and less directly bound to his sources. Vanhoozer is also far more entertaining, in his use of, for example, the metaphor of the theo-drama. As a result, Thiselton provides the more sober and rigorous exposition, while Vanhoozer provides a synthetic treatment of admittedly complex notions.

Reference Works

Adam, A. K. M. *What Is Postmodern Biblical Criticism?* Minneapolis: Augsburg Fortress, 1995.

Adam, A. K. M., Stephen E. Fowl, Kevin J. Vanhoozer, and Francis Watson. *Reading Scripture with the Church: Toward a Hermeneutic for Theological Interpretation.* Grand Rapids: Baker, 2006.

Austin, J. L. *How to Do Things with Words.* Oxford: Clarendon, 1962.

Balthasar, Hans Urs von. *Theo-Drama: Theological Dramatic Theory.* 4 vols. San Francisco: Ignatius, 1984-94.

Barr, James. *The Semantics of Biblical Language.* Oxford: Oxford University Press, 1961.

————. *Biblical Words for Time.* London: SCM Press, 1962.

Bartholomew, Craig G. "Three Horizons: Hermeneutics from the Other End — An Evaluation of Anthony Thiselton's Hermeneutic Proposals." *European Journal of Theology* 5, no. 2 (1996): 121-35.

Bartholomew, Craig, Colin Greene, and Karl Möller, eds. *After Pentecost: Language and Biblical Interpretation.* Carlisle, UK: Paternoster, 2001.

Bogen, David. *Order without Rules: Critical Theory and the Logic of Conversation.* Albany: State University of New York Press, 1999.

Bühler, Karl. *Theory of Language: The Representational Function of Language,* trans. Donald Fraser Goodwin. Amsterdam: Benjamins, 1990 (1934).

Fowl, Stephen E. *Engaging Scripture: A Model for Theological Interpretation.* Oxford: Blackwell, 1998.

————. *Philippians.* The Two Horizons New Testament Commentary. Grand Rapids: Eerdmans, 2005.

————. *Theological Interpretation of Scripture.* Eugene, OR: Cascade, 2009.

Fowl, Stephen E., ed. *The Theological Interpretation of Scripture: Classic and Contemporary Readings.* Oxford: Blackwell, 1997.

Frei, Hans. *The Eclipse of Biblical Narrative.* New Haven: Yale University Press, 1974.

Gunderson, Steven R. "Thiselton, Anthony C. (1937-)." In *Dictionary of Biblical Criticism and Interpretation,* ed. Stanley E. Porter, pp. 356-57. London: Routledge, 2007.

Kelsey, David. *Proving Doctrine: The Uses of Scripture in Recent Theology.* Harrisburg, PA: Trinity Press International, 1999.

Lakatos, Imre. "Falsification and Methodology of Scientific Research Programmes." In *Criticism and the Growth of Knowledge,* ed. Imre Lakatos and Alan Musgrave, pp. 91-196. Cambridge: Cambridge University Press, 1970.

Levinson, Stephen C. *Pragmatics*. Cambridge: Cambridge University Press, 1983.

Lindbeck, George. *The Nature of Doctrine: Religion and Theology in a Post-liberal Age*. Philadelphia: Westminster, 1984.

Lundin, Roger, Anthony C. Thiselton, and Clarence Walhout. *The Responsibility of Hermeneutics*. Grand Rapids: Eerdmans, 1985.

Lundin, Roger, Clarence Walhout, and Anthony C. Thiselton. *The Promise of Hermeneutics*. Grand Rapids: Eerdmans, 1999.

Porter, Stanley E. "Hermeneutics, Biblical Interpretation, and Theology: Hunch, Holy Spirit, or Hard Work?" In *Beyond the Bible: Moving from Scripture to Theology*, ed. I. Howard Marshall, pp. 97-127. Grand Rapids: Baker, 2004.

—————. "What Difference Does Hermeneutics Make? Hermeneutical Theory Applied." *Jian Dao* 34/*Pastoral Journal* 27 (July 2010): 1-50.

Ricoeur, Paul. *Time and Narrative*, trans. Kathleen McLaughlin, Kathleen Blamey, and David Pellauer, 3 vols. Chicago: University of Chicago Press, 1984, 1985, 1988 (1983-1985).

Searle, John R. *Speech Acts: An Essay in the Philosophy of Language*. Cambridge: Cambridge University Press, 1969.

Thiselton, Anthony C. *1 and 2 Thessalonians: Through the Centuries*. Chichester: Wiley-Blackwell, 2011.

—————. "Biblical Interpretation." In *The Modern Theologians: An Introduction to Christian Theology since 1918*, ed. David Ford, pp. 287-307. 3rd ed. Oxford: Blackwell, 2005.

—————. "Biblical Studies and Theoretical Hermeneutics." In *The Cambridge Companion to Biblical Interpretation*, ed. John Barton, pp. 95-113. Cambridge: Cambridge University Press, 1998.

—————. "Christology in Luke, Speech-Act Theory, and the Problem of Dualism in Christology after Kant." In *Jesus of Nazareth: Lord and Christ. Essays on the Historical Jesus and New Testament Christology*, ed. Joel B. Green and Max Turner, pp. 453-72. Grand Rapids: Eerdmans, 1994.

—————. *A Concise Encyclopedia of the Philosophy of Religion*. Grand Rapids: Baker, 2002.

—————. *The First Epistle to the Corinthians*. New International Greek Testament Commentary. Grand Rapids: Eerdmans, 2006.

—————. *Hermeneutics: An Introduction*. Grand Rapids: Eerdmans, 2009.

—————. *The Hermeneutics of Doctrine*. Grand Rapids: Eerdmans, 2007.

—————. *Interpreting God and the Postmodern Self: On Meaning, Manipulation and Promise*. Edinburgh: T. & T. Clark, 1995.

————. *Living Paul.* London: SPCK, 2009.

————. "The New Hermeneutic." In *New Testament Interpretation: Essays on Principles and Methods,* ed. I. Howard Marshall, pp. 308-33. Grand Rapids: Eerdmans, 1977.

————. *New Horizons in Hermeneutics: The Theory and Practice of Transforming Biblical Reading.* Grand Rapids: Zondervan, 1992.

————. "The Supposed Power of Words in the Biblical Writings." *Journal of Theological Studies* 25 (1974): 283-99.

————. "New Testament Interpretation in Historical Perspective." In *Hearing the New Testament: Strategies for Interpretation,* ed. Joel B. Green, pp. 10-36. Grand Rapids: Eerdmans, 1995.

————. "Speaking and Hearing." In *Christian Faith and Practice in the Modern World,* ed. Mark A. Noll and David F. Wells, pp. 139-51. Grand Rapids: Eerdmans, 1988.

————. *Thiselton on Hermeneutics: Collected Works with New Essays.* Grand Rapids: Eerdmans, 2006.

————. *The Two Horizons: New Testament Hermeneutics and Philosophical Description with Special Reference to Heidegger, Bultmann, Gadamer, and Wittgenstein.* Grand Rapids: Eerdmans, 1980.

Treier, Daniel J. *Introducing Theological Interpretation of Scripture: Recovering a Christian Practice.* Grand Rapids: Baker, 2008.

Vanhoozer, Kevin J. *The Drama of Doctrine: A Canonical-Linguistic Approach to Christian Theology.* Louisville: Westminster/John Knox, 2005.

————. "A Drama-of-Redemption Model." In *Four Views on Moving Beyond the Bible to Theology,* ed. Gary T. Meadors, pp. 151-99. Grand Rapids: Zondervan, 2009.

————. *First Theology: God, Scripture, and Hermeneutics.* Downers Grove, IL: InterVarsity Press, 2002.

————. "Imprisoned or Free? Text, Status, and Theological Interpretation in the Master/Slave Discourse of Philemon" and "Four Theological Faces of Biblical Interpretation." In *Reading Scripture with the Church: Toward a Hermeneutic for Theological Interpretation,* by A. K. M. Adam, Stephen E. Fowl, Kevin J. Vanhoozer, and Francis Watson. Grand Rapids: Baker, 2006.

————. *Is There a Meaning in This Text? The Bible, the Reader, and the Morality of Literary Knowledge.* Grand Rapids: Zondervan, 1998.

————. "Lost in Interpretation? Truth, Scripture, and Hermeneutics." *Journal of the Evangelical Theological Society* 48, no. 1 (2005): 89-114.

————. "Pilgrim's Digress: Christian Thinking on and about the Post/Modern

Way" and "Disputing about Words? Of Fallible Foundations and Modest Metanarratives." In *Christianity and the Postmodern Turn,* ed. Myron Penner, pp. 71-103, 187-200. Grand Rapids: Baker, 2005.

―――. *Remythologizing Theology: Divine Action, Passion, and Authorship.* Cambridge: Cambridge University Press, 2010.

―――. "The Semantics of Biblical Literature: Truth and Scripture's Diverse Literary Forms." In *Hermeneutics, Authority, and Canon,* ed. D. A. Carson and John D. Woodbridge, pp. 49-104. Grand Rapids: Zondervan, 1986.

―――. "The Voice and the Actor: A Dramatic Proposal about the Ministry and Minstrelsy of Theology." In *Evangelical Futures: A Conversation on Theological Method,* ed. John G. Stackhouse, Jr., pp. 61-106. Grand Rapids: Baker, 2000.

Vanhoozer, Kevin J., ed. *Cambridge Companion to Postmodern Theology.* Cambridge: Cambridge University Press, 2003.

―――, ed. *Dictionary for Theological Interpretation of the Bible.* Grand Rapids: Baker, 2005.

Vanhoozer, Kevin J., James K. A. Smith, and Bruce Ellis Benson, eds. *Hermeneutics at the Crossroads.* Bloomington: Indiana University Press, 2006.

Watson, Francis. *Eros, Agape, Gender: Towards a Pauline Sexual Ethic.* Cambridge: Cambridge University Press, 2000.

―――. *Paul and the Hermeneutics of Faith.* London: Clark International, 2004.

―――. *Paul, Judaism and the Gentiles: A Sociological Approach.* Society for New Testament Studies Monograph Series 56. Cambridge: Cambridge University Press, 1986. Revised and expanded edition: *Paul, Judaism, and the Gentiles: Beyond the New Perspective.* Grand Rapids: Eerdmans, 2007.

―――. *Text and Truth: Redefining Biblical Theology.* Edinburgh: T. & T. Clark, 1997.

―――. *Text, Church, and World: Biblical Interpretation in Theological Perspective.* Grand Rapids: Eerdmans, 1994.

Watson, Francis, ed. *The Open Text: New Directions for Biblical Studies?* London: SCM Press, 1993.

Wolterstorff, Nicholas. *Divine Discourse.* Cambridge: Cambridge University Press, 1995.

―――. "Authorial Discourse Interpretation," in *Dictionary for Theological Interpretation of the Bible,* ed. Kevin J. Vanhoozer, pp. 78-80. Grand Rapids: Baker, 2005.

Zimmermann, Jens. *Recovering Theological Hermeneutics: An Incarnational-Trinitarian Theory of Interpretation.* Grand Rapids: Baker, 2004.

ELEVEN

Literary Hermeneutics:
Alan Culpepper and Stephen Moore

Introduction

One of the most widely practiced and most accessible hermeneutical models is that of literary criticism. The relationship of various forms of literary criticism to other hermeneutical approaches should be clear by this point. Literary criticism is the heir to a variety of interpretive methods, including various types of phenomenology, structuralism, poststructuralism, philosophical hermeneutics with its reception-orientation, and other forms of critical thought. Often the relationship of literary criticism to these hermeneutical models is not formally recognized or taken into practical consideration, especially when the emphasis of much literary criticism becomes that of simply reading the text. However, the best literary interpreters, such as Alan Culpepper and Stephen Moore, are keenly aware of the philosophical and hermeneutical roots of their literary interpretive models, even if, as is the case with someone like Culpepper and even Moore to some extent, their individual theoretical contributions are somewhat limited. Along with other significant literary interpreters, they have been responsible for bridging the gap between hermeneutical theory and literary interpretation, and the result has been development of a literary hermeneutics. This hermeneutics continues to develop as theoretical questions continue to be asked of the process of reading and interpreting, and various other hermeneutical developments are taken into account.

R. Alan Culpepper

For many scholars, R. Alan Culpepper (1945-) marks the development of a distinct literary hermeneutics for students of the Bible, especially the New Testament. The emergence of literary hermeneutics has marked one of the most significant recent interpretive developments in relation to the Bible, as the tyranny of the historical-critical method, asserted since the time of the Enlightenment, has lost its stranglehold on biblical exegesis. Culpepper has enabled scholars to understand some of the hermeneutical issues and implications of reading the Bible as literature.

Life and Influences

Culpepper was born in 1945, and received his undergraduate education at Baylor University in Waco, Texas, and theological training at the Southern Baptist Theological Seminary in Louisville, Kentucky, before receiving his Ph.D. in Biblical Studies from Duke University in Durham, North Carolina, in 1974. Culpepper has spent his teaching career at three institutions in the United States: the Southern Baptist Theological Seminary, where he became the James Buchanan Harrison Professor of New Testament Interpretation, Baylor University, and McAfee School of Theology at Mercer University in Atlanta, Georgia, where he is professor of New Testament and Dean.

Like many other scholars who have been attracted to literary interpretation of the Bible, Culpepper did not formally train in the field of literary criticism, nor did he publish his first works in this area. His first book, a revision of his doctoral dissertation, was titled *The Johannine School* (1975). Following in a line of historical critics who had previously pursued this topic, Culpepper wrote a traditional historically based analysis of the concept of a Johannine school on the basis of the nature of "schools" in the ancient world. It was his second book, however, that marked Culpepper's entrance into literary interpretation. In 1983, he published *Anatomy of the Fourth Gospel: A Study in Literary Design,* with a preface by the renowned English literature scholar Frank Kermode (1919-2010), with whom Culpepper worked while writing the book. Since that important work, Culpepper has continued to publish, especially on the Johannine writings of the New Testament, although he has also branched out into other Gospels. Besides commentaries on Luke's Gospel (1996) and Mark's Gospel (2007),

Culpepper has written a commentary on the Johannine letters (1985); *John the Son of Zebedee* (1994), a biography and survey of the history of discussion of John; and *The Gospel and Letters of John* (1998), a survey of the Johannine writings. Culpepper also wrote an extended introduction to three studies of the Johannine writings (2000), and has edited several volumes, including a collection of essays on John in honor of D. Moody Smith (1996), his doctoral supervisor at Duke, and a volume of readings of John 6 (1997). He also wrote a biography of his father, Hugo Culpepper, a well-known Baptist missionary and professor (2002).

The major hermeneutical method that Culpepper helped to introduce to and promote in New Testament scholarship — literary hermeneutics — has been subsequently utilized in various ways in much of his research, even if it does not dominate it. This is seen in the variety of approaches found in his published works, besides his more overtly literary readings (e.g., "The Johannine Hypodeigma" and "Johannine Irony"). His treatment of John the Son of Zebedee is in some ways a reception-history of John, and hence has similarities to the reception aesthetics associated with Wolfgang Iser (1926-2007) and Hans-Robert Jauss (1921-1997) of the Constance University school of thought; his general treatment of the Johannine writings has a lengthy introduction that covers literary and other topics; and his commentary on Mark reads the final form of the text, while appreciating the history of interpretation in the church (2007). He revisits the topic of literary interpretation in a brief way in an essay in a recent book that commemorates *Anatomy of the Fourth Gospel* twenty-five years later ("Symbolism and History") and lists those he sees as having followed in his wake in another article ("Looking Downstream"). As this last article illustrates, Culpepper's literary hermeneutic has had a significant effect on literary interpretation of the New Testament, because of its method that combines phenomenological (New Criticism) and reader-oriented criticism. This paved the way for further developments in literary interpretation and in what has come to be characterized as narrative criticism, along with a variety of literary methods that eventually led to poststructuralism.

Defining a Literary Hermeneutics

In his *Anatomy of the Fourth Gospel,* Culpepper introduces an inclusive model of literary hermeneutics that draws on a range of theoretical thought. This is perhaps not surprising when one notices that Kermode, who (it is well known) introduced French literary criticism to the British scene, writes the foreword to Culpepper's major initiatory work. Culpepper is not, however, the first to utilize literary criticism to examine the Bible. There has long been appreciation of literary features of the biblical text, as analyzed in the works of such well-known writers as Robert Lowth (1710-1787), Eric Auerbach (1892-1957), Mary Chase (1887-1973), Northrop Frye (1912-1991), and Kermode, among many others. There was also the Bible-as-literature movement active in various religion departments that had promoted study of the Bible as a collection of literary documents. A number of Old Testament scholars, influenced by a seminal paper by James Muilenburg read in 1968 (published in 1969), had also already begun literary interpretation of the Bible, including such contemporary authors as Meir Sternberg, Adele Berlin, David Gunn, David Clines, and Robert Alter. In New Testament studies, which came to literary interpretation later than those studying the Old Testament, Charles Talbert, Werner Kelber, David Rhoads, Robert Tannehill, and Jack Kingsbury undertook similar kinds of investigations. Only one of these New Testament literary explorations attempted to be highly explicit in method, the one co-authored by Rhoads and an English literature professor named Donald Michie (1982). Written independently of each other, the two literary treatments by Culpepper and Rhoads/Michie have much in common and draw upon many of the same literary critics in developing a similar literary-hermeneutical method. Culpepper's work, however, has more representatively defined the field for New Testament scholars because of his eclectic approach that positioned his method within the stream of both literary, especially narratological, and biblical scholarship.

In *Anatomy of the Fourth Gospel,* Culpepper encapsulates his literary hermeneutic in two major emphases. The first is in relation to the metaphor of the text as window or mirror. Drawing upon the distinguished New Critic Murray Krieger (1923-2000), Culpepper wishes to reposition the study of John's Gospel, and by implication the New Testament as a whole, from being a window to being a mirror. The metaphor of the window is that the text serves as a point of access to the history of the community behind the Gospel, and behind that to the life and teaching of Jesus. Instead, if the text is seen as a mirror, the metaphor shifts the point of focus from going beyond the text to seeing meaning reside between the observer and the mirror, or between the reader and the text. Therefore, rather than origins, historical background, and matters behind the text having preeminence, the focus is upon the text and its readers, both implied and real.

The second major emphasis of Culpepper's literary hermeneutic is upon the implications of such a mirror-like reading. Drawing freely upon the work of American narratologist Seymour Chatman (1928-), and his interpretation and extension of the communications model of the structuralist Roman Jakobson (1896-1982), Culpepper develops a communications model that moves from the real author through the implied author to the narrator and then the story, and from the story to the narratee and then to the implied and real reader. Involved in the communication between implied author and implied reader is both explicit and implicit commentary. Within the scope of the narrator-narratee relation, there is the world of narrative time, within which lies the story time. The story involves events, settings, characters, and plot, and stands at the center of the communications model. The major components of this communications model form the basic elements of Culpepper's literary and especially narrative-focused hermeneutics.

Before the major categories and operative practices of this literary hermeneutics can be suitably explicated, there are, according to Culpepper, three potential objections to such an interpretive stance that merit attention. These three objections include the question of the legitimacy of applying modern literary interpretive models to the study of ancient texts, the appropriateness of applying interpretive methods developed for fiction to the study of religious texts, especially the Christian literary texts, and the apparent disregard in the practice of literary criticism for what has been learned through historical criticism, including consideration of the historical context of the Gospels. These are legitimate objections to raise, and they have continued to be asked by a variety of interpreters, in particular historical critics of the New Testament.

There is no doubt, according to Culpepper, that there are differences between ancient and modern literatures, and that the type of narrative that comprises the Gospels — with connections to other realistic narrative but apparently constituting their own genre — would merit use of literary criteria specifically geared toward them. However, in the absence of such literary-interpretive criteria, perhaps those used in modern literature could prove useful. The division between secular and sacred literature is one that has traditionally been maintained by interpreters on both sides, with few exceptions. Most literary critics, however, have held to a common epistemology that does not warrant such a separation. Finally, there is an important distinction to be made between drawing upon historical information to reconstruct a historical situation and drawing upon this same information to aid in literary interpretation. In this situation, the use of historical information is a necessity.

In Culpepper's analysis, the narrator and point of view are the first major consideration in a literary hermeneutics. The three essential components are the real author, the implied author, and the narrator. In this literary hermeneutical stance, the real author, though the object of much traditional analysis, is of relatively little concern. More important is the "implied author" who is called forth by the narrative. This term was formulated by the neo-Aristotelian literary critic of the Chicago school, Wayne Booth (1921-2005), and denotes the reconstructed author as implied by and indirectly accessed through the narrative. The narrator may be construed in a number of different ways within a narrative, sometimes overtly and other times simply as the surrogate voice of the implied author, or even real author. In any case, the narrator cannot necessarily be equated with either author, but is the force, either as a character or not, that guides the reader through the text. Narrators do this by various means, by either revealing much initially or a little incrementally, in either a trustworthy or an untrustworthy manner, and as either omniscient or limited in knowledge. The point of view of the narrator has also been analyzed in detail by numerous scholars. Here Culpepper draws on the narratologist Gérard Genette (1930-), the structuralist Boris Uspensky (1937-), and the American New Critics Cleanth Brooks (1906-1994) and Robert Penn Warren (1905-1989). Culpepper adopts a model in which the narrator may be located either internal or external to the events of the narrative, and may or may not function as a character in that narrative. This grid provides four different narrative points of view. Further, Culpepper notes, with Uspensky (and followed by Gary Yamasaki), the five planes on which point of view may be articulated: ideological, concerning evaluation of the narrative (reliable or unreliable); phraseological, regarding the linguistic patterns of the text; spatial, concerning the narrator's location (omnipresent or limited); temporal, with regard to the narrator's time (contemporary or retrospective); and psychological, concerning the internal and external relation to the characters in the narrative (omniscient or limited). Each of these frameworks attempts to access the same basic issues involving point of view, i.e., the relationship of the narrator to the action of the narrative. Finally, the narrator may be defined without regard for the narrative but in relation to other characters, including the depicted characters and the implied author.

The next interpretive category for Culpepper is that of narrative time. There are several distinctions to be made regarding time in narrative. One of these, based on the categories of Genette (*Narrative Discourse,* 1980), is the distinction between the narrative *per se* and the story of the narrative. This is a fundamental distinction made in much narratological theorizing. There are several ways that this relationship can be categorized. One is to speak of narrative as text that conveys the story. Another is to speak of the relationship of *signifier* to *signified,* or narrative story to text, or discourse to content, or even the "how" to the "what." The result is that the temporal sphere of each may be distinguished, so that narrative time and story time are differentiated (note that the relation to real time need not be raised in this context). Narrative time is concerned with the events that occur in the narrative and their order and duration, as opposed to story time. These elements of order, duration, and frequency require further development. Order is concerned with the ordering of the presentation of events within the narrative. When the events in the narrative are seen to be discordant with the events in the stories, the dis-orders are identified, according to Genette, as anachronies. Often, however, the order of events in the story can only be determined on the basis of reconstructing such an order from the indicators within the narrative. Duration concerns the imprecise and relative relationship that exists between the length of transpiration of the narrative and that of the story. Genette has referred to this narrative speed as either duration as measured in units of time or length as measured in written length, such as pages. A narrative may utilize a number of different durative lengths, depending upon the events being narrated. Those that are of approximately equal length to the events in the story are said to be scenes; those that occur more quickly in the narrative are summaries. When the narrative omits material from the story, there is ellipsis. The final category is frequency. Frequency concerns the number of times that a given event of the story is transmitted in the narrative. Narrative frequency can vary from conveying of a singular incident once in the narrative to repeated conveyance, and from narrating once an event that happened repeatedly to narrating such an event repeatedly. One of the means of judging the significance of an event is relative to how many times and in what way it is told within the narrative.

Plot, in Culpepper's scheme, constitutes an important concept in a literary hermeneutics of narrative. In his *Poetics,* Aristotle (384-322 BC) himself was concerned with plot, which he defined in its essential characteristics of order, amplitude, unity, and connection as either probable or necessary. Under the influence of Aristotle, nearly as many definitions of plot have been derived as there have been plots to which to give the label. Aristotle's concept of mimesis or imitation has been instrumental in the development of various theories of how the elements of the story relate to the world outside of the text. Also important are Aristotle's notions of *peripeteia* or reversal and *anagnorisis* or recognition. As a result, Culpepper recounts, a number of classifications of types of plots that draw on these essential features. The neo-Aristotelian Chicago school literary scholar R. S. Crane (1886-1967) defines three types of plot: of action, of character, and of thought, in which the major change or reversal *(peripeteia)* of the plot occurs in relation to one of these elements. Chatman defines six types of plot based on Aristotle: a good person falls, which is improbable; a villain falls, which is simply justice; a noble person falls, which arouses pity and fear; a villain succeeds, which is against probability; a good person succeeds, which is satisfying; and a noble person temporarily falls, whose vindication is welcome. Arguably the best-known contemporary typology of plot was developed by the archetypal literary critic Frye. Frye determines that there are four grand myths or literary genres: the romance, the tragedy, the comedy, and the irony or satire, potentially involving five types of characters: the myth of the divine hero, the romance of the super being, the high mimetic of the superior being, the low mimetic of the person equal to his environment, and the ironic of the inferior hero. There have been various attempts to classify the narratives of the Gospels into one of the above (or other) categories. A prior question that must be asked, however, is whether a Gospel even has a plot. The answer to such a question comes from both internal and external criteria. The internal criteria are that there are four Gospels: three synoptics and John's. The relationship among these Gospels, in which there are four different narratives that convey the same basic story of the life and teaching of Jesus, indicates that there is a plot, in that the authors of the Gospels had to make choices about the arrangement and shape of their individual Gospels that resulted in the different emphases of their narratives. The external criteria revolve around the reality that there was a literary tradition within both Jewish and Greek cultures in which stories were told that involved a variety of characters and means by which the events of these stories were conveyed. Thus, the search for a plot within biblical narrative appears to be a warranted exercise in an attempt to interpret and understand each Gospel author's unique perspective.

Related to plot in a number of ways is the concept of character. Aristotle again forms the basis for definition of character, when he notes that characters should have four primary characteristics: being morally good, suitability, life-likeness, and consistency. Whereas these criteria are useful for assessing character, they do not tell much about the determination and development of character. There are two major views of character within literary criticism that Culpepper draws upon. The first is the view that characters function as autonomous and independent beings with their own distinct personalities and characteristics. Chapman holds to this position, although Culpepper does not favor it in developing a literary hermeneutics geared toward John's Gospel. Instead, he opts for the position that sees characters as functionaries within the plot, in which they fulfill various tasks that they are commissioned to do. This is the position that is taken by structuralism and formalism. This is also the one that he believes is most useful in analyzing the Gospels. The categorization of character by the novelist E. M. Forster (1879-1970) plays into this analysis. Forster differentiates between flat and round characters. Round characters are those who are complex in orientation and motivation, whereas flat characters are created around a primary idea or trait, and are more typical than developmental. Forster also notes that the lives of characters are lived either "by values" or "by time," i.e., either in response to important moments or in response to temporal succession. Culpepper finds that this set of characteristics fits the New Testament evidence regarding characterization, as Jesus is a static character who does not change or develop, although Culpepper admits that some minor characters, such as the Samaritan woman, do experience change. Another distinction is that of protagonist, intermediate character, foil (or ficelle), and background character. Jesus is the protagonist in the narrative of the Gospels, with the characters often divided into two opposed camps, depending upon whether they do or do not follow him. The choice that is conveyed is whether the character chooses one or the other of the two clear choices. In John's Gospel, Jesus as protagonist enters into relationship with God, the disciples, the Jews, and a host of minor characters. The result of these interactions is designed to explicate the various elements of Jesus' character on the basis of his interaction with other characters, and to draw attention to responses to Jesus that differ from each other, and push the reader to follow the consequences of such responses.

Implicit commentary is a part of the communication that occurs between the author and the reader, but it is a very important element of that communication. The heart of implicit commentary is the ability to communicate meaningful comment on the plots and the characters, without coming out and explicitly stating it. Thus, even if the plot itself is relatively simple and straightforward, the implied author can implicitly state much more than appears to be said, through a variety of indirect communicative signals. Three are developed by Culpepper: misunderstanding, irony, and symbolism. Misunderstanding may occur at any number of different levels. Traditional criticism has tended to confine it to the historical level, where it can be found within the narrative itself as a means of communication about the characters and their motives. Irony is typically characterized as a simple inconsistency between appearance and reality. There is much more to irony than this, however. Irony involves the realization that the appearance is only an appearance and that there is a certain comic effect when one observes it from a detached position as one not involved in the irony. Finally, symbolism is designed to open up the meanings shared between the author and reader, with the symbol providing the vehicle by which the meaning is conveyed. Some of these symbols may be authorial creations, while others may be drawn from other sources; some may reflect archetypal or universal notions, while others are based on the contexts of the author and reader. In creating or utilizing any of these symbols, the author may draw upon any number of types of vehicles or images.

In developing what may be the most important notion in his reading of John's Gospel, Culpepper treats the concept of the implied reader. As a way of setting the stage for discussion of the implied reader, Culpepper explicates the various types of audiences. The narratologist Peter J. Rabinowitz states that there are four audiences in narrative: actual audience, authorial audience, narrative audience, and ideal narrative audience. The actual audience, for the sake of developing a biblical literary hermeneutics, can mean the original first-century audience of John's Gospel or a contemporary reading audience, and can be determined on the basis of reconstructed contextual knowledge. The authorial audience reflects the audience that the real author envisions when writing, and to whom the work is addressed. Distance between these two audiences increases the level of difficulty for the actual reader, as the reader will have less access to the shared suppositions that make understanding possible. The narrative audience is the audience that accepts the worldview of the narrative and accepts the conditions under which the story unfolds. The fourth audience, the ideal narrative audience, goes further than simply the narrative audience and believes the narrator. Other narratologists add other "readers" to the equation. For example, Culpepper draws on the work of the narratologist Gerald Prince to introduce the notion of the narratee, positioned between the authorial and narrative audiences, as, in some ways, another interpretive

HERMENEUTICS

layer between the text and the actual audience. Culpepper now turns to the notion of the implied reader. The most important definition of the implied reader is by reader-response critic Wolfgang Iser. Iser's contribution rests in drawing attention to not only identifying the stance the reader must assume when reading but the larger and perhaps more significant question of what a narrative requires its reader to do. For Iser, the text requires that the reader be involved in producing or actualizing the meaning of the text. The notion of the implied reader grows from this conception in that the implied reader responds to the narratological movement and thereby is involved in the production of meaning. This process can involve all kinds of narrative-based movements of affirmation and denial, as expectations are encouraged or thwarted. In that way, the reader through the implied reader becomes a part of the narrative as they unfold its meaning.

Culpepper defines a literary hermeneutics that is crafted out of the materials from a number of types of contemporary literary criticism. As we have noted above, the influence of the New Criticism is significant, specifically for defining narrative itself. However, the Chicago literary school is also important, helping to articulate formal and structural elements of the text, such as plot. There is also an influence from structuralism and narratology, as the literary model defines what it is that makes a narrative function. The influence of reader-response criticism helps to define the role of the reader. Thus, to summarize this literary hermeneutic, it is concerned with the text as text, as defined by its major constituents, such as plot, character, and the like, and with the reader both within and outside the literary text.

This framework has laid the groundwork for a number of developments in literary interpretation of the New Testament. The first and most direct is the growth of what has come to be called narrative criticism in New Testament studies. Rhoads apparently used the term "narrative criticism" for the first time in a paper delivered in 1980 and published in 1982. The term has caught on in New Testament studies, with many using the title to characterize their interpretive work (e.g., David Howell and Mark Stibbe) and others articulating it as a method in its own right (e.g., Mark Alan Powell and James Resseguie). Narrative criticism, generally lacking the same theoretical and methodological rigor that Culpepper displays in developing his literary hermeneutical model, to say nothing of showing little influence of the major French or other narratologists, has in some circles come to be equated with literary criticism of the New Testament and in particular with the reading of New Testament narratives. Narrative crit-

284

icism is less a hermeneutical model than it is a set of techniques for reading narrative, based for the most part in formalist and related types of methods. The result is appreciation for the work as a whole, the parts of that work including plot and characters, and (often) the role of the implied reader in understanding. A second major trajectory developing from this literary hermeneutics includes those who have followed more progressive hermeneutical paths, such as more reader-oriented criticism, and others who have followed the way of deconstruction. At least some, if not all, of these developments are somewhere on the path toward or have become forms of poststructuralism.

Stephen Moore

In biblical studies, Stephen Moore (1954-) is one of the major literary hermeneutical figures heading down the path of poststructuralism. There have been many developments in literary hermeneutics since Culpepper and his contemporaries wrote their important works of literary criticism. In the 1990s and beyond, they were followed in this hermeneutical endeavor by a number of other literary critics of the New Testament, including such scholars as Elizabeth Struthers Malbon, David Gowler, James Williams, Warren Carter, John Darr, and Janice Capel Anderson. Some, such as Robert Fowler, Jeffrey Staley, and Mary Ann Beavis, moved from narrative criticism to more explicitly reader-response oriented criticism. As noted above in discussion of Culpepper, one of the strands of development in his literary hermeneutic involves reader-response criticism. For Culpepper, this entails the relatively moderate form of criticism defined by Wolfgang Iser, in which the reader in effect fills in the indeterminate gaps in the text. The progression from the New Criticism to various reader-oriented criticisms logically follows as the locus of interpretation shifts from the text, the focus of various phenomenological criticisms, to the reader. Whereas Culpepper introduces reader-oriented criticism into his literary hermeneutic, Moore takes readerly notions several steps further, and develops a more robust poststructuralist criticism. Its very robustness as it shifts the focus of attention from text to reader contains the seeds of its own further development, both in the work of Moore and in the literary criticism of others, so that it continues down the road to deconstruction and poststructuralism. In this way, the literary hermeneutic developed by Moore is a direct consequence of the narrative criticism of Culpepper.

Life and Influences

Moore was born in 1954 in Ireland. He was educated at Trinity College Dublin, from which he received his undergraduate degree and his Ph.D. in New Testament in 1986, with a thesis on "Narrative Homiletics: Lukan Rhetoric and the Making of the Reader," written under the direction of Professor Sean Freyne. After a time as a postdoctoral fellow at Yale Divinity School in New Haven, Connecticut, Moore's first teaching position was at Wichita State University in Kansas, where he was an assistant professor. He then returned to the British Isles, and took up a position in the Department of Biblical Studies at the University of Sheffield, reaching the rank of senior lecturer, before returning once more to North America as professor of New Testament at the Theological School of Drew University in Madison, New Jersey, in 1999.

Through the years, there has been a steady progression and development in Moore's work, much of it motivated by acute literary interests that are increasingly exposed to a variety of cultural influences. His first book, which grew out of his doctorate, provides the basis for his reader-response hermeneutic, and was titled *Literary Criticism and the Gospels: The Theoretical Challenge* (1989). He continued to pay attention to the biblical text, while increasingly moving toward deconstruction and poststructuralism in his next several books. In *Mark and Luke in Poststructuralist Perspectives* (1992), Moore offers an interpretation of Mark's and Luke's Gospels through the deconstructive poststructuralism of Jacques Derrida (1930-2004), Jacques Lacan (1901-1981), and Michel Foucault (1926-1984). It is in this poststructuralist work that signs glimpsed in his earlier work emerge more fully. Moore does not write as your typical New Testament scholar, but as a witty and clever manipulator of the English language. More importantly, he brings this cleverness to bear in fundamental ways in his interpretation of Mark and Luke. As he states in the introduction to *Mark and Luke in Poststructuralist Perspectives*, "Graphic imagery, creative anachronism, sustained wordplay (wordwork, rather), and surrealistic stories of reading make up my method in this book" (xviii). He takes the written texts of the Gospels and makes them into visual substances to be manipulated in his hands. In *Poststructuralism and the New Testament: Derrida and Foucault at the Foot of the Cross* (1994), Moore offers a student's guide to the work of Derrida and Foucault. In this book, he wants (among other things) to show at least two things regarding deconstruction: that it is not inimical to theology, and that it is not without a political conscience. Moore followed this volume with a collaborative effort (under the authorial label the Bible and Culture Collective) titled *The Postmodern Bible* (1995). He notes in *Post-structuralism and the New Testament* that, at this stage, he is already making connections with and learning from a variety of ideologically based criticisms, such as feminism. Many of these interests are explicitly pursued in some of his subsequent writing, such as *God's Gym: Divine Male Bodies of the Bible* (1996), *God's Beauty Parlor: And Other Queer Spaces in and around the Bible* (2001), and *Empire and Apocalypse: Postcolonialism and the New Testament* (2006). In his most recent work, Moore has toyed with forms of post-poststructuralism, such as postcolonialism, queer theory, masculinity studies, autobiographical criticism, and especially cultural hermeneutics or cultural studies, the last of which he believes have potential for moving biblical studies beyond methodological preoccupation. Indicative of how far he has moved, Moore reflects back on the influence of narrative criticism on his own scholarly work in his 2008 essay "Afterword."

Moore has also edited a number of books that support his theoretical work in his authored volumes. These include, with Janice Capel Anderson, *Mark and Method* (1992; rev. ed. 2008), with David J. A. Clines, *Auguries: The Jubilee Volume of the Sheffield Department of Biblical Studies* (1998) with J. Cheryl Exum, *Biblical Studies/Cultural Studies* (1998), with Janice Capel Anderson, *New Testament Masculinities* (2003), with Fernando Segovia, *Postcolonial Biblical Criticism: Interdisciplinary Intersections* (2006), and, with Tom Thatcher, *Anatomies of Narrative Criticism: The Past, Present, and Futures of the Fourth Gospel as Literature* (2008), a volume offered in tribute to Culpepper's *Anatomy of the Fourth Gospel* twenty-five years later. Moore has also edited several issues of the experimental journal *Semeia*, and served as the editor and on the editorial board of a number of the standard journals in the field of New Testament and related studies. His research continues to bring biblical studies together with other critical modes, including those that are literarily oriented but also those that are involved with gender, culture, and postcolonialism.

The Consequences of Literary Criticism

The literary hermeneutics that Moore develops in his *Literary Criticism and the Gospels* is not the same kind of working model that Culpepper initiates and that has become enshrined in what is now known as narrative criticism. To the contrary, what Moore does is illustrate the consequences

287

of literary criticism, especially as one moves down the interpretive path from the New Criticism to reader-response criticism to deconstruction and poststructuralism.

There are three important interpretive signposts that mark out Moore's terrain. These three signposts represent turning points in criticism that are embedded within a larger narrative regarding the development of New Testament literary criticism as a whole (which will not be analyzed here except as it is germane to the larger discussion). Each of these three merits treatment in its own right for signaling major developments in New Testament scholarship.

The first significant literary hermeneutical marker is Moore's observation that redaction criticism and literary criticism have much more in common than most scholars imagine. After extensively surveying the development of narrative criticism, Moore brings it into dialogue with traditional historical criticism, especially redaction criticism. He first observes that theology is another way of speaking of an ideological point of view, and it therefore functions as one of the points of view within a poetics of the New Testament. Redaction criticism, however, retains a closer relation, or even creates a bond, between theology and the historical situation of the text. In Moore's configuration, narrative criticism is less interested in the historical situation, although it is concerned with all of the internal dynamics of the text, such as plot and character. However, most of these concerns are also the concerns of redaction criticism, including the theology of the Gospels. There are, according to Moore, two further factors to consider. One is the relation of content to form, and the other is the notion of mediation. Narrative criticism wishes to distinguish between the "what" and the "how" of a narrative, but such a distinction is not easily made, leaving the content or theology as a part of the form of the text itself. Narrative criticism is then better able to describe the thought of the text than is redaction criticism, which does not recognize the narrative nature of the text and hence does not describe the content of the text as well. Concerning mediation, narrative criticism tends to be either plot oriented or geared toward mediating features between the action and the story. Redaction criticism, with its concern for the specific generic and verbal characteristics mediated by the text, is arguably (and perhaps surprisingly) more literarily oriented than narrative criticism. This prompts consideration of reader-response criticism as a means of focusing upon the importance of narrative, as the reader is closely involved with the narrative itself.

The second significant marker, therefore, concerns reader-response criticism. Moore first examines a number of reader-response efforts in New Testament studies, by such scholars as Robert Tannehill, Jouette Bassler, Robert Fowler, Culpepper, and Gary Phillips, with the resulting critical opinion of their readings that, as he so succinctly concludes, "For biblical studies the moral is plain: criticism is an institution to which real readers need not apply" (*Literary Criticism*, 106). Moore examines two important works in an attempt to enlighten and clarify the notion of reading. The first is Kermode's *The Genesis of Secrecy* (1979), and the other is Stanley Fish's (1937-) *Is There a Text in This Class?* (1980). In *The Genesis of Secrecy* by Kermode, who introduced French structuralism to British study of literature in the 1970s, the reader of the Gospel is like the disciples in the Gospel itself — seeing but not understanding. The reader reads the Gospel as a complex allegory with multiple meanings, as the various equations of meaning and emblem are explored. Even what appear to be straightforward stories end up being full of ambiguity to the modern reader. Kermode ends up calling into question what it means for readers to interpret. Whereas in some ways Kermode's perspective leads to the disappearance of the reader, according to Moore, Fish leads to the disappearance of the text itself. Whereas the earlier Fish was similar to Iser in offering readers a chance to deal closely with the text as a means of developing their responses, the later Fish makes us aware of the consequences of a reader-oriented stance. All reading, even of grammar, involves interpretation, to the point that there is no firm foundation for interpretation that does not involve assumptions. This pragmatic view of language has roots in American neo-pragmatism and the thought of Ludwig Wittgenstein (1889-1951). It is resolved in the notion of interpretive communities, those who share common assumptions about how it is that readers create meaning in texts. Here Kermode's multiple interpretations and Fish's interpretive communities come together, with Kermode's many meanings representing various views that communities have adopted. The result is a critical interpretive position that does not demonstrate that certain readings are better but attempts to persuade that such is the case. The rationalism of modern interpretation must give way to postmodern politics of influence. Nevertheless, even with this pragmatic view of texts replacing an ontological one, when it comes to interpretation itself the text reappears and is the subject of discussion, questions of epistemology aside.

The third landmark on the interpretive terrain for Moore is Derridaean poststructural deconstruction. Despite the results of Fish's perspective, one is not compelled to deconstruction. Fish still maintains, while not providing the ability to create definitive interpretations of texts, that there is what Moore calls "a definitive interpretation of interpretation" (*Literary Criticism,* 135), and by that a kind of transcendent discourse. Going back to the fundamental distinction between sign and signified, and all of the meaningful oppositions derived since then, Derrida calls into question all of the major points of departure for interpretation. Whereas some biblical interpreters have tried to adopt various "soft" forms of deconstruction, in which criticism still remains even if the fixed points are now moving, the "hard" form of deconstruction attempts to break completely with the foundations of criticism itself, with the interpreter becoming alienated from meaning and an exile and outsider to the interpretive task. Despite this, Derrida prefers to refer to this as "play," the only thing one can affirm in the midst of such interpretive alienation.

With his theory of literary hermeneutical dependence, Moore thus accounts for how one gets from narrative criticism to deconstruction, and why it is that reader-response criticism, despite the efforts of some, has been generally unsatisfying in New Testament literary studies. For most New Testament biblical scholars, their attempts at reader-response criticism have made the reader text-immanent, rather than leaving the reader text-external, and hence they have fallen back into performing the kinds of criticism defined by Culpepper and formalized in narrative criticism. This kind of criticism, which generally embraces Iser's immanent reader, has come to represent literary hermeneutics as practiced by numerous New Testament scholars. Once one breaks out of text-immanency, however, as Fish has shown, there are logical and almost inevitable consequences of such reader-oriented approaches that move beyond interpretation into the realm of deconstruction. As a result, reader-response efforts that have utilized Fish's more aggressively pragmatic approach have been limited. Such readings have been few, and the sustainability of the approach has been demonstrated by even fewer. As this move illustrates, deconstruction has identified the arbitrariness of the sign, and wishes to move beyond the easy polarities of structuralism and later foundationalist thought. The major polar opposition that deconstruction rejects is the antithesis of speech and writing. Deconstruction itself, however, has the makings of its own deconstruction within it. Deconstruction emphasizes difference, contradiction, and alienation. The result is texts that are fragmentary and divided against themselves. In some ways, deconstruction therefore leads inevitably back to historical criticism, but without the same kind of optimism regarding interpretation. Historical criticism, though acutely aware of inconsistencies in the text, believes that these apparent problems can either be constructively overcome and give insight into the meaning of the text, or be analyzed so as to give insight into the history behind the text. Deconstruction, without such optimism, simply affirms the tension between text and external reader. One can argue that, in this dimension at least, deconstruction throws interpretation back to the epoch before historical criticism, to a time when interpreters perceived textual inconsistencies, but did not have a meaningful apparatus for explaining and understanding them. The result at that time was to theologically override textual difficulties and to relegate them to the status of their being apparent problems only. Deconstruction, with no overriding theology, Moore concludes, is reduced simply to "play."

A Critical Appraisal of Literary Hermeneutics

Literary hermeneutics has garnered a significant following among recent biblical interpreters, as well as developing in a number of important directions. There are a number of critical questions that should be raised in regard to the development and practice of literary hermeneutics.

The first is whether the literary interpretive model that Culpepper developed, and that has come to be known and practiced as narrative criticism, is a hermeneutical method, or simply a set of exegetical techniques. Culpepper's literary hermeneutics was a creative composite of a number of different literary practices, but it was driven by a conception of literary theorizing. Narrative criticism has tended to emphasize the results of the theorizing as interpretive practice.

The second question is whether any literary hermeneutic can be so combinatory in nature, without losing its interpretive focus. As we have seen, literary hermeneutics is a product of various other hermeneutics, as it draws freely from various literary approaches, including New Criticism with its ties to logical positivism, and reader-oriented literary criticism with its links to phenomenology. Nevertheless, as is evident in many hermeneutical stances, their creative dialogue with each other is what often generates creative theoretical development.

The third question interrogates the relationship between literary hermeneutics developed for the interpretation of secular literature, and the interpretation of the Bible. This is a question that has been raised from the advent of the development of biblically focused literary hermeneutics. Such a question involves more than simply querying the appropriate literary practices and techniques for study of the Bible. It probes issues of possible philosophical and literary difference between secular and religious texts, especially with regard to such fundamental concepts as referentiality, historicity, transcendence, and truth claims.

The fourth question notices that the locus of meaning in literary hermeneutics appears to be shifting, and hence raises the question of its foundation of meaning. The ground of meaning in literary studies has focused on one or more of three loci — author, text, or reader — and their relative importance has been under scrutiny as the various literary hermeneutics have developed.

The fifth question focuses upon the reader. Particularly problematic, as we have seen in the work of Culpepper and especially in the analysis of Moore, is the role of the reader. As long as the reader is equated with the original reader, interpretation remains relatively stable, because there seems to be a sense that the reader is identifiable and discernible. When the reader is equated with an implied reader, and hence is text-immanent, the reader-response options are limited by the construct of the text, and this type of reader-response criticism can be incorporated in a robust literary-critical model. When the reader becomes external to the text and functions as a contemporary reader outside textual constraint, there seems to be a resulting epistemological crisis. This emphasizes the question of how meaning is created, because the external contemporary reader becomes the locus of understanding.

This raises the further question of the status of the text. In Fish's reader-response criticism, the reader becomes the one who generates the meaning of the text, and adjudicates between meanings on the basis of interpretive communities. The transference of meaning to interpretive communities does not alleviate the ontological anxiety, but instead makes meaning a more unstable and tentative concept. Textual meaning becomes a negotiated response done in community, not necessarily a result of a process focused upon the text.

The last question concerns the future of literary hermeneutics for New Testament studies. This question addresses issues both of further methodological development and of continued viability. Narrative criticism may well continue to be practiced, but the method as it currently stands has limited its potential for further constructive theoretical development. It is hard to imagine in what ways narrative criticism can develop, and this may well call into question the continuing viability of literary hermeneutics as presently defined. However, other forms of literary hermeneutics may well continue to be developed as viable interpretive methods.

292

Conclusion

There have been two major trends in literary hermeneutics. The first is the further formalization and application of literary hermeneutics to the reading of texts. This is seen especially in types of narrative criticism, which has become one of the standard, recognized forms of critical orthodoxy in contemporary biblical interpretation. In this sense, literary hermeneutics will continue to be utilized in a variety of ways, especially in biblical studies. The second trend concerns theoretical developments in literary hermeneutics. It is worth noting that the theoretical developments that occurred in the 1980s have not been duplicated insofar as producing new literary hermeneutics that are not self-destructing or self-negating. The developments in the area have moved beyond literary criticism and into other forms of poststructural analysis, such as deconstruction and various other types of postmodern interpretation. Moore is representative of this type of hermeneutical development. Nevertheless, the model that Culpepper generated continues to have currency in a number of areas.

REFERENCE WORKS

Anderson, Janice Capel, and Stephen D. Moore, eds. *Mark and Method: New Approaches in Biblical Studies.* Minneapolis: Fortress, 1992; rev. ed. 2008.

The Bible and Culture Collective. *The Postmodern Bible.* New Haven: Yale University Press, 1995.

Booth, Wayne. *The Rhetoric of Fiction.* Chicago: University of Chicago Press, 1961.

Brooks, Cleanth, and Robert Penn Warren. *Understanding Fiction.* New York: Crofts, 1943.

Chatman, Seymour. *Story and Discourse: Narrative Structure in Fiction and Film.* Ithaca, NY: Cornell University Press, 1978.

Clines, David J. A., and Stephen D. Moore, eds. *Auguries: The Jubilee Volume of the Sheffield Department of Biblical Studies.* Sheffield: Sheffield Academic Press, 1998.

Crane, R. S. "The Concept of the Plot." In *Approaches to the Novel,* ed. Robert Scholes, pp. 233-43. Rev. ed. San Francisco: Chandler, 1966.

Culpepper, R. Alan. *Anatomy of the Fourth Gospel: A Study in Literary Design.* Philadelphia: Fortress, 1983.

———. *The Gospel and Letters of John.* Interpreting Biblical Texts. Nashville: Abingdon, 1998.

————. "An Introduction to the Johannine Writings." In *The Johannine Litera-ture,* by Barnabas Lindars, Ruth B. Edwards, and John M. Court. Shef-field: Sheffield Academic Press, 2000.

————. "The Johannine *Hypodeigma:* A Reading of John 13:1-38." *Semeia* 53 (1991): 133-52.

————. *The Johannine School: An Evaluation of the Johannine-School Hypothe-sis Based on an Investigation of the Nature of Ancient Schools.* SBL Disser-tation Series 26. Missoula, MT: Scholars Press, 1975.

————. *John, the Son of Zebedee: The Life of a Legend.* Columbia: University of South Carolina Press, 1994.

————. "Luke." *New Interpreter's Bible, IX: Luke-John,* ed. Leander Keck. Nashville: Abingdon, 1996.

————. "Looking Downstream: Where Will the New Currents Take Us?" In *New Currents through John: A Global Perspective,* ed. Francisco Lozada Jr. and Tom Thatcher, pp. 199-209. Atlanta: Society of Biblical Literature, 2006.

————. *Mark.* Smyth and Helwys Bible Commentary. Macon, GA: Smyth and Helwys, 2007.

————. "Reading Johannine Irony." In *Exploring the Gospel of John: In Honor of D. Moody Smith,* ed. R. Alan Culpepper and C. Clifton Black, pp. 193-207. Louisville: Westminster/John Knox, 1996.

————. "Symbolism and History in John's Account of Jesus' Death." In *Anat-omies of Narrative Criticism: The Past, Present, and Future of the Fourth Gospel as Literature,* ed. Tom Thatcher and Stephen D. Moore, pp. 39-54. Resources for Biblical Study 55. Atlanta: Society of Biblical Literature, 2008.

Culpepper, R. Alan, ed. *Critical Readings of John 6.* Biblical Interpretation Se-ries 22. Leiden: Brill, 1997.

Culpepper, R. Alan, and Carl Clifton Black, eds. *Exploring the Gospel of John: In Honor of D. Moody Smith.* Louisville: Westminster/John Knox, 1996.

Culpepper, R. Alan, and Fernando Segovia, eds. *The Fourth Gospel from a Lit-erary Perspective.* Semeia 53. Atlanta: Scholars Press, 1991.

Exum, J. Cheryl, and Stephen D. Moore, eds. *Biblical Studies/Cultural Studies: The Third Sheffield Colloquium.* Sheffield: Sheffield Academic Press, 1998.

Fish, Stanley E. *Is There a Text in This Class? The Authority of Interpretive Communities.* Cambridge, MA: Harvard University Press, 1980.

Forster, E. M. *Aspects of the Novel.* New York: Penguin, 1962.

Frye, Northrop. *Anatomy of Criticism: Four Essays.* Princeton: Princeton University Press, 1957.

Genette, Gérard. *Narrative Discourse: An Essay in Method,* trans. Jane E. Lewin. Ithaca, NY: Cornell University Press, 1980.

———. *Narrative Discourse Revisited,* trans. Jane E. Lewin. Ithaca, NY: Cornell University Press, 1988.

Iser, Wolfgang. *The Implied Reader: Patterns of Communication in Prose Fiction from Bunyan to Beckett.* Baltimore: Johns Hopkins University Press, 1974.

Jakobson, Roman. "Linguistics and Poetics." In *Style in Language,* ed. Thomas A. Sebeok, pp. 350-77. Cambridge, MA: MIT Press, 1960.

Jauss, Hans Robert. *Toward an Aesthetic of Reception,* trans. Timothy Bahti. Brighton, UK: Harvester, 1982.

Jobling, David, and Stephen D. Moore, eds. "Poststructuralism as Exegesis." *Semeia* 54 (1992).

Kermode, Frank. *The Genesis of Secrecy: On the Interpretation of Narrative.* Cambridge, MA: Harvard University Press, 1979.

Moore, Stephen D. "Afterword: Things Not Written in This Book." In *Anatomies of Narrative Criticism: The Past, Present, and Future of the Fourth Gospel as Literature,* ed. Tom Thatcher and Stephen D. Moore, pp. 253-58. Resources for Biblical Study 55. Atlanta: Society of Biblical Literature, 2008.

———. "Between Birmingham and Jerusalem: Cultural Studies and Biblical Studies." *Semeia* 82 (1998): 1-32.

———. *Empire and Apocalypse: Postcolonialism and the New Testament.* Sheffield: Sheffield Phoenix Press, 2006.

———. *God's Beauty Parlor: And Other Queer Spaces in and around the Bible.* Stanford, CA: Stanford University Press, 2001.

———. *God's Gym: Divine Male Bodies of the Bible.* London: Routledge, 1996.

———. *Literary Criticism and the Gospels: The Theoretical Challenge.* New Haven: Yale University Press, 1989.

———. *Mark and Luke in Poststructuralist Perspectives: Jesus Begins to Write.* New Haven: Yale University Press, 1992.

———. "A Modest Manifesto for New Testament Literary Criticism: How to Interface with a Literary Studies Field That Is Post-Literary, Post-Theoretical, and Post-Methodological." *Biblical Interpretation* 15 (2007): 1-25.

———. *Poststructuralism and the New Testament: Derrida and Foucault at the Foot of the Cross.* Minneapolis: Fortress, 1994.

————. "True Confessions and Weird Obsessions: Autobiographical Interventions in Literary and Biblical Studies." *Semeia* 72 (1995): 19-50.

Moore, Stephen D., and Janice Capel Anderson, eds. *New Testament Masculinities.* Semeia Studies. Atlanta: Society of Biblical Literature, 2003.

Moore, Stephen D., and Fernando Segovia, eds. *Postcolonial Biblical Criticism: Interdisciplinary Intersections.* London: Clark International, 2005.

Muilenburg, James. "Form Criticism and Beyond." *Journal of Biblical Literature* 88 (1969): 1-18.

Porter, Stanley E. "Literary Approaches to the New Testament: From Formalism to Deconstruction and Back." In *Approaches to New Testament Study,* ed. Stanley E. Porter and David Tombs, pp. 77-128. JSNT Supplement Series 120. Sheffield: Sheffield Academic Press, 1995.

————. "What Difference Does Hermeneutics Make? Hermeneutical Theory Applied." *Jian Dao* 34/*Pastoral Journal* 27 (July 2010): 1-50.

————. "Why Hasn't Reader-Response Criticism Caught on in New Testament Studies?" *Journal of Literature and Theology* 4, no. 3 (1990): 278-92.

Powell, Mark Allen. *What Is Narrative Criticism? A New Approach to the Bible.* London: SPCK, 1990.

Prince, Gerald. "Notes Toward a Categorization of Fictional 'Narratees.'" *Genre* 4 (1971): 100-105.

Rabinowitz, Peter J. "Truth in Fiction: A Reexamination of Audiences." *Critical Inquiry* 4 (1977): 121-41.

Resseguie, James L. *Narrative Criticism of the New Testament: An Introduction.* Grand Rapids: Baker, 2005.

Rhoads, David. "Narrative Criticism and the Gospel of Mark." *Journal of the American Academy of Religion* 50 (1980): 411-34.

Rhoads, David, and Donald Michie. *Mark as Story: An Introduction to the Narrative of a Gospel.* Philadelphia: Fortress, 1982; 2nd ed. with Joanna Dewey, Minneapolis: Fortress, 1999.

Thatcher, Tom, and Stephen D. Moore, eds. *Anatomies of Narrative Criticism: The Past, Present, and Futures of the Fourth Gospel as Literature.* Resources for Biblical Study 55. Atlanta: Society of Biblical Literature, 2008.

Uspensky, Boris. *A Poetics of Composition: The Structure of the Artistic Text and Typology of a Compositional Form,* trans. Valentina Zavarin and Susan Wittig. Berkeley: University of California Press, 1973.

Yamasaki, Gary. *Watching a Biblical Narrative: Point of View in Biblical Exegesis.* New York: T. & T. Clark, 2007.

TWELVE Conclusion

What Is Hermeneutics?

When asked what hermeneutics is, we will, of necessity, have to request re-
finement in the question if there is to be much substance in the answer.
Are we curious about contemporary or early hermeneutics? Are we interested in a disciplinary-specific hermeneutics or a general theory? Are our
concerns mostly literary, theological, or philosophical? Do we want an ontological description or a methodological program? Are we interested in
primarily the natural sciences or the humanities? However, even then, after having narrowed the range of potential answers as to what hermeneutics might be, we cannot give a univocal and completely unambiguous definition. If asked the same question one hundred years ago, the answer
would have been much simpler. It was fairly clear what hermeneutics was
meant for, what it was capable of doing, and to which disciplines it be-
longed. This is no longer the case.

While many hermeneuts are inclined to think of hermeneutics as a
literary method for reading texts, others — an ever-growing majority —
take hermeneutics to represent a description of human understanding
generally, a way of thinking about our ontology, and the means of challenging dominant ideals of truth, reason, and knowledge that do not capture the full range of human experience. Hermeneutics has become a way
of describing our encounters with art and our own self-understandings as
historical beings. What is hermeneutics? The simple answer is that we are
doing it right now. It is our mode of understanding the meanings on this

page, a mode in which truth is disclosed by virtue of incorporating our previous experiences and understandings. It is both the theory "and" practice of interpretation. As Hans-Georg Gadamer (1900-2002) has framed it, hermeneutics is the attitude of someone who wants to understand someone or something else.

As a way of both seeing and resolving, when possible, the many obstacles that stand in the way of understanding someone or something else, hermeneutics represents an ongoing challenge to our preconceptions, beliefs, and ideals. If we consider more recent versions such as critical and philosophical hermeneutics, we see that hermeneutics calls each of us to return to our own practical and moral responsibilities in which we are obligated to find the best form of relationship possible to texts, people, art, religion, science, technology — all of life. As something involved in the concrete affairs of our everyday lives, hermeneutics, in both theory and practice, describes the ways in which we try to overcome inhibiting and often invisible boundaries to critical-rational dialogue and a healthy way of being — of seeing and engaging the world. By doing what we can to be critical, involved, and morally conscious thinkers, one of the highest goals and most worthy of hermeneutical aims is to attain, in Gadamer's words, a "sense of what is feasible, what is possible, what is correct, here and now" (*Truth and Method*, xxxviii).

While there may be no universal agreement as to which hermeneutical theory to accept, there are many positive and provocative approaches that encourage us to think deeply and critically about our own interpretive theories. In doing so, we are required to examine our own beliefs and opinions, and the connections those have with our culturally contingent worldviews. Hermeneutics challenges us to find a sense of what is feasible, possible, and correct today. As we have seen, it is far more than merely a theoretical activity in which we speculate about abstract matters. It is a way of thinking about everyday matters such as how to generate common accord, how to understand what someone is desperately searching for the rights words to say, how to make sense of why someone would do what they did and what that means, and so on. Hermeneutics does not claim to guarantee universal, absolute, and certain knowledge or completely rational and clear thinking, but only to help us foster the best means we have at our disposal of searching for meaning and truth — our finite and prejudiced curiosity for enlightenment, insight, solidarity, and common accord through our interactions with likewise conditioned and fallible human beings.

In order to know better what hermeneutics is, we must know its history by having walked down many of its divergent paths. To answer the question requires that we step into the ongoing conversation — by no means a settled one — as to how we might better describe the act of interpretation and understanding. We cannot answer about hermeneutics except that we recognize the family of themes and concerns that continue to gain attention, such as tradition, language, objectivity, subjectivity, science, and art. And then, after we have learned about these things in greater detail we still cannot say exactly what hermeneutics is, for we will have been doing it, practicing it, all the time — questioning, debating, ruminating on what all of this means. We are the hermeneutical spiral that reaches constantly upward, yearning for new insight and truth — changing to meet the demands encountered in our experiences of the other.

Hermeneutics has a story of both abrupt dead-ends and surprising new beginnings. Framing a notion of hermeneutics within the context of the many questions it has asked is a difficult thing to do, for many questions have simply been dropped from popular interest and attention. As we have witnessed, the questions that Friedrich Schleiermacher (1768-1835) took to be of paramount importance are much different from those of Martin Heidegger (1889-1976) or Jacques Derrida (1930-2004), or most of the other hermeneuts treated in the preceding chapters. The direction of hermeneutical questions has been less a matter of finding resolution and more about finding redirection and revaluation. Indeed, the very underpinnings of what early hermeneuts took to be the foundation of hermeneutics have vanished from the mainstream. Thus, again, we find ourselves able to appreciate hermeneutics best by relying on one of its principles, namely that to understand a thing one must have a shared sense of its history. A study of hermeneutics, like ourselves, belongs to its history — to understand means to be historical.

Without a unifying definition for hermeneutics, it may seem like an impossibly difficult task to begin a study of interpretive theory. The openness of hermeneutics, however, reflects its positive flexibility to be relevant in different contexts, as well as its ability to provide enough room for new and unpredictable developments in interpretive theories. Moreover, because this openness is limited to a family of readily identifiable concerns, hermeneuts are able to offer critical perspectives on specific issues and problems that add to the ongoing dialogue. Deciding which issues and problems are most worthy remains part of the overall challenge. We have tried to leave those decisions up to our readers.

Ongoing Debates

Having surveyed the history of hermeneutics as represented by many of its major thinkers and writers, we are now in a better position to speak of its future. Hermeneutics is adaptive, open, and evolving. Where, then, might we expect it to go from here? That is, which questions remain important and which are no longer worthy avenues of pursuit? We began this book by pointing out an important debate in hermeneutics over which elements to emphasize in the tripartite relationship of author, text, and reader, for the purpose of bridging gaps in understanding — whether to highlight (a) the author and the intention placed within the text, (b) the text and its cultural-historical context, or (c) the reader's present situation and socio-historically conditioned way of understanding the text. To these basic considerations we went on to add a multitude of further, highly controversial questions such as:

(1) In interpretation should we look primarily for another's mind, maybe the original creative act? Should we seek to know the surrounding socio-historical circumstances of the author? Perhaps we should seek a dialogue with something that the author could not have foreseen, and something that his or her circumstances cannot control, namely an experience in which we ask the text questions and it asks of us.

(2) Does misunderstanding and radical difference come first in every experience? Or does a common accord, however slight, pre-exist, thereby enabling understanding?

(3) To what degree should we rely on methods, principles, or laws of understanding?

(4) What does it mean to cultivate a critical and reflective attitude? Is that mutually exclusive from methods? What is the proper role, if any, of practical wisdom and personal responsibility in hermeneutics?

(5) Is interpretation an objective or subjective act? Perhaps it is neither. Perhaps it is a play, an intersubjective accord, or maybe even something so fluid that we cannot really call it anything specific at all.

(6) Is there then a correct interpretation? Maybe we should concern ourselves with the best interpretation possible at that moment. Further still, perhaps we should reject the idea of a correct or best interpretation and seek instead merely to enjoy reading for its pleasure value

alone, recognizing that there is no real transhistorical or transcultural truth involved.

(7) What is the proper role of hermeneutics in theological and biblical interpretation?

We have not answered these questions, because we believe that it is best left to the reader to explore the controversies, having been equipped in the previous chapters with a knowledge of important alternative conceptions. Naturally our biases are evident throughout this book, whether we recognize them or not, yet our hope is that readers are able to see past our limitations to the valuable questions hermeneutics continues to ask, for there are many more than we have listed here.

Language, Tradition, and Rationality

It is easy to predict with confidence that the future of hermeneutics will continue to center on discussions about the natures and proper roles of language, tradition, and reason. These, of course, rely on particular views about the human subject and its limit and possibility for understanding. Language has become a preoccupation for many in recent years. The linguistic turn has taken hold among virtually every academic enterprise. One of the major questions has to do with whether and in what way understanding is language-bound. If all understanding is in some way mediated through language, what are the limits of such understanding? May we transcend our own linguistically mediated traditions and prejudices or must we work through them — with them — in order to see the world and ourselves?

Again, as we have seen, many hermeneuts are concerned with language, in particular, that our (linguistic) understanding of the world has been co-opted by technological and scientific ideologies such that we are able scarcely to see past their limitations. Have we allowed ourselves to be dominated by narrow conceptions of truth? Have we allowed our preoccupations with specific epistemological and scientific versions of "progress" to blind us to other experiences of truth and meaning? For some, the very notion of what it means to be rational has been lost to popular discourse in which objective certainty remains the key determining factor of genuine and reliable knowledge. For others, it remains an important task to rethink the nature of interpretation "within" the boundaries demarcated by objectivity and subjectivity, for it is only there that a thorough description of interpretation is possible. Whatever the case, it is clear that views of language, tradition, and reason will continue to be important and to evolve. Perhaps a more important question relates to how attentive we are to our own participation in language. Will art, critical theory, method, or radical difference be our structural exemplar of the experience of dialogue and understanding? Will mathematical symbolism, formulae, and universal principles and laws be our primary means of conversation? Or will we find a happy medium in which all of these forms of language become useful and constructive to the human situation?

Ontology or Epistemology or What?

As we have seen, the development of hermeneutics is marked by a crisis of meaning, understanding, and truth — however we choose to define these terms — for it remains unclear just what these things represent. Added to the complexity is that the history of hermeneutics incorporates the many changing ideals and views of Western intellectual thought, which is a truly breathtaking panorama. If, however, we were to paint the recent history of Western thought with two very general brushstrokes, we would see that the dominant ways of investigating human understanding appear to be either ontologically (and phenomenologically) driven or epistemologically driven. While these may overlap in certain regards — including the acceptance of the "linguistic turn" — many treat these two camps as mutually exclusive. Indeed, as we have also seen, how the linguistic turn finds expression for developing an interpretive theory is often very different depending upon one's starting-point, itself determined by one's ontological or epistemological commitments.

The important point to remind ourselves of here is that it is a mistake to rely on absolute categories when thinking about hermeneutics. We cannot rightly divide ways of thinking about hermeneutics into bipolar camps of either structuralism or poststructuralism, foundationalism or antifoundationalism, ontology or epistemology, textual or authorial, literary or philosophical, etc. These categories represent uneven tensions within hermeneutics that transgress simple boundaries and disciplinary lines, most obviously so in the works of those such as Jürgen Habermas (1929-) and Paul Ricoeur (1913-2005), as two ready examples of thinkers who incorporate different traditions and styles of thought into their interpretive theories.

Hermeneutics is a hybrid of that which is, that which came before, and that which is becoming. It is ontological, epistemological, and far more. Moreover, it currently shows no signs of coming to rest in any one camp. On the contrary, hermeneutics and interpretive theories continue to expand and develop in new directions. To be sure, there have been many radical changes in philosophical and theological hermeneutics over the last century. From Schleiermacher to the present, the purposes and means of interpretive approaches have evolved and changed in ways that none could have predicted. Our belief is that the future of hermeneutics will be one in which the very conception of what it means for humans to understand will continue to develop, most especially so as we find new and more helpful ways of describing our being-in-the-world and being-with-others — including our very complex and changing relationships with the written word. We welcome the future of hermeneutics with these exciting questions and possibilities in mind.

REFERENCE WORKS

Gadamer, Hans-Georg. *Truth and Method,* trans. Joel Weinsheimer and Donald G. Marshall. 2nd rev. ed. New York: Continuum, 2002 (1960).

Author Index